BEYOND BAKING

For the children who, even in the hardest places,
dare to dream of something sweeter.

And for those who will build new worlds
from what we leave behind.

'Trust in dreams, for in them is hidden the gate to eternity.'
KHALIL GIBRAN

'We have on this earth what makes life worth living.'
MAHMOUD DARWISH

BEYOND BAKING

PHILIP KHOURY

PHOTOGRAPHY BY MATT RUSSELL

Quadrille

Introduction 7
A brief history of cake 11
Essential tools 13
The weigh to bake 15
The plantry 16

SWEET RISEN MORNINGS 49

Olive Oil Butter 55
Vrioche 56
Croissant Dough 60
Croissants 65
Almond Croissants 66
Pains au Chocolat 69
Mixed Berry Custard Danishes 70
Pains aux Raisins 72
Glazed Doughnuts 76
Chocolate-glazed Cream Buns 79
Pistachio Babka 80

A COOKIE (AND BISCUIT) A DAY 83

Peanut Butter Choc Chip Cookies 86
Hazelnut and Toasted Vanilla Cookies 88
Macadamia Shortbread 91
Orange and Maple Spiced Biscuits 92
Stuffed Almond Croissant Cookies 95
Fig Newtons 96

A PIECE OF CAKE 99

Light Fruit Cake 102
Pistachio and Matcha Loaf Cake 104
Pineapple, Coconut & Lime Drizzle Cake 107
Peanut Butter and Jelly Sandwich Cake 110
Peach and Hazelnut Crumble Cake 112

About the author 248
Acknowledgements 249
Index 250

CAKE FOR A SPECTACLE 115

Strawberry and Cream Basket Cake 118
Pecan and Muscovado Medovik Cake 120
Pure Chocolate Delice 124
Tarte Tropézienne 126
Pistachio and Raspberry Cream Dream 129
Coconut Millefeuille 132
Black Forest Cake 136
Pistachio Yule Log 139

SWEET AS PIE 143

Flaky Pastry 146
Short Sweet Pastry 147
Perfect Peach Pie 148
Yuzu Meringue Pie 152
Pure Pistachio Tart 155
Figwell Tart 157
Apricot Tarte Tatin 161
Mango Lemongrass Tart 162
Grape Tart 166
Anzac Muscovado Custard Pie 168

SOME ROOM FOR DESSERT 171

Chocolate Mousse Three Ways 175
Baklava Parfait Roll 179
Mango and Vanilla Bombe Alaska 180
Roasted Almond, Pear and Saffron Trifle 184
A Perfect Summer Dessert 187

A COLLECTION TO SAVOUR 191

Puffy Pastry 194
Puff Pastry 195
Blind-baked Flaky Pastry 196
Savoury Royale Custard 197
Corn-ish Pasty 199
Nightshade Quiche 202
Squash, Hazelnut and Sage Quiche 204
Mushroom and Truffle Quiche 206
Caramelised Onion, Pepper and Za'atar Quiche 209
Spinach Roll 210
Sausy Roll 213
Tempeh and Mushroom Pie 214
Courgette Galette 218
Creamy Leek and Tofu Pie 220
Savoury Summer Gateau 223
Corn and Jalapeño Muffins 227
Cheesy Sun Buns 228
Bread Sticks 231

A SELECTION OF STAPLES 235

Fresh Whipping Cream 238
Crème Pâtissière 239
Chocolate Crème Pâtissière 239
Oat Crumble 240
Candied Peel 240
Baking Glaze 242
Exotic Clear Glaze 242
Aquafaba from Dried Chickpeas 244
Aquafaba from Tinned Chickpeas 244
Classic Hummus 244
Tomato Ketchup 246
Mayonnaise 246

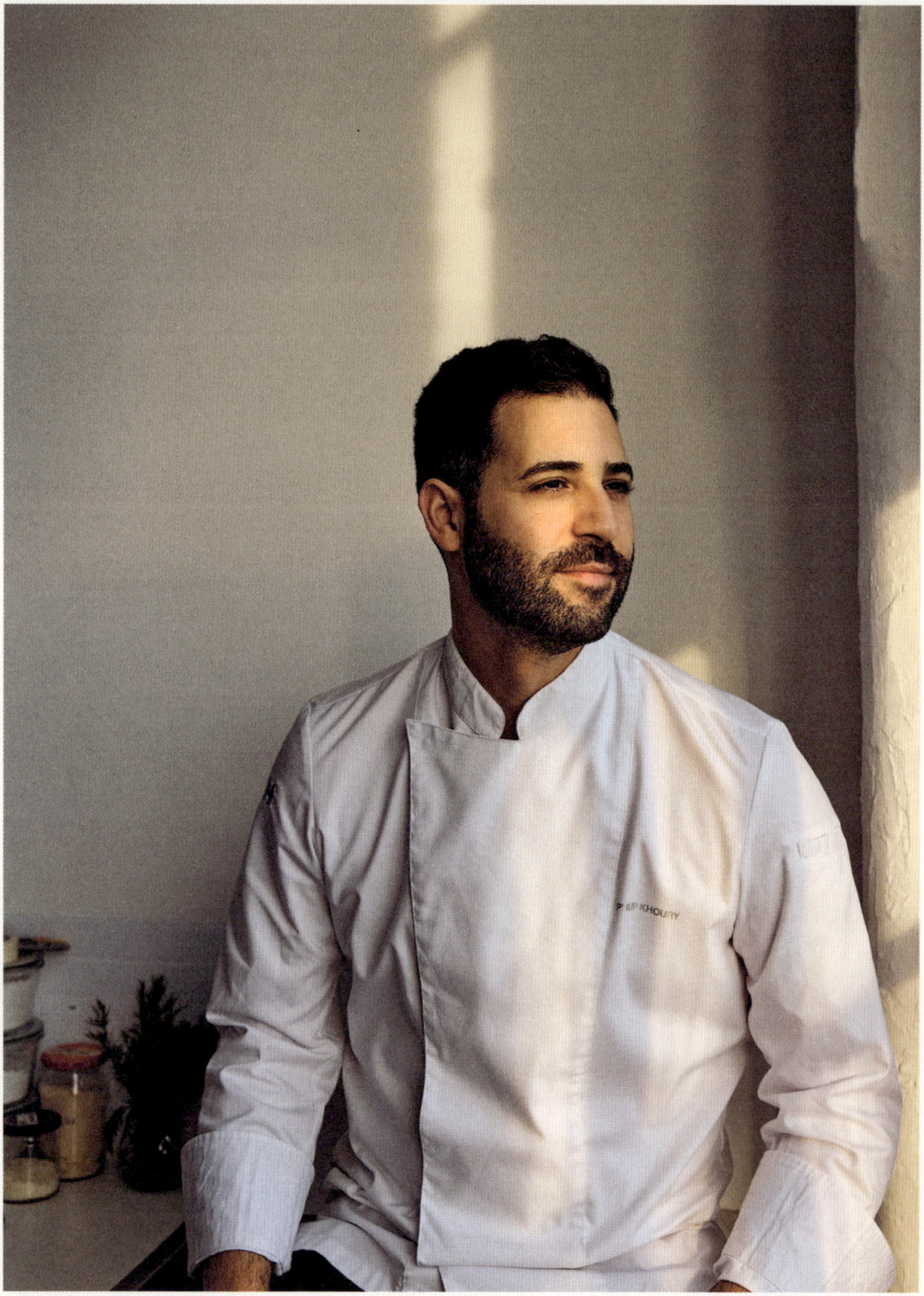
KHOURY

INTRODUCTION

There is no single way to bake. If my first book, *A New Way to Bake*, was about proving that, then *Beyond Baking* is about pushing those ideas even further – showing not just an alternative, but an evolution. This book isn't about making substitutes or tiptoeing around tradition. It's about rethinking what's possible and unlocking new ways to create flavour, texture and indulgence by using what we've had in our pantries all along.

Baking is about transformation – the alchemy of simple ingredients turning into something greater than the sum of their parts. For centuries, eggs and dairy have been the glue that holds this process together, and for good reason. Without them, we wouldn't have the rich, laminated layers of pastry, the delicate aeration of sponge or the emulsification of custards and creams. They helped shape the very foundations of modern pâtisserie.

But just as baking evolved to embrace these ingredients, it can evolve again. The question isn't whether eggs and dairy *work* – they clearly do. The question is: *are they the only way?*

What happens if we strip baking back to its fundamentals? Instead of seeing eggs as 'essential', can we rethink structure? Instead of assuming that butter is the only route to flakiness, can we explore how fats interact with flour and hydration? That's what I've spent the last decade exploring – not through imitation, but by embracing the natural properties of everyday pantry staples. Flour provides structure. Sugars caramelise and tenderise. Starches bind and emulsify. Fat enriches and crisps. The elements are all there – we just have to use them differently.

This book builds on everything I learned while writing *A New Way to Bake*. That book was about proving what was possible. This book goes further. The sweet chapters go beyond the familiar, rethinking how cakes, pastries and desserts are made. The savoury chapter explores a side of baking that often gets overlooked, proving that indulgent, deeply satisfying flavours aren't limited to sweet dishes. And for those who believe that laminated pastries – croissants, viennoiseries, anything crisp and golden – are impossible without conventional butter, this book will change that perception entirely, with step-by-step guidance on making them with my homemade plant-based butter.

WHY THIS MATTERS

A big part of my philosophy is that there's more than one way to roll out a perfect pastry. This is not *the* way to bake. It's not *the best way* to bake. It's simply another way – one that happens to be kinder to the planet, to people and to animals.

I don't believe in putting baking into boxes. Too often, the word 'vegan' is polarising. It makes people judge a pastry before they've even taken a bite. So, my goal has always been simple: don't tell them. Just let them taste. When something is good – flaky, buttery, crisp or tender, moist and flavoursome – it speaks for itself.

But I do believe in being informed. The way we produce food today is vastly different from when these traditions first developed. The same ingredients that shaped pâtisserie have also spawned industrial-scale, energy-intensive and often cruel industries.

Take butter. A single 250 g (8.8 oz) block requires *5 litres (1.3 gallons) of milk* to produce. That means a single batch of croissants or a few cakes might use up the daily milk output of an entire dairy cow. Eggs tell a similar story. A century ago, a hen laid around 20 eggs per year. Today, through selective breeding and intensive farming, that number has risen to *over 300 per year*. The demand for these ingredients has driven mass production, changing the way we farm and consume food on an industrial scale.

THE INGREDIENTS YOU ALREADY HAVE

This book isn't about restriction or artificial substitutes. The ingredients I use are the same pantry staples that have been used in kitchens for generations – flour, sugar, cornflour (cornflour) and natural oils. The difference is in how we use them. Instead of following convention, we tweak, rebalance and refine. We lean into their natural properties to create textures and flavours that feel both familiar and fresh.

This isn't about taking things away. It's about expanding what's possible.

THE FUTURE OF BAKING STARTS HERE

Baking has always evolved. The cakes we consider traditional today were once considered revolutionary. Pastry chefs throughout history have challenged convention, asked new questions and redefined what's possible.

I believe we're at the start of a new era – one where we stop seeing plant-based baking as an alternative and start seeing it as an evolution.

In professional kitchens, I've seen this shift first hand. Pastry chefs trained in classical French technique are beginning to question the rigidity of old methods, not because they must, but because they *can* – because baking has never been a fixed discipline. It's a craft that thrives on reinvention. So why should we, as home bakers, not do the same? Why should we not embrace the idea that there is more than one way to make a perfect croissant? That a cake can be just as rich, just as tender and just as indulgent without the ingredients we've been taught are non-negotiable? Why should we limit ourselves to convention, when convention itself has always been fluid?

So, if you loved *A New Way to Bake*, welcome back. There's more to discover. If this is your first time picking up one of my books, I hope these pages challenge, excite and inspire you. I hope they show you that baking has no boundaries – only possibilities.

THE RULES

1 Read the recipe first

If you're making something for the first time, the recipe is there to help you, so read and watch it from start to finish before you get going. The QR codes link to videos of the recipe, so I can show you exactly how and why to do things.

2 Use scales!

Digital scales are affordable and easy to use. Grab the bowl or jug (pitcher) mentioned in the recipe and weigh your ingredients directly into it for fuss-free and consistent baking.

3 Don't substitute

I have tried to build plenty of flexibility into the recipes to cater for different allergies. As a general rule, however, don't substitute different ingredients, as they will work differently. Gluten-free options are included where appropriate. By all means, use the recipes as a foundation for experimentation, but do try them as they are written first.

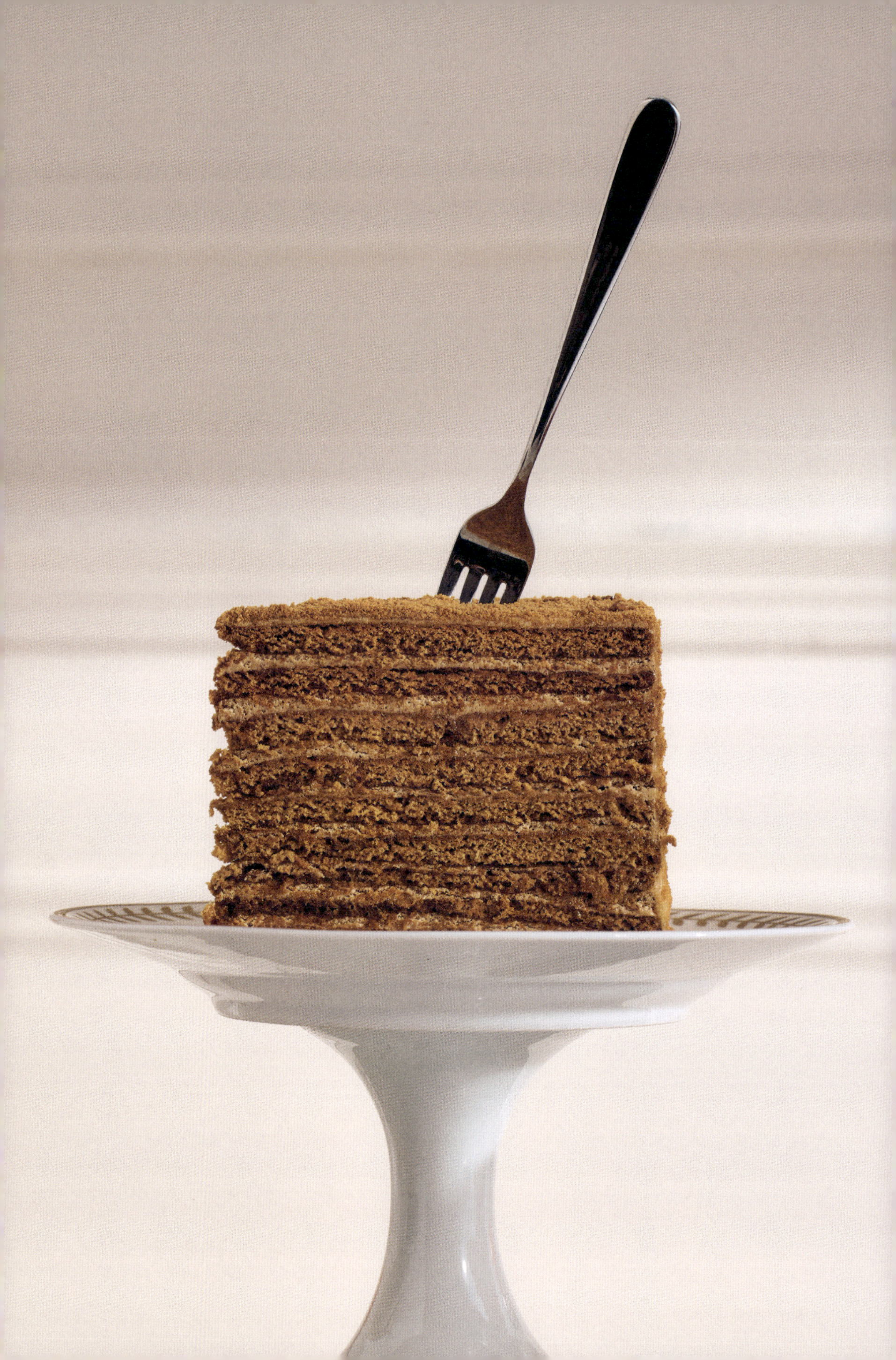

A BRIEF HISTORY OF CAKE

Cake as we know it is a new innovation in the history of mankind, evolved from a number of transformations in farming and agriculture, chemistry and technology.

In fact, most foods that we consider traditional are relatively new and are the products of industrialisation. Many of them were hailed as modern inventions not so long ago. Moist sponge cakes and other similar cakes evolved from breads that were enriched with honey and milk, and later sugar, butter and eggs. Cooks eventually discovered that if you beat eggs or butter you could incorporate air, which led to the creation of recipes that resemble cakes as we know them today.

Domesticated animals have long been tied to the history of agriculture. They were needed to till fields and help sow crops, while their waste was used as fertiliser and they were killed for their meat. Using dairy and eggs seemed like the natural thing to do. After all, butter is a healthy and delicious fat when eaten in moderation.

About 60–80 g (2–2.8 oz) butter can be produced from 1 litre (33.8 fl oz) milk. In the 1970s, the average Holstein-Friesian cow produced 10 litres (2.6 gallons) of milk a day, while in 2012, the average was 21 litres (5.5 gallons). A standard 23 cm (9 in) round cake can contain up to 250 g (8.8 oz) of butter, which will have needed 5 litres (1.3 gallons) of milk to make.

The ancestors of egg-laying hens used to lay 20 eggs a year. Now, the modern broiler chicken will lay almost an egg per day. An average cake uses 5–8 eggs, so we can see how our demand for eggs has led to cruel and intensive industries.

Two hundred years ago, if you owned a few chickens, using their unfertilised eggs as food and to enrich cakes may have seemed like a natural evolution. But chickens have since been selectively bred and put into manipulated environments that are arguably the worst of any farmed animal. Living in extreme confinement and unable to perform any of their natural behaviours, they suffer daily in conditions that no living creature should ever have to endure.

My intention is not to make you feel uncomfortable by describing how intensively farmed animals are raised, but the reality is confronting and it is uncomfortable.

We have become so disconnected to where and how our food is produced. We live to eat whatever we want, on demand. Instead of this, we need more options that are less impactful on the planet and which don't rely on animal exploitation. Sure, there are organic and high-welfare options, but most can't afford those. I believe there is a better way to get our sugar fix.

This book aims to provide you with a new outlook and the tools to bake a better future.

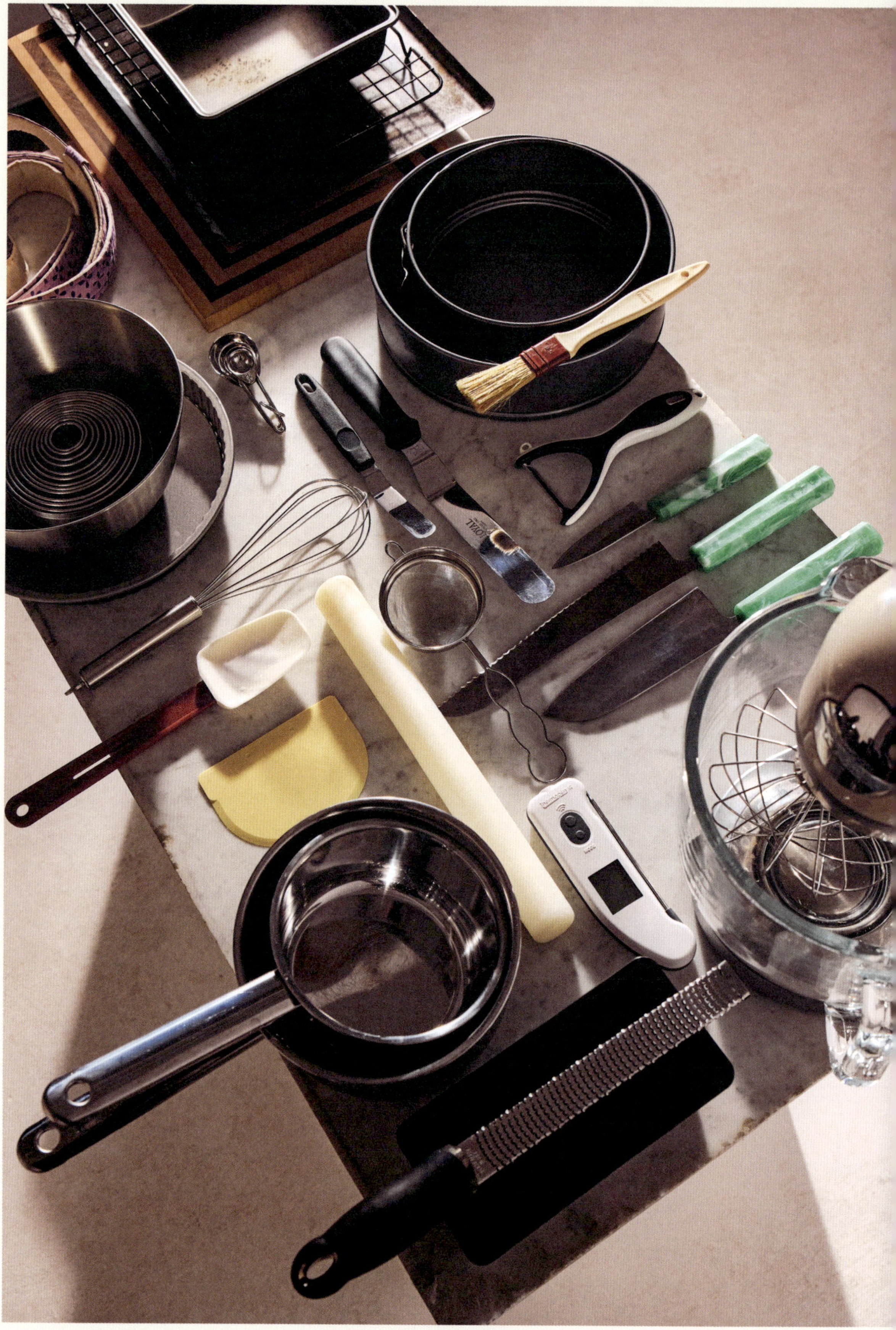

ESSENTIAL TOOLS

Tools and equipment for repeatable results.

Oven
Most ovens are electric and will have a conventional setting (top and bottom element) and fan-forced/convection setting. I recommend using the fan setting for most bakes, so if you are cooking in a conventional, non-fan-assisted oven, you should increase the temperature by 10–20°C (50–60°F).

A stand mixer (with whisk, dough hook and paddle attachments)
Personally, I mix all batters by hand because they're really easy, but I use a stand mixer for whipping cream, meringues and kneading dough quickly, efficiently and with less mess – although even doughs can be kneaded by hand. Kenwood or KitchenAid machines both work great and come with many attachments.

Digital scales
More accessible and accurate than ever, these come in slim, easy-to-store shapes and sizes.

Microscales
Available online, these are great for measuring very small amounts (for me, that's anything less than 10 g/0.4 oz), where an extra gram greatly affects the finished product.

High-powered blenders
Very useful for grinding nuts and blending emulsions. Nutribullet, Vitamix or Thermomix are great machines.

Hand-held blender
I love using a hand-held blender and they often come with a number of attachments. Find one that has a sturdy metal blender mechanism. Bamix, Waring and Braun make great blenders. I use a hand-held blender to emulsify my homemade Whipping Cream (page 238) or ganaches, where there is fat and water that needs to be combined thoroughly, as well as for any liquids, gels, custards and so on. Helps minimise washing-up, too!

Silicone spatula
This is indispensable for mixing. Select a spatula that's firm but with some flexibility, which will allow you to scrape against a bowl and combine ingredients.

Metal whisk
Great for combining ingredients swiftly. I don't sift dry ingredients; I just stir my flours and other dry ingredients in a bowl to gently mix and 'lighten' them and break up any clumps.

Saucepans
When making caramels, use a saucepan with high sides that has plenty of space for the liquid to expand as it boils. I prefer stainless-steel saucepans, especially for caramel, so that I can see the colour as it cooks.

Wire rack
Used to cool things quicker and prevent moisture condensing on a baked good.

Cake tins (pans)
I like springform cake tins (which are easy to line and remove cakes from) or cake rings for baking round cakes. Here is my list of must-haves:

- 20 cm (8 in) springform cake tin
- 23 cm (9 in) springform tin (the size I use for large single-layer cakes)
- 23 × 33 × 5 cm (9 × 13 × 2 in) rectangular cake tin
- 20 × 20 × 5 cm (8 × 8 × 2 in) square cake tin
- a small 450 g (1 lb) / 15 × 6 × 6 cm (6 × 2½ × 2½ in) loaf tin

Silicone dome or mini muffin moulds
One 45 mm (1¾ in) diameter mould tray for making soft centres for the Cheesy Sun Buns (page 228).

Non-stick silicone baking mat
This is a great alternative to baking parchment.

Large serrated knife
For trimming and halving sponge cakes.

Small paring knife
Serrated ones are versatile and great for cutting fruits and vegetables.

Silicone piping (pastry) bags and nozzles (tips)
Buy a small and a large one.

Microplane
These are invaluable for extracting the precious and explosively flavoursome essential oils from citrus. Rotate and press the citrus as you move it along the microplane, directly over the bowl.

Set of round cutters

Pastry brush

Rolling pin

A range of bowl sizes

Large and fine sieves (fine-mesh strainers)

43 × 30 cm (17 × 11 ¾ in) baking sheet

THE WEIGH TO BAKE

I'd like you to cast your imagination back 100 years, to a time when ingredients didn't come in neat little packages, the home oven was fuelled by temperamental and dangerous fire rather than electricity, cups and teaspoons were all different sizes and scales were cumbersome, difficult to use and even harder to transport.

Believe it or not, baking today is easier and better than it ever has been. One of the reasons for this is that digital scales are compact, cheap and accurate. Using ingredients in the exact quantities specified in a recipe is one of the best ways to guarantee success for experienced and non-experienced bakers alike.

Professional bakers use formulae and tables of ingredients that can be precisely calculated to produce the batches or volumes that each day calls for. The same technique has been used in this book so that you can enjoy the same flexibility, precision and confidence that your recipe will turn out with consistency every time.

In this new way of baking, especially for recipes that produce small quantities, such as a batch of 10 biscuits (cookies), precision is critical – a few extra grams of baking powder (the difference between a standard or non-standard spoon) can drastically alter the finished product. For this reason, you can even use microscales – I use these for weighing anything under 10 g (0.4 oz) with supreme confidence, especially ingredients like baking powder, agar-agar powder or salt.

As a pastry chef, I can vouch that baking professionals universally weigh their ingredients – it's the secret to perfectly consistent bakes.

Weighing in grams produces the best results, but I wanted the book to be as accessible as possible, so I have also included imperial measurements as an alternative.

ADAPTING RECIPES FOR DIFFERENT-SIZED TINS

Round tins (pans)
A 20 cm (8 in) tin provides 8 generous portions or 12 sensible portions.

My recipes for single-layer cakes are in 23 cm (9 in) round tins, and the ones that call for two baked layers use two 20 cm (8 in) tins.

Loaf tin (pans)
I have used a 450 g (1 lb) loaf tin, measuring 15 cm (6 in) long, 6 cm (2½ in) wide and 6 cm (2½ in) tall, which serves 8–10. If you're using the more common 900 g (2 lb) loaf tins, double the recipe.

Fluted tart tin (pan)
A 23 cm (9 in) tart serves 10–12.

If you'd like to make any of the other common sizes, simply multiply each amount by the numbers in each chart.

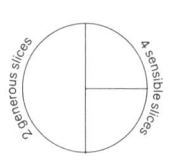

10 cm (4 in) x 0.18

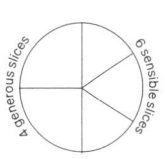

13 cm (5 in) x 0.31

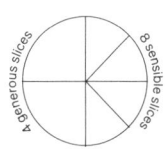

15 cm (6 in) x 0.42

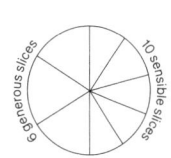

18 cm (7 in) x 0.61

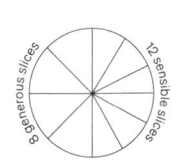

20 cm (8 in) x 0.75

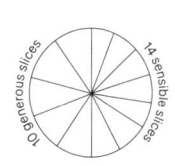

23 cm (9 in) x 1

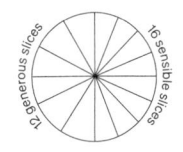

25 cm (10) x 1.18

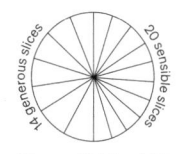

28 cm (11 in) x 1.48

THE PLANTRY

A new way of looking at the naturally plant-based, nutritious ingredients already in our pantry. By revisiting formulas, adjusting ratios or starting from scratch, I let these familiar ingredients shine in new and unexpected ways. This section outlines the key components of my plant-based pantry – my 'plantry' – with insights into how they're produced, how they function in recipes and my personal recommendations.

FLOURS

Flour is a staple ingredient in cooking and baking, made by grinding whole grains, seeds or roots into a fine powder. The production process typically involves cleaning the raw materials, milling them to break down the structure, then sifting the resulting substance in various stages to achieve a uniform texture. Flour serves as the foundation for a wide range of dishes, providing structure, texture and thickness. It's used in everything from bread and cakes to sauces and coatings, making it an essential component in many kitchens.

Wheat flour

Wheat flour is the most common type of flour used in cooking and baking. It forms a humble yet vital foundation that nearly all baked goods and many foods have evolved from. It's made by milling wheat grains and comes in various forms, such as plain (all-purpose), bread and cake flour. Wheat flour is known for its high gluten content, which gives baked goods their structure and chewiness. Bread flour, with its high protein content, is perfect for yeasted breads, while cake and pastry flour, which is finely milled and lower in protein, produces tender bakes.

Humans have consumed wheat flour for thousands of years – records date back to the Egyptians. Picture vast swathes of wheat fields, uniform and impressive, yet hiding a secret. These monoculture systems, though efficient, have unintended consequences. Much has changed in the farming of wheat in the last 200 years thanks to the advent of industrial and intensive farming and the use of fertilisers. Modern farming uses pesticides to eliminate pests, herbicides to remove weeds and fertilisers to feed the wheat, resulting in soil that is lacking in biodiversity and micronutrients and which leaches carbon out of the ground when it is tilled. It leads to soil degradation and the depletion of natural resources, while the use of synthetic chemicals to maintain high yields harm both the environment and our health. Some experts estimate that with traditional monoculture farming, we have a mere 60–100 years of crops left, primarily due to soil degradation.

Fear not, for there is hope on the horizon. It comes in the form of the wildfarmed method. This more sustainable, regenerative approach to wheat cultivation nurtures the land by incorporating a diverse mix of up to four plants alongside our precious wheat. The benefits are abundant: healthier soil through enhanced fertility and structure, a thriving ecosystem with increased biodiversity, CO_2 capture and a reduced reliance on synthetic chemicals. This method ensures that the healthy, live soil will bear crops of nutritious, flavoursome wheat in perpetuity.

The art of milling is crucial to the transformation of wheat into flour. The usual milling process involves cleaning the wheat to remove impurities, followed by grinding the grains to separate the endosperm, bran and germ. Finally, the flour particles are sifted to obtain the desired granulation. Within this process lies a beautiful alternative: the stoneground milling method.

By gently grinding the grains between two large stones, the bran and germ are preserved, resulting in a more nutritious and flavoursome flour. So, next time you are gathering your ingredients for your next culinary adventure, take a moment to consider the story behind the flour you will use. Seek out regeneratively farmed wheat and traditional stoneground milling, as they help to preserve our precious planet and also elevate our baking.

When flour is mixed with water to make a batter or dough, a network of protein called gluten develops, which provides a web-like structure and strength. When the batter or dough is baked, the proteins and starches create a gelling effect, so the mixture becomes firm.

Flours are made from different types of wheat, grown under different conditions or in different seasons to achieve specific profiles and protein levels. While there's an incredible range of flours, the two main flours I use for the recipes in this book are:

Plain (all-purpose) flour
(10–13 per cent protein)
For cakes.

Strong bread flour
(12–15 per cent protein)
For yeasted/sweet risen doughs.

Gluten-free flour
Many people have developed a sensitivity and intolerance to gluten, the protein that develops when flour is mixed with water, while others with coeliac disease are downright allergic to it. Symptoms can vary from mild discomfort to intense agony and distressing physiological symptoms after consuming foods containing even a trace of gluten. More people are diagnosed with gluten sensitivities each year, meaning they must avoid products containing gluten, while coeliacs must eliminate it from their diet completely.

There are many flours that don't contain gluten, such as buckwheat, teff, hemp, oat, rice, coconut, almond and potato flours, but I would never recommend swapping ANY flour directly for wheat flour as it will not work the same way.

Gluten-free replacements for plain (all-purpose) flour have become increasingly popular. These are usually a combination of very finely milled rice flour with potato, tapioca or cornflour (cornstarch). A common formula for a versatile gluten-free flour contains two parts finely milled rice flour, one-part potato starch and one-part tapioca starch. For recipes in which moisture retention is important, 1 teaspoon of xanthan gum can be added per 120 g (4.2 oz) gluten-free flour blend.

Some cake and biscuit (cookie) recipes allow for the simple substitution of a plain gluten-free flour for regular plain flour, so I have noted these where applicable. I have also kept some recipes intentionally gluten-free.

Rice flour
Rice flour, made from finely milled rice, is a popular gluten-free alternative to wheat flour. It has a light texture and is used in a variety of dishes, from Asian dumplings and noodles to gluten-free baked goods. Rice flour is great for creating smooth, silky textures in sauces and soups, and it's also used as a crispy coating for fried foods. Its neutral flavour means it can be used in both sweet and savoury recipes, but I strongly favour and recommend you seek out rice flour from Asian supermarkets from brands like Foo Lung, which is very finely milled and provides a superior texture.

Chickpea (gram) flour
Chickpea flour, also known as gram flour or besan, is made from ground chickpeas (garbanzos). It's a staple in Indian and Middle Eastern cuisines and is praised for its high protein and fibre content. Chickpea flour has a slightly nutty flavour and is used in dishes like flatbreads, pancakes and fritters. It's also a great thickening agent for soups and stews. Its binding properties make it an excellent substitute for eggs in vegan savoury recipes, and its nutritional benefits add value to many dishes, though I find its flavour too strong for use in delicate sweet recipes.

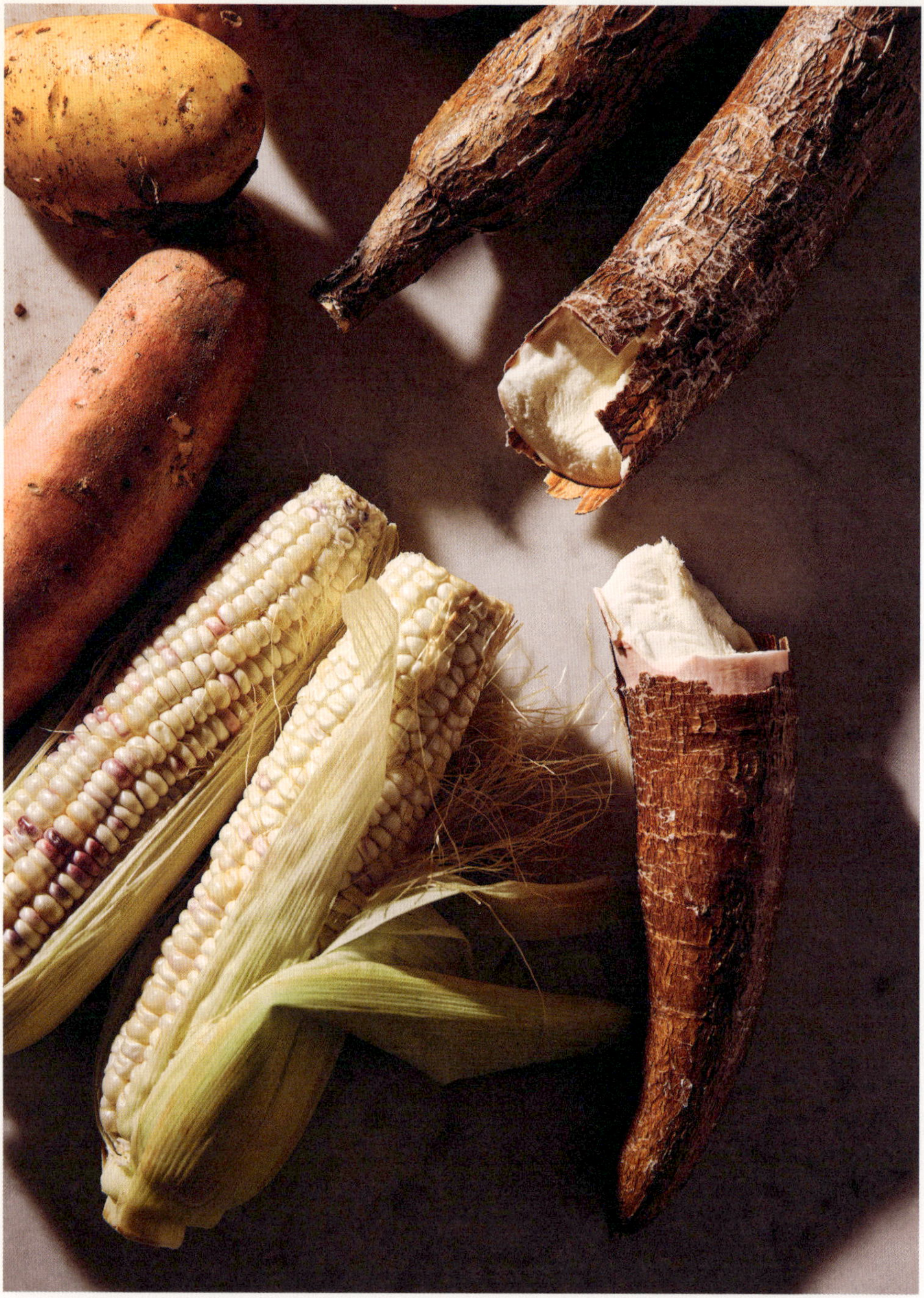

STARCHES: THE THICK OF IT

Starches are derived from various plants, such as corn, potatoes, cassava and wheat, through a straightforward extraction process. The raw material, like corn kernels or cassava roots, is first cleaned and then crushed or ground into a pulp. This pulp is mixed with water to separate the starch granules from the fibrous material. The mixture is then strained and allowed to settle, so that the starch sinks to the bottom. After draining the excess water, the starch is dried to form a fine powder ready for packaging.

In cooking, starches are versatile and invaluable. They are primarily used as thickeners in soups, sauces and gravies, providing a smooth and glossy texture. Their neutral flavour allows them to blend seamlessly into both sweet and savoury dishes, making them essential in recipes like puddings, pie fillings and baked goods. Starches also contribute to the texture of foods, such as giving a chewy consistency to tapioca pearls in bubble tea.

Starches vary in their features and characteristics and can't be substituted for one another in a lot of pastry recipes. As thickeners for soups or gravies, it might not matter, but in custards, for example, if the starch is substituted with potato starch in the same amount the texture will be very gummy and unappetising.

Cornflour (cornstarch)
Cornflour is a go-to thickener in cooking, prized for its ability to create opaque, glossy sauces and gravies. Despite some confusing naming conventions, cornstarch is the more accurate name. Cornflour, as it is called in the UK, is a more accurate name for finely milled corn kernels, which is a different ingredient altogether.

The corn that's used for making starch isn't much like the sweetcorn that you eat from the cob. The cultivars meant for eating are sweeter and are harvested before they mature. The kind meant for milling is starchy rather than sweet and it's left on the cob until it's rock hard. The first step in extracting the starch is to soak the corn kernels for a day or two in huge vats. This loosens the husks and moistens the grain. After this, the corn passes through a series of screens, designed to separate the grain into its various parts. The hulls and germ are removed to be processed into corn bran and corn oil. The endosperm, which has a lot of protein as well as starch, is separated out for a variety of other uses. What's left is a wet slurry that's made up of water and starch. The water is drained and replaced with fresh water to wash and purify the starches. Finally, the starch is dried and milled to a fine powder. That's the cornflour you buy from the supermarket.

Cornflour is nearly flavourless, so it blends well into both sweet and savoury dishes without changing the taste. It also thickens quickly at high temperatures, making it perfect for stir-fries and quick sauces. It's a key ingredient in baking, helping to give cakes and biscuits (cookies) a light, tender texture.

Tapioca starch

Tapioca starch comes from the cassava root and is valued for its stability and unique texture. It forms a clear, smooth gel that remains consistent even after freezing and thawing, which is perfect for frozen desserts and reheatable dishes. Tapioca starch is famous for creating a chewy texture, ideal for bubble tea and puddings. Its neutral taste and smooth finish make it a favourite in various recipes without overpowering other flavours.

Arrowroot

Arrowroot, derived from tropical plant rhizomes (underground stems), is a versatile thickener that works well even in acidic dishes. It doesn't break down like cornflour (cornstarch) can, making it great for fruit sauces and glazes. Arrowroot thickens at lower temperatures, preserving the colour and flavour of delicate ingredients. Its light, silky texture is perfect for gluten-free baking, achieving a tender, moist crumb. Arrowroot is also easily digestible, making it a preferred thickener for those with dietary restrictions or sensitive digestive systems.

Starch type	Best applications	Reaction to acidity	Reaction to sugar	Reaction to heat
Potato starch	Sauces, soups and baked goods. Ideal for clear, glossy sauces.	Moderate resistance	Moderately stable	High heat tolerance
Tapioca starch	Puddings, pie fillings and clear sauces. Great for freezing.	Good resistance	Moderately stable	High heat tolerance
Cornflour (cornstarch)	Thickening soups, gravies and sauces. Common in baked goods.	Moderate resistance	Less stable in high-sugar environments	Moderate heat tolerance
Waxy maize starch	Acidic sauces, frozen foods and products requiring freeze-thaw stability.	Good resistance	Stable	High heat tolerance
Rice starch	Dairy products, sauces and baby foods. Good for smooth textures.	Moderate resistance	Stable	Moderate heat tolerance
Wheat starch	Soups, sauces and certain baked goods.	Low resistance	Less stable	Moderate heat tolerance
Arrowroot	Sauces, gravies and desserts. Ideal for clear, glossy and light sauces.	Good resistance	Stable	Low to moderate heat tolerance

Potato starch

Potato starch, derived from potatoes, is known for its strong thickening power at lower temperatures. This makes it ideal for creamy soups, stews and sauces. It's also excellent in gluten-free baking, providing a light, fluffy texture to cakes and breads. Potato starch doesn't get grainy or pasty, even with prolonged heating, and maintains its consistency well. These qualities make it a versatile and essential ingredient in many recipes.

Clarity and texture	Thickening power	Freeze-thaw stability	Shear tolerance (blending)	Other considerations
High clarity, smooth and glossy texture	High	Low	Low	High water-binding capacity, tends to break down in prolonged heating.
Excellent clarity, chewy texture	High	Excellent	Moderate	Excellent freeze-thaw stability, elastic texture.
Moderate clarity, smooth texture	Moderate	Low	Low	Prone to syneresis (water release) during storage.
Moderate clarity, smooth texture	Moderate	Excellent	High	Excellent freeze-thaw stability, low tendency to retrogradation.
Fine, smooth texture, slightly cloudy appearance	Moderate	Low to Moderate	Moderate	Hypoallergenic, suitable for sensitive diets.
Cloudy appearance, slightly grainy texture	Moderate	Low	Low	Contains gluten, which may limit its use for those with a gluten intolerance.
High clarity, smooth and light texture	Moderate	Excellent	High	Easily digestible, often used in gluten-free and allergen-free products.

THE PLANTRY

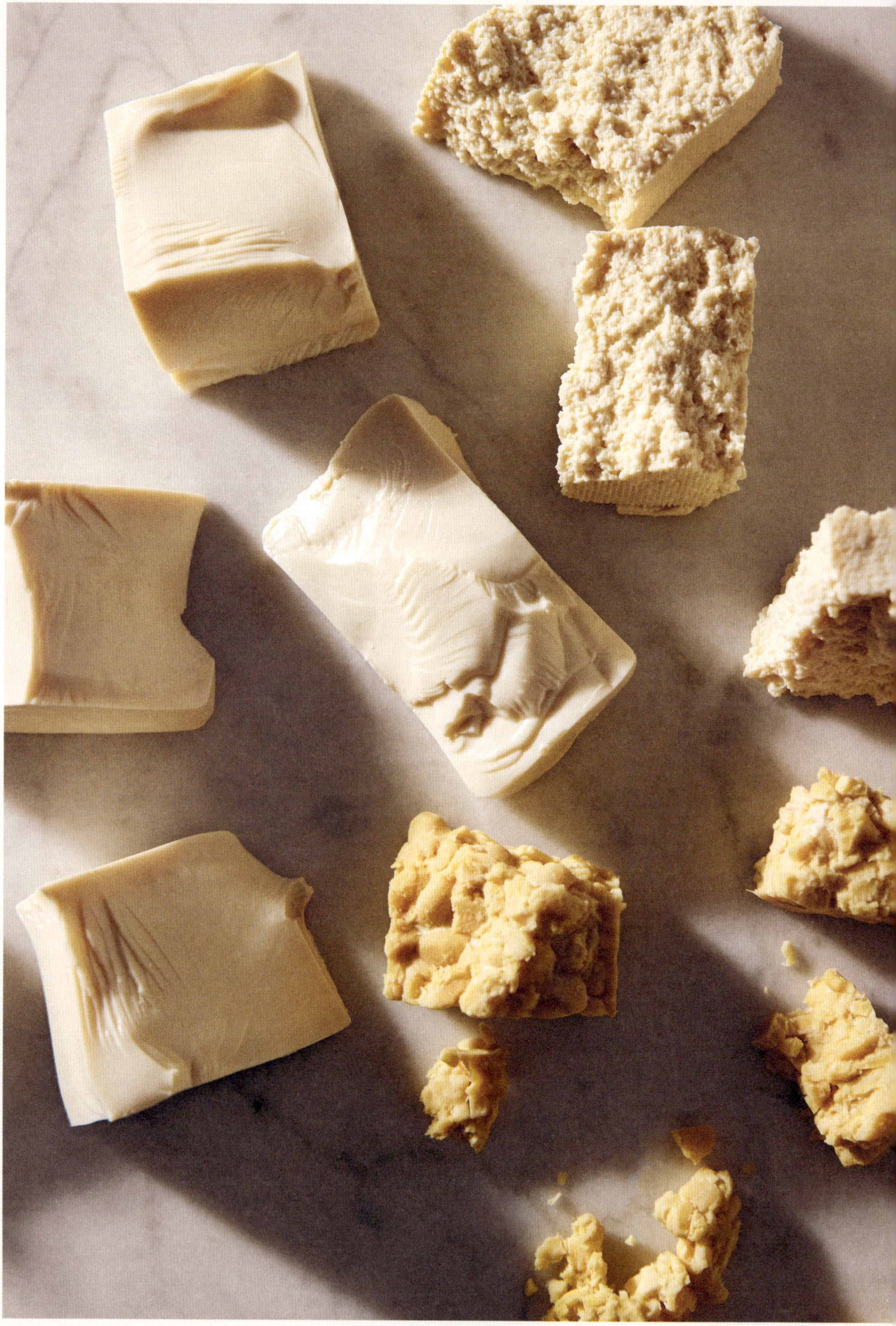

THE QUEEN BEAN SOYA

The use of soya beans as an ingredient dates back 9,000 years, with archaeological evidence suggesting that they were domesticated in China around 7000 BCE. By the time of the Zhou dynasty (1046–256 BCE), soya beans had become a staple crop in Chinese agriculture and an integral part of the diet.

Soya products eventually spread to neighbouring countries like Japan, Korea and Indonesia, where they became deeply embedded in local cuisines and food cultures.

Legumes like soya beans are the unsung heroes of sustainable agriculture, thanks to their superpower: nitrogen fixation. These plants pull nitrogen from the air and tuck it into the soil, boosting fertility and making the land more productive for other crops. Nitrogen is a vital nutrient for plant growth, essential for the formation of proteins, amino acids and DNA. Without sufficient nitrogen, plants cannot grow properly, resulting in poor yields and less nutritious crops. By fixing atmospheric nitrogen in the soil, legumes reduce the need for synthetic fertilisers, which can be costly and harmful to the environment. Among these green champions, soya beans stand tall as the 'queen bean', thanks to their pivotal role in agriculture and deep-rooted significance in the cuisines of East Asian cultures, especially in China, Japan, Indonesia and Korea, for thousands of years.

A NUTRITIONAL POWERHOUSE

Soya beans have been revered for their versatility and nutritional richness since ancient times. Chinese farmers quickly recognised soya's dual benefits: it not only nourished their families with its high protein content and essential nutrients but also enriched their fields. The Chinese transformed these humble beans into a variety of food products, creating a culinary tradition that has been passed down through generations.

Nutritionally, soya beans are powerhouses. They provide complete protein, containing all essential amino acids, making them an excellent alternative to animal-based proteins. Soya is also packed with vitamins, minerals and beneficial plant compounds like isoflavones.

MUCH MALIGNED, BUT OFT MISUNDERSTOOD

Despite its numerous benefits, soya has become somewhat maligned in recent years. Much of the controversy stems from the prevalence of genetically modified (GMO) soya and its extensive use in animal feed (about 80 per cent of global soya production is used for this purpose). This massive demand for soya as animal feed has led to significant habitat destruction, particularly in regions like the Amazon rainforest, where forests are cleared to make way for soya plantations. This environmental impact has fuelled negative perceptions of soya.

Organic soya beans are cultivated without synthetic pesticides or fertilisers, making them a more environmentally friendly choice. Organic farming practices enhance biodiversity, improve soil health and reduce pollution, contributing to a more sustainable agricultural system. Many regenerative farmers include soya beans along with other members of the legume family like peas and beans in their cover crops as a way of bringing nitrogen into the soil and to avoid the use of synthetic fertilisers completely.

EMBRACING THE QUEEN BEAN

When consumed as an ingredient in human diets, soya offers substantial health benefits. The artistry and tradition behind soya products in East Asian cultures can be likened to the crafts of cheesemaking, pickling and fermentation in the West. Both involve meticulous processes that transform basic ingredients into something wonderfully complex and delicious. By exploring the diverse range of soya products and understanding their nutritional value, we can appreciate the queen bean's rightful place in our kitchens. The processes that transform soya beans into these products highlight the ingenuity and versatility of this remarkable legume, proving that soya is truly a culinary and nutritional gem. Embracing organic soya beans not only enhances our diets but also plays a crucial role in creating a sustainable future.

THE MARVELLOUS TRANSFORMATIONS OF SOYA

From soya beans, we get a diverse array of products, each with unique characteristics and culinary uses. Here's how some of the most popular soya products are made:

Tofu: the versatile bean curd

Tofu, often referred to as bean curd, is made by coagulating soya milk – a process akin to Western cheesemaking. The process begins by soaking and grinding soya beans to extract soya milk. A coagulant, such as calcium sulfate or magnesium chloride, is then added to the soya milk, causing it to curdle. These curds are then pressed into blocks of varying firmness, resulting in tofu that can be soft, firm or extra-firm. Tofu's versatility makes it suitable for stir-frying, steaming, grilling (broiling) and even blending into smoothies.

Tempeh: the nutty ferment

Tempeh, a fermented soya bean cake from Indonesia, offers a nutty flavour and dense texture. To make tempeh, whole soya beans are dehulled, cooked and inoculated with a starter culture of Rhizopus mould. The beans are then spread into a thin layer and incubated at a warm temperature for 24–48 hours. During this fermentation process, the mould binds the beans into a firm, cake-like consistency. Tempeh is rich in protein, fibre and probiotics, making it an excellent addition to a healthy diet.

Miso: the umami paste

Miso is a quintessential Japanese ingredient. It is made by fermenting soya beans with salt and kōji, a type of mould (*Aspergillus oryzae*). The mixture is left to ferment for several months or even years, depending on the desired flavour profile. The result is a thick, savoury paste that adds umami depth to soups, marinades and sauces. Miso is not only flavourful but also packed with beneficial probiotics that support gut health.

Soy sauce: liquid gold

Soy sauce, another staple of Japanese cuisine, undergoes an intricate fermentation process. To make soy sauce, soya beans and wheat are cooked, mashed and inoculated with kōji. This mixture is then combined with a saltwater brine and left to ferment for several months. The fermentation process breaks down the proteins and starches, producing a rich, salty liquid. After fermentation, the mixture is pressed to extract the liquid soy sauce, which is then pasteurised and bottled.

Soya milk and soya yoghurt

Soya milk is made by soaking and grinding soya beans with water, then straining the mixture to remove the solid residues. The resulting milk can be consumed as it is or used as a base for other products. Soya yoghurt is made by fermenting soya milk with live cultures, similar to dairy yoghurt. The fermentation process gives soya yogurt its creamy texture and tangy flavour. Both soya milk and soya yoghurt are excellent dairy-free alternatives.

Textured vegetable protein

Textured vegetable protein (TVP) was invented in the 1960s by the Archer Daniels Midland Company (ADM), as a way to make use of the protein-rich defatted soya flour left over from soya oil production (soya beans naturally contain about 20 per cent fat, which can be extracted to make oil). ADM developed a method to turn the flour into a high-protein, fibrous product that could serve as a meat substitute. Over time, TVP gained popularity as a versatile, plant-based ingredient that could be easily incorporated into vegetarian and vegan diets. Although soya is the most common base for TVP, it can also be made from other vegetable proteins like peas, lentils and wheat, offering more options for diverse protein sources and allergen considerations.

Once the oil has been extracted from the soya beans, TVP is produced by mixing the resulting flour with water, then heating it and passing it through an extruder, creating a fibrous, meat-like texture. Although the industrial method uses specialised machinery, the process itself isn't overly complex. In fact, similar products can be made at home using soya flour or other plant proteins, although they may not have the exact texture of commercially produced TVP. Fortunately, TVP is now widely available in shops, in a variety of sizes from fine granules to larger chunks.

To prepare TVP, it must be rehydrated before cooking. The most common method is to soak it in hot water or broth, often at a ratio of 1:1. It absorbs flavours well and offers a flexible, nutritious addition to plant-based meals.

OTHER INGREDIENTS THAT FORM GELS

Pectins

Pectin is found in fruit fibres. It is usually extracted from citrus fruits and comes in a powder. This powder is mixed with sugar (so it doesn't clump) before being added to liquid and simmered, which forms a gel when cooled. It is often used in jam (jelly) making.

There are a few types of pectin available, but the one I use in this book is pectin NH – a type of pectin that gels with low sugar and acidity, meaning you can make jams and preserves that freeze and defrost very well. If you are not freezing your cake, feel free to use agar-agar powder instead.

Pectin NH is available in nearly all countries, although you may need to find an online supplier – 20–30 g (0.7–1 oz) is required to set 1 kg (2 lb 4 oz) of gel or jam, so a little goes a long way. There are other types of pectin available, such as Ball RealFruit Low or No-Sugar Needed Pectin or Pomona's Universal Pectin, which should be used according to the packet instructions.

The most common type of pectin is often just called 'pectin' or 'yellow pectin' and requires a high quantity of sugar and acid to create a gel. This is desirable in a jam, which has a lot of sugar and acid from lemon juice.

Agar-agar

Agar-agar is extracted from red algae (*Rhodophyceae*). It can be added in very small amounts to liquids and then boiled to make a gel at 38–40°C (100–104°F) as it cools. Agar-agar mainly comes in two forms – a powder and strips. The powder is made from grinding down the strips and is the one I recommend using, as it's easier to weigh and use. Use high-accuracy microscales when dealing with agar-agar, because only a small amount is needed to set a large amount of liquid. Recipes will usually specify small amounts. When using acidic liquids, such as cranberry juice, lime juice or pineapple juice, you may need to use more.

A soft jam or gel with very low sweetness can be made by blending a set agar gel and used in a fresh cake. These jams contain significantly less sugar than most commercial varieties, which are often as much as one part sugar to one part fruit. A low-sugar agar jam will have a short shelf life but can be a delicious addition to fresh cakes that don't need to be stored at room temperature for extended periods.

LEAVENERS AND RAISING AGENTS

Originally, yeast was just a crude preparation of flour and water that was affected by the weather and prone to spoiling and funky flavours. Baking was a heavily skills-based and time-consuming activity that was the domain of wives and daughters. Cooks in those days also had very different ovens and inconsistent flour, which they even had to dry in the oven. Chemical leaveners, such as potash and pearl ash (the ancestors of baking powder), first made an appearance in recipes as early as the 1780s, when they were mixed with an acidic ingredient, such as lemon juice, vinegar or buttermilk. The reaction created air (gases) that was trapped within the structure of the bake, lightening the recipe as the batter or dough heated and firmed up during cooking.

CHEMICAL

Bicarbonate of soda (baking soda)
In recipes, bicarbonate of soda provides the 'first rise' or leavening of a batter or dough. This is what happens when the bicarbonate of soda and an acidic ingredient (like lemon juice or brown sugar) combine in the presence of water. It also promotes browning and caramelisation in biscuits (cookies) and sponges when it is included without an acidic ingredient to neutralise it.

Baking powder
Baking powder as we know it came to exist in the 1840s. The British inventor and food scientist Alfred Bird created a 'single-acting' baking powder for his wife, who was allergic to yeast (he also created custard powder for his wife, as she was also allergic to eggs). He mixed bicarbonate of soda (baking soda) and cream of tartar (an acidic powder leftover from wine production). When added to a recipe, the baking powder created an instant reaction without requiring an acidic ingredient to be added to the recipe.

In the 1860s, 'double-acting' baking powder was invented by Eben Norton Horsford. This type of baking powder first becomes active when combined with a liquid and then, as the mixture is heated to above 60°C (140°F), a second acidic compound dissolves and gives the mixture a second rise. Starches start to gel at this temperature, too. Nearly all blends of baking powder have had formulations that have been the same for the last 200 years. 'Single-acting' baking powder is only available to industrial bakers for specific applications, so all baking powder you buy in the shops is 'double-acting'.

BIOLOGICAL

Yeast

Yeast as we know it (in fresh or dried form) is a relatively modern invention – in fact, it is newer than baking powder. Prior to 1876, when it was introduced by the Fleischmann brothers at the Centennial Exposition in Philadelphia, 'yeast' was prepared in the same way as a sourdough starter, by combining flour and water and leaving it to ferment. The brothers' impressive invention isolated *Saccharomyces cerevisiae* (brewer's yeast), a single-celled fungus responsible for many fermentation processes and also one of the most widely studied organisms. These simple organisms consume starch and simple sugars and produce carbon dioxide as a result of dividing and multiplying. How yeast is added to a recipe depends on how it has been processed or dried. Fresh and instant types can be added directly to a recipe, whereas active yeast needs to be 'activated' or dissolved in lukewarm liquid first. The water temperature should not exceed 59°C (138°F), as this will kill the yeast and make it useless. In this book, I use the most commonly available yeast – fast-action dried yeast, also called instant yeast – for everyone's convenience. It can be purchased in packets or small tins and has a very long shelf life (two years from date of manufacture) and doesn't need to be refrigerated like fresh yeast.

If you can, I recommend seeking out an organic brand of instant dried yeast, as it will only contain the active yeast – the ingredients will list *Saccharomyces cerevisiae*. Organic yeast is produced using organic cereals without the use of chemical additives during fermentation. Selected strains of yeast and lactic acid bacteria cultures are bred in a wholly organic nutrient solution made from organic grain, pure spring water and enzymes. All microorganisms and raw materials used are guaranteed non-GMO, organic ingredients.

Fast-action dried yeast or instant yeast is a fine granule that can usually be added directly to a recipe.

Active dry yeast has been dried at a slightly higher temperature, so it has a coating of deactivated (dead) yeast cells that need to be dissolved or 'activated' in lukewarm water or liquid before use. Multiply the instant amount by 1.3 if you want to use active dry yeast.

Compressed fresh (cake) yeast contains 70 per cent water and can be added directly to a recipe. It is popular with bakers who can use it in its short use-by (expiration) date as it typically doesn't last more than a week or two. If you prefer to use fresh yeast, you must multiply the amount of instant yeast by 3.

I recommend using instant dry yeast. It can be purchased in packs or in small cans and has a very long shelf life (2 years from date of manufacture) and doesn't need to be refrigerated like fresh.

OILS: GOOD PLANT FATS

Oils are naturally plant-based fats that are liquid at room temperature. This critical characteristic makes them incredibly useful for cooking and baking many delicious foods. In a sponge, for example, they penetrate the batter readily, creating a tender, moist crumb. This is different to solid fats, which must be manipulated (beaten or melted) in order to be incorporated into a recipe. When the temperature drops below 20°C (68°F), cakes made with butter and other solid fats tend to become firm and take on a 'dry mouthfeel', especially if they have been refrigerated – it takes a lot to warm them back up to the temperature at which a solid fat might become soft again. My recipes use significantly less fat compared to traditional bakes, and I use high-quality oils as the expense is comparative. Cheap, highly refined oils should be avoided (see right).

I hope that people will discover the beautiful flavour and qualities of cold-pressed and organic oils. To my mind, they should be celebrated for their provenance and flavour in the way we celebrate wine and honey.

UNREFINED VS REFINED OILS

Unrefined oils are those that have been mechanically processed – usually by some form of pressing. Oils that are certified organic will have been processed this way too. These oils usually contain higher amounts of vitamins and minerals and of residual compounds that flavour the oil. These compounds also increase the chance of the oil oxidising and spoiling faster as well as reducing their smoke point (the temperature an oil can be heated to before it starts to break down and release harmful chemicals and taste bitter). All unrefined or low-processed oils have a lower smoke point for frying, but this isn't relevant to baking, as the batter or dough never exceeds 100°C (212°F), which is well below the smoking point for most oils. These oils should be used at the peak of freshness and stored in cool, dark places or containers. Choose oils that have mild or complementary flavours. I use extra virgin olive oil and organic or virgin sunflower oil in nearly everything, from pastry to cakes. Some organic oils may be steam-refined, which is a gentler method of deodorising the oil in which steam is pumped into a chamber under vacuum to help remove volatile aroma compounds. This is still a far cry from the harmful processes used for many refined oils.

Refined oils are extracted using chemical solvents and should be avoided. They are ultra-processed ingredients. For this reason, I purposefully formulate recipes without margarines, which are made from refined oils (sometimes hydrogenated to make them solid at room temperature).

Some oils are very high in omega-6 fatty acids and can contribute to known health risks if not kept in check.

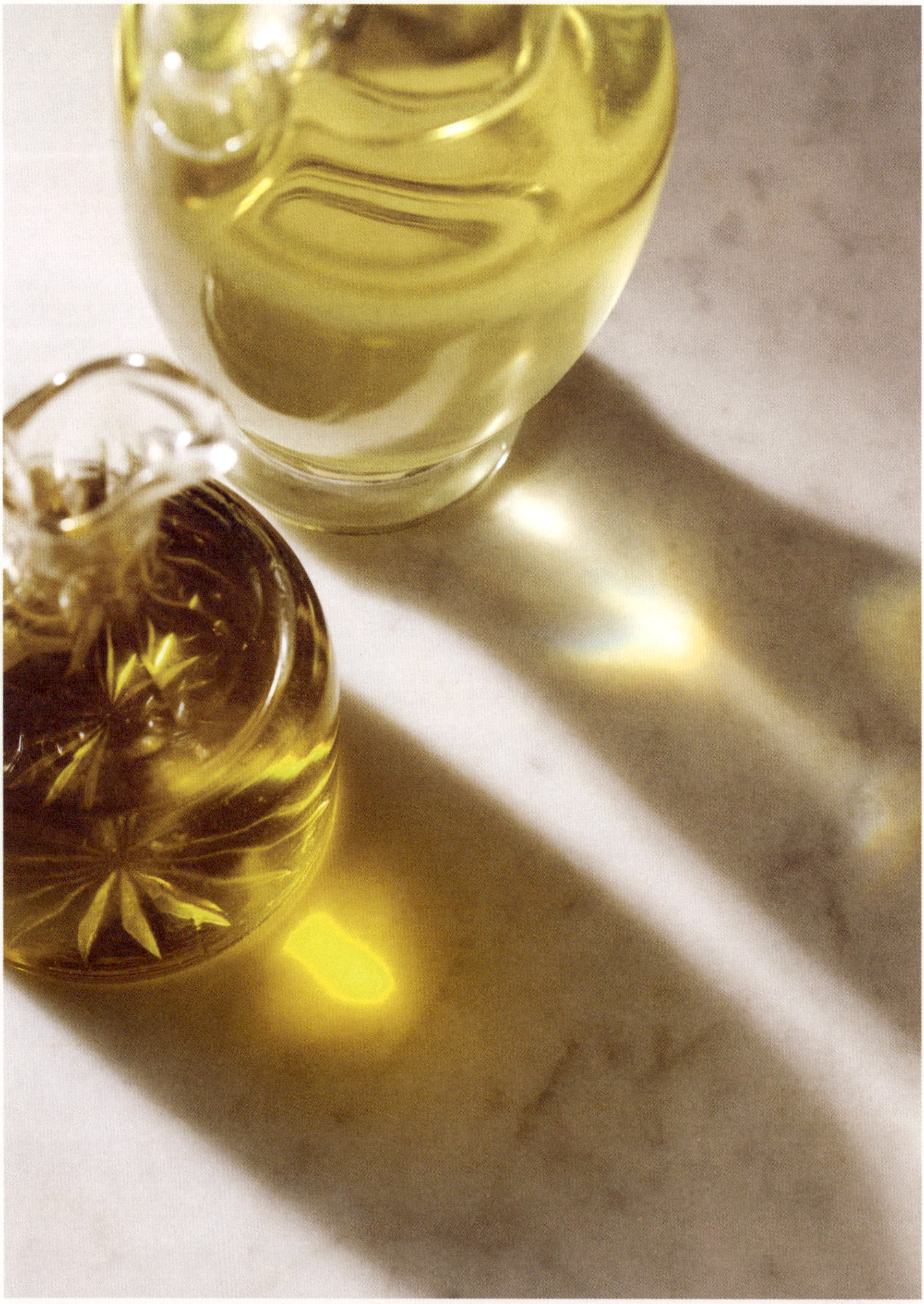

OLIVE'S REIGN CONTINUES

Olive oil, a staple in Mediterranean cuisine, has a history dating back thousands of years. Ancient civilizations such as the Egyptians, Greeks and Romans revered olive oil not only as a food ingredient but also for its medicinal and ritualistic properties. Its production and use can be traced back to around 4000 BCE in the Mediterranean basin, where olive trees were first cultivated. The Phoenicians played a crucial role in the spread of olive cultivation and olive oil production techniques. As skilled seafarers and traders, they established trade routes across the Mediterranean, introducing olive oil to new regions and cultures, significantly contributing to its widespread use and significance in ancient societies. The Greeks and Romans later refined these techniques, establishing olive oil as a crucial element of their diet and trade. Over time, olive oil became synonymous with the Mediterranean lifestyle, symbolising health, wealth and culinary sophistication.

Extra Virgin Olive Oil

Extra virgin olive oil (EVOO) is the highest-quality olive oil. The production of EVOO involves harvesting olives at their optimal ripeness and then cold-pressing them within hours to extract the oil. This method preserves the oil's natural flavours, aromas and nutritional properties. EVOO is celebrated for its robust taste and its high levels of polyphenols and antioxidants, which contribute to its health benefits and long shelf life. Its rising popularity in recent years can be attributed to growing awareness of its health benefits, including heart health and anti-inflammatory properties, as well as its versatility in culinary applications. Climatic changes, olive tree diseases and increased production costs have contributed to a rise in olive oil prices over the last decade. As consumers increasingly seek natural and high-quality ingredients, EVOO has become more prized than ever. I use it in so much of my baking – it works beautifully when paired with any bakes that have a fruity component, or even when I want some contrast with a nutty or chocolatey flavour.

Groundnut (peanut) oil

Peanuts, or groundnuts, have been cultivated for thousands of years, particularly in South America, where they were first domesticated around 3,500 years ago. The Spanish explorers introduced peanuts to Europe in the 16th century, from where they spread to Africa and Asia. Groundnut oil, extracted from pressing the kernels of the peanut plant, has been used in cooking for centuries, especially in regions where peanuts are a staple crop. Its rich nutritional profile makes it a healthy cooking oil, packed with monounsaturated fats that help lower bad cholesterol (LDL) and raise good cholesterol (HDL). Additionally, groundnut oil is a good source of vitamin E, an antioxidant that protects cells, and resveratrol, known for its anti-inflammatory and heart-protective properties.

Groundnut oil is highly regarded in the kitchen for its mild flavour with a subtle nutty hint, which enhances dishes without overwhelming other ingredients. There are different types of groundnut oil, each offering unique flavour profiles: deodorised groundnut oil, with a neutral taste and high smoke point, which is perfect for frying, baking and sautéing; cold-pressed groundnut oil, which retains more of the natural peanut flavour and aroma; and roasted groundnut oil, which has a deep peanut flavour.

Groundnut oil's high smoke point (about 232°C/450°F) makes it ideal for deep-frying and stir-frying, delivering crispy and evenly cooked results. The mild flavour also makes it a great substitute for other oils or fats in baking, adding moisture without changing the taste significantly. Cold-pressed groundnut oil can be used to create flavourful dressings and marinades, enhancing salads with its nutty notes. Its stability at high temperatures also makes it perfect for sautéing and roasting. Peanut oil's blend of health benefits, high heat tolerance and versatile flavour make it one of my favourite oils to bake with, period. Where allergies are concerned, a cold-pressed sunflower oil can be a great replacement.

Coconut oil

The pressed oil from coconut flesh is a saturated fat that may raise the levels of good cholesterol.

Virgin coconut oil is made by cold-pressing fresh coconut flesh to making coconut milk, which separates, leaving the oil on top. Unrefined or virgin coconut oil has a very strong coconut flavour, a slightly lower smoking point and is prone to faster rancidity. It can be used in baking but only in recipes where the flavour would be complementary. I generally don't use it.

Refined coconut oil is made from dried organic coconut meat, or copra. It is gently steam-refined through a certified organic process to achieve a neutral scent and flavour. If it's organic, absolutely no chemicals will be used, but if not, it will likely go through additional refining steps to purify the oil. I recommend seeking out a steam-deodorised, odourless coconut oil. I use coconut oil in recipes where I need some hardness, or for a creamy texture when blended, such as in a custard or to make your own whipping cream.

Sunflower oil

Sunflower oil is produced by pressing sunflower seeds and has a mild, nutty flavour. This oil originates in the cooler climates of Eastern Europe (Ukraine and Russia account for half of global production), where it is the most popular oil to cook with. I recommend a cold-pressed or organic sunflower oil in items where chocolate, caramel or other 'brown' flavours are being highlighted.

VANILLA: ANYTHING BUT

Vanilla is one of the world's most prized and labour-intensive spices, derived from the seed pods of a tropical orchid (*Vanilla planifolia* and related species). Each delicate flower must be pollinated by hand, and the harvested pods go through a slow, complex curing process that can take several months. The result is a richly aromatic ingredient with sweet, earthy tones and often unexpected depth. There are three main varieties, each with distinct flavour profiles: Madagascar bourbon vanilla is bold and woody, Mexican vanilla has a spicy, almost smoky edge, and Tahitian vanilla is floral and perfumed, with subtle hints of cherry or anise.

Because real vanilla is so costly to produce, it has long been imitated. Synthetic vanillin – the main compound responsible for vanilla's familiar flavour – flooded the market and contributed to vanilla being seen as a 'default' or bland option. In reality, true vanilla is anything but bland: it's complex, nuanced and transformative when used well. I often use Heilala vanilla, grown in Tonga and known for its ethical sourcing, transparency and beautifully balanced flavour.

Vanilla bean or paste
For home bakers, I generally recommend vanilla bean paste. It's a convenient way to add the depth and visual appeal of real vanilla seeds without needing to split pods (beans) or wonder what to do with the leftovers. In professional kitchens, we dry used pods and grind them into powder to extract every last bit of aroma, but at home you're unlikely to use enough to make that worthwhile. Paste is an elegant solution, offering consistent flavour, minimal waste and easy measurement. In my recipes, 1 teaspoon is interchangeable with ½ vanilla pod.

Vanilla extract
Vanilla extract – made by steeping vanilla pods in alcohol – is another excellent option, especially in liquid-based recipes or batters where it disperses evenly. A good-quality extract brings warmth and richness, and it's often more affordable than paste or pods. Just be sure to look for pure extract rather than imitation, which lacks the complexity and depth of the real thing.

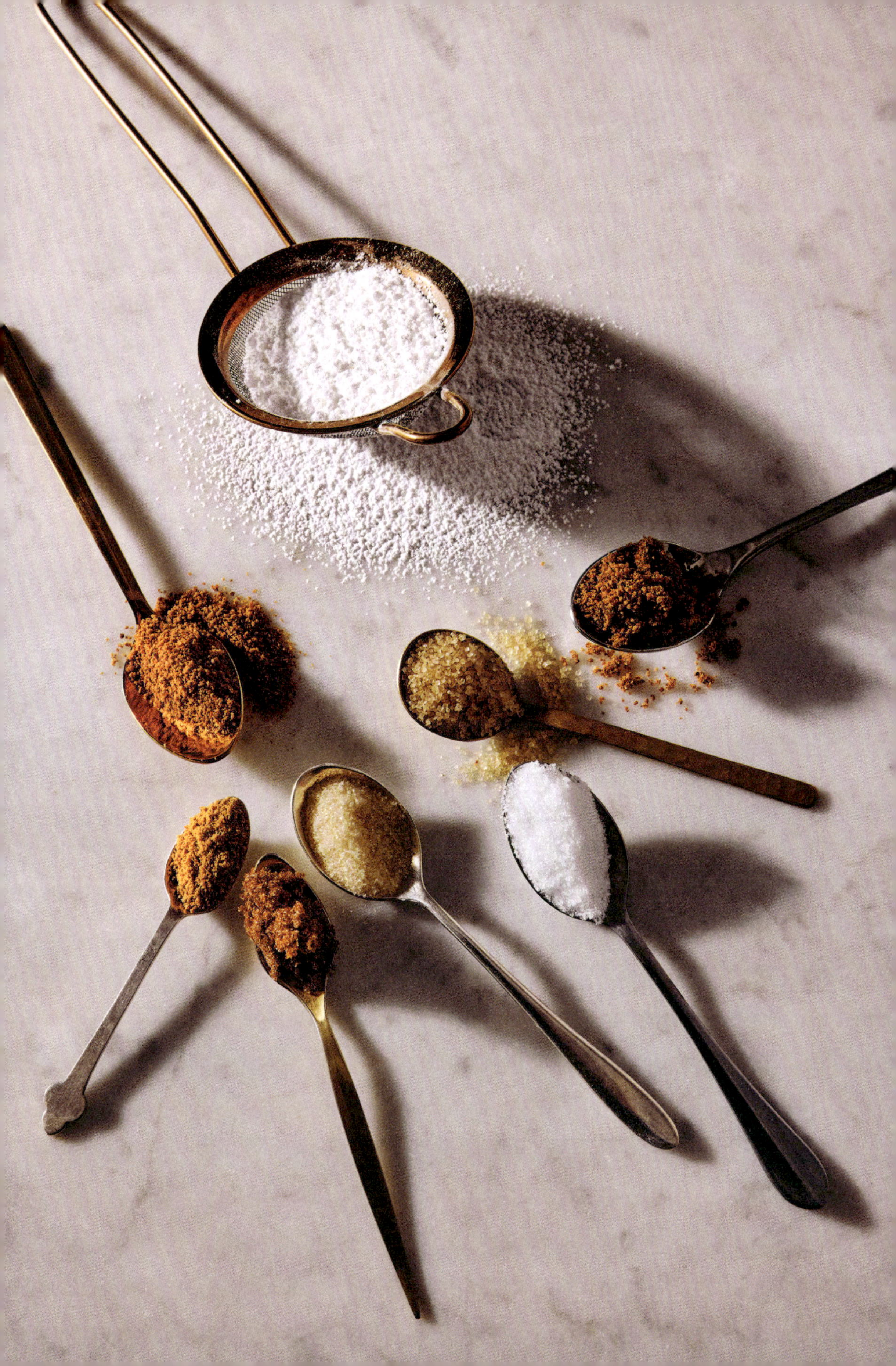

SUGAR BY ANY OTHER NAME WOULD TASTE AS SWEET

Who knew that one base ingredient could have over 50 names and forms! They mostly vary by the amount of molasses and how 'purified' they are, but how they are named comes down to marketing, local laws and politics. The difference in processing between types of sugar can be small, but the finished product can appear very different. Take light and dark brown sugars: these are technically more processed than white sugar because they are made by first making white sugar and then adding molasses back into it. This is different to muscovado sugars, which have a similar but richer flavour and are less processed.

UNREFINED VS REFINED OR CENTRIFUGED VS NON-CENTRIFUGED

Even 'unrefined' sugars go through a refining process. With the exception of panela (rapadura), other artisanal dark sugars and muscovado sugars (which are only made from sugar cane juice), nearly all sugars will need to be refined to remove the molasses.

Non-centrifuged sugar has all the molasses content retained and has trace amounts of nutrients. But even sugars we consider 'raw' or which are marketed as non-refined have often simply been through fewer 'centrifuges' in the final stages of production.

Because of their high molasses content, brown sugars are often used to add beautiful toffee and caramel flavours to baked goods, but they are rarely used alone as they may add too much of these lovely flavours (too much of anything can be a bad thing – a fitting sentiment to discuss in the sugar section of a baking book!). They also melt and behave differently to more refined sugars because the higher molasses content can burn easily, giving off a burned or overpowering flavour when used in caramels, for example.

No matter what the marketing says, anything other than this is 'processed', which isn't necessarily always a bad thing, as manufacturers have found cleaner ways of processing and refining sugar. Below, I have outlined how sugars are produced and refined.

Crushing: sugar juice is obtained by crushing or milling sugar cane or beets.

Clarification: impurities are removed from the juice by heating and adding lime, followed by filtration.

Evaporation: the clarified juice is concentrated by evaporating the water, resulting in a thick syrup.

Crystallisation: sugar crystallisation is encouraged by boiling the syrup in vacuum pans.

Centrifugation: a centrifuge is used to separate sugar crystals from the syrup (molasses).

Washing: the purity of sugar crystals is increased by washing them with hot water or steam.

Drying and cooling: the sugar crystals are dried and cooled before packaging or further refining.

TYPES OF SUGARS

Common white

White sugar (sucrose) is what we are most commonly familiar with and what we measure sweetness by. It comes from two main crops: sugar cane (a grass), which accounts for 70 per cent of all white sugar and is grown in warmer climates, and sugar beets (related to beetroot), which is grown in temperate climates. In processing, beets will always be refined to produce white sugar products (which can then be made into 'brown' sugar), whereas sugar cane can produce various types of sugar. The juice from both plants is extracted and then boiled under vacuum to concentrate the sugars. It is then crystallised and washed to remove the dark molasses before being made into syrups that are progressively clarified.

White sugar has been refined to be 99.95 per cent sucrose. It is pure white, with no other flavour than sweetness. Meanwhile, 'raw' sugar (see right) is refined to about 99 per cent sucrose and has traces of molasses, which give it a light golden colour and a light toffee flavour.

White sugar is available in various granule sizes: granulated, the sugar you stir into coffee; finer-ground sugar like caster (superfine) sugar, used in baking – the type that I recommend for the way it dissolves into recipes; and icing (powdered) sugar, which is further pulverised and is great for icings (frostings). In an emergency, you can make icing sugar yourself by blending either granulated or caster sugar in a high-powered blender and then sifting the fine powder.

Raw sugar (also called golden/blonde, plantation white, turbinado or Demerara)

The crystals of these sugars have just a hint of molasses flavour and a pale blonde colour, thanks to trace amounts of the original cane molasses, which is retained around the crystals. They contain less than 2 per cent molasses and their crystals are medium-sized or slightly larger than granulated sugar. Golden or blonde sugars are slightly less refined than granulated sugar but much less processed and contain about 99 per cent sucrose. Both of these sugars are purified by crystallisation and centrifugation. The difference is white sugar goes through more series of crystallisation and centrifugation cycles to achieve higher 'purity'.

Light or dark brown sugar

Brown sugar is refined white sugar that has had molasses added back into it. The amount of molasses determines whether sugar is 'light' or 'dark': the darker the sugar, the more molasses it contains. It is technically more processed than white sugar, as it has been through more centrifuges before the molasses is added back in. Dark brown sugar is a suitable substitute for muscovado sugar, with a similar flavour and texture.

Muscovado sugar

Muscovado sugar is made by extracting sugar cane juice, then clarifying and cooking it until it crystallises and the moisture evaporates. The brown, syrupy molasses created during cooking remains in the final product, resulting in a moist, dark brown sugar that has the texture of wet sand. The high molasses content gives the sugar a complex flavour with hints of toffee and a slightly bitter aftertaste. Some companies that produce muscovado remove a small amount of the molasses to create a light variety. Muscovado is often called an 'artisanal' sugar, as the production methods are relatively low-tech and labour intensive. In many cases, it is a non-centrifuged sugar, depending on the manufacturing process and country of origin, but some processing can be partially refined.

Traditional artisan sugars

Artisan sugar is a non-centrifugal sugar that is traditionally produced close to cane fields and is made from freshly harvested cane using hundreds of years of knowledge. These sugars are often made on a small scale for local markets with simple equipment and little capital. The process involves collecting the cane juice, clarifying it and boiling off the water through slow simmering in open kettles. Dark artisan sugars include muscovado from Mauritius and the Philippines, rapadura from Brazil, panela from Colombia, piloncillo from Mexico, kokutō from Japan and jaggery from India. Each of these have specific flavour profiles derived from their terroir, much like wines, coffee or chocolate. In this book, I use the below types of sugar:

Golden or white caster (superfine) sugar

I use this sugar as it can be easily incorporated into batters and doughs and dissolves quickly when making a syrup. Use white caster sugar for making caramels, as the molasses in other sugars is prone to burning.

Pure icing (powdered) sugar, with no added starches or anti-caking agents

This is used for icings (frostings) that recrystallise beautifully. If you would like to use raw sugar, blend it in a high-powered blender first.

Dark muscovado or dark brown sugars

These are used for their toffee and butterscotch flavour and colour. In recipes where I specify muscovado, I am referring to dark muscovado.

Glucose (corn syrup)

Maize (corn) is the crop most commonly used to make this type of sugar in the US, where it is called 'light corn syrup', but glucose syrup can also be made from potatoes, wheat and even cassava or rice. Glucose syrup is created by hydrolysing, or breaking apart, the strings of glucose molecules that make up starchy foods by cooking them with water and introducing an acid or enzyme. These syrups are great at keeping things moist and help to give an elastic texture to caramels.

Golden syrup or light treacle

With the texture of honey, golden syrup is produced in a number of ways around the world. Generally, it is a dense sugar syrup that has been cooked for a long time. When citric acid (or another acid) is added, the composition of the sugar changes to invert sugar, meaning the resulting syrup doesn't crystallise. It is a popular topping syrup and a fantastic and easy-to-use inverted sugar with a unique light molasses flavour. Invert sugar helps to retain moisture in cakes and biscuits (cookies) and promotes caramelisation. If you can't get hold of golden syrup, agave syrup or light corn syrup are suitable direct substitutes.

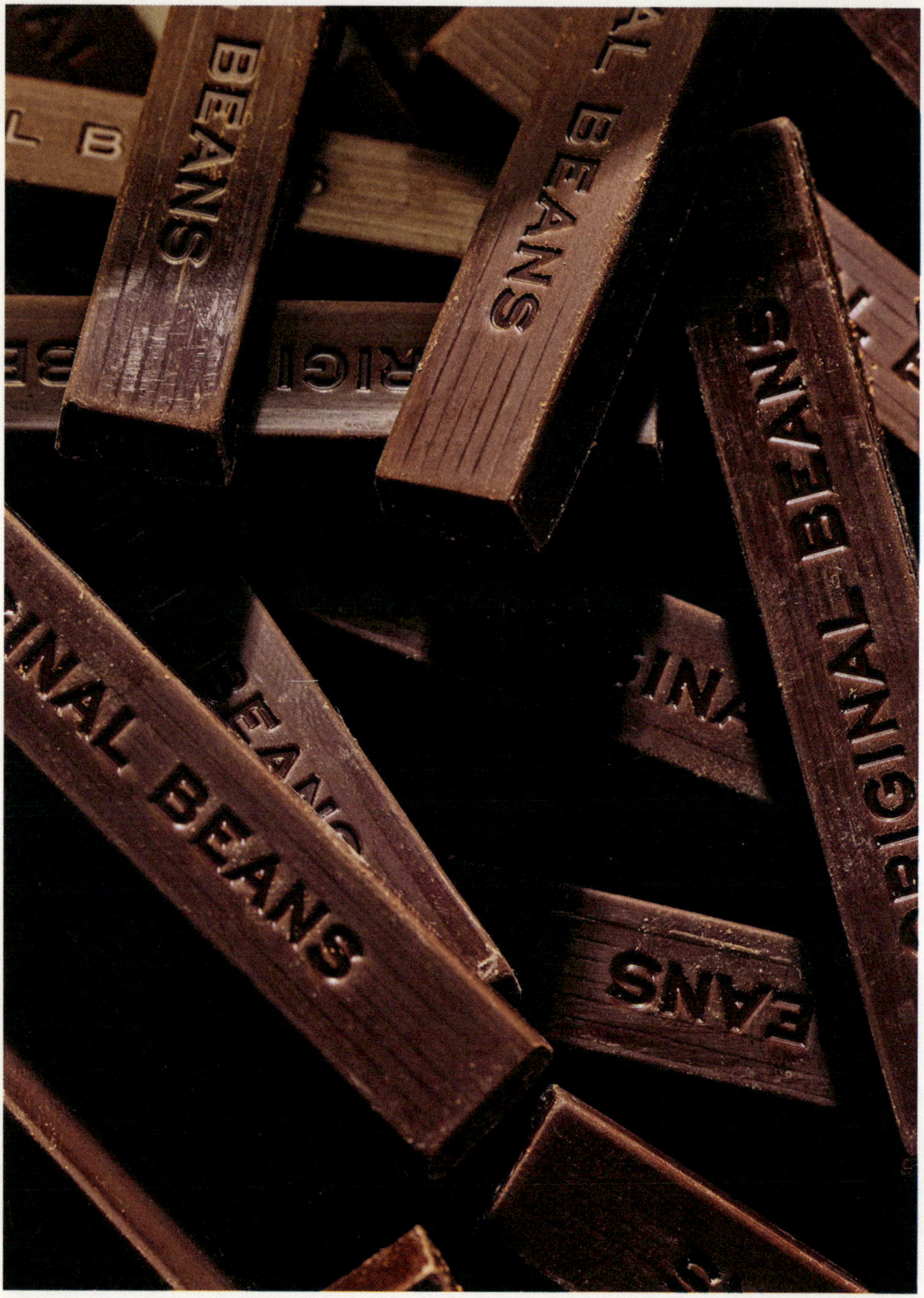
ORIGINAL BEANS

CACAO

Cacaofruit or *Theobroma cacao* is the fruit of a cacao tree. In each fruit pod, about 30 per cent is the beans (the seeds of the fruit) and the rest is mucilage, a pulp surrounding them. This has a delightful, tropical sweet flavour that reminds me of mango, pineapple, passion fruit and lychee. The whole beans are fermented with the mucilage, which imparts lots of fruity flavours to the beans, which are then roasted to develop cocoa flavours. The outer shells, or husks, of the beans are then removed to leave the cocoa nibs, which are about 50 per cent cocoa solids and 50 per cent cocoa butter. The nib is then conched (rolled between stone or steel rollers) with sugar for hours until glossy and smooth with a particle size that is imperceptible to the tongue and melts to nothing.

Chocolate can be used as an ingredient or tempered for coating and decoration. Buy from chocolate makers or brands that can guarantee they don't use child slave labour, pay their farmers fairly and that guarantee traceability. Cocoa is hard to produce, so should be treated with care and respect. It should be expensive and traceable, so you know exploitation (usually of children) hasn't taken place in its farming.

Dark chocolate
High-quality dark (bittersweet) chocolate should only have two or three ingredients: cacao, sugar and maybe lecithin (page 45). The percentage on packets of dark chocolate refers to the cocoa content (percentage of cocoa solids and cocoa butter). The rest is sugar. Some brands will add vanilla and/or additional cocoa butter to make it more fluid for professionals. Use a high-quality dark chocolate for chocolate recipes and try to find 'couverture', a grade that has more cocoa butter. I use dark chocolate with at least 65–70 per cent cocoa solids (couverture grade) in my recipes.

Cocoa (unsweetened) powder
When cocoa nibs are pressed to make cocoa butter, the cake of solids left over is the cocoa powder. It can be further processed to alter the fat content. Natural cocoa powder has a slightly fruitier and more acidic flavour because cocoa is naturally slightly acidic. An alkali (potassium carbonate) can be added and results in a woodier flavour profile and darker colour (called Dutch process). You can use any type of cocoa powder you like; the main difference will be the colour.

Cocoa butter
Cocoa butter is the fat pressed from the nib. It can be virgin, which has a very strong flavour that can be rather overpowering, or it can be deodorised gently with steam processing. I only use deodorised cocoa butter as an ingredient.

To make batons
If you can't find ready-made chocolate batons, you can easily make your own from a bar of good-quality dark chocolate. Choose a thinner-style tablet (with least 55–70 per cent cocoa solids) for easier slicing. Dip a sharp knife in a jug (pitcher) of hot water, wipe it dry, then gently cut the bar into sticks measuring 8 × 1 cm (3 x ½ in). Chill the batons until you're ready to use them.

NUTS

Technically speaking, what we think of as nuts actually includes a range of seeds, legumes and drupes (a type of fruit). A nut is a fruit encapsulated by a hard shell; true nuts include hazelnuts, chestnuts and acorns, but culinary nuts include pecans, walnuts, pistachios, almonds, macadamias, pine nuts, and so on. Nuts are nutritionally dense and contain lots of protein and unsaturated fats. They can be pressed to make oils and ground to make butters or coarse flours. Nuts can go rancid or oxidise if kept too long, so store them in airtight containers and taste them before using if you've had them for a long time. They should smell and taste nutty rather than plasticky or bitter. Using rancid nuts is an easy way to ruin a bake.

Grind with flour
A great way to use nuts in cookie and cake batters is to grind them with the flour to extract their oils and flavour, plus it also coats the gluten, making the cookie or sponge softer. Each nut has a beautiful characteristic flavour. Explore as many as you can!

Roasting nuts
I like to use nuts with their skin on, as the skin is often a rich source of fibre and antioxidants. To roast nuts, preheat the oven to 150°C fan (350°F), then spread them on a large baking sheet in a single layer. Roast for 15–20 minutes. This lower oven temperature allows the nuts to roast evenly and all the way through to the centre.

Nut butter
To make a nut butter, you will need to fill your food blender or food processor about three-quarters full to generate enough friction to blend them efficiently. Blend the roasted nuts until they start to clump as the oils are released. As they blend, the mixture will start to look wet and generate some heat. Continue blending until the mixture is smooth. Store in an airtight jar away from direct sunlight and stir well before use as there will be some separation over time. I have also successfully used a small high-powered blender, too. Just make sure to pulse it, then scrape the sides of the blender down regularly between pulses, and blend until smooth and liquid.

PLANT-BASED MILKS

Cow's milk is highly nutritious and is necessary to grow a 36 kg (79 lb) newborn calf into a 600 kg (1,323 lb) cow within two years. But it is estimated that almost 70 per cent of the world has a form of lactose (the sugar naturally present in milk) intolerance, as many of us lack the enzyme needed to break it down. A huge variety of milk alternatives now exist, including everything from nuts like almonds to soya, oats, seeds, rice and coconut! Plant-based milk lends a creamy flavour and body to baking. In many cases, water could be used without much fuss, but I often prefer the 'milky' flavour that these milks provide.

I rank milk alternatives according to nutrition, flavour and functionality. 'Barista' and professional milks are also widely available – these have had a stabiliser like a gum added to them, to stop the milk from separating when added to coffee or foam when steamed when making espresso-based beverages. Some have had oils blended into them to make them creamier. I recommend reading the label before buying any milk so that you can seek out plant-based milks that are unsweetened and which contain the fewest ingredients. Try to buy organic if possible as these contain fewer ingredients and will not contain any synthetic ingredients or additives.

Soya milk
This milk has the most protein of all natural milk alternatives and has a creamy texture and mild flavour. The protein content has lots of functionalities, too, as it helps with emulsification. Soya milk is my preferred plant-based milk because of its natural protein and fat content and body.

Oat milk
Oat milk has a lovely cereal flavour to it. It is prepared by grinding oats with water, then adding an enzyme that breaks down the starches into sugars. This stops the starches from becoming slimy and gelling when heated. Oat milk may contain gluten due to processing or growing near wheat crops, but you can find oat products that are certified gluten-free. I would recommend 'barista' oat milks – find an organic brand with as few ingredients as possible.

Almond milk
Almond milk is made by grinding almonds and water with a tiny bit of salt. Sweeteners and stabilisers may be added. A number of issues have arisen due to the industrialisation of almond farming. Almonds are a thirsty crop requiring a lot of water and need bees to pollinate the flowers. Specific species of bees are shipped around to pollinate these farms, but many die and spread diseases that kill off other native species of bees, which are crucial to pollination and biodiversity of the area. I don't use almond milk for this reason, as well as because some people may be allergic to it and it can make a recipe that might otherwise have been nut-free contain nuts.

SWEET POTATO

I use sweet potatoes in sweet yeasted doughs to soften the texture by adding extra moisture, as well as to add a golden, sweet, aromatic tinge to baked goods. I recommend preparing them in advance and freezing them so that they're always ready to use.

To prepare sweet potatoes, peel them with a vegetable peeler, then cut them into 2 cm (¾ in) thick rounds. Place in a saucepan of simmering water set over a medium heat. Set a timer for 15–20 minutes and cook until a knife inserted into the potatoes meets no resistance. Drain and cool at room temperature, then freeze in a freezer-proof container.

AQUAFABA

In 2014, a musician called Joel Roussel made the exciting discovery that the water from tinned beans and chickpeas (garbanzos) showed some foaming capabilities. This is due to the trace amounts of protein, starch and other soluble solids in the liquid. In my experience, aquafaba is great for making meringues, foams and for emulsifying mayonnaise, but it does not gel or coagulate and set like an egg white, so I would not call it an egg white or egg replacer, broadly speaking.

For sweet recipes and bakes, tinned white beans and chickpeas work well. Make sure to use beans that are in water and not brine. When using aquafaba from tinned chickpeas, it is best to reduce it by half in order to concentrate its foaming abilities (see page 244 for instructions on how to do this).

GLUTEN PRODUCTS

Wheat gluten was first isolated and described in 1745 by Jacopo Beccari, a chemistry professor at the University of Bologna. Also called 'vital wheat gluten', it is a concentrated protein derived from wheat flour. It is produced by hydrating wheat flour to activate the gluten and then rinsing it to remove the starch, leaving behind a highly concentrated form of gluten. This is then dried and ground into a fine powder. Vital wheat gluten is primarily used to improve the elasticity and chewiness of dough, making it essential in wholemeal (whole-wheat) loaves, wraps and other baked goods. It's also a key ingredient in seitan, a popular meat substitute for vegetarians and vegans due to its high protein content and meat-like texture.

Seitan, also known as wheat meat, originated in ancient China, where Buddhist monks developed it as a vegetarian protein source. Traditionally, seitan is made by washing wheat flour dough to remove starch, leaving behind the gluten protein network, which is then cooked in a savoury broth. Modern production often uses vital wheat gluten powder to simplify the process, making it quicker and more consistent.

LECITHIN

Lecithin was first isolated as a food ingredient in the mid-19th century. It was discovered by the French chemist and pharmacist Théodore Gobley in 1845. Gobley initially extracted lecithin from egg yolks, recognising it as a key component of cell membranes. Over time, lecithin's emulsifying properties were understood, and it began to be used more widely in the food industry. By the early 20th century, lecithin derived from soya beans became common due to its abundance and cost-effectiveness. Sunflower lecithin has also become increasingly popular due to soya being an allergen that some people avoid. Today, lecithin is widely used as an emulsifier and stabiliser in a variety of food products, including margarine, chocolate and baked goods. I've included it here to give some background into its use in the laminating butter (page 55).

NUTRITIONAL YEAST

The use of yeast in general has a long history, with yeasts being used for fermentation and baking for thousands of years. The specific production and marketing of yeast as a nutritional supplement, distinct from baking and brewing yeasts, became more prominent in the early 1900s. In the 1920s and 1930s, yeast extracts were marketed for their nutritional benefits, particularly in Europe and North America.

The production of nutritional yeast specifically as a dietary supplement was influenced by the discovery of its high B vitamin content (except B12, which is added), which was particularly important during periods when deficiencies were common, such as during the Great Depression and World War II.

Nutritional yeast is derived from the yeast species *Saccharomyces cerevisiae* and is cultivated on a sugar-rich medium, such as molasses or sugarcane. During fermentation, yeast cells metabolise the sugars, multiplying and producing B vitamins. Once cultivated, the yeast is deactivated through pasteurisation or steaming at high temperatures, which stops it from being able to ferment or leaven bread. The deactivated yeast is then washed, dried and flaked into small pieces or made into a powder, making it easy to sprinkle on foods or incorporate into recipes.

Nutritional yeast is naturally rich in several B vitamins, including B1 (thiamine), B2 (riboflavin), B3 (niacin), B5 (pantothenic acid) and B6 (pyridoxine), which play crucial roles in energy metabolism, brain function and red blood cell production. Since vitamin B12 is not naturally present in *Saccharomyces cerevisiae*, many nutritional yeast products are fortified with B12 by adding a synthetic form of B12, often derived from bacterial fermentation, during or after the deactivation process. This ensures the nutritional yeast provides a comprehensive range of B vitamins, including B12, essential for nerve function and DNA synthesis. Nutritional yeast is also a good source of protein and dietary fibre. It has a unique cheesy and nutty flavour, which makes it a popular ingredient in vegan cooking as a cheese substitute. It is also used to add umami flavour to dishes like sauces, soups, dips and baked goods. It is versatile and can be stored for long periods.

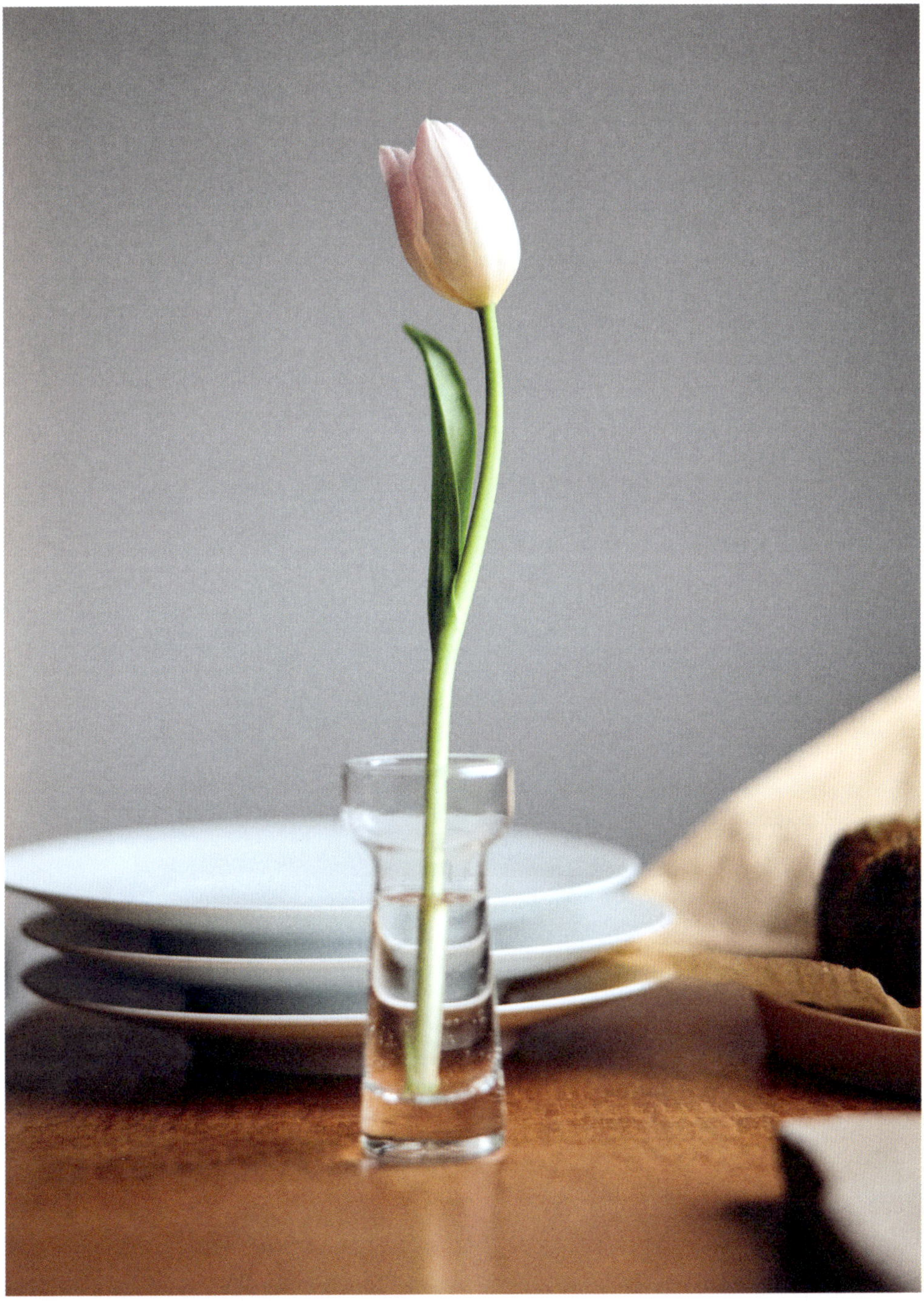

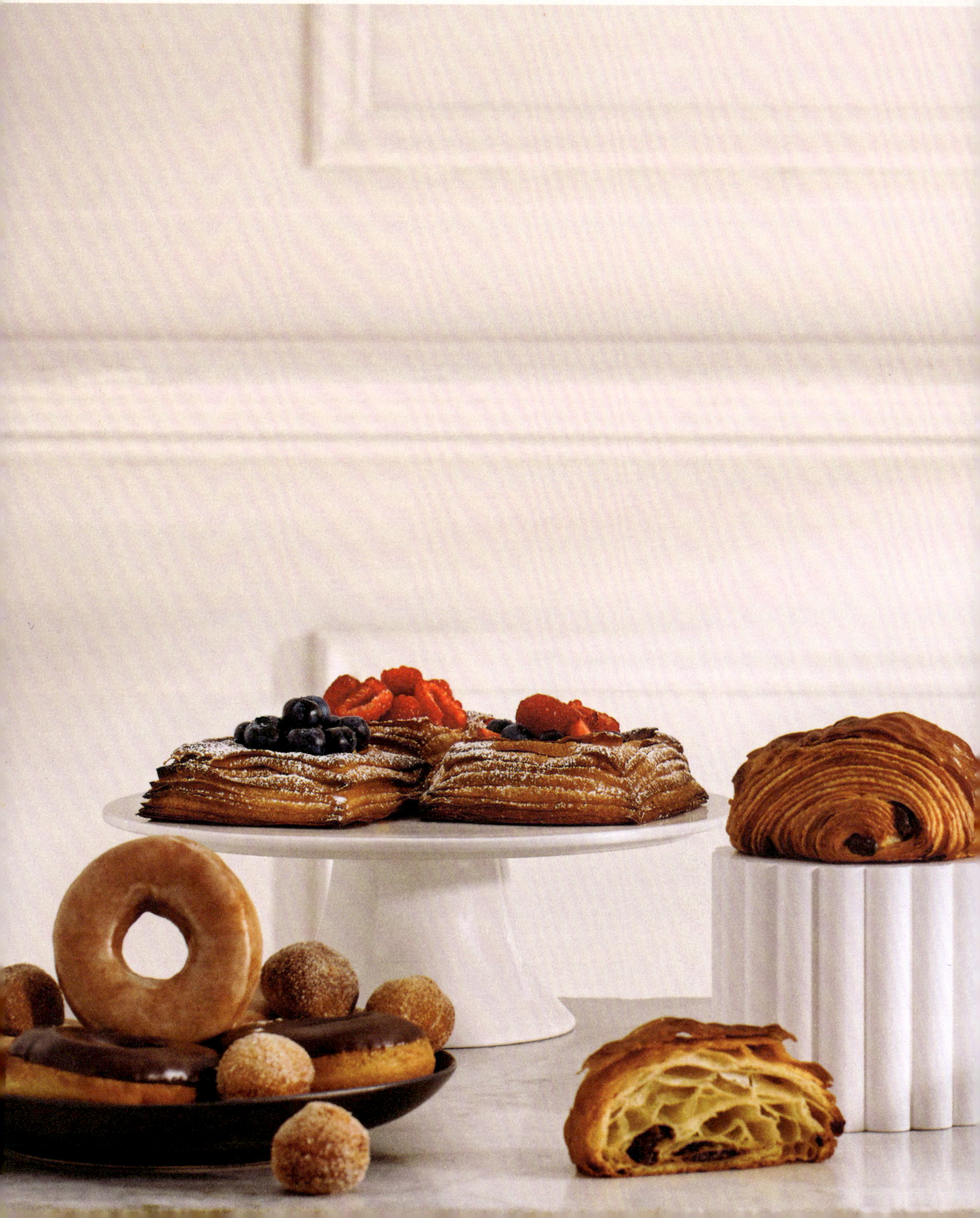

1 SWEET RISEN MORNINGS

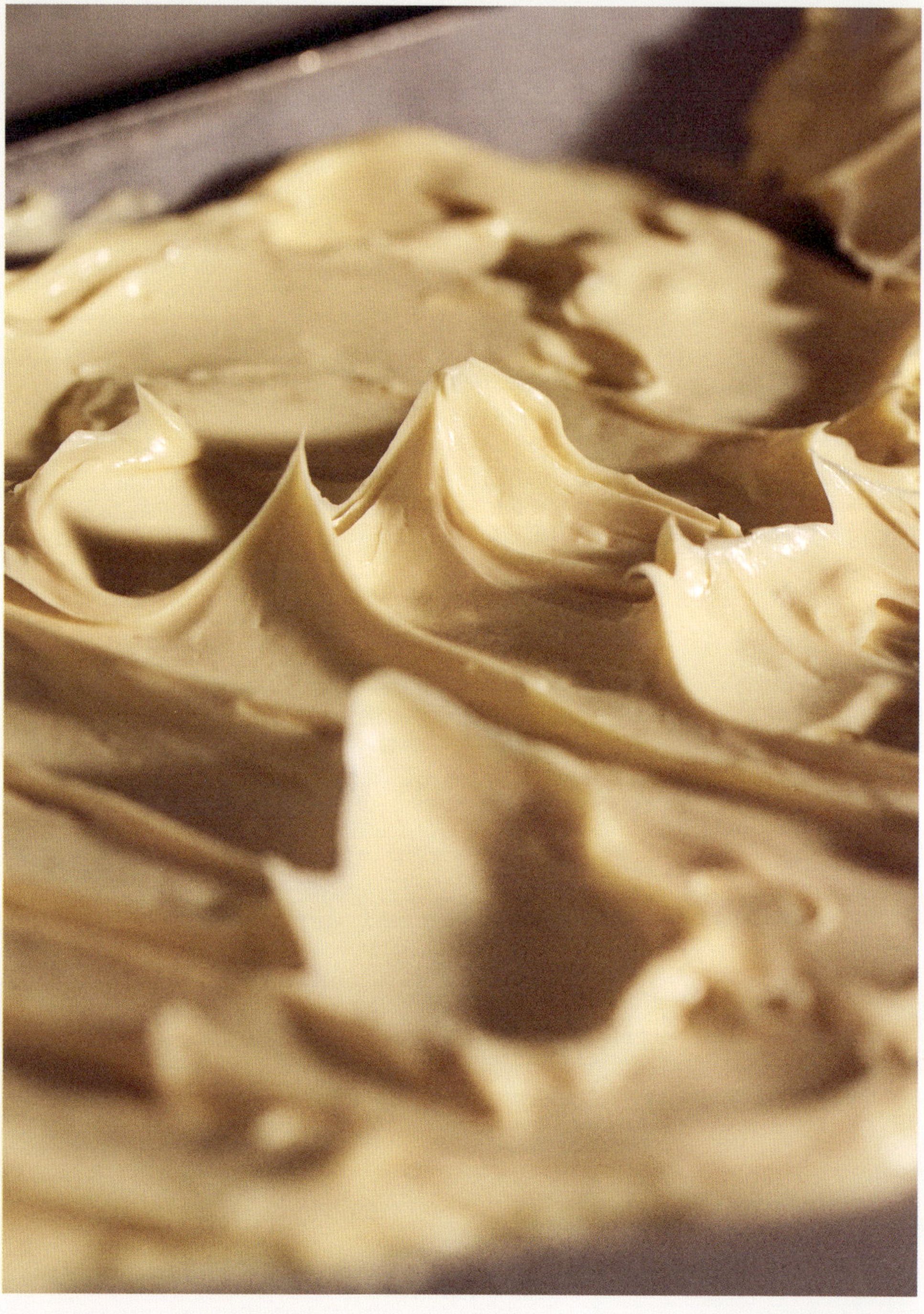

MASTERING LAMINATED PASTRY AT HOME

There is something undeniably magical about laminated pastry. The crisp, golden shell that shatters at the first bite, revealing delicate honeycomb layers within. The deep, complex aroma that fills the kitchen as the pastry bakes. The contrast of textures – crisp, flaky, tender – all achieved through a method that requires time, precision and patience. A perfect croissant or pain au chocolat is more than just a pastry – it's a testament to technique.

For years, home bakers were led to believe that true laminated dough was the domain of professionals, requiring industrial dough sheeters, temperature-controlled conditions and years of training. But I believe that home bakers deserve access to truly great pastry – not a shortcut version or a compromise, but the real thing.

This chapter is dedicated to exactly that: an approachable, foolproof method for making croissants and other laminated pastries at home. Whether you use shop-bought block butter or my carefully developed alternative (a combination of olive oil and cocoa butter, see page 55), you'll achieve incredible bakery-quality results, without industrial equipment or bakery conditions. This method has been developed specifically for home baking, from lamination to proving and final baking, ensuring that the process is not only manageable but also delivers exceptional flavour and texture.

WHY BUTTER MATTERS – AND WHY THERE'S ANOTHER WAY

Butter is at the heart of laminated pastry. It's responsible for those impossibly thin layers, the crisp exterior and the deep, satisfying richness that defines a well-made croissant. Its function in lamination is critical, as it creates the distinct layering effect when folded and rolled into dough.

For much of history, butter was a luxury. In fact, for a time, margarine was more widely used than butter in French viennoiserie – not because it was better, but because industrialisation made it a necessity. At the height of mass production, meeting the demand for butter wasn't feasible at a price most could afford. That later changed, but at a hidden cost.

Producing butter on a commercial scale is resource intensive. As mentioned previously (page 8), to make just 250 g (8.8 oz) of butter – the amount needed for a batch of six to eight croissants – 5 litres (1.3 gallons) of milk are required.

Scale that up to the millions of croissants consumed daily, and the environmental and ethical impact of dairy production becomes hard to ignore. Beyond butter, the industrialisation of cheese for mass export has placed even greater strain on dairy production, prioritising high-yield farming at an enormous scale.

So, what if we could achieve the same result in a different way? Not by cutting corners, but by refining the process – re-examining how structure, richness and flavour develop in laminated dough? A new approach to laminated pastry.

While I was testing and developing my own plant-based laminated pastry recipe, I realised something crucial: so much of the flavour in laminated pastry doesn't just come from the fat – it comes from the fermentation of the dough itself.

Good lamination isn't just about layering – it requires time. A minimum amount of resting is essential to prevent the final roll-out from undoing all the hard work of laminating. Too often, rolling out the dough too soon results in butter (or, in my case, my plant-based alternative) breaking through the layers, destroying the carefully built structure.

That's why my method is structured as a two-day process:

Day one | The dough is laminated and rested.

Day two | The dough is rolled out, proved and baked.

This approach has a threefold benefit:

1 **Better lamination** | By giving the dough time to rest, it becomes more elastic and cooperative, preventing the hard work of lamination from being destroyed at the final roll-out.

2 **Superior flavour development** | The overnight rest allows the dough to undergo slow fermentation, unlocking deeper, more complex flavours that would otherwise be missed.

3 **A more sociable baking schedule based on professional schedules** | No more waiting until the evening to enjoy fresh pastries. With this method, you can prove and bake at a reasonable hour, ensuring that your croissants are ready for breakfast or brunch on your day off.

Ironically, none of this would have been discovered had I not set out to develop a butter-free version of laminated dough. Without butter acting as a flavour crutch, I had to look elsewhere for complexity, and that led me to fermentation, resting times and refining every step of the process. In the end, the quest for an alternative didn't just yield a substitute; it led to a better method altogether.

This is how great baking evolves – not by avoiding tradition, but by questioning it, refining it, and sometimes, surpassing it.

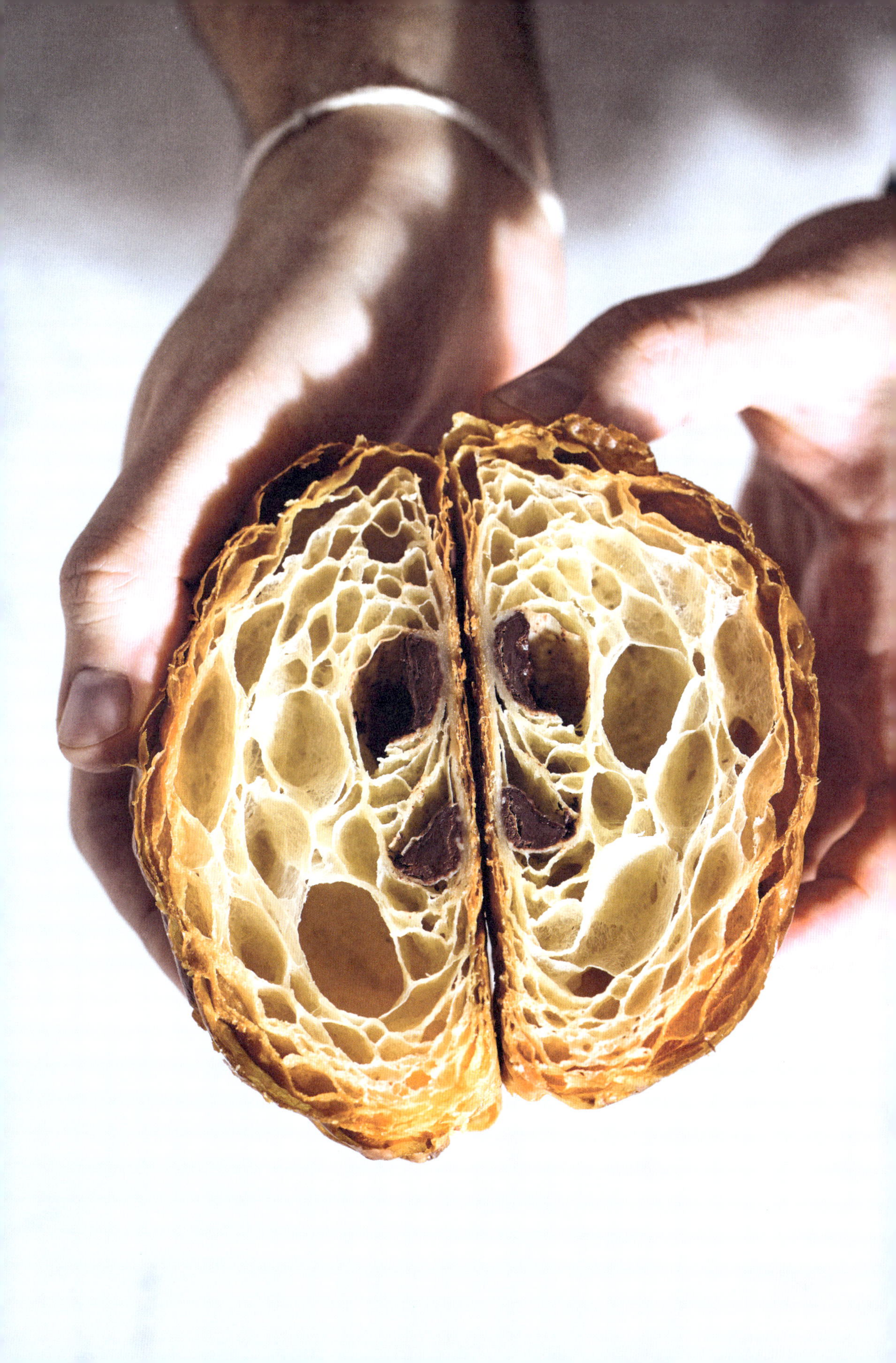

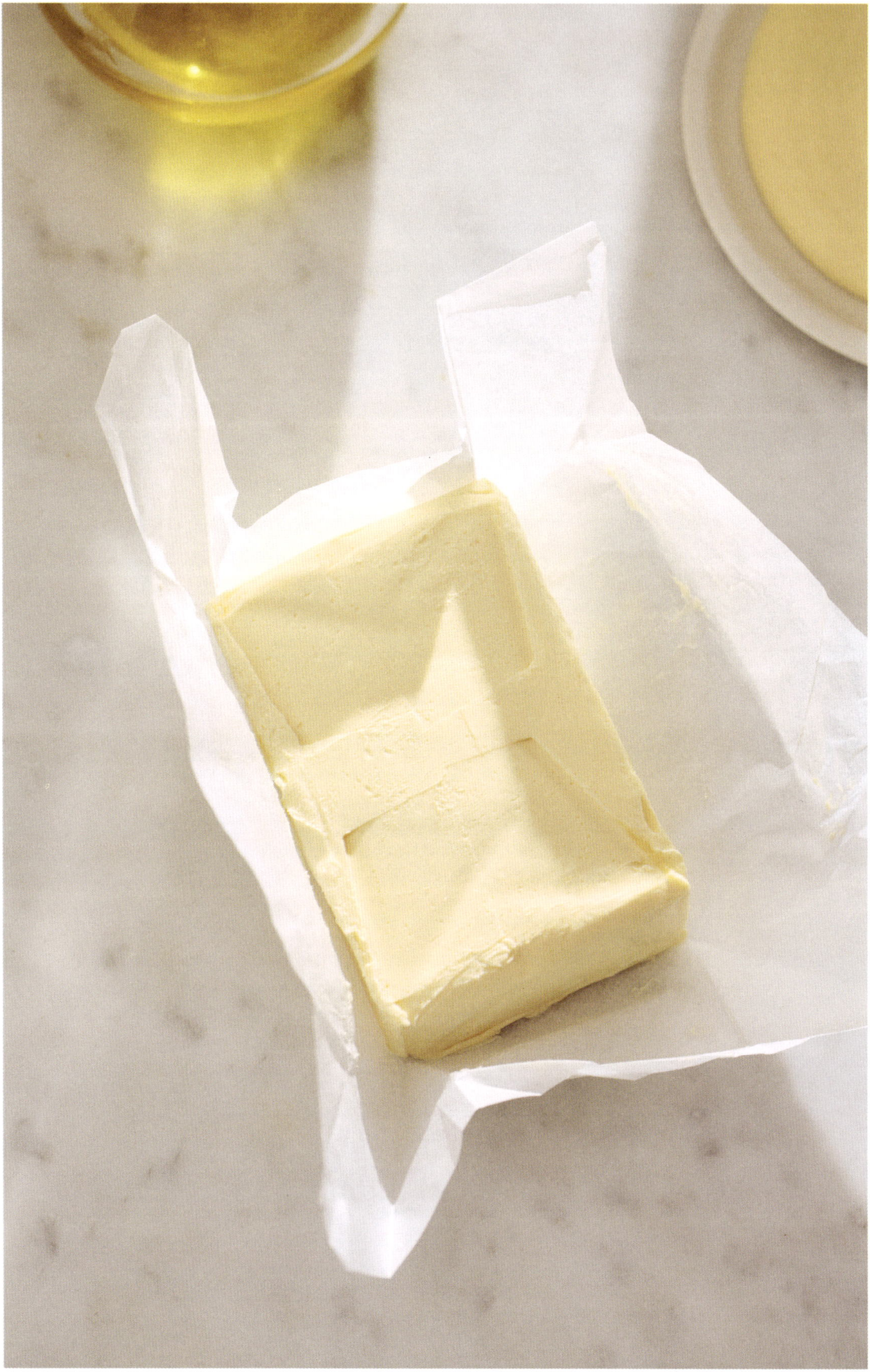

OLIVE OIL BUTTER

Making your own plant-based margarine or butter using cocoa butter and olive oil allows you to control exactly which fats you're using, avoiding ingredients like palm oil or solvent-extracted seed oils that some may wish to avoid. This homemade blend maintains the total fat percentage of traditional butter but in a precise ratio that provides excellent texture for laminating pastry – just as dairy butter does. Given that it takes about 5 litres (1¼ gallons) of milk to produce 300 g (10.6 oz) of butter, crafting your own plant-based alternative offers a unique and ethical choice without compromising on quality. While some excellent plant-based butters do exist, they require careful label-checking and experimentation to achieve the right texture and flavour. In the UK, for example, Naturli Organic Vegan Block has worked well for me for laminating. However, the combination of cocoa butter and olive oil creates a distinct, luxurious flavour – different from dairy butter but still exceptional in its own right. Although cocoa butter can be expensive, the cost per batch is comparable to premium dairy butter, making it a worthy investment for pastry enthusiasts. Cocoa butter should be refined or deodorised (this involves heating it in the presence of steam, which absorbs some of the stronger aroma).

1. Line a 20 × 20 cm (8 × 8 in) square cake tin (pan) with baking parchment, neatly folding the corners to ensure a smooth, even block of butter.

2. Melt the cocoa butter in a heatproof bowl over a bain-marie or in short bursts in the microwave until it reaches 70°C (158°F) on a thermometer.

3. Once fully melted, add the cocoa butter and all remaining ingredients to the blender or food processor (a NutriBullet works perfectly for this) to combine. Pour half the mixture into a shallow ceramic dish and refrigerate for 30 minutes until it is cooled and set at refrigerator temperature – 5°C (41°F).

4. Once the cooled half of the mixture is ready, use a pairing knife to cut the chilled mixture into 2–3 cm (1 in) squares. Check the warm mixture is 40°C (104°F), and warm up gently in the microwave if required.

5. Add the cooled pieces to the blender with the melted mixture and blend until it becomes thick and creamy. Be careful not to over blend, as the mixture can heat up too much and become too soft.

6. Pour the mixture into the pre-prepared tin and place in the refrigerator for at least 6 hours.

7. Once solid, remove from the tin, wrap in baking parchment and store in the refrigerator for up to 3 weeks, or freeze for up to 3 months.

	%		
cocoa butter (deodorised)	27	95 g	3.4 oz
lecithin powder	1	3.5 g	1 tsp
extra virgin olive oil	55	193 g	6.8 oz
soya milk	15	53 g	1.9 oz
nutritional yeast	0.2	1 g	1 tsp
fine sea salt	1.8	6 g	1 tsp

TIP

If your mixture seems too soft, 'melty' or even liquid, repeat the temperature treatment from step 4 (melt half and chill half) and then blend again to achieve a very creamy texture.

VRIOCHE

Traditional brioche gets its beautiful feathered texture, softness and flavour from a lot of butter and the shaping technique. Here, I have developed a recipe that, in conjunction with the tangzhong technique and the inclusion of a healthy dose of olive oil, produces a beautiful and versatile dough. Prepare and chill the tangzhong, then proceed to mix the dough before adding the tangzhong last, once the dough has developed. This recipe can be prepared by hand, but a stand mixer will make much lighter work of it.

	500 g	1 lb 2 oz	650 g	1 lb 7 oz	750 g	1 lb 10 oz	1 kg	2 lb 4 oz
TANGZHONG								
strong white bread flour (1)	12 g	0.4 oz	15 g	0.5 oz	18 g	0.6 oz	24 g	0.9 oz
water	60 g	2 oz	75 g	2.6 oz	90 g	3.2 oz	120 g	4.2 oz
VRIOCHE								
soya milk, at room temperature	96 g	3.4 oz	120 g	4.2 oz	144 g	5.1 oz	192 g	6.8 oz
instant yeast	4 g	1 tsp	5 g	1 tsp	6 g	1½ tsp	8 g	2 tsp
strong white bread flour (2)	240 g	8.5 oz	300 g	10.6 oz	360 g	12.7 oz	480 g	16.9 oz
caster (superfine) sugar	20 g	0.7 oz	25 g	0.9 oz	30 g	1 oz	32 g	1.1 oz
golden (or agave) syrup	20 g	0.7 oz	25 g	0.9 oz	30 g	1 oz	40 g	1.4 oz
fine sea salt	5 g	1 tsp	6 g	1¼ tsp	7 g	1½ tsp	8 g	1½ tsp
cooked and cooled sweet potato (page 44)	40 g	1.4 oz	50 g	1.8 oz	60 g	2 oz	80 g	2.8 oz
extra virgin olive oil, plus extra for greasing	32 g	1.1 oz	40 g	1.4 oz	48 g	1.7 oz	64 g	2.3 oz
Tangzhong (from above)	70 g	2.5 oz	90 g	3.2 oz	105 g	3.7 oz	140 g	4.9 oz

SIZE AND WEIGHT GUIDE FOR BUNS AND LOAVES

STANDARD BUN SIZES	WEIGHT		BAKING TEMPERATURE		BAKING TIME
burger bun (large)	130 g	4.6 oz	190°C	375°F	13–14 minutes
burger bun / roll (standard)	100 g	3.5 oz	190°C	375°F	13 minutes
small bun / dinner roll	60 g	2 oz	190°C	375°F	11–12 minutes
slider buns	30 g	1 oz	190°C	375°F	11–12 minutes
bostock	75 g	2.6 oz	190°C	375°F	13 minutes
hot dog roll	90 g	3.2 oz	190°C	375°F	13 minutes
nanterre balls for loaves	50 g	1.8 oz	180°C	350°F	20 minutes
small loaf tin (pan)	450 g	15.9 oz	180°C	350°F	25–30 minutes
standard loaf tin (pan)	750–850 g	1 lb 10– 1 lb 14 oz	180°C	350°F	35–40 minutes

SWEET RISEN MORNINGS

1. Prepare the tangzhong by combining the bread flour (1) and water in a small saucepan over a medium heat, mixing it together to dissolve the flour. Cook, stirring constantly with a silicone spatula so it doesn't catch, until thickened (a temperature probe will read 65°C/149°F minimum). I have not had any ill effects from just bringing it to the boil while stirring well. Pour the tangzhong into a shallow dish and cover the surface with cling film (plastic wrap), then leave to chill in the refrigerator for 1 hour, or until cool to the touch.

2. Now prepare the dough. Pour the milk into a bowl, add the instant yeast and stir to dissolve. If using active dry yeast, you may need to leave it to stand for 10 minutes to dissolve the coating.

3. Combine the bread flour (2), sugar, golden syrup, salt, sweet potato and olive oil in a stand mixer fitted with the dough hook attachment. Add the milk and yeast mixture and start mixing on low speed. A dough will start to form. Once all the flour is combined, increase the speed slightly and mix for about 5 minutes – the dough should be smooth and developed. Keep kneading until a windowpane test (page 61) shows a well-developed dough.

4. Add the chilled tangzhong to the dough and mix for 3–5 minutes until it is incorporated and smooth. The dough may look like it's beginning to become wet and separated, but keep mixing until the dough starts to climb up the hook and come away from the sides of the bowl. Tip the dough out onto a lightly oiled work surface to shape it into a ball, then place it back into the bowl, cover with cling film and leave to rise in a warm place for 1½–2 hours, or until doubled in size.

5. When the dough is ready to use, knock it back by punching the air out in the bowl. Try to avoid mixing it at this stage, as you want to keep the dough flexible for rolling or shaping into your desired shape – although if it isn't, this can be remedied by a 15-minute rest on the work surface before shaping.

6. Use a scraper or knife to cut the dough into your desired weights, then proceed to shape according to the recipe.

TIP

This initial rise – or what professionals call a 'bulk ferment' – allows the dough to develop flavour and to rest. Timings are always a guide, based on a room temperature of 20–22°C (68–72°C). If your room is warmer or colder, your timings may need to shift.

Yeast is a living organism and if it's warmer it works quicker and if colder it's much slower, so read your dough for its visual cues rather than rigidly sticking to timings.

7. Once you have shaped the dough, arrange it on a sheet of baking parchment or on a lightly greased and floured baking sheet. Make sure there is just over the width of one item distance between each item and just over half the distance from the edge of the baking sheet.

8. When proving, I recommend brushing a layer of water on the dough to keep it supple, then placing the baking sheet in a large, clean storage container with a clip-on lid that fits the sheet (I have bought a couple of slim storage containers for this purpose that can be stacked and stowed away once done). Alternatively, place a piece of cling film loosely on top of the baking sheet. Try to keep them in a warm place (about 25°C/77°F), although at room temperature (20–22°C/68–72°F) it should take roughly 1 hour for them to double in size.

9. About 30 minutes into proving, preheat the oven to 190°C fan (400°F) and position a shelf in the middle of the oven.

10. Once proved, bake the buns or loaves until golden all over the top, or for larger loaves (especially babkas) until a temperature probe reads 90°C (194°F).

11. Once baked, remove the items from the oven and transfer to a wire rack to cool.

12. Once completely cool, wrap or place in an airtight bag and store at room temperature for up to 4 days, or freeze for up to 3 months.

TIP

Make sure there is plenty of space if baking individual shapes. A bun will expand by twice its initial size during the proving stage. Mark this size as a guide, either in flour or with a pencil, so you know when it is proved and how far apart you need to place your buns.

TIP

Proving is the one stage most inexperienced bakers will rush, but it is crucial to ensure light, fluffy products that eat beautifully. Underproved doughs result in a dense, unenjoyable eat. You will know most doughs have fully proved once they have doubled in size or pass the jiggle test – when a gently wobbled baking sheet makes the buns jiggle.

NOTE

Ovens do vary, so take a visual check that they are nice and golden all over – then you know they will be ready. This excludes babka and large loaves, which can brown on top before the centre is fully cooked – the internal temperature measured with a temperature probe should be 90°C (194°F).

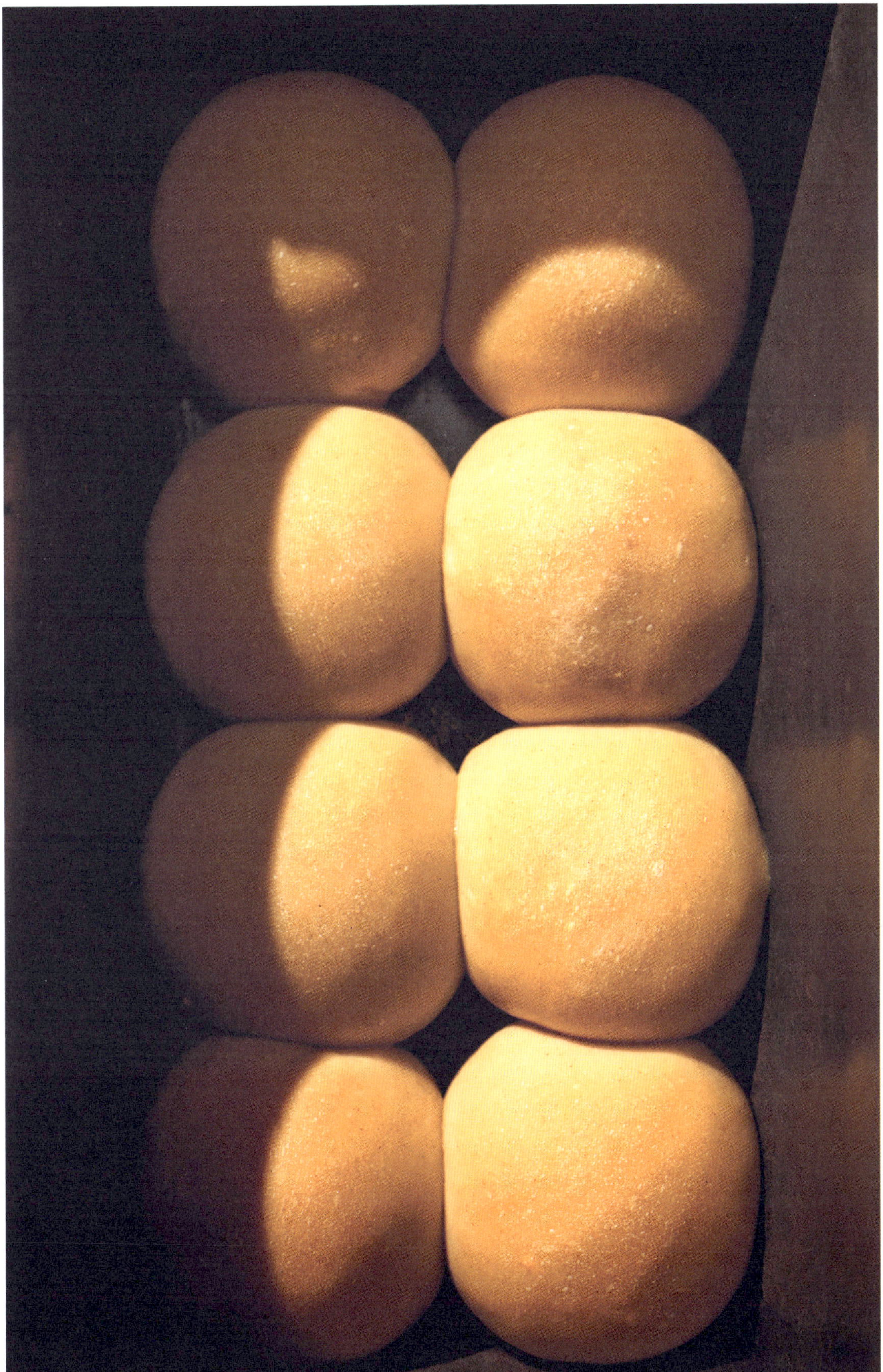

CROISSANT DOUGH

Makes 8–9 croissants or 12 pains au chocolat/pastries

This exquisite dough forms the foundation of an exceptional croissant and serves as the base for a variety of other viennoiseries featured in this chapter. A traditional butter croissant owes much of its flavour to the quality of the butter itself, but equally vital is the fermentation process, which develops the beautifully complex, toasty, yeasted notes that define these iconic pastries.

In professional bakeries, croissant-making is a meticulous two-day process: the dough is mixed, laminated and shaped on the first day, then left to prove in temperature-controlled, timed provers overnight before being baked the next morning. This distinction is crucial, as it influences how the dough rolls out, the integrity of the lamination, and – most importantly – the depth of flavour. Many home recipes attempt to condense this into a single day, often yielding sub-par results – croissants that are rushed, difficult to handle, and inconveniently ready late in the afternoon or evening.

A key challenge of the one-day method is that, by the time you reach the final and most consequential roll-out before cutting and shaping, the dough has become tight and resistant, making it difficult to achieve the proper thickness and shape. This can undo all your hard work, compromising both texture and structure. My approach, however, allows you to work at your own pace: you mix and laminate the dough on day one (either in the morning or afternoon), then let it rest overnight. By the next morning, the dough is far more pliable, making the final roll-out effortless and the resulting pastries significantly superior in both texture and taste. And, crucially, this schedule allows you to enjoy freshly baked croissants at a civilised hour – around 10 or 11 a.m. – rather than in the middle of the night.

Once shaped, croissants require a slow and steady proving process to develop their delicate, airy texture without compromising lamination. Unlike many breads, which prove at higher temperatures, croissants must be kept cooler to prevent the butter from melting prematurely. At 26°C (79°F), this dough typically takes about 3 hours to prove, although in colder environments it may take even longer. I recommend creating a controlled proving setup at home (see Tip on page 65), as depending on your location, your ambient temperature may vary significantly; in London, for instance, it is often quite cool, making this setup particularly cost-effective and reliable.

If you're using the dough to make other pastries, follow the instructions up to step 8, then use in the recipe of your choice the following day.

1. Weigh all the ingredients except the butter (2) for laminating directly into the bowl of a stand mixer, adding the yeast and liquids last.

2. Mix on low speed for 1–2 minutes until a dough forms, then increase to the second speed for 6–8 minutes, mixing until the dough reaches 24–25°C (75–77°F). To check the gluten development, perform the windowpane test: take a small piece of dough, roll it out with a rolling pin, then gently stretch it between your fingers. It should stretch thinly enough to become translucent without tearing. Proper gluten development is essential for the dough to expand, trap air and form the light, honeycomb-like structure characteristic of a well-made croissant.

3. Shape the dough into a smooth ball, cover it with cling film (plastic wrap), then leave to rest at room temperature for 20 minutes.

4. Once rested, cut an X shape into the ball, slicing halfway into it, then stretch each corner outward to create a square shape – this will make rolling out the dough easier later. Aim for clean, square corners. Wrap the dough in a large sheet of baking parchment and place it in the freezer for 30 minutes to chill rapidly.

5. While the dough chills, remove the butter (2) from the refrigerator. Plasticise it by placing a piece of baking parchment underneath and on top of it, and press down at 1 cm (½ in) increments with a rolling pin, and as it flattens, fold the paper underneath the block at 20 × 20 cm (8 in) to create a border the butter can be rolled up to. The butter should be cold but flexible for lamination.

6. Roll the chilled dough into a rectangle just over 20 × 40 cm (8 × 16 in). Place the plasticised but still cold butter in the centre, ensuring it covers the middle third of the dough. Fold the two exposed sides of dough over the butter so they meet in the centre, then press the edges together to seal the butter inside (see diagram, overleaf).

7. Lightly flour the work surface as needed but brush off any excess flour before folding to prevent it from being incorporated into the dough, which would make the final pastry dry. Always roll in the direction of the open edges of the dough (so the folded edges are on the sides). Roll the dough out to roughly 20 × 60 cm (8 × 24 in), keeping the edges as straight as possible and running your hand underneath the dough occasionally to make sure it does not get stuck to the work surface. Complete the first double book fold by folding both ends of the dough toward the centre, leaving a small gap between them, then folding the dough in half like a book to create four layers (see diagram overleaf). Wrap in baking parchment and refrigerate for 1 hour to allow the gluten to relax and prevent the butter from melting during the next roll.

8. Remove the dough from the refrigerator again, roll it out and complete one single fold (folding the dough into thirds like a letter – see overleaf). Wrap and refrigerate overnight to allow the gluten to relax and fermentation to take place, which will enhance the pastry's flavour.

plain (all-purpose) flour (T45 if you can get it), plus extra for dusting	500 g	1 lb 2 oz
caster (superfine) sugar	70 g	2.5 oz
fine sea salt	10 g	1¾ tsp
instant yeast	6 g	2 tsp
Olive Oil Butter (page 55) or shop-bought vegan block butter (1), at room temperature	50 g	1.8 oz
soya milk	125 g	4.4 oz
water	120 g	4.2 oz
Olive Oil Butter (page 55) or shop-bought vegan block butter (2), for laminating	275 g	9.7 oz

TIPS

Fast-action or instant dried yeast and fresh yeast (use double the amount specified above) can be added directly to the dough mixture. Active dry yeast (same weight as instant) must first be dissolved in water to remove its protective coating before adding it to the mix.

If you want to make both croissants and pains au chocolat for breakfast or brunch, you can use this recipe to make six croissants and four pains au chocolat in one batch (follow the instructions for rolling and shaping the pains au chocolat on page 69).

DAY 1

Butter lock-in

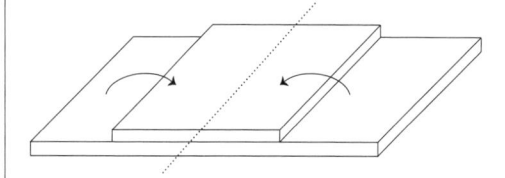

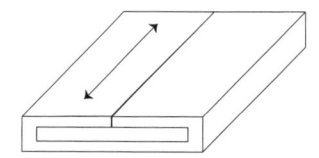

Double fold

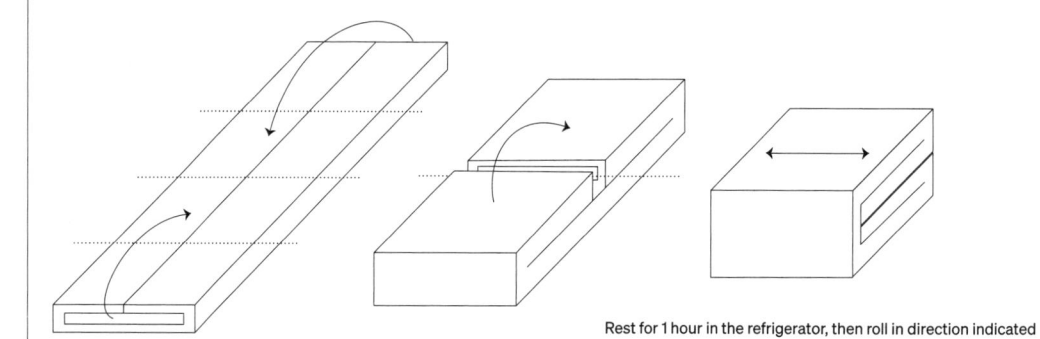

Rest for 1 hour in the refrigerator, then roll in direction indicated

Single fold

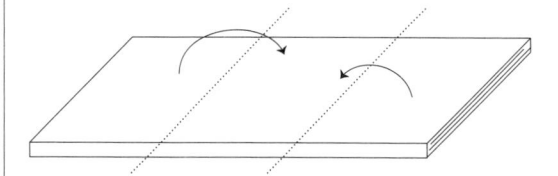

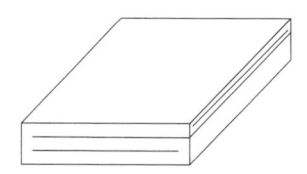

Wrap and refrigerate overnight

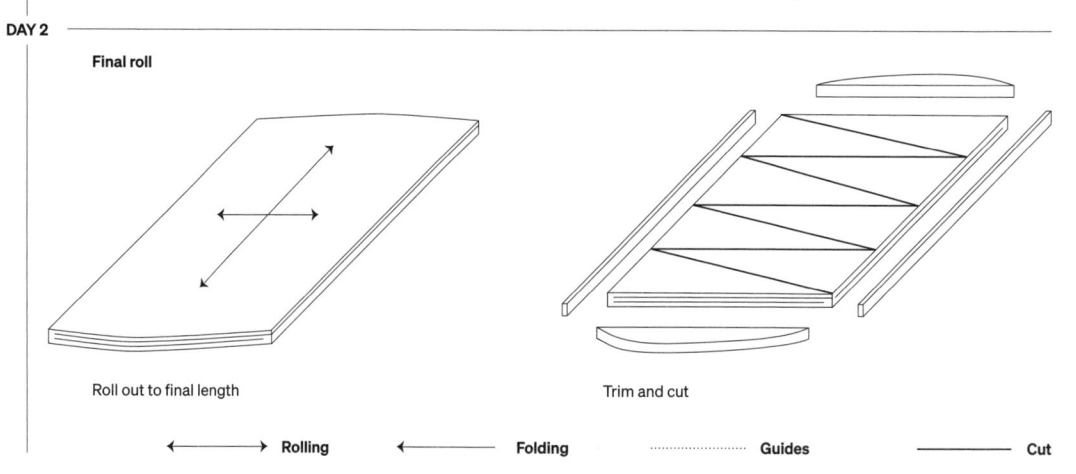

DAY 2

Final roll

Roll out to final length

Trim and cut

⟵⟶ Rolling ⟵ Folding ········ Guides ⎯⎯ Cut

62   **SWEET RISEN MORNINGS**

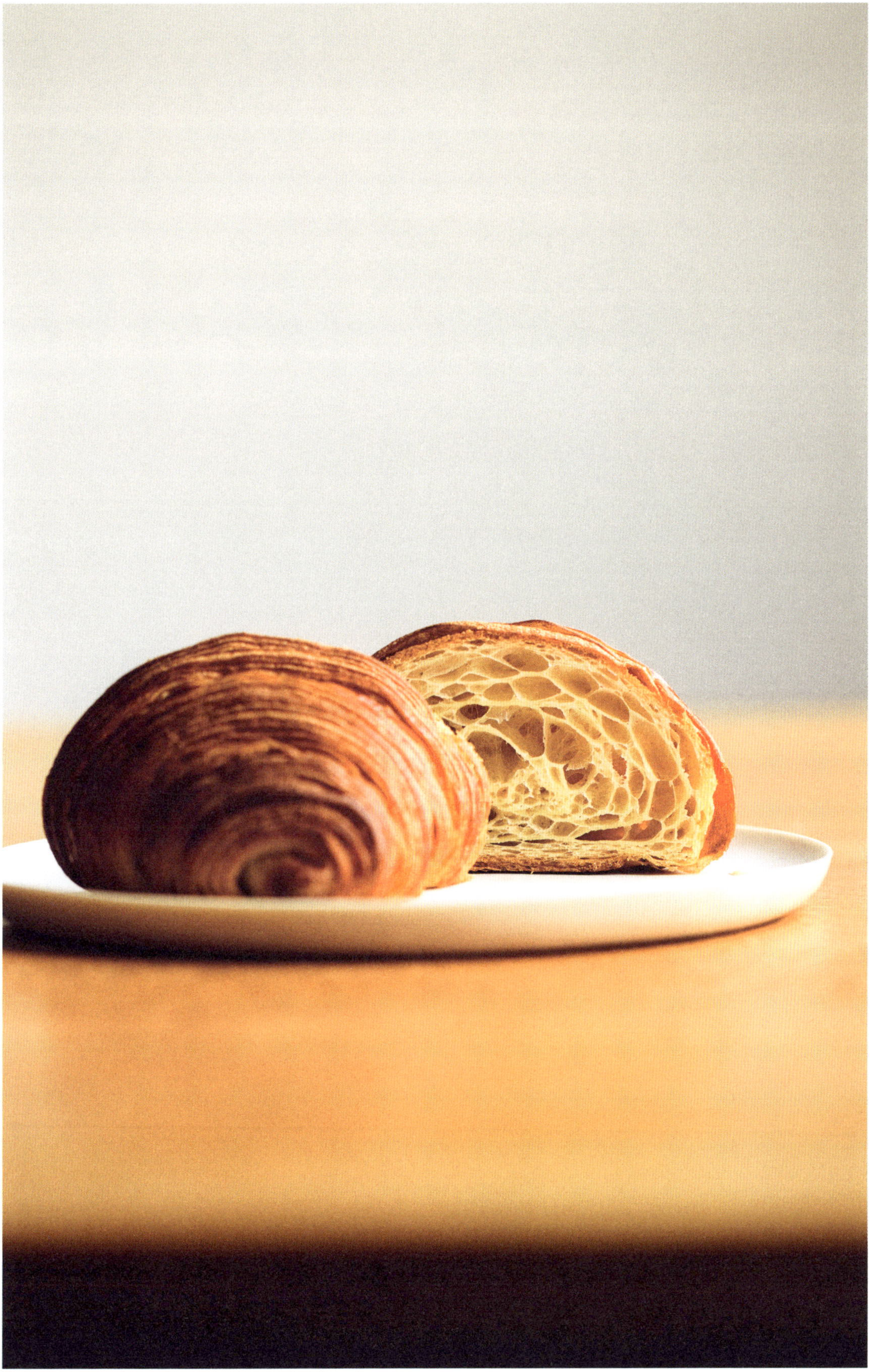

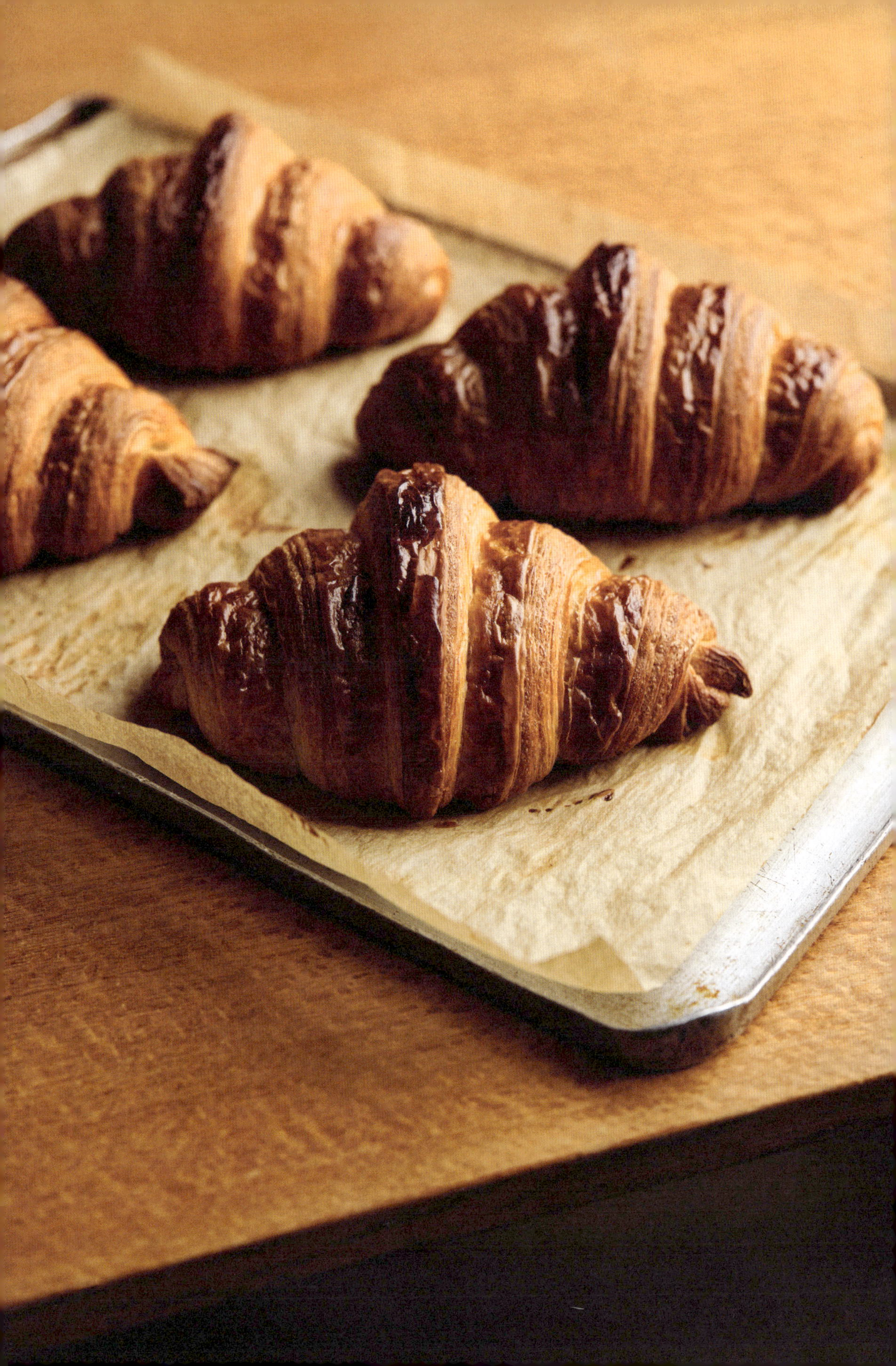

CROISSANTS

Makes 8–9 croissants

Making croissants at home is no small undertaking, but it is an immensely rewarding craft. With practise, your technique will refine, your results will improve and the satisfaction of creating bakery-quality croissants in your own kitchen will make every effort worthwhile. If they are not perfect, stress not, they will make a delicious Almond Croissant (page 66).

Croissant Dough (page 60)	1 quantity
Baking Glaze (page 242)	

1. On day one, follow the instructions on pages 60–62 to make the croissant dough.

2. The next day, roll the dough out to 30 × 45 cm (12 × 18 in) and 5 mm (¼ in) thick (see diagram on page 62). Trim 1 cm (½ in) off the edges to ensure clean, well-defined layers (leaving the edge is fine for the flavour but does result in sections of the croissant being a tiny bit denser/bready).

3. Measure and mark 10 cm (4 in) increments along the long side of the dough. Using a sharp knife or pastry cutter, cut the dough diagonally to form triangles (see diagram on page 62). Reserve the offcuts as these can be braided or placed in an individual pie or quiche dish to make a little monkey bread.

4. Shape the croissants by gently stretching the base of each triangle and rolling it up tightly from the base to the tip. There should be layers or steps of pastry. I like to very gently press the shaped croissant down on the thin end to secure it underneath the croissant on the tray. Place all the pastries on a baking sheet lined with baking parchment, spacing them apart to allow for expansion.

5. Prove in a warm but controlled environment at 26°C (79°F) for about 3 hours (see Tip). If your kitchen is colder, proving may take longer. In warmer climates, be cautious not to overprove. When fully proved, the croissants should be noticeably puffy and should slightly wobble when the baking sheet is gently shaken.

6. Preheat the oven to 180°C fan (400°F).

7. Once proved, lightly brush the tops of the croissants with baking glaze, ensuring none drips onto the exposed layers, as this can seal them and inhibit rising.

8. Bake in the oven for 18–22 minutes until deep golden brown. Rotate the trays halfway through for even baking.

9. Remove from the oven and leave to cool on a wire rack before eating, as this will help to set the flaky layers.

10. To reheat baked croissants, place in an oven preheated to 150°C fan (350°F) for 5–8 minutes until warm and crisp. Avoid microwaving, as this will make them soft rather than flaky.

TIP

To achieve the perfect light, airy texture, the dough must prove slowly at a controlled temperature to develop volume without compromising lamination. Since this dough contains butter, it is essential to keep the proving temperature at 26°C (79°F) so that the butter stays firm and does not melt prematurely. To create a controlled proving setup at home, I recommend using a large plastic storage container with a small heater – often used in 3D printing – to maintain a consistent temperature. A fine mist of water from a spray bottle over the pastries helps maintain humidity, preventing the dough from drying out.

ALMOND CROISSANTS

Makes 8–9 croissants

The twice-baked almond croissant is among the most beloved pastries for good reason. I've sampled many versions with fillings baked inside, but there's something uniquely indulgent about this recipe – perhaps it's the generous soak in vanilla and rum-infused syrup or the exceptionally moist almond cream tucked within. Whatever it is, these croissants deliver flavour and texture that's undeniably indulgent for a breakfast or afternoon treat.

ALMOND FRANGIPANE

1. Pulse the almonds, sugar and cornflour in a small food processor or high-powered blender until finely ground and starting to clump together.

2. Add the milk, olive oil and bitter almond extract (if using). Pulse again until the mixture becomes a thick, creamy paste. Transfer the frangipane to a piping (pastry) bag and set aside until ready to use.

raw almonds	200 g	7 oz
caster (superfine) sugar	130 g	4.6 oz
cornflour (cornstarch)	30 g	1 oz
plant-based milk	125 g	4.4 oz
extra virgin olive oil	13 g	0.5 oz
bitter almond extract (optional)	¼ tsp	

VANILLA SYRUP

3. Put all the ingredients into a wide, shallow saucepan and bring to a simmer, then remove from the heat and set aside.

water	200 g	7 oz
caster (superfine) sugar	250 g	8.8 oz
used vanilla pod (bean) or vanilla paste	1 pod or 1 tsp paste	
rum (optional)	30 g	1 oz

TO ASSEMBLE AND BAKE

4. Preheat the oven to 160°C fan (350°F) and line two baking sheets with baking parchment.

5. Using a sharp, serrated knife, carefully slice each croissant in half lengthways to create a top and bottom half.

6. Dip both halves of each croissant briefly into the vanilla syrup, ensuring they absorb some of the syrup without becoming overly saturated. Let any excess syrup drip off.

7. Pipe a layer of almond frangipane onto the bottom half of each croissant, spreading it out slightly if needed. Replace the top of the croissant to sandwich the frangipane and then pipe a line of frangipane lengthways along the top.

8. Spread the flaked almonds evenly on a dinner plate or tray. Gently press the top of each croissant into the almonds.

9. Arrange the assembled croissants on the prepared baking sheets (five per tray) and bake in the oven for 12–15 minutes, or until golden brown and crisp.

10. Remove from the oven and transfer the croissants to a wire rack to cool before serving. These are best enjoyed on the same day, dusted with icing sugar.

Croissants (page 65), baked	8–9	
flaked (slivered) almonds	100 g	3.5 oz
icing (powdered) sugar	for dusting	

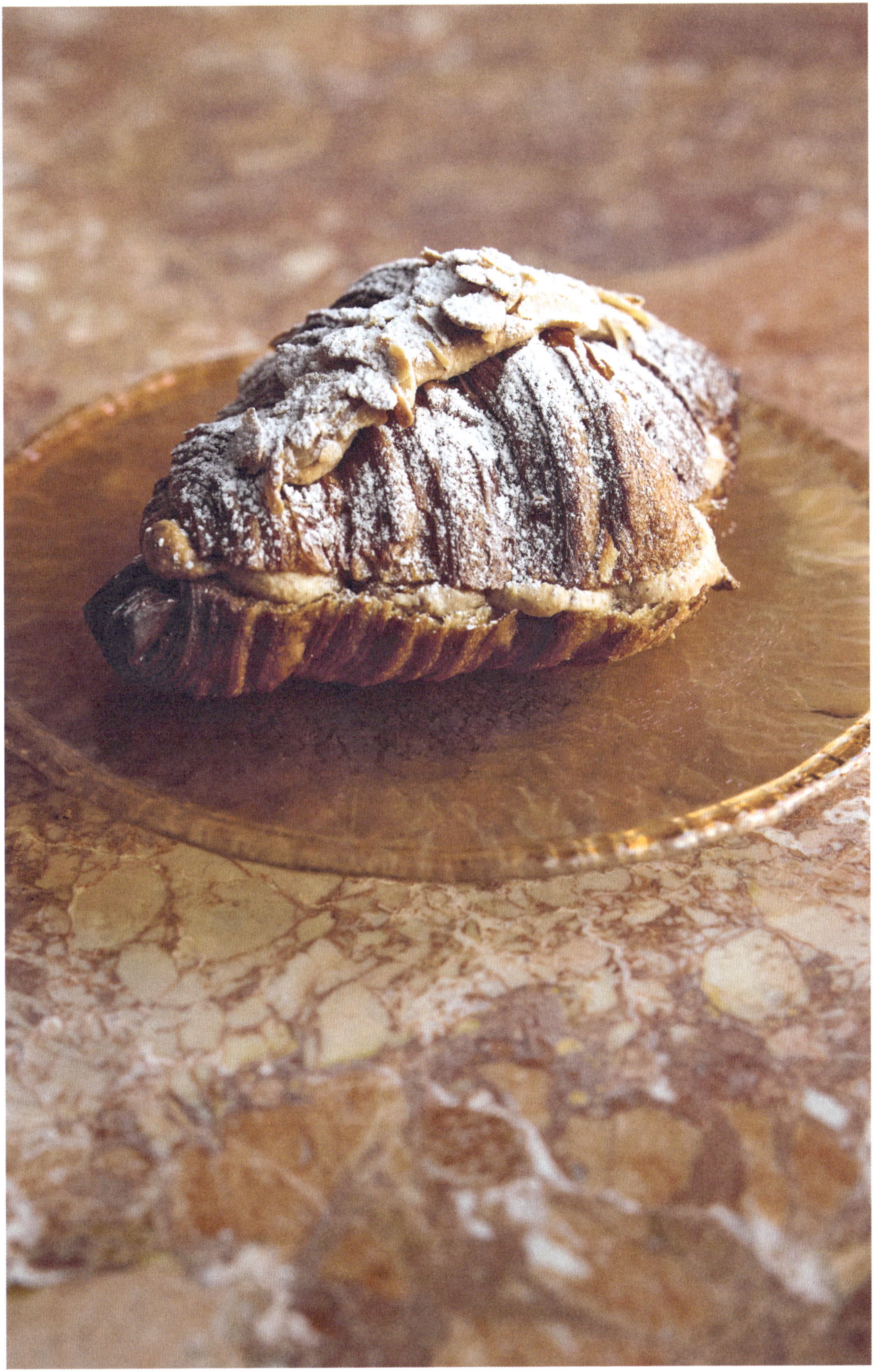

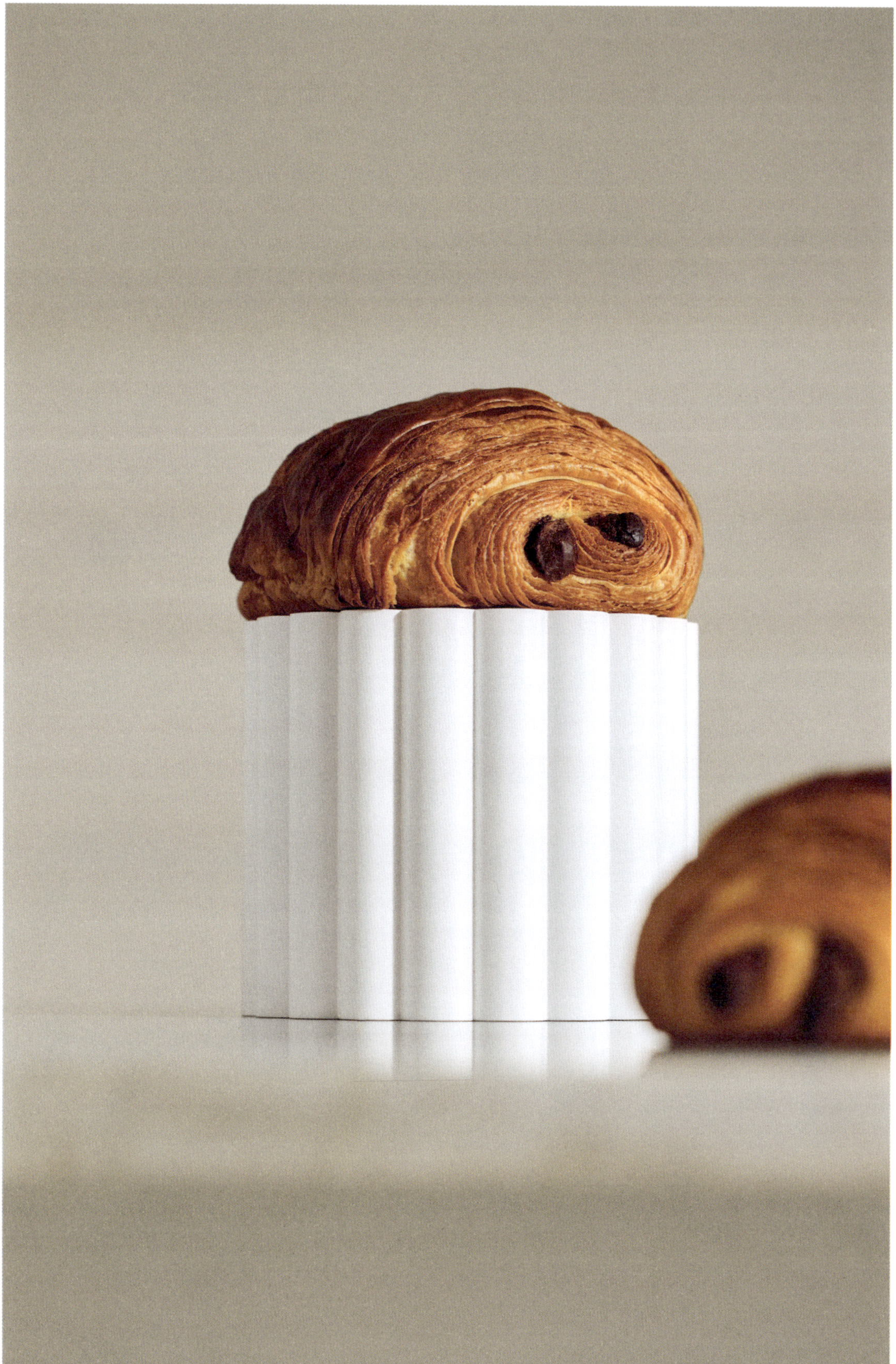

PAINS AU CHOCOLAT

Makes 12 pains au chocolate

This might be my favourite pastry. Not too sweet, but still a treat. So easy to get wrong and often difficult to get perfectly right! Chocolate batons are a ingredient made by chocolate brands that are available to the professional market. You can typically buy them in 1–2 kg (2 lb 4 oz–8 lb 8 oz) boxes, which is a bit more than you need for home baking. Some are available from speciality online suppliers, as home baking boomed during the 2020 Covid-19 pandemic. I am lucky to use the exceptional dark chocolate batons from regenerative cocoa company Original Beans.

Croissant Dough (page 60)	1 quantity
dark chocolate batons	24
Baking Glaze (page 242)	

1. On day one, follow the instructions on pages 60–62 to make the croissant dough.

2. The next day, roll out the dough into a 32 × 42 cm (12½ × 16½ in) rectangle, about 5 mm (¼ in) thick (see diagram on page 62). Lightly flour the work surface as needed, but brush off any excess, as too much flour will dry out the dough and interfere with lamination.

3. Trim 1 cm (½ in) off all edges to ensure clean, well-defined layers. On the long sides, mark 7 cm (2¾ in) intervals; on the short sides, mark and cut two 16 cm (6¼ in) strips. Use a sharp knife or pastry cutter to cut out 12 rectangles measuring 16 × 7 cm (6¼ × 2¾ in). Precision is key – keeping the cuts straight and uniform helps ensure the layers bake evenly and produce that signature, professional finish.

4. Place a chocolate baton 1 cm (½ in) from the bottom edge of each rectangle. Roll up the dough just enough to encase the baton, then place a second chocolate baton just above the first and continue rolling, keeping the roll snug but not too tight.

TIP
This layering ensures that the chocolate remains evenly distributed within the pastry.

5. Place the shaped pains au chocolat seam-side down on a baking sheet lined with baking parchment, leaving enough space between them for expansion.

6. Prove in a warm but controlled environment at 26°C (79°F) for about 3 hours (see Tip on page 65). The pains au chocolat are fully proved when they appear visibly puffed up and should slightly wobble when the tray is gently shaken.

TIP
If your kitchen is colder, proving may take longer. In warmer climates, be cautious not to overprove.

7. Preheat the oven to 180°C fan (400°F).

8. Once proved, lightly and evenly brush the top of the pastries with the baking glaze. Focus on glazing the flat surfaces, avoiding the exposed layers.

9. Bake in the oven for 18–22 minutes, rotating the tray halfway through, until the pastries are deep golden brown and crisp on the outside.

10. These are best enjoyed still slightly warm, when the chocolate inside is still soft and slightly melted. Any leftovers can be gently wrapped (or put in a container) and frozen. To reheat them, place in an oven preheated to 150°C fan (350°F) for 5–8 minutes until warm and crisp. Avoid microwaving, as this will make them soft rather than flaky.

MIXED BERRY CUSTARD DANISHES

Makes 12–15 pastries

I don't like unnecessary wastage, especially when it comes to a dough as beautifully laminated as this one. That's why I prefer to cut these Danish pastries into clean 10 cm (4 in) squares – it ensures that every bit of dough is used efficiently, with no awkward scraps left behind. While some might suggest re-rolling the excess dough, this completely disrupts the lamination and compromises the final texture. Instead of crisp, defined layers, you'd end up with a denser, less structured pastry.

Crème Pâtissière (page 239)	500 g	1 lb 2 oz
Croissant Dough (page 60)	1 quantity	
Berry Compôte (page 111)		
mixed berries of your choice	400 g	14.1 oz
Exotic Clear Glaze (page 242), melted	150 g	5.3 oz
icing (powdered) sugar	for dusting	

1. Pipe fifteen 30 g (1 oz) portions of crème pâtissière into 5 cm (2 in) silicone muffin moulds and freeze for at least 1 hour.
2. Roll out the dough to just over 5 mm (¼ in) thick, keeping the shape as square as possible – it should be just over 30 × 50 cm (12 × 20 in). Lightly flour the work surface as needed but brush off any excess.
3. Trim the edges to ensure clean, well-defined layers and a piece of dough that measures 30 × 50 cm (12 × 20 in). Using a sharp knife or pastry cutter, cut the dough into 10 × 10 cm (4 × 4 in) squares.
4. Transfer six squares to a 30 × 40 cm (12 × 16 in) baking tray (pan) lined with baking parchment, ensuring they are evenly spaced to allow for expansion. Repeat with a second tray for the remaining six squares.
5. Cover loosely with a dish towel or cling film (plastic wrap) and leave to prove in a warm but controlled environment at 26°C (79°F) for about 3 hours (see Tip on page 65). When fully proved, the pastries should be visibly puffed up and should slightly wobble when the tray is gently shaken.
6. Preheat the oven to 180°C fan (400°F).
7. Once fully proved, remove the frozen crème pâtissière from the freezer and press a frozen puck into the centre of each dough square until it can go no further into the dough.
8. Bake the pastries in the oven for 18–22 minutes, rotating the trays halfway through, until the edges are deep golden brown and crisp.
9. Remove the pastries from the oven and transfer them to a wire rack, then leave them to cool fully.
10. Once cool, spoon 1 tablespoon of berry compôte into the well of each pastry, spreading it slightly if needed. Arrange the fresh berries on top of the compôte.
11. Lightly brush the fresh fruit with melted exotic clear glaze to give a glossy, professional sheen. Finally, dust the edges of the pastry with icing sugar.
12. These Danish pastries are best enjoyed fresh, with their crisp, buttery layers complementing the creamy custard and juicy berries.

TIP

If your kitchen is colder, proving may take longer. In warmer climates, be cautious not to overprove.

TIP

This creates a well for the filling while maintaining the distinct laminated layers around the edges.

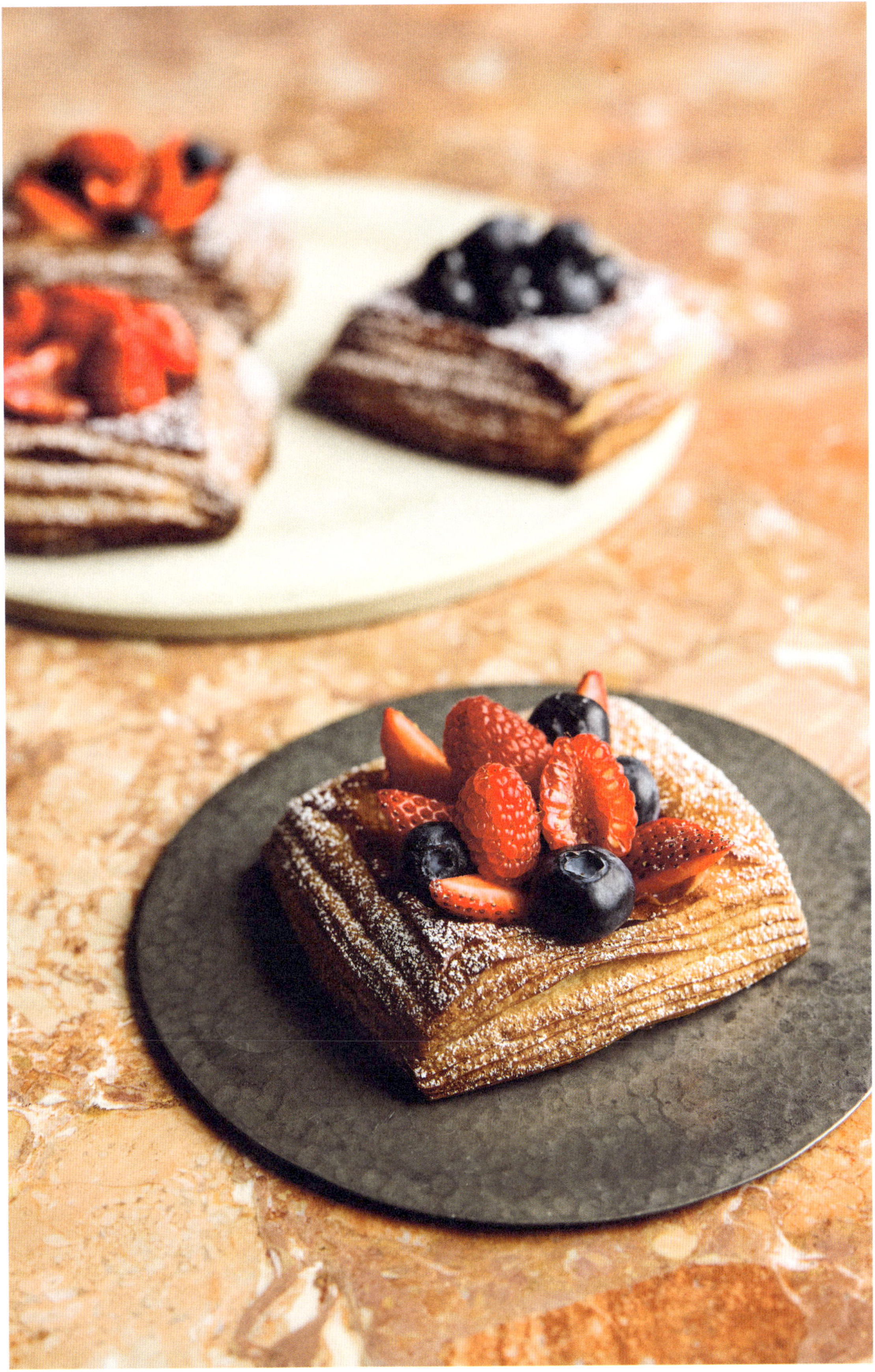

PAINS AUX RAISINS

Makes 12 pains au raisins

A well-made pain aux raisins is easily one of my all-time favourite pastries. The best ones are anything but dry – every swirl should be laced with silky crème pâtissière and studded with plump, orange-soaked raisins and sultanas (golden raisins), evenly distributed for the perfect balance of sweetness and texture. One step I never skip is glazing the pastries as they cool – this not only locks in moisture but also creates a lustrous sheen that highlights the delicate lamination.

SOAKED SULTANAS AND RAISINS

1. Put the sultanas and raisins into a bowl and pour over the orange juice. Cover and leave to soak at room temperature overnight, stirring occasionally to ensure even hydration. The next day, drain any excess juice.

sultanas (golden raisins)	100 g	3.5 oz
raisins	100 g	3.5 oz
orange juice	150 g	5.3 oz

CROISSANT DOUGH

2. Follow the instructions on pages 60–62 to make the croissant dough.

Croissant Dough (page 60)		1 quantity
Crème Pâtissière (page 239)	400 g	14.1 oz
Exotic Clear Glaze (page 242), melted	100 g	3.5 oz

TO ASSEMBLE AND BAKE

3. Roll out the dough to just over 5 mm (¼ in) thick, aiming for a 25 × 40 cm (10 × 16 in) rectangle. Lightly flour the work surface as needed, but brush off any excess flour to prevent drying out the dough.

4. Using an offset spatula, evenly spread the crème pâtissière over the entire surface of the dough, leaving a 1 cm (½ in) border along the top edge to help seal the roll.

5. Evenly scatter 200 g (7 oz) of the soaked, drained sultanas and raisins over the crème pâtissière, ensuring they are well distributed. Starting from the bottom long edge, roll the dough up tightly but without stretching it, maintaining an even cylindrical shape. Once fully rolled, gently press along the seam to seal.

6. Transfer the rolled dough to a tray and chill in the refrigerator for 20 minutes to firm up before slicing.

7. Using a sharp knife, cut the roll into 12 equal pieces, each approximately 3 cm (1¼ in) wide. Picking up each scroll, pull the outermost part of the scroll (the 'tail') stretching it slightly and tucking it underneath to secure the shape.

8. Place six pastries each on two 30 × 40 cm (12 × 16 in) baking trays (pans) lined with baking parchment, spacing them well apart to allow for expansion.

9. Cover loosely and leave to prove in a warm but controlled environment at 26°C (79°F) for about 3 hours (see Tip on page 65). When fully proved, the pastries should be visibly doubled in size.

10. Preheat the oven to 180°C fan (400°F).

11. Once proved, bake the pastries in the oven for 18–22 minutes until deep golden brown.

12. Remove from the oven and transfer the pastries to a wire rack, then brush with the melted exotic clear glaze while still warm to lock in moisture and give them a glossy finish.

13. Leave to cool completely before serving.

TIP
If your kitchen is colder, proving may take longer. In warmer climates, be cautious not to overprove.

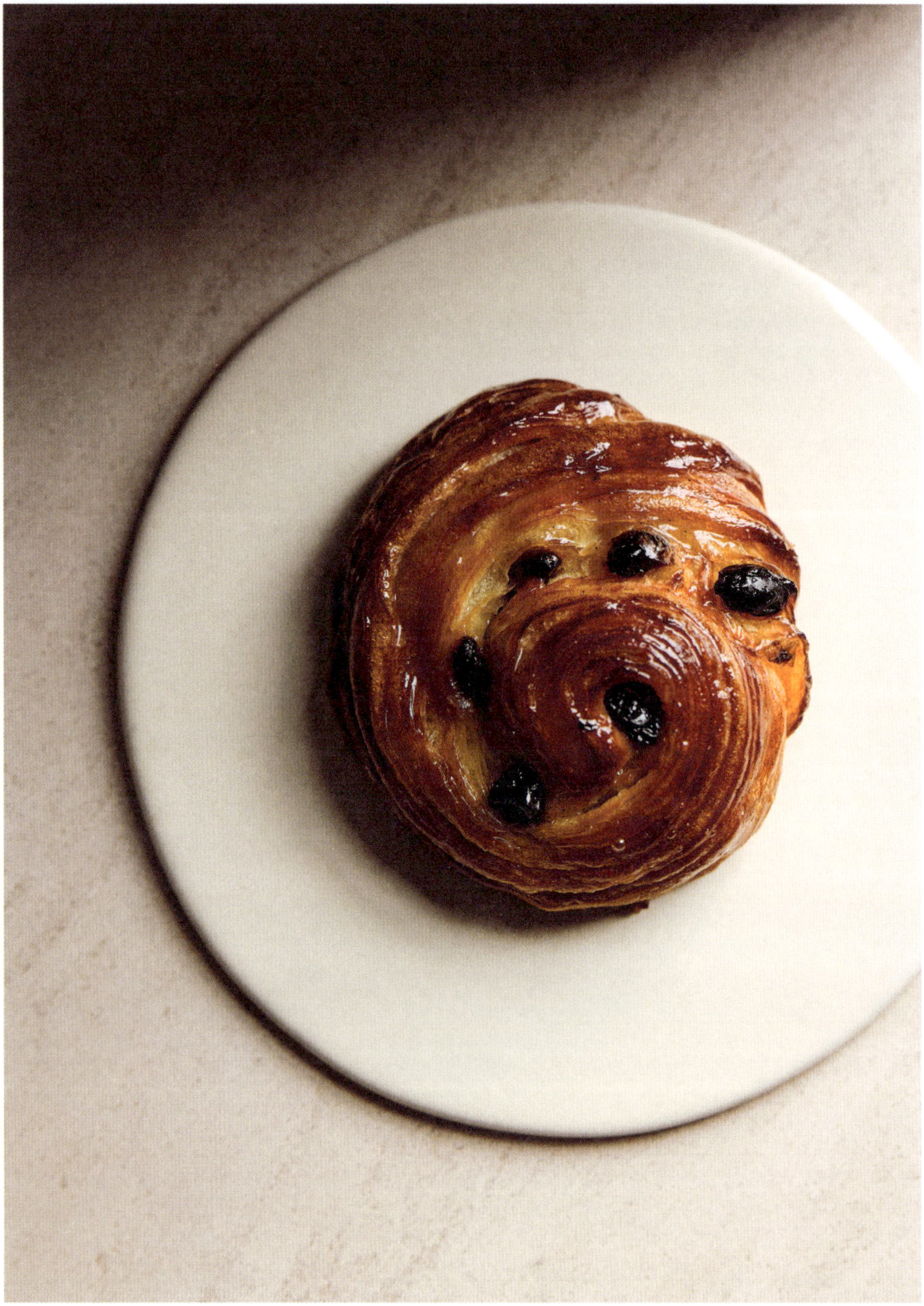

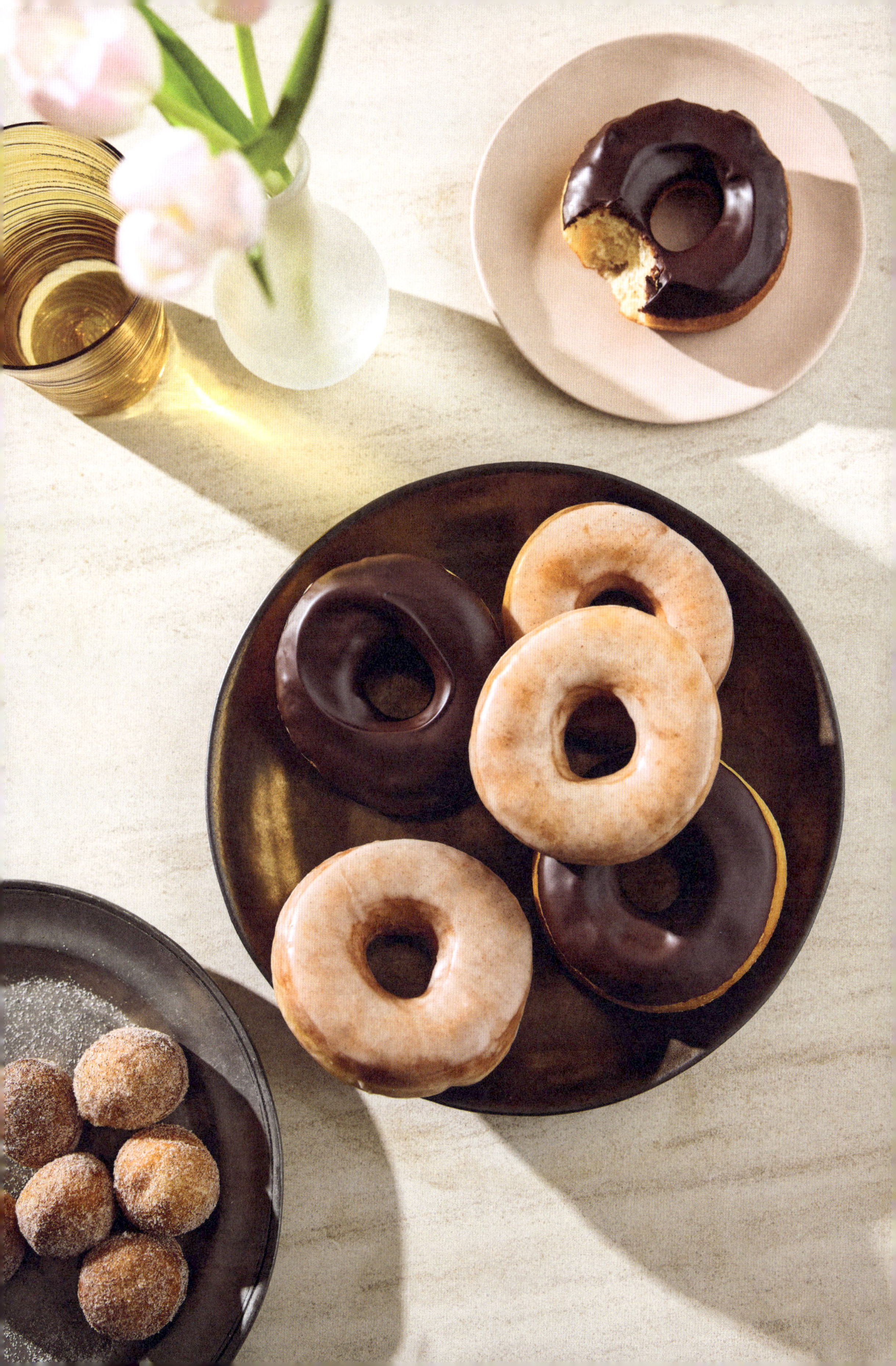

GLAZED DOUGHNUTS

Makes 10 doughnuts

Light and fluffy with just the right chew, these classic yeasted doughnuts are a joy to make and even more satisfying to finish with your choice of glaze. A simple icing (frosting) made from icing (powdered) sugar and water is the most familiar, but the liquid can be flavoured with anything: try lemon juice, coffee or even a splash of rum. For a bakery-style chocolate glaze, use the one from the Chocolate Glazed Cream Buns on page 79. Also, if you're making ring doughnuts, don't forget to fry the little holes and toss them in some cinnamon sugar – count them as a baker's treat. The doughnuts are best eaten on the day they're made.

1. Gently warm the milk and water in a small saucepan until lukewarm (35–40°C/95–104°F). Transfer to a blender and blend with the cooked sweet potato until smooth.

2. In a large bowl or the bowl of a stand mixer fitted with the dough hook attachment, combine the flours, sugar, yeast and salt. Add the blended milk mixture and mix until a dough forms.

3. Add the butter in small pieces and continue to knead on low speed for 8–10 minutes (or by hand for 10–12 minutes) until smooth, elastic and slightly tacky but not sticky. If kneading by hand, lightly flour the work surface only as needed to prevent sticking.

4. Shape the dough into a ball, place it in a lightly oiled bowl, cover with a damp dish towel or cling film (plastic wrap) and leave to rise in a warm place (24–26°C/75–79°F) for 1½–2 hours, or until doubled in size. This is very much temperature dependant, so go by the visual doubling in size.

5. Once proved, lightly flour the work surface, then roll out the dough out to 1.5 cm (⅔ in) thick. Use a 7–8 cm (2¾–3 in) round cutter to cut out doughnut shapes. For ring doughnuts, use a smaller cutter (2–3 cm/¾–1 in) to remove the centres. Re-roll scraps as needed. I like to fry the small dough balls from the centres as they are.

6. Place the doughnuts on individual squares of baking parchment on a tray, spacing them apart. Cover loosely with a damp dish towel and leave to rise at room temperature for 45–60 minutes, or until puffy and slightly jiggly when touched.

7. Heat at least 5 cm (2 in) of oil in a deep saucepan or deep-fat fryer to 175°C (350°F).

8. Carefully lower the doughnuts into the oil, a few at a time to avoid overcrowding. Fry for approximately 1 minute per side, flipping once, until deep golden brown. Transfer to a wire rack lined with paper towels to drain any excess oil. If you prefer not to make the glaze opposite, these can be tossed in caster sugar while warm.

soya milk	240 g	8.5 oz
water	75 g	2.6 oz
cooked sweet potato (page 44)	30 g	1 oz
strong white bread flour	230 g	8.1 oz
plain (all-purpose) flour, plus extra for dusting	230 g	8.1 oz
caster (superfine) sugar	60 g	2 oz
instant yeast	6 g	2 tsp
fine sea salt	5 g	1 tsp
Olive Oil Butter (page 55) or shop-bought block butter, at room temperature	60 g	2 oz
groundnut (peanut) or sunflower seed oil	for greasing and frying	

CINNAMON GLAZE

9 Whisk the icing sugar and cinnamon together in a bowl until evenly combined.

10 Add the milk and vanilla extract, then whisk until smooth.

11 Adjust the consistency, if needed, with a little more icing sugar if it's too thin or a splash more milk if it's too thick.

12 Dip the warm doughnuts into the glaze, then place on a wire rack and leave to set for 10–15 minutes before serving.

13 These doughnuts are best eaten the same day, but if for some reason you have some left over, finished doughnuts can be frozen in an airtight container and microwaved for 10 seconds.

icing (powdered) sugar	170 g	6 oz
ground cinnamon	0.5 g	½ tsp
soya milk (or other plant-based milk)	45 g	1.6 oz
vanilla extract	3 g	½ tsp

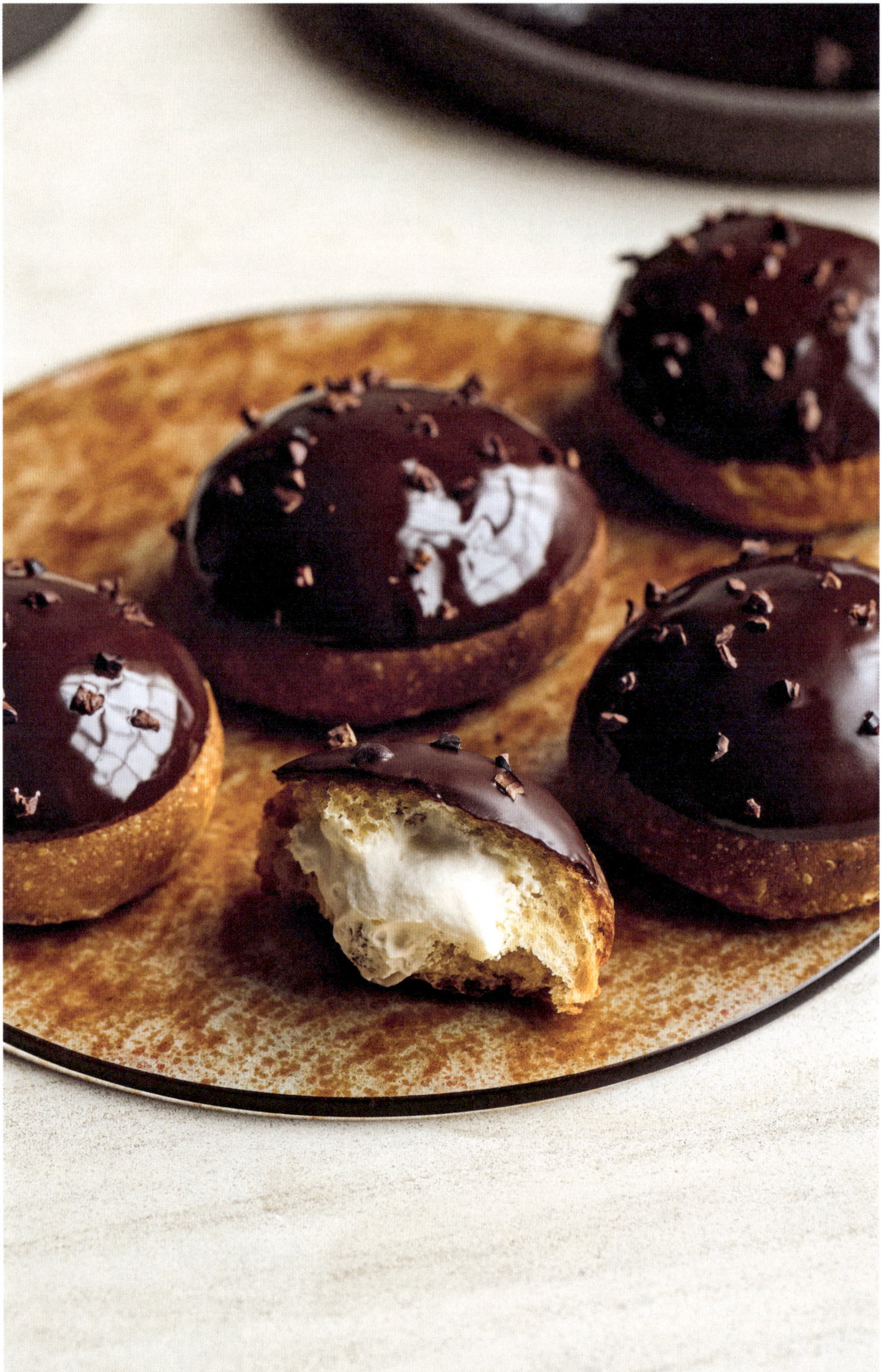

CHOCOLATE-GLAZED CREAM BUNS

Makes 12 buns

Fluffy, soft and unapologetically nostalgic, these filled buns are made with a cloud-like 'vrioche' dough and injected with a light crème diplomat. A glossy chocolate glaze cloaks the top – simple, elegant and deeply satisfying. They sit somewhere between a bakery classic and a celebration treat, best served freshly filled for slightly messy and rich yet ethereal indulgence.

CREAM BUNS

Vrioche dough (page 56)	600 g	1 lb 5 oz
Crème Diplomat (page 126), chilled	500 g	1 lb 2 oz

1. Punch down the proved dough to release the air and turn it out onto a lightly floured surface.
2. Divide the dough into 12 equal portions, each weighing approximately 60–70 g (2–2.5 oz). Shape each portion into a smooth ball.
3. Place the dough balls on a baking sheet lined with baking parchment, spacing them evenly apart.
4. Cover the shaped buns with a damp dish towel and let them rise for 30–45 minutes in a warm place, or until they have doubled in size. It is crucial that these double in size to get the lightest bun that will be delicious to eat (and fit in a generous amount of crème diplomat!).
5. Preheat the oven to 180°C fan (400°F).
6. Once the buns have risen, bake them in the oven for 12–15 minutes, or until golden brown.
7. Remove the buns from the oven and transfer them to a wire rack to cool.
8. Once cooled, use a piping (pastry) bag fitted with a small nozzle (tip) to fill each bun with the chilled crème diplomat.

CHOCOLATE GANACHE GLAZE

dark chocolate with at least 70% cocoa solids	200 g	7 oz
plant-based milk	100 g	3.5 oz
caster (superfine) sugar	100 g	3.5 oz

9. Chop the chocolate and place it in a small heatproof bowl.
10. Heat the milk and sugar in a small saucepan over a medium heat until just simmering.
11. Pour the hot milk mixture over the chopped chocolate and let it sit for 1–2 minutes to soften the chocolate.
12. Stir until the chocolate has completely melted and the ganache is smooth and glossy. I recommend using a hand-held blender to blend it well, although some blenders do incorporate air. If you're not sure, stirring well with a silicone spatula will work nicely. Set aside to cool slightly.
13. Dip the top of each filled bun into the chocolate ganache glaze, then place the glazed buns back on the wire rack and leave to set before serving.

PISTACHIO BABKA

Makes 2 small loaves or 1 large loaf

This babka showcases the deep, naturally buttery flavour of real pistachio in all its glory, with a luscious pistachio filling woven through soft, enriched dough. The result is a beautifully layered, aromatic loaf that highlights why this flavour has taken centre stage in modern baking.

PISTACHIO FILLING

1. Pulse the pistachios, sugar, cornflour, salt and vanilla paste in a food processor or high-powered blender until finely ground and starting to clump.
2. Add the milk and coconut oil and continue blending until the mixture becomes glossy and smooth. Scrape down the sides as needed to ensure even blending.
3. Set aside until ready to use.

shelled pistachios	130 g	4.6 oz
caster (superfine) sugar	130g	4.6 oz
cornflour (cornstarch)	20 g	0.7 oz
flaky sea salt	2 g	½ tsp
vanilla paste	5 g	1 tsp
plant-based milk	35 g	1.2 oz
coconut oil (deodorised)	50 g	1.8 oz

TO SHAPE AND BAKE

4. Roll out the dough into a 22 × 30 cm (9 × 12 in) rectangle, then place on a baking tray (pan) lined with baking parchment.
5. Spread the filling over the dough, leaving a 2 cm (¾ in) border at one short edge. Chill in the freezer for 15 minutes to set the filling so it is easier to roll and shape.
6. Line a 900 g (2 lb) loaf tin (pan) or two 450 g (1 lb) loaf tins with baking parchment.
7. Roll up the chilled dough, starting from the short edge without the border, then brush the border with water and stretch and press it to seal the log. Using a serrated knife, cut the log in half lengthways using a gentle sawing motion to cut all the way through. Place the long halves in a cross with the pistachio layers showing.
8. Twist the two halves around each other so that the cut side showing the pistachio is on top, then tuck the ends in. Place the 'braid' in the prepared loaf tin or tins, brush the top/s lightly with water to keep it supple, then wrap the tin/s loosely with cling film (plastic wrap) and leave to prove in a warm place for 1–1½ hours until doubled in size.
9. Preheat the oven to 190°C fan (400°F).
10. Once proved, place a piece of foil loosely on top of the loaf/loaves. Bake in the oven for 25 minutes, then remove the foil and bake for a further 5 minutes, or until a probe thermometer reads 90°C (194°F). Babka loaves can be deceptive because they will brown nicely on top before they are fully baked inside due to the size and shape of the loaf.
11. Remove from the oven and cool in the tin/s for 15 minutes, then remove gently. You might need to run a sharp knife around the edge of the tin to help ease it out. Once cool, brush the top of the loaf/loaves with the exotic clear glaze.
12. Wrap well and store at room temperature for up to 4 days, or frozen for 3 months.

Vrioche dough (page 56)	600 g	1 lb 5 oz
Exotic Clear Glaze (page 242), melted		for brushing

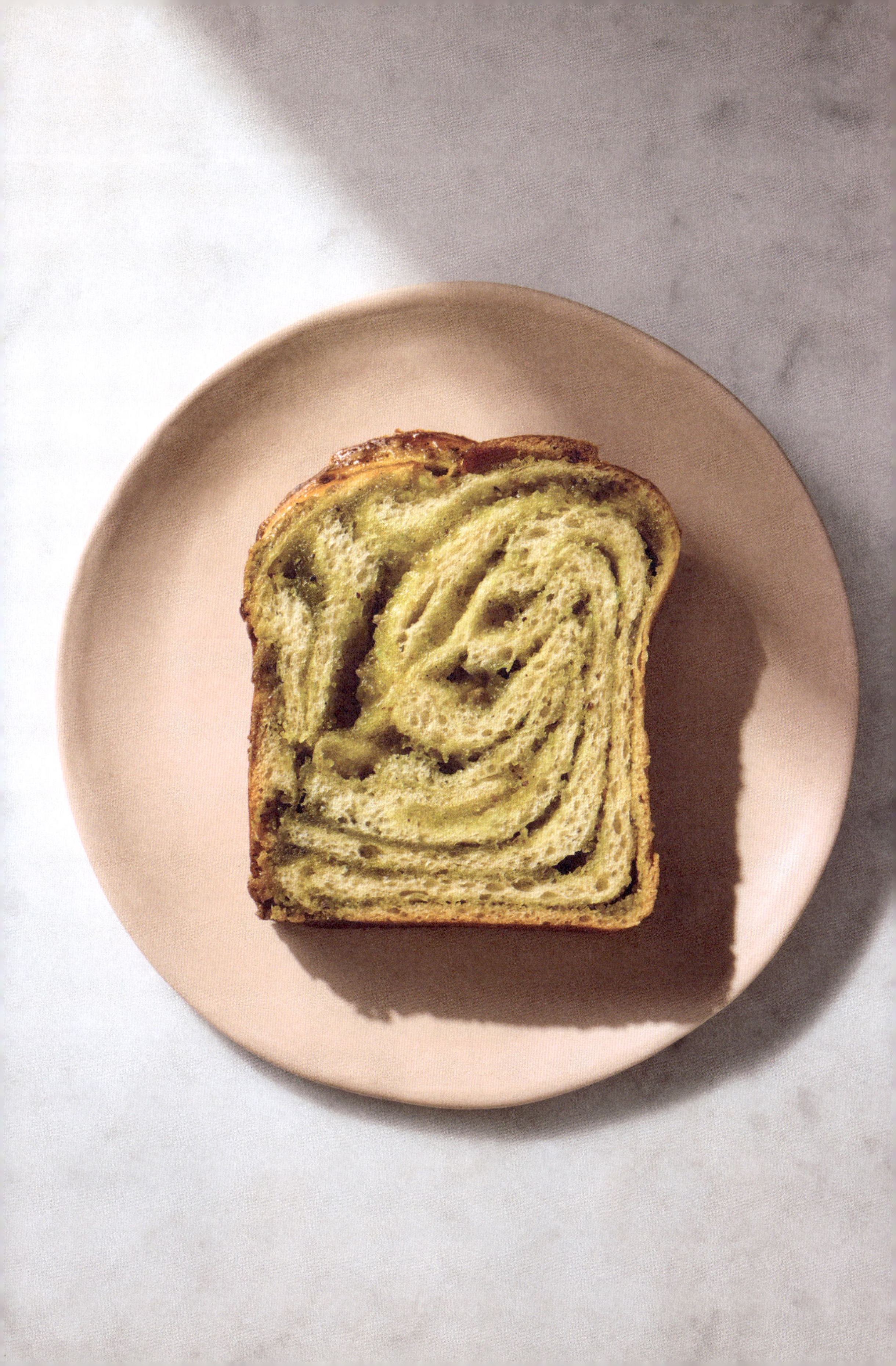

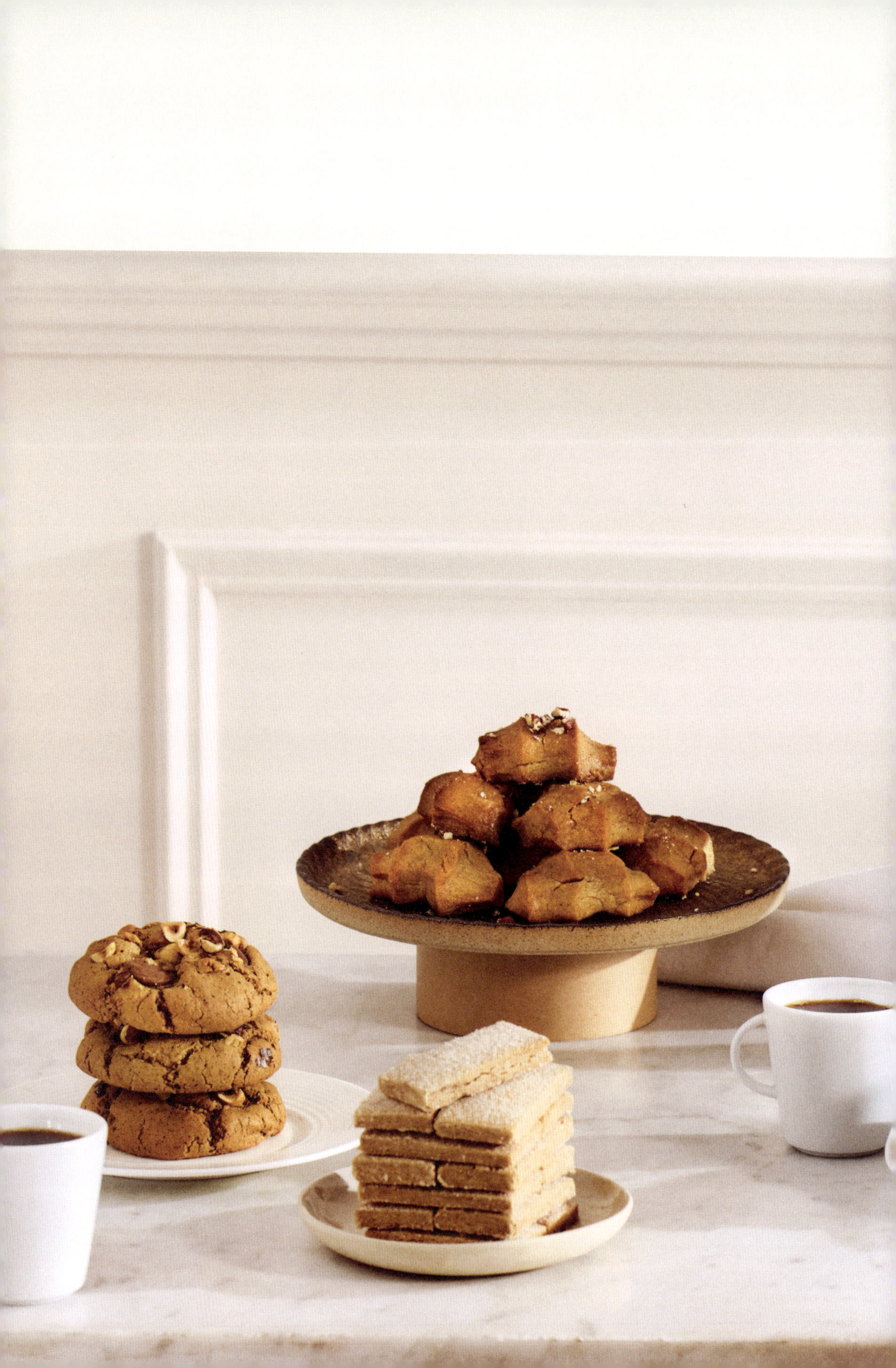

2   A COOKIE (AND BISCUIT) A DAY

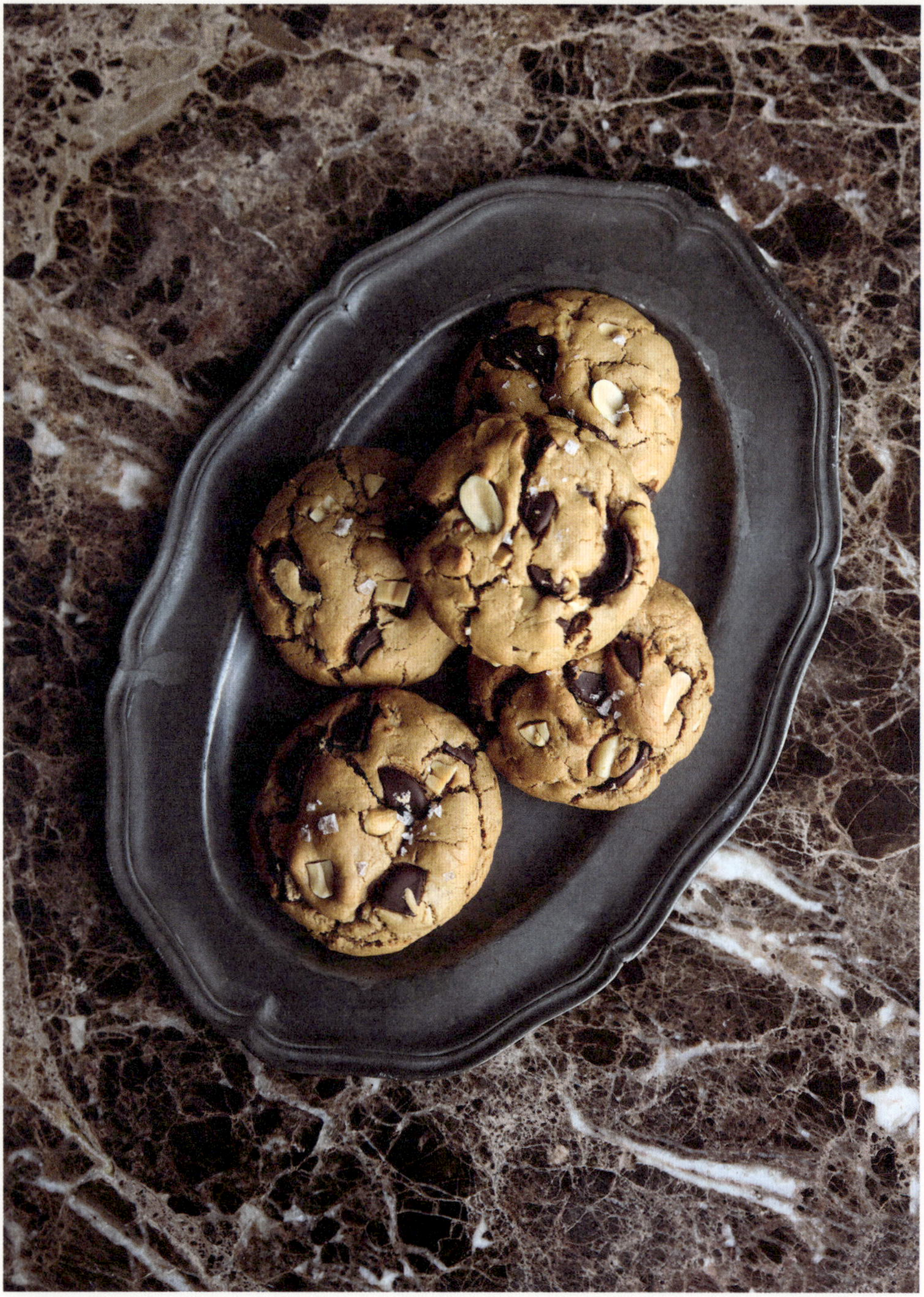

THE SUGAR SYRUP METHOD: BAKING STREAMLINED

This chapter is about more than just baking sweet treats – it's about finding new and creative ways to bring ingredients together to form that perfect cookie texture: crisp at the edges, soft and gooey in the middle, and endlessly satisfying.

At the heart of many of these recipes is a simple but powerful method: I whisk (or blend) oil, water (or plant-based milk) and sugar together to form a thick, syrup-like emulsion. This step is essential. The sugar acts as a bridge, helping oil and water to combine evenly, creating a smooth base that hydrates the flour uniformly when folded into the dry ingredients. Skipping this step and adding those elements separately often results in a dry, crumbly dough that refuses to cooperate – one that's difficult to roll, scoop or shape, and which bakes into something far less than it could be.

You'll find that this dough is slightly softer than traditional biscuit or cookie dough made with solid fats like butter, but this is easily resolved with a 30-minute rest in the refrigerator. The bonus? These cookies tend to use less fat overall, keep beautifully and offer a clean canvas for deep and varied flavours.

Within this chapter, I also explore two different approaches to nut-based cookies. In some recipes, I use nut butters as a rich, flavourful fat base. In others, I grind whole nuts directly into the flour, allowing their natural oils to release and enrich the dough as it mixes and bakes. These subtle differences create unique textures and flavour profiles, offering something special in every bite.

PEANUT BUTTER CHOC CHIP COOKIES

Makes 10 cookies

Need I say more? This decadent cookie takes inspiration from the chunky, indulgent style made famous by New York's Levain Bakery. It's perfect for when you want to whip up cookies using ready-made nut butter, as opposed to recipes like the Hazelnut and Toasted Vanilla Cookies (page 88), which derive flavour and fat from freshly ground roasted nuts. With rivulets of melted chocolate weaving through a nutty, tender morsel, these cookies are best enjoyed slightly warm, but their magic doesn't end there. Stored in an airtight container, they will keep well for up to a week. When you're ready for that molten, gooey goodness, simply pop one in the microwave for 8 seconds for swift revival.

peanut butter	100 g	3.5 oz
groundnut (peanut) oil	40 g	1.4 oz
dark brown sugar	210 g	7.4 oz
water	100 g	3.5 oz
plain (all-purpose) flour	260 g	9.2 oz
baking powder	5 g	1 tsp
bicarbonate of soda (baking soda)	4 g	½ tsp
fine sea salt	2 g	½ tsp
dark chocolate	120 g	4.2 oz
roasted peanuts	60 g	2 oz
flaky sea salt		for sprinkling

1. Put the peanut butter, groundnut oil, sugar and water into a large bowl and whisk until fully combined and the mixture is smooth, homogenous and there are no oily streaks.

2. In a separate large bowl, whisk together the flour, baking powder, bicarbonate of soda and salt.

3. Add the wet ingredients to the dry ingredients and mix with a silicone spatula until a dough forms. Chop the chocolate and peanuts, then mix them into the dough.

4. Leave the dough to rest for at least 2 hours, or wrap in cling film (plastic wrap) and rest overnight in the refrigerator – the dough can be stored in the refrigerator for up to 3 days.

5. Preheat the oven to 180°C fan (350°F) and line two large baking sheets with baking parchment.

6. Divide the dough into 70 g (2.5 oz) portions (about the size of a golf ball), then roll these into balls and arrange them on the prepared baking sheets, spaced 5 cm (2 in) apart and away from the edge (you should be able to fit 12 per baking sheet). Top each with a sprinkle of flaky sea salt.

7. Bake in the oven for about 12 minutes for soft, fudgy cookies, or 15 minutes for crispier edges.

8. While the cookies are still warm, you can make them sexy and perfectly round – use a large plain cutter or ring and rotate it around the cookies quickly to tuck in and 'round' the edges.

9. These will keep well for up to 1 week in an airtight container, although they are especially good on the first day before the chocolate has cooled down and reset into chunks.

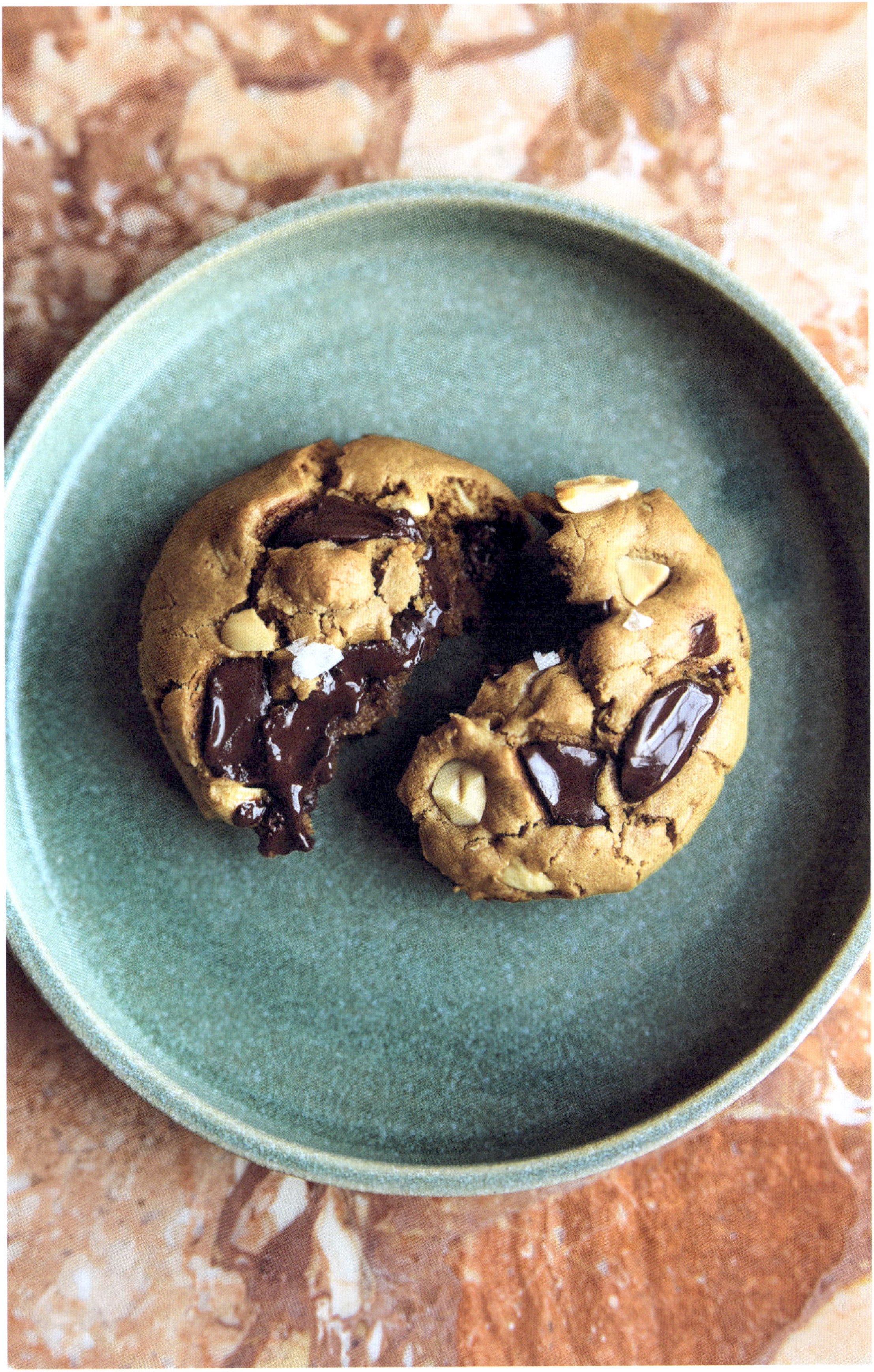

HAZELNUT AND TOASTED VANILLA COOKIES

Makes 12 cookies

Inspired by the flavours of a certain iconic chocolate and hazelnut treat, these cookies are chewy, nutty and utterly irresistible. They also happen to be a brilliant way to repurpose a scraped vanilla pod (bean). A quick zap in the microwave (or a toast in the oven) dries it out perfectly, making it easy to blend with the toasted hazelnuts that bring deep flavour and a satisfying crunch. This recipe method is a great way of incorporating nut flavours into a cookie when you don't have a nut butter available.

skin-on hazelnuts	100 g	3.5 oz
muscovado or dark brown sugar	120 g	4.2 oz
caster (superfine) sugar	120 g	4.2 oz
water	85 g	3 oz
groundnut (peanut) or olive oil	30 g	1 oz
vanilla pod (bean), already used	1 pod	
plain (all-purpose) flour	300 g	10.6 oz
baking powder	8 g	2 tsp
bicarbonate soda (baking soda)	5 g	1 tsp
fine sea salt	2 g	½ tsp
dairy-free milk or dark chocolate, chopped	120 g	4.2 oz
flaky sea salt	for sprinkling	

1. Preheat the oven to 160°C fan (350°F). Spread the hazelnuts in a baking tray (pan) and toast in the oven for 15–18 minutes until golden inside when halved. Remove from the oven and leave to cool, then roughly chop half of them (half will be whizzed up with the flour and half are folded in for texture).

2. Put the sugars, water and oil into a large bowl and whisk until fully combined and the mixture is smooth, homogenous and there are no oily streaks.

3. Microwave the vanilla pod for 20 seconds – it will puff up as the moisture evaporates. Once cooled, break it up and then transfer to a food processor along with the cooled whole hazelnuts, flour, baking powder, bicarbonate of soda and fine salt. Blend to a fine powder – it will start to clump as the oils are released from the hazelnuts.

4. Add the wet ingredients to the dry ingredients along with the chopped chocolate and hazelnuts (reserving a few hazelnut pieces for the tops) and mix well with a silicone spatula until a dough forms. Cover and refrigerate for at least 2 hours, or overnight. The dough will keep for up to 3 days in the refrigerator.

5. Preheat the oven to 180°C fan (400°F) and line a baking sheet with baking parchment.

6. Divide the dough into 70 g (2.5 oz) portions (about the size of a golf ball), then roll these into balls and arrange them on the prepared baking sheet, spaced 5 cm (2 in) apart and away from the edge. Place a few extra pieces of hazelnut on top and add a sprinkle of flaky sea salt for a pop of seasoning.

7. Bake in the oven for 12 minutes for soft, fudgy cookies, or 15 minutes for crispier edges.

8. Remove from the oven and leave to cool on the baking sheet for a few minutes, then transfer to a wire rack to cool completely.

9. These will keep well for up to 5 days in an airtight container.

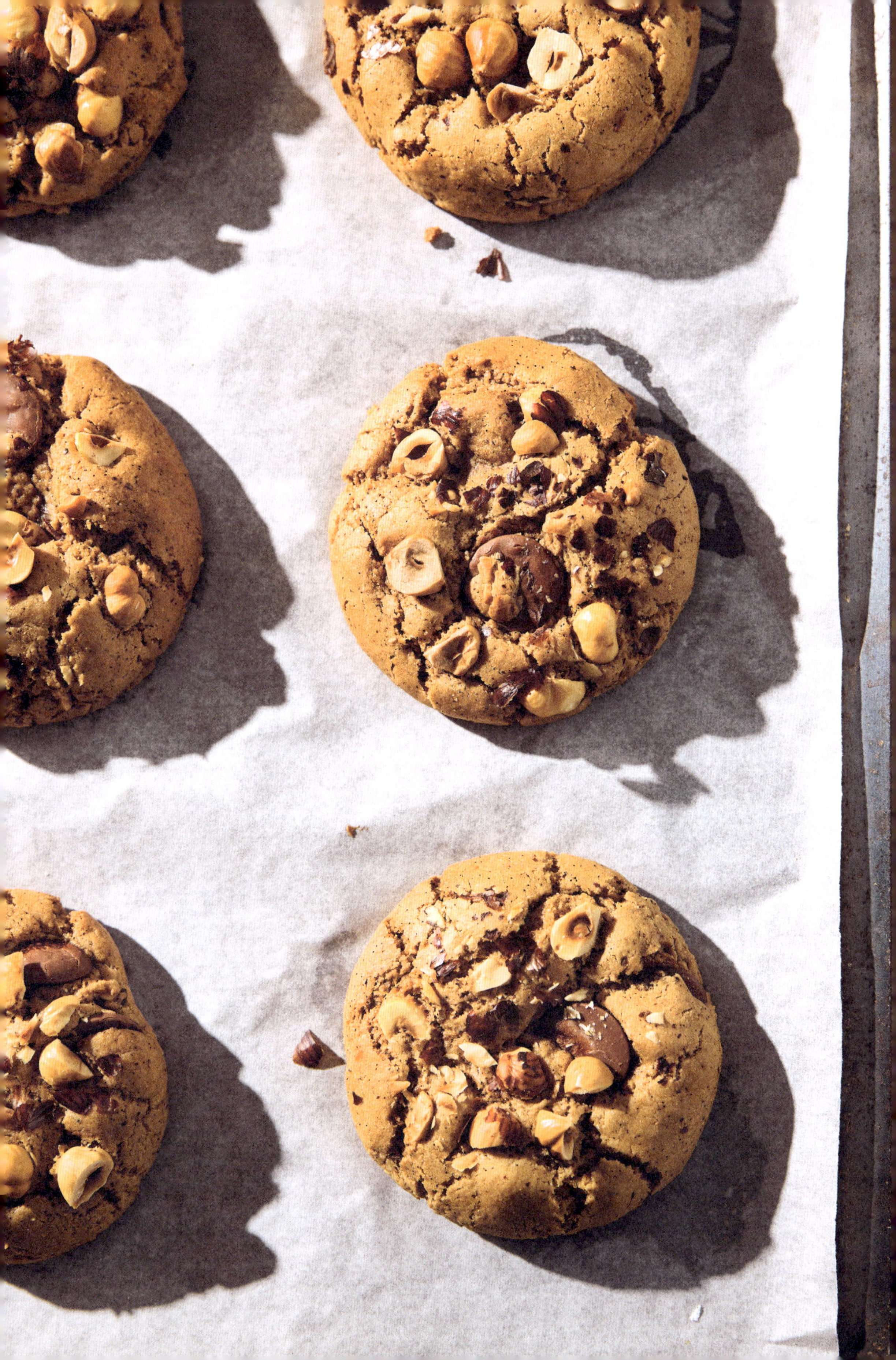

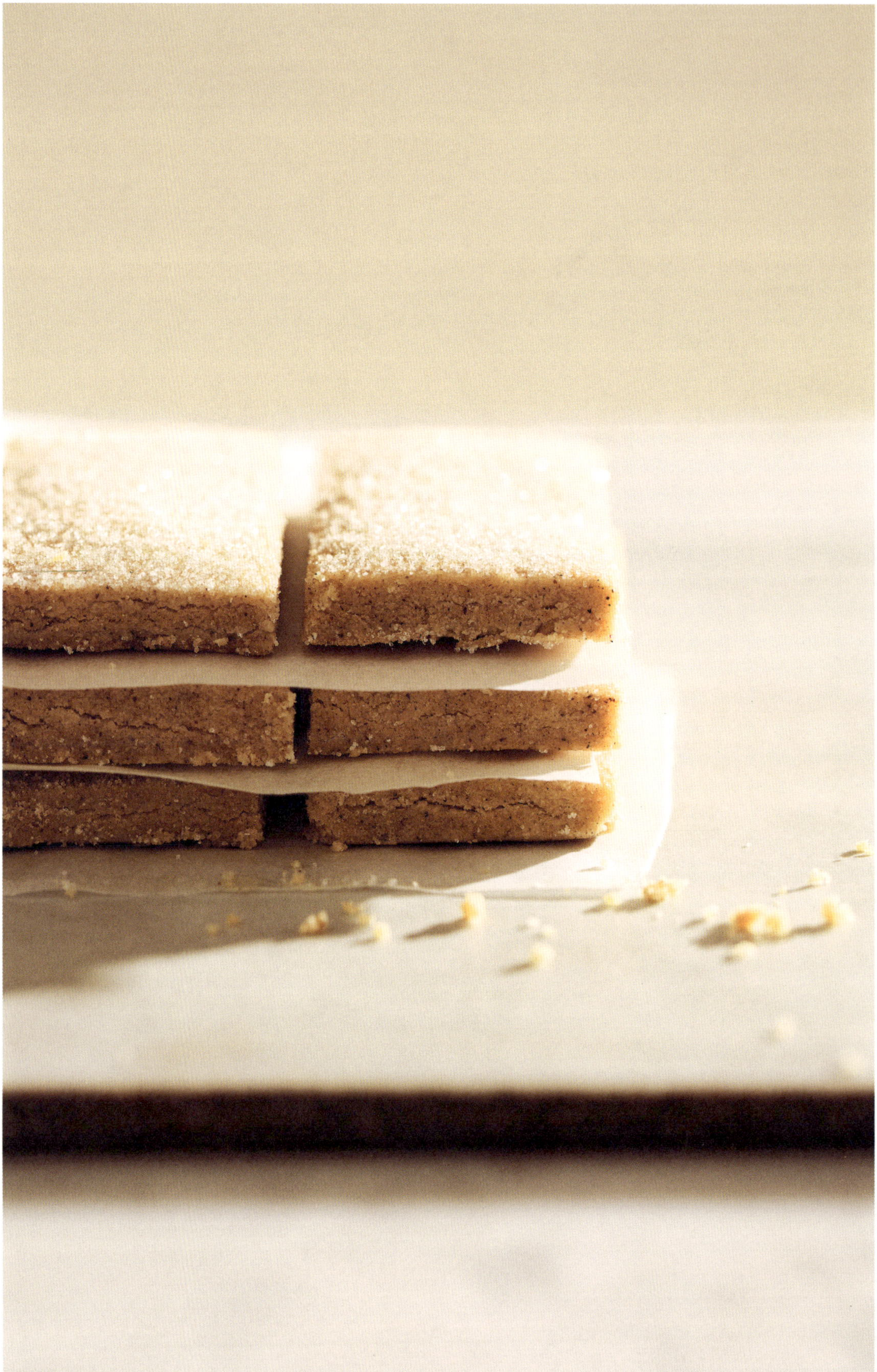

MACADAMIA SHORTBREAD

Makes 10–15 shortbread pieces

This melt-in-your-mouth macadamia shortbread is rich, buttery and endlessly adaptable. Its delicate crumb pairs beautifully with spices, citrus zest, herbs or extracts, allowing for endless variations. If macadamias are hard to find, Brazil nuts make a perfect substitute. Whether kept classic or infused with bold flavours, this shortbread delivers a luxuriously tender bite.

macadamia or Brazil nuts	200 g	7 oz
plain (all-purpose) flour	340 g	12 oz
caster (superfine) sugar, plus extra for dusting	100 g	3.5 oz
flaky sea salt, crushed	2 g	½ tsp
ground cinnamon	5 g	1 tsp

1. Preheat the oven to 160°C fan (350°F) and line a 20 × 20 cm (8 in) baking tin with baking parchment.
2. Put the nuts, flour, sugar, salt and cinnamon into a food processor and pulse until the nuts blend into the flour, clump together. It's very important to use a good blender for this to extract as much of the nut's oils.
3. Tip out into the lined tin, and press down well with an angled palette knife, and sprinkle some caster sugar on top. Press a knife gently into the mixture to cut desired strips.
4. Bake in the oven for 15 minutes until golden.
5. Remove from the oven and leave to cool to room temperature. Gently lift out of the tin using the parchment paper. These will keep well for 1 week in an airtight container.

ORANGE AND MAPLE SPICED BISCUITS

Makes 16 biscuits

Melomakarona, the quintessential Greek Christmas biscuit (cookie), is a symphony of honey, spice and festive delight. This version takes a subtle detour, swapping honey for maple syrup and folding walnuts into the dough for an irresistibly tender bite. A small twist on tradition, but one that feels right.

MAPLE SOAKING SYRUP

1. Combine the maple syrup, water, sugar, cinnamon and ground cloves in a saucepan over a medium heat and bring to a simmer, stirring occasionally.
2. Remove the syrup from the heat and discard the cinnamon stick (if using). Set aside while the biscuits are prepared.

maple syrup	150 g	5.3 oz
water	100 g	3.5 oz
caster (superfine) sugar	100 g	3.5 oz
cinnamon stick or		1
ground cinnamon	1 g	¼ tsp
ground cloves	1 g	¼ tsp

SPICED ORANGE COOKIE DOUGH

3. Preheat the oven to 180°C fan (400°F) and line a baking sheet with baking parchment.
4. Put the oil, orange juice, sugar and orange zest into a large bowl and whisk until fully combined and the mixture is smooth, homogenous and there are no oily streaks.
5. In a separate large bowl, whisk together the flour, semolina, baking powder, bicarbonate of soda, ground spices and chopped walnuts (1).
6. Gradually add the dry ingredients to the wet ingredients, stirring until a soft dough forms. The dough should be slightly sticky but should hold together well.
7. Shape the dough into small oval biscuits, about 4 cm (1.5 in) in length. Place them on the prepared baking sheet, spacing them about 3 cm (1¼ in) apart.
8. Bake in the oven for 20–25 minutes, or until the cookies are golden brown and firm to the touch.
9. Remove the biscuits from the oven. While they are still hot, dip each biscuit into the slightly cooled soaking syrup for about 5 seconds, ensuring they are fully coated.
10. Place the soaked cookies back on the baking sheet still lined with parchment.
11. Sprinkle the tops of the biscuits with the chopped walnuts (2) and a light dusting of ground cinnamon.
12. Let the biscuits sit for a few hours, or overnight, to absorb the syrup and develop their full flavour. Store in an airtight container for up to 2 weeks.

olive oil	110 g	3.9 oz
orange juice (about 1 orange)	60 g	2 oz
caster (superfine) sugar	70 g	2.5 oz
orange zest	1 orange	
plain (all-purpose) flour	250 g	8.8 oz
fine semolina	50 g	1.8 oz
baking powder	4 g	1 tsp
bicarbonate of soda (baking soda)	2 g	¼ tsp
ground cinnamon, plus extra for sprinkling	1 g	½ tsp
ground cloves	1 g	¼ tsp
chopped walnuts (1)	50 g	1.8 oz
chopped walnuts (2)	30 g	1 oz

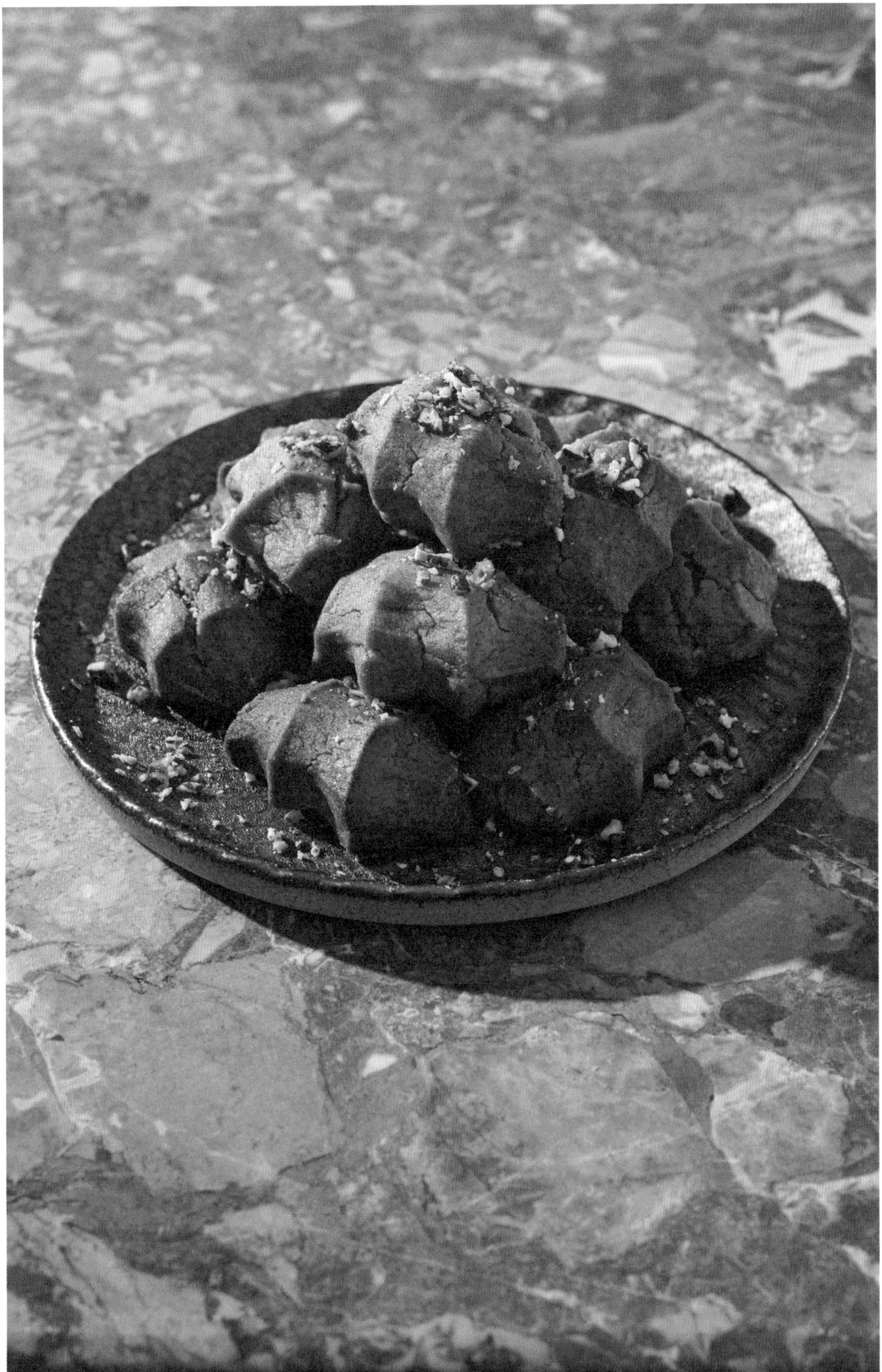

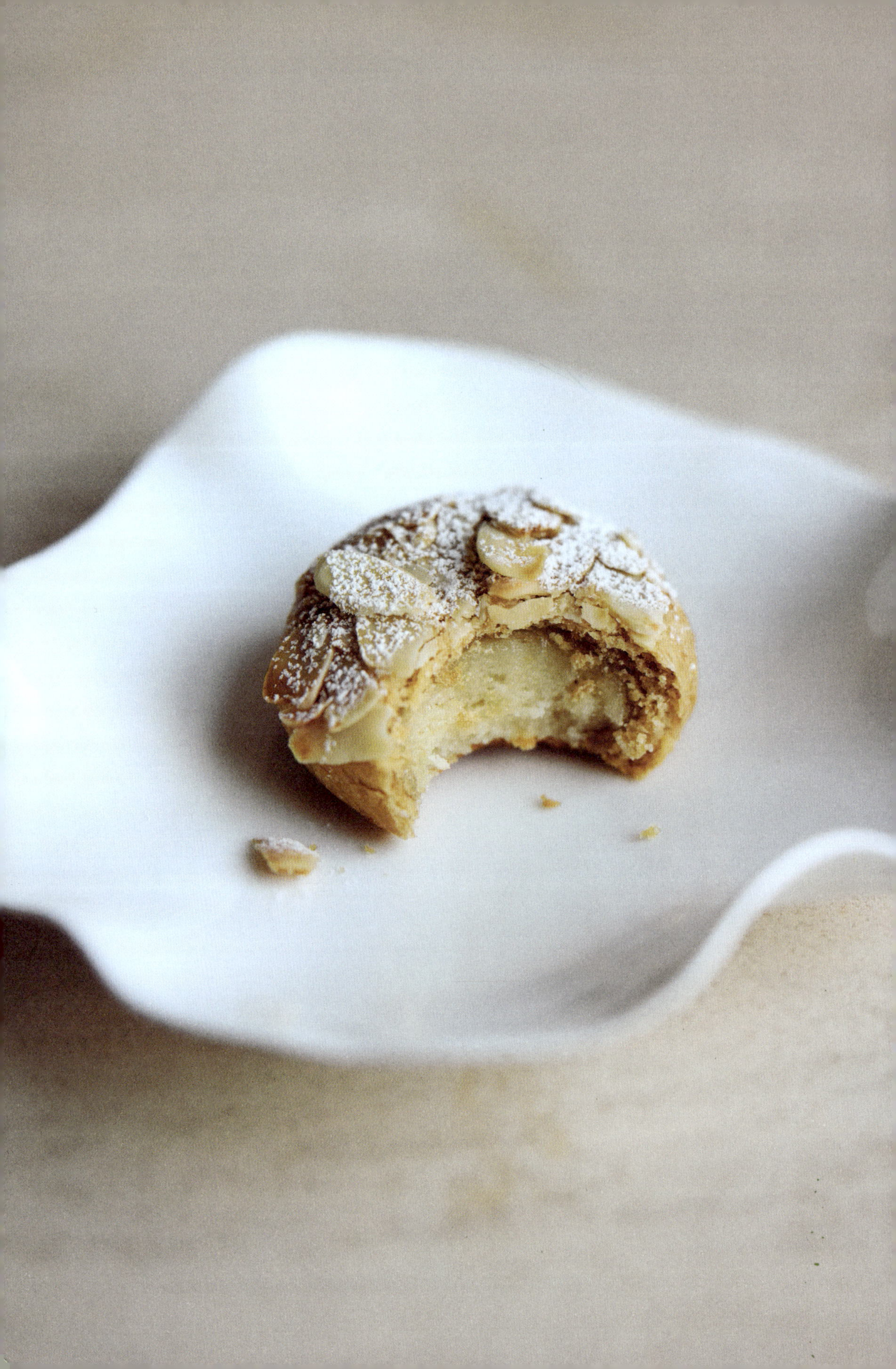

STUFFED ALMOND CROISSANT COOKIES

Makes 12 cookies

At the heart of this creation is a homemade marzipan filling, crafted from scratch in a food processor – an incredibly rewarding process that allows complete control over sweetness and quality. To elevate the almond flavour, I add a drop or two of bitter almond extract, which enhances the nuttiness and brings out the essence of marzipan. Each bite is a balance of crisp, golden edges, the soft almond-rich interior and just the right touch of sweetness.

MARZIPAN

1. Put the almonds and icing sugar in a food processor and blend well until a very fine powder is achieved.

2. Add the bitter almond extract (if using) and the water and continue blending until a dough forms. You need to keep blending until it forms a smooth mass – this will heat up quite a lot from the friction. If it doesn't become a smooth dough, add ½ teaspoon water and continue blending.

3. Scrape the dough out onto a sheet of baking parchment and fold it over the top to cover. Flatten the dough inside the parchment, then leave until cool. This can be stored at room temperature for up to 1 week, well wrapped.

4. Once cool, weigh out 25 g (1 oz) pieces of marzipan and roll them into balls. Set aside.

raw, skin-on almonds	200 g	7 oz
icing (powdered) sugar	100 g	3.5 oz
bitter almond oil extract (optional)	1–2 drops	
water	6 g	1½ tsp

FLAKY PASTRY DOUGH

5. Preheat the oven to 180°C fan (400°F) and line a baking sheet with baking parchment.

6. Put the flour, salt and sugar into a large bowl and mix together.

7. Add the oil and use a silicone spatula or your hands to mix it into the flour. The oil should coat all the flour.

8. Add the sweet potato and water and mix until the dough just comes together. Don't overmix, because the dough will start to separate and become more difficult to handle, but even if this happens it will still work out fine.

9. Weigh out the dough into 35 g (1.2 oz) balls and then press them down into large, flat discs.

10. Wrap the discs of dough around the balls of marzipan and pinch the edges closed.

11. Brush the cookies with maple syrup and top with flaked almonds, pressing them into the tops until flat. Place on the prepared baking sheet with the almonds facing upwards, then bake in the oven for 15 minutes until golden.

12. Remove from the oven and leave to cool, then dust with icing sugar to finish.

plain (all-purpose) flour	250 g	8.8 oz
fine sea salt	3 g	¾ tsp
caster (superfine) sugar	40 g	1.4 oz
olive oil	100 g	3.5 oz
sweet potato, cooked and cooled (page 44)	20 g	0.7 oz
cold water	40 g	1.4 oz
maple syrup	for brushing	
flaked (slivered) almonds	for topping	
icing (powdered) sugar	for dusting	

FIG NEWTONS

Makes 30 cookies

These are clever cookies indeed. The recipe is endlessly versatile – try dried dates, apricots or even apples with some cinnamon. Other fruits work just as beautifully, too – no added sugar required. I also recommend playing around with the dough by adding flavours like orange blossom water or rosewater, almond extract or other spices depending on the fruit you choose to try.

FIG PASTE

1. Trim any hard stalks from the figs, then put them into a food processor. If they are very dry, add 2 tablespoons water.
2. Pulse until a thick paste is achieved, then transfer to a piping (pastry) bag.

VANILLA PASTRY

3. Put the olive oil, both sugars, the salt, water and vanilla paste into a large bowl and whisk until fully combined and the mixture is smooth, homogenous and there are no oily streaks. This is key to a dough that doesn't separate when mixed.
4. In a separate large bowl, whisk together the flour and baking powder.
5. Add the wet ingredients to the dry ingredients and mix well with a silicone spatula, then turn the mixture out onto a work surface and knead for about 5 minutes until the dough comes together into a cohesive mixture. You can also use a stand mixer fitted with the paddle attachment and mix for 1–2 minutes. The dough can look as though it isn't coming together, but continue mixing on low speed until it does!
6. Wrap the dough well in cling film (plastic wrap) and leave to rest in the refrigerator for 1 hour before using.
7. Preheat the oven to 180°C fan (400°F) and line a large baking sheet with baking parchment.
8. Roll out the dough into a rectangle about 20 × 30 cm (6 × 12 in) and 4 mm (¼ in) thick, then slice into four even strips, each 10 cm (4 in) wide.
9. Pipe the filling evenly down the middle of each strip, then fold one side of the strip over the filling. Brush the other side of each strip with water and fold over, then gently press down to seal. Gently roll over so the seam is on the bottom. Repeat until all the strips are filled.
10. Brush the tops with milk and sprinkle with some Demerara sugar, then cut each strip into five 4 cm (1½ in) pieces and transfer to the prepared baking sheet, spacing them about 2 cm (¾ in) apart.
11. Bake in the oven for 10 minutes until puffed up, then remove from the oven and leave to cool completely.
12. These will keep well for 1 week in an airtight container.

dried figs	400 g	14.1 oz
extra virgin olive oil	60 g	2 oz
caster (superfine) sugar	80 g	2.8 oz
muscovado or dark brown sugar	20 g	0.7 oz
fine sea salt	2 g	½ tsp
water	60 g	2 oz
vanilla paste	5 g	1 tsp
plain (all-purpose) flour	300 g	10.6 oz
baking powder	4 g	1 tsp
plant-based milk	for brushing	
Demerara sugar	for sprinkling	

TIP

Some figs can be dried but still juicy enough to be blendable. It's the same with other dried fruits – their texture and level of dryness can vary, so this may need to be adjusted with a teaspoon at a time of water in order to achieve a paste.

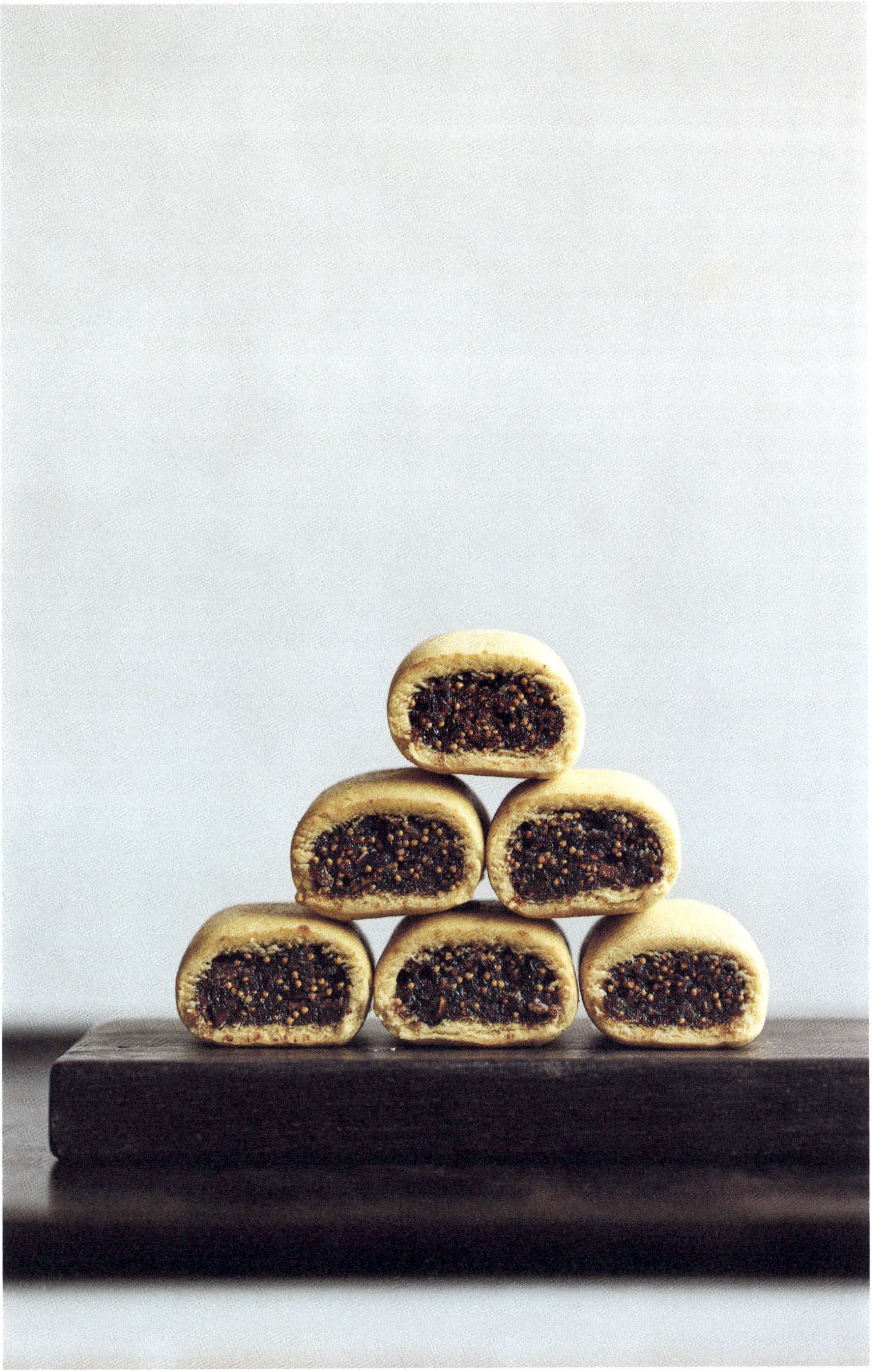

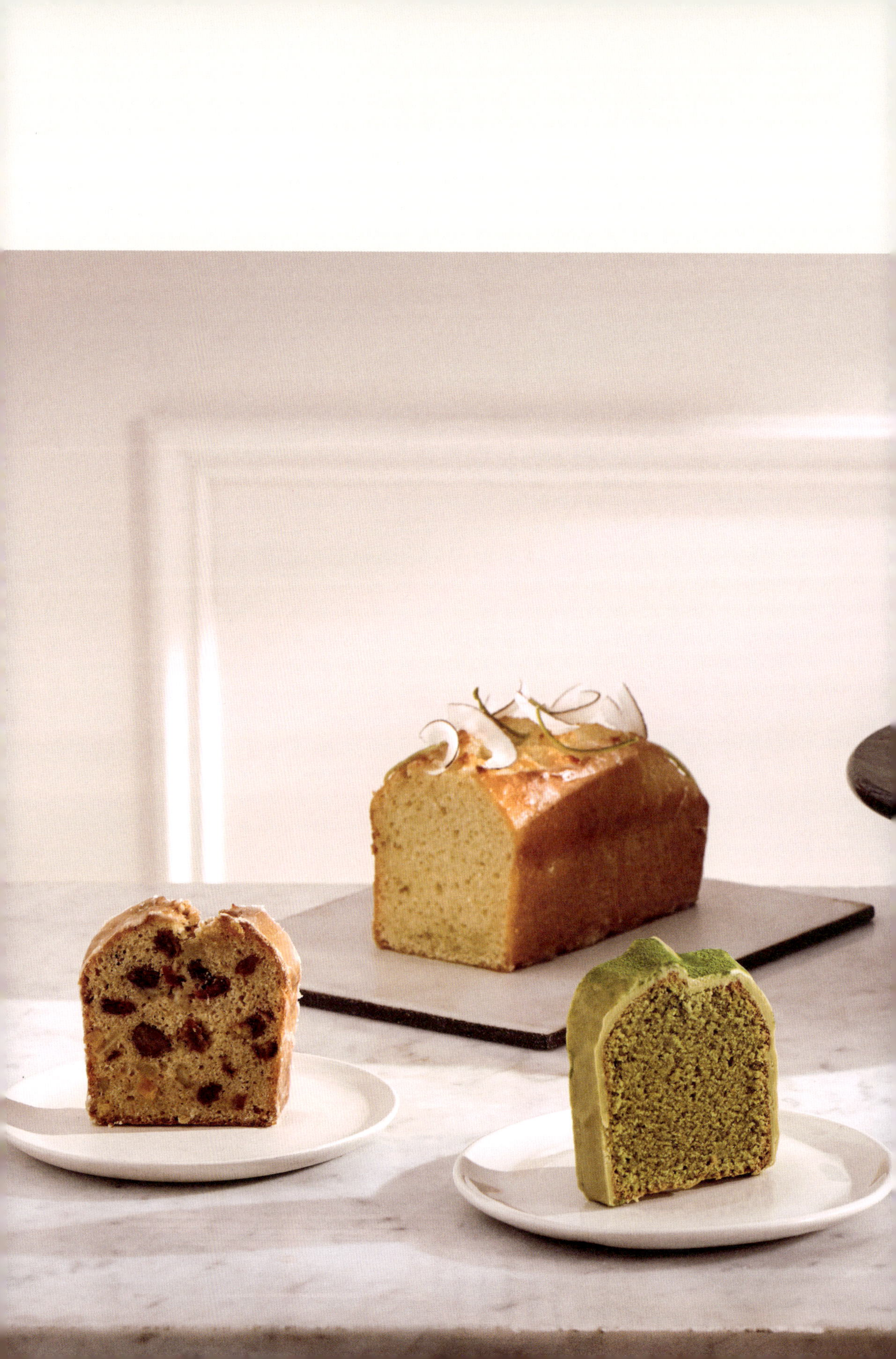

3 A PIECE OF CAKE

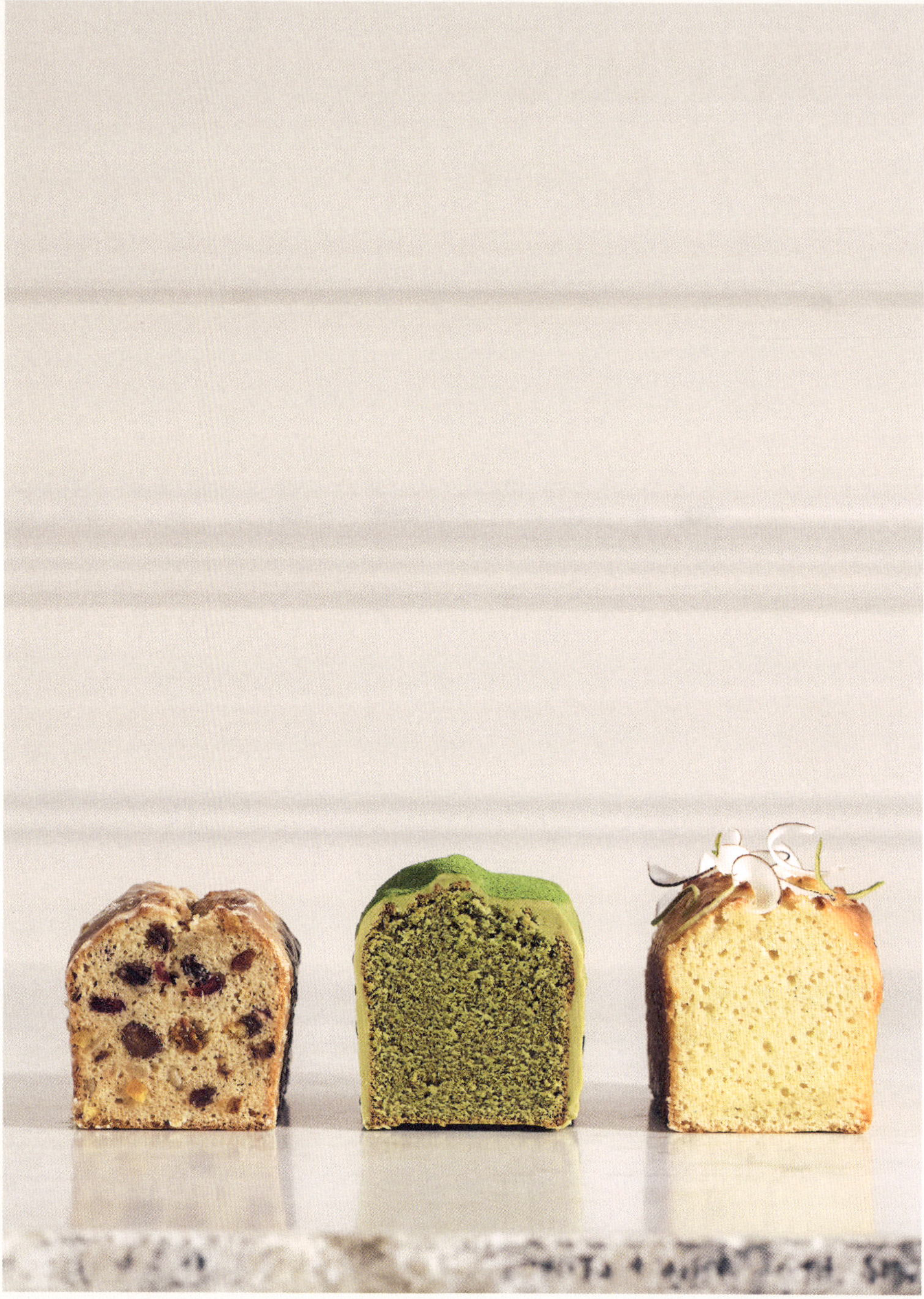

SIMPLE METHODS, BOLDER FLAVOURS

Reworking cake batters without eggs meant unlearning much of what I thought I knew about baking. The first and most surprising discovery? I had to drastically reduce the fat – sometimes by as much as 60 per cent. In traditional sponge cakes, eggs and flour team up to form a gelling structure as they bake. Fat then tenderises this structure, creating that soft, sumptuous crumb we associate with great cake. Remove the eggs and that balance shifts – there's less structure to tenderise, so too much fat simply overwhelms the flour, weakening the gluten and leaving the cake dense, oily or fragile.

The second key consideration is air. A light, fluffy texture depends on it. In classic baking, air is introduced by creaming butter and sugar or whipping egg whites. But the real revolution came in the 19th century, with the invention of baking powder – a scientific breakthrough that changed home baking forever. Unlike temperamental sourdough starters and slow-rising breads (often viewed with suspicion at the time), baking powder offered consistency and speed. Just add water and heat, and it releases gas to lift the batter. Suddenly, cakes became quicker, easier and more accessible – particularly for women, who bore the brunt of labour-intensive breadmaking.

This leap in convenience gave rise to a whole new category of cakes: soft sponges, loaves, cupcakes, scones and quick breads – simple cakes that didn't rely on beaten eggs or long fermentation but rose beautifully with just a few pantry staples. Many of the recipes in this chapter honour that tradition. They're designed to be straightforward and forgiving, using thoughtfully balanced plant-based ingredients to recreate the lightness, moisture and tender crumb we all love – no eggs or mixers required.

But simplicity doesn't mean plain. In fact, these cakes offer the perfect framework for introducing bold and exciting flavours. By carefully infusing the batter with fruits, nuts, spices, teas and botanical extracts, we can take something humble and make it unforgettable.

LIGHT FRUIT CAKE

Makes 1 × 450 g (1 lb) loaf

I've always had a soft spot for the little fruit cakes from Bonne Maman that come wrapped in paper – they're soft-crumbed, never too dark or dense. This is a quiet ode to them. It's tender and fragrant, with just enough fruit – rum-soaked sultanas (golden raisins), dried cranberries and candied citrus peel – to add interest without overwhelming. The rum is there too, but only just. This is a fruit cake for people who don't like fruit cake – light, fragrant and impossible not to finish.

1. The night before, combine the raisins and rum in a bowl and leave to soak overnight. If you're short on time, you can also microwave the raisins and rum in a covered dish for 30 seconds, then let them sit for 30 minutes to absorb the liquid.

2. On the day of making the batter, preheat the oven to 180°C fan (400°F) and position a shelf in the middle of the oven. Line a 450 g (1 lb) loaf tin (pan) with baking parchment, ensuring the paper extends slightly over the edges for easy removal.

3. Sift the flour, baking powder and salt into a large bowl.

4. In a separate bowl or jug (pitcher), whisk together the milk, oil, sugar, orange zest and vanilla. Mix until the sugar begins to dissolve.

5. Add the wet ingredients to the dry ingredients, folding gently until just combined and there are no streaks.

6. Drain any excess rum from the raisins and fold them into the batter along with the candied orange pieces and dried cranberries. Ensure the fruit is evenly distributed throughout the batter.

7. Pour the batter into the prepared tin, spreading it out evenly with a spatula.

8. Bake in the oven for 40–45 minutes, or until the top is golden brown and a skewer inserted into the centre of the cake comes out clean.

9. Remove from the oven and leave the cake to cool in the tin for 10 minutes before lifting it out using the parchment paper and transferring it to a wire rack to cool completely.

raisins	60 g	2 oz
dark rum	30 g	1 oz
plain (all-purpose) flour	150 g	5.3 oz
baking powder	5 g	1¼ tsp
fine sea salt	1 g	¼ tsp
plant-based milk	120 g	4.2 oz
groundnut (peanut) oil	40 g	1.4 oz
golden caster (superfine) sugar	125 g	4.4 oz
orange zest	4 g	½ orange
vanilla paste	5 g	1 tsp
candied orange pieces	50 g	1.8 oz
dried cranberries	30 g	1 oz

RUM WATER ICING

10. Slowly mix the icing sugar, rum and water together in a small bowl or jug (pitcher) until it is fully combined and smooth.

11. Use a pastry brush to generously dab or brush the glaze over the whole cake, then leave to set for 30–60 minutes.

12. The cake can be stored in cling film (plastic wrap) or in an airtight container for up to 5 days.

icing (powdered) sugar	80 g	2.8 oz
dark rum	10 g	2 tsp
water	10 g	2 tsp

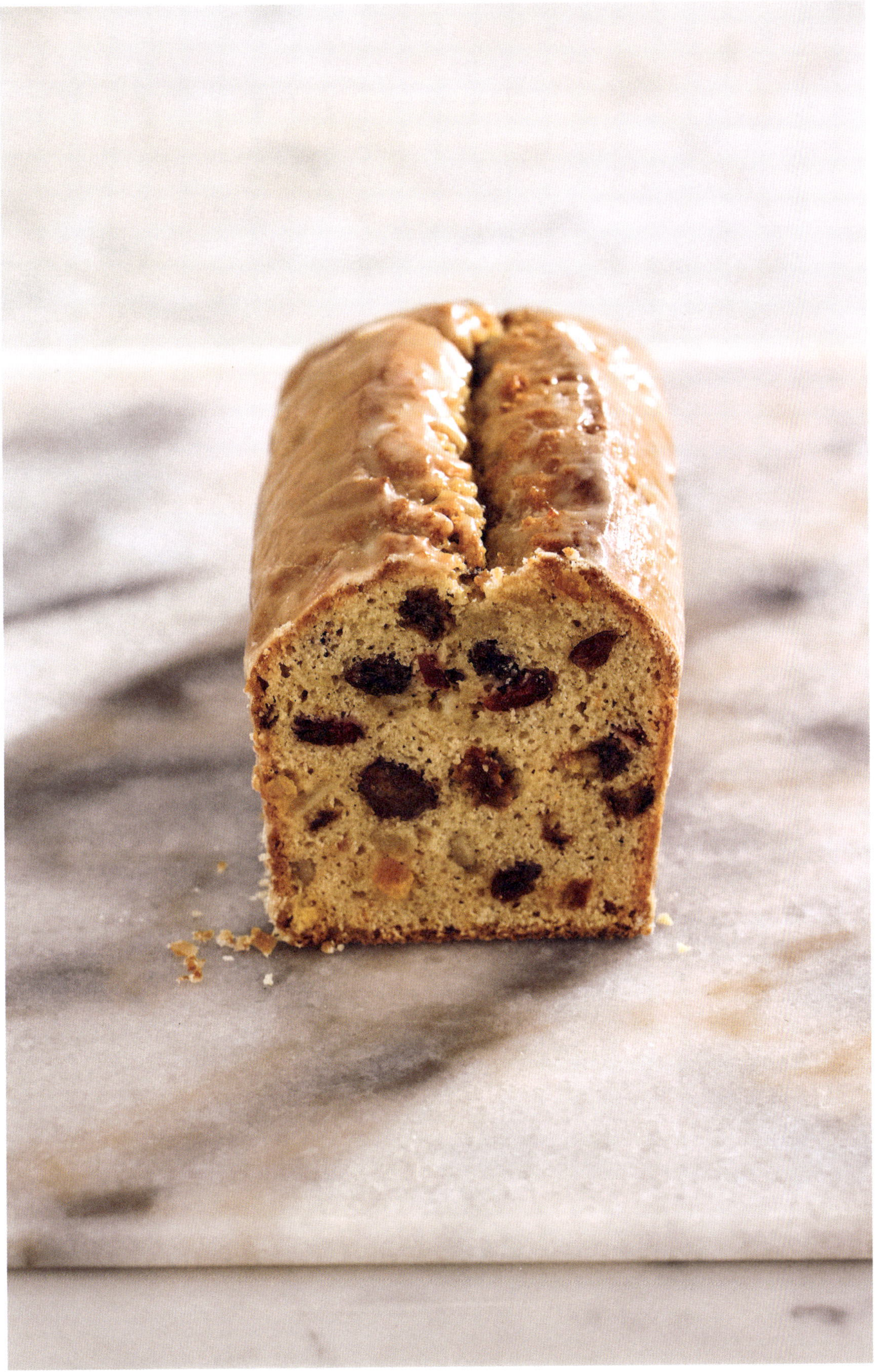

PISTACHIO AND MATCHA LOAF CAKE

Makes 1 × 450 g (1 lb) loaf

There's a deep, buttery richness to pistachios that comes out best when they're finely ground with flour – the oils release, the texture softens and the flavour becomes more pronounced. Just a little matcha adds a quiet bitterness and depth, enough to hold its own without overpowering. The cake is close-crumbed and tender, finished with a thin glaze of matcha icing (frosting) that sets to a soft, pale-green sheen. It's a loaf that feels composed – not flashy, but quietly fragrant, with just the right amount of earthiness.

plain (all-purpose) flour	150 g	5.3 oz
baking powder	4 g	1 tsp
shelled pistachios	100 g	3.5 oz
matcha powder	3 g	2 tsp
fine sea salt	2 g	½ tsp
golden caster (superfine) sugar	150 g	5.3 oz
plant-based milk	150 g	5.3 oz
olive oil	20 g	0.7 oz

1. Preheat the oven to 180°C fan (400°F) and position a shelf in the middle of the oven. Line a 450 g (1 lb) loaf tin (pan) with baking parchment, ensuring the paper extends slightly over the edges for easy removal.

2. Put the flour, baking powder, pistachios, matcha powder and salt into a food processor and pulse until the pistachios are finely ground and the mixture begins to clump together slightly. This clumping indicates the oils from the pistachios have been released and are evenly distributed through the dry ingredients.

3. Pour the sugar, milk and oil into the food processor and pulse to combine, scraping down the sides to make sure everything is nicely incorporated. You can also transfer the dry ingredients to a bowl and whisk in the sugar, milk and oil with a balloon whisk until the batter is smooth and lump-free. Take care not to overmix, but ensure all the dry ingredients are fully incorporated and there are no streaks left.

4. Pour the batter into the prepared tin and spread it out evenly with a spatula to ensure a smooth top.

5. Bake in the oven for 45–50 minutes, or until the top is golden and a skewer inserted into the centre of the cake comes out clean. Don't open the oven until at least 35 minutes – this ensures it doesn't collapse. The cake should have risen slightly and feel springy to the touch.

6. Remove the cake from the oven and leave it to cool in the tin for 10 minutes before using the parchment paper to lift it out and gently peeling back the parchment paper from the sides. Place on a wire rack to cool completely before coating.

MATCHA ICING

cocoa butter (deodorised)	30 g	1 oz
groundnut (peanut) oil	20 g	0.7 oz
icing (powdered) sugar	100 g	3.5 oz
matcha powder, plus extra for sprinkling	2 g	1 tsp

7. Melt the cocoa butter in a saucepan over a low heat. Add the oil, followed by the icing sugar and matcha powder and whisk well to combine and form a glossy and smooth glaze.

8. Place the cooled cake on a wire rack, then pour the glaze over the top, using a dry pastry brush to help spread the glaze if needed. Leave to set at room temperature. The cake can be stored in an airtight container at room temperature for up to 3 days. For longer storage, wrap the loaf tightly in cling film (plastic wrap) and freeze for up to 3 months. Defrost at room temperature.

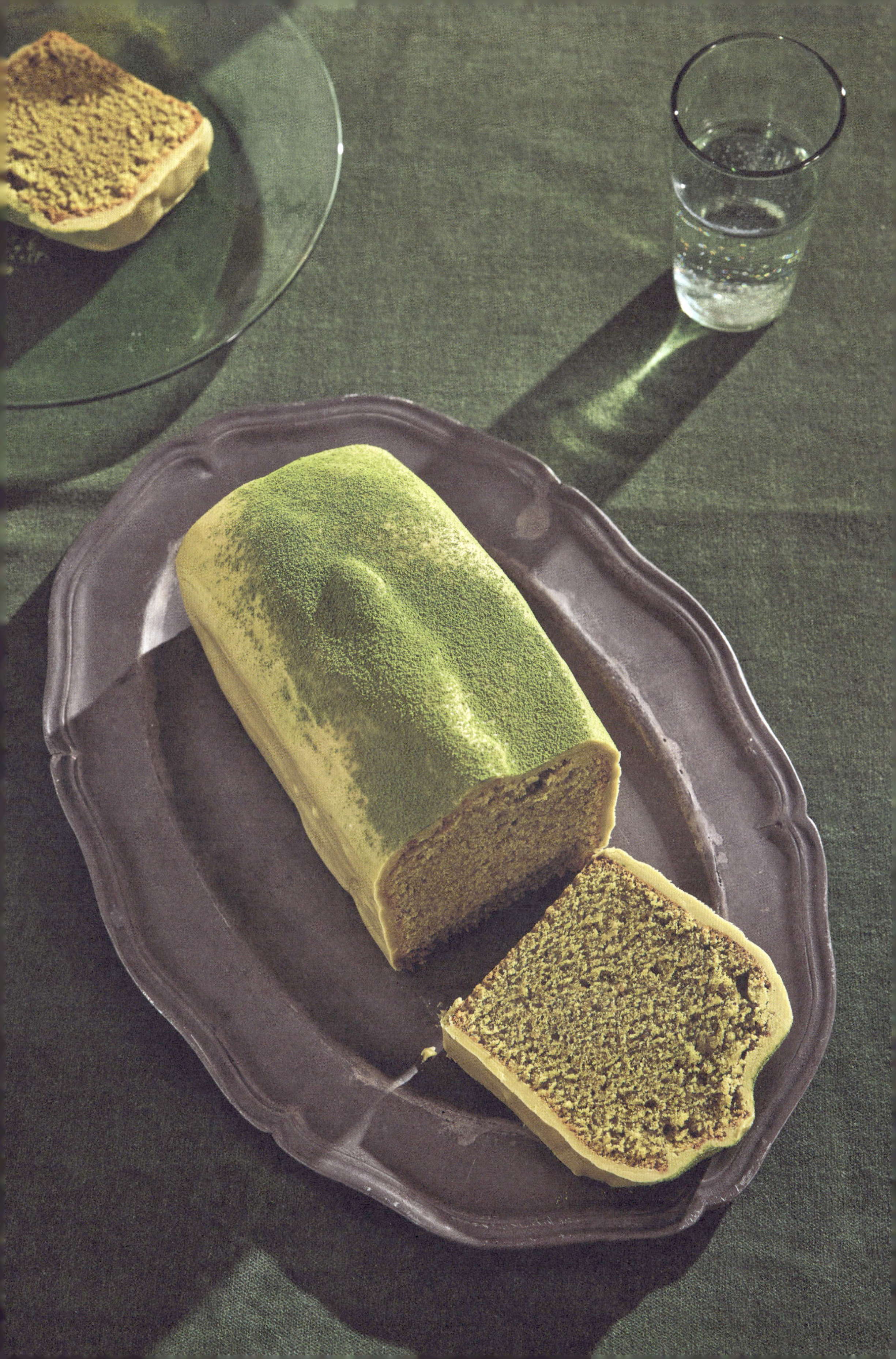

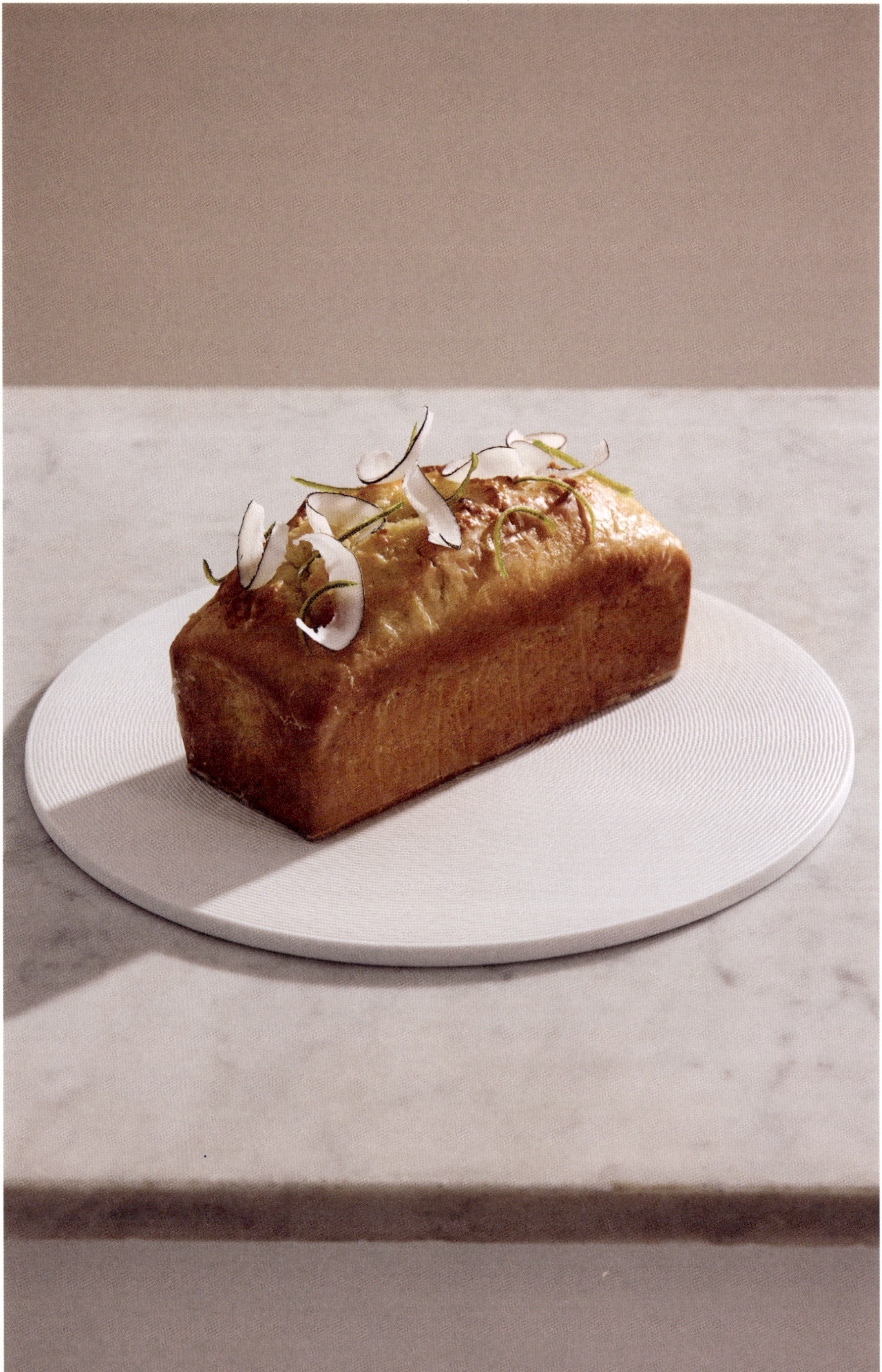

PINEAPPLE, COCONUT AND LIME DRIZZLE CAKE

Makes 1 × 450 g (1 lb) loaf

I don't usually go for the texture of dried coconut – too dry, too chewy – but mixed into this batter, it softens just enough to give a gentle bite and a resounding sensation of moisture in every slice. Coconut cream adds richness, the pineapple brings body and tropical perfume, and everything's lifted with the brightness of lime: zest in the batter, juice in the glaze. It's sweet but certainly not cloying, and better still the next day.

1. Preheat the oven to 180°C fan (400°F) and position a shelf in the middle of the oven. Line a 450 g (1 lb) loaf tin (pan) with baking parchment, ensuring the paper extends slightly over the edges for easy removal.

2. In a small upright blender or in a bowl using a hand-held blender, blend the pineapple, coconut cream, lime zest, sugar, oil and vanilla extract or paste. Blend until the mixture is smooth and creamy, ensuring the pineapple is fully puréed. The mixture should look pale and slightly thick.

3. Place the flour, baking powder and desiccated coconut in a bowl and whisk them to combine.

4. Pour the wet ingredients into the dry ingredients. Using a balloon whisk or spatula, gently mix until just combined. Be careful not to overmix; overworking the batter can result in a dense cake. The batter should be smooth but not over-stirred.

5. Pour the batter into the prepared tin, spreading it out evenly with a spatula to ensure a level top.

6. Bake in the oven for 45–50 minutes, or until the top is golden brown and a skewer inserted into the centre of the cake comes out clean. The cake should have risen slightly and feel springy to the touch.

7. Remove from the oven and leave the cake to cool in the tin for 5 minutes before using the baking parchment to lift it out. Transfer to a wire rack to cool completely, gently peeling back the parchment paper from the sides.

tinned pineapple, drained	130 g	4.6 oz
coconut cream	100 g	3.5 oz
lime zest	3 g	1 lime
caster (superfine) sugar	120 g	4.2 oz
groundnut (peanut) oil	40 g	1.4 oz
vanilla extract or paste	5 g	1 tsp
plain (all-purpose) flour	150 g	5.3 oz
baking powder	6 g	1½ tsp
desiccated (dried shredded) coconut	28 g	1 oz

LIME DRIZZLE

8. As it cools, mix together the icing sugar and lime juice and pour it over the top of the cake, using a pastry brush to brush it over the top and sides of the cake in a nice thin layer.

9. Decorate with strips of lime zest and shaved coconut.

10. The cake can be stored in an airtight container at room temperature for up to 3 days. For longer storage, wrap the cake tightly in cling film (plastic wrap) and freeze for up to 3 months. Defrost at room temperature until fully thawed.

icing (powdered) sugar	110 g	3.9 oz
lime juice	30 g	1 oz
thin strips of lime zest		for topping
shaved coconut		for topping

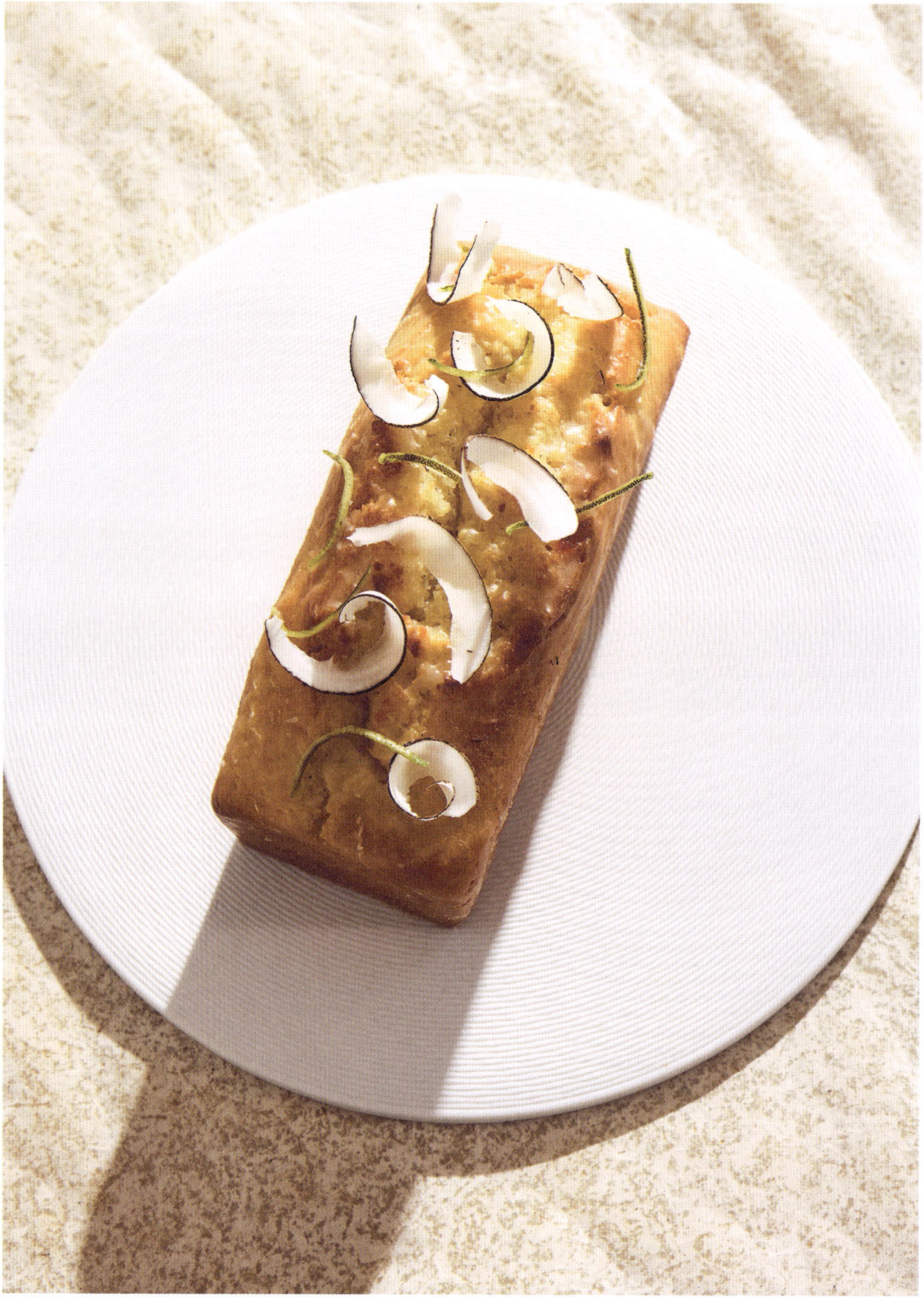

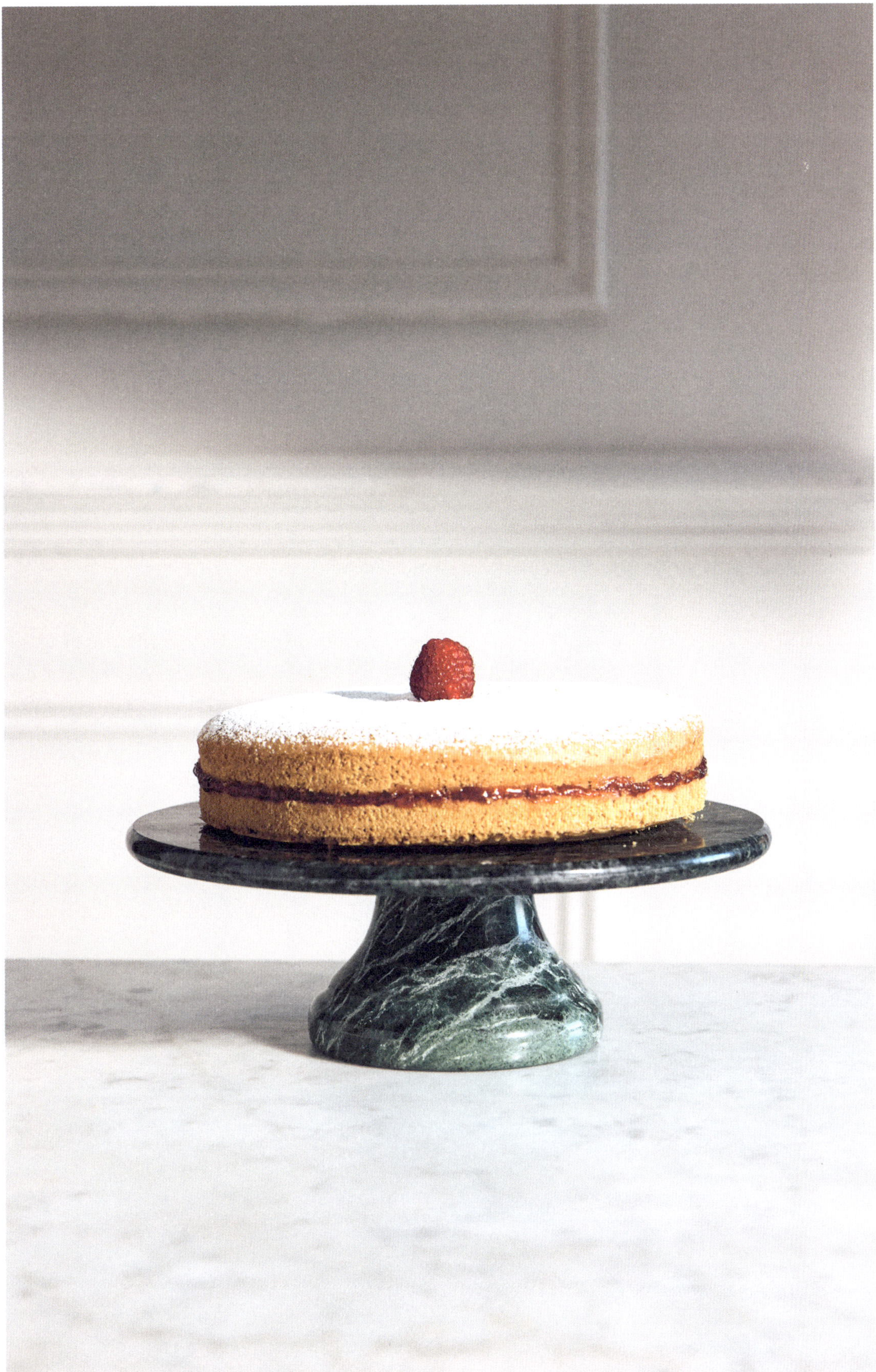

PEANUT BUTTER AND JELLY SANDWICH CAKE

Makes 1 × 20 cm (8 in) sandwich cake

Blending nuts directly with the flour to extract the fat offers a way to add flavour and richness all at once, without relying on added oils or butter. In this case, it's peanuts: roasted and blended until fine, they bring a warm nuttiness and just enough fat to create a soft, golden crumb. It's the kind of base you could adapt with other nuts – almonds, hazelnuts, cashews – depending on what you want to highlight. Here, it's paired with a layer of berry jam for something familiar, unfussy and quietly satisfying.

PEANUT SPONGE

1. Preheat the oven to 150°C fan (350°F). Spread the peanuts over a roasting tray (pan) and roast in the oven for 15 minutes, or until aromatic and golden. Remove from the oven and leave them to cool completely. You can skip this step if using pre-roasted peanuts.

2. Increase the oven temperature to 180°C fan (400°F). Line the base of a 20 cm (8 in) springform cake tin (pan) with baking parchment.

3. Combine the roasted peanuts, flour, baking powder, bicarbonate of soda, salt and sugar in a food processor. Blend until the mixture forms a fine powder and starts to clump together, indicating that the oils from the peanuts have been released.

4. Gently warm the milk in a saucepan or in 30-second bursts in the microwave to around 30°C (86°F) to ensure an evenly rising batter. Pour the warm milk into a large bowl, then whisk in the oil, vinegar and vanilla extract.

5. Pour the blended dry ingredients into the bowl and gently whisk by hand with a balloon whisk until smooth and combined. Avoid overmixing, as this can result in 'tunnelling' – the appearance of unattractive air bubbles rising up through the cake.

6. Pour the batter into the prepared tin, smoothing the top with a spatula. Cover the tin loosely with foil to prevent it browning too quickly. Bake in the oven for 40 minutes, then remove the foil and bake for an additional 10–15 minutes, or until the top is golden and springs back when gently pressed with your fingertips.

7. Remove the cake from the oven and leave it to cool in the tin for 10 minutes. Run a sharp knife around the edges of the tin to release the cake, then turn it out onto a wire rack to cool completely.

blanched peanuts or roasted peanuts	110 g	3.6 oz
plain (all-purpose) flour	150 g	5.3 oz
baking powder	4 g	1 tsp
bicarbonate of soda (baking soda)	2 g	¼ tsp
fine sea salt	1 g	¼ tsp
caster (superfine) sugar	140 g	5 oz
soya milk	200 g	7.1 oz
groundnut (peanut) oil	28 g	1 oz
apple cider vinegar	8 g	2 tsp
vanilla extract	5 g	1 tsp

BERRY JAM LAYER

8 To make the berry jam, mix the caster sugar and agar-agar together in a bowl. Add to a blender along with the berries and lemon juice and blend to a purée. Transfer to a saucepan and bring to the boil, then pour into a shallow container. Allow to cool, then place in the refrigerator to set. When ready to serve, blend or whisk the jam until smooth. Alternatively, you can use 100 g (3.5 oz) shop-bought raspberry jam.

caster (superfine) sugar	30 g	1.1 oz
agar-agar	2 g	½ tsp
strawberries, trimmed	120 g	4.2 oz
raspberries	110 g	3.9 oz
lemon juice	22 g	0.8 oz

TO ASSEMBLE

9 Ensure the sponge has completely cooled before assembling the cake. To cut the sponge in half, position a serrated knife halfway up the sponge, keeping the blade flat and steady by resting your knuckles or the side of your hand on the work surface. With your other hand, slowly rotate the cake, gently sawing about 1–2 cm (½–¾ in) in to create a guide. Continue turning and deepening the cut – the knife will follow the guide and glide cleanly through the sponge.

10 Place the bottom half of the sponge on a serving dish and spread the raspberry jam evenly over the top of the first sponge layer.

11 Place the second sponge layer on top of the jam, pressing down gently to secure it.

12 Dust the top with some icing sugar, and place a fresh raspberry in the middle.

icing (powdered) sugar	for dusting
raspberry	1

PEACH AND HAZELNUT CRUMBLE CAKE

Makes 1 × 23 cm (9 in) cake

This is the kind of cake that feels generous and golden – soft-crumbed with a jammy layer of peaches, and a crisp hazelnut crumble on top. It makes the most of two 400 g (15 oz) tins of drained peaches split between the batter and baked on top. These bring texture and a sweet acidity without needing to be peeled or sliced perfectly. The crumble is blitzed together in a blender or food processor, for a quick and satisfying topping that contrasts beautifully with the soft and moist cake.

HAZELNUT CRUMB

1. Pulse the flour, hazelnuts and sugar in a small food processor or high-powered blender until clumping together – if you grab a fistful, it will hold its shape. Add the water, then pulse again. Reserve to sprinkle on top of the cake batter.

plain (all-purpose) flour	35 g	1.2 oz
hazelnuts	20 g	0.7 oz
caster (superfine) sugar	20 g	0.7 oz
water	10 g	0.4 oz

CAKE

2. Preheat the oven to 180°C fan (400°F) with an oven shelf in the middle of the oven. Line the base of a 23 cm (9 in) cake tin (pan) with baking parchment.

3. Add the drained tinned peaches (1) to a high-powered blender or food processor with the vanilla paste, sugar, oil and milk and blend until smooth.

4. Add the flour and baking powder to a large bowl and gently whisk to 'sieve' and combine the ingredients. Add the peach mixture, and chopped peaches (2) and mix well with a silicone spatula until just combined and there are no dry streaks.

5. Pour the batter into the lined tin and top with the drained tinned peach slices (3), hazelnut crumb and chopped hazelnuts sprinkled across the batter, avoid covering the peach slices.

6. Bake for 40 minutes until golden and the top springs back when gently pressed with your fingertips, or a skewer inserted into the centre of the cake comes out clean.

7. Leave to cool completely on a wire rack, then remove from the tin. Serve with a dusting of icing sugar. This cake keeps very well in an airtight container at room temperature for up to 3 days.

tinned peaches, drained (1)	200 g	7 oz
vanilla paste	5 g	1 tsp
caster (superfine) sugar	180 g	6.3 oz
extra virgin olive oil	80 g	2.8 oz
plant-based milk	90 g	3.2 oz
plain (all-purpose) flour	225 g	7.9 oz
baking powder	8 g	2 tsp
tinned peaches, drained, chopped (2)	125 g	4.4 oz
tinned peaches, drained, to layer on top (3)	125 g	4.4 oz
hazelnuts, for topping	40 g	1.4 oz
icing (powdered) sugar	for dusting	

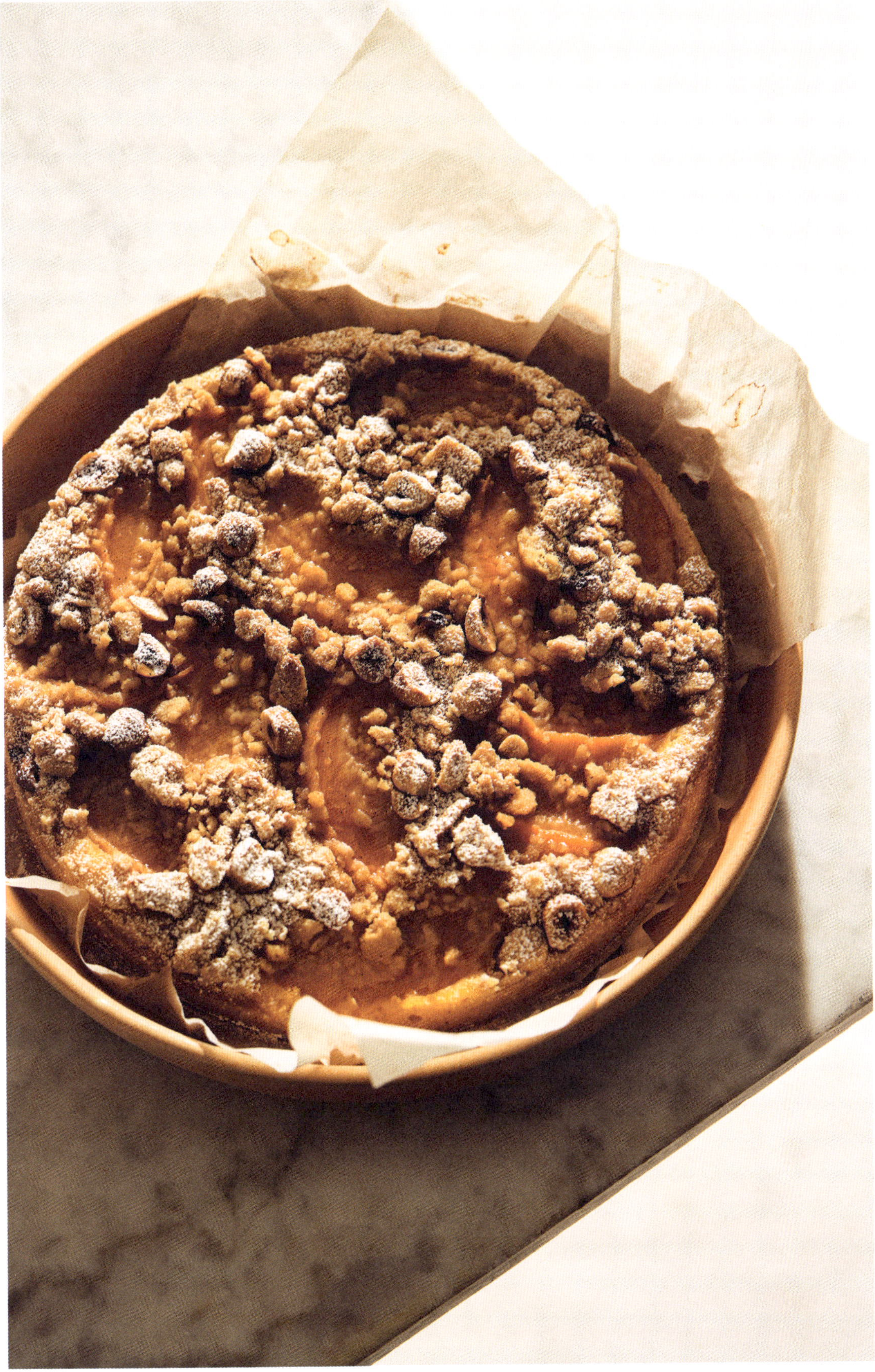

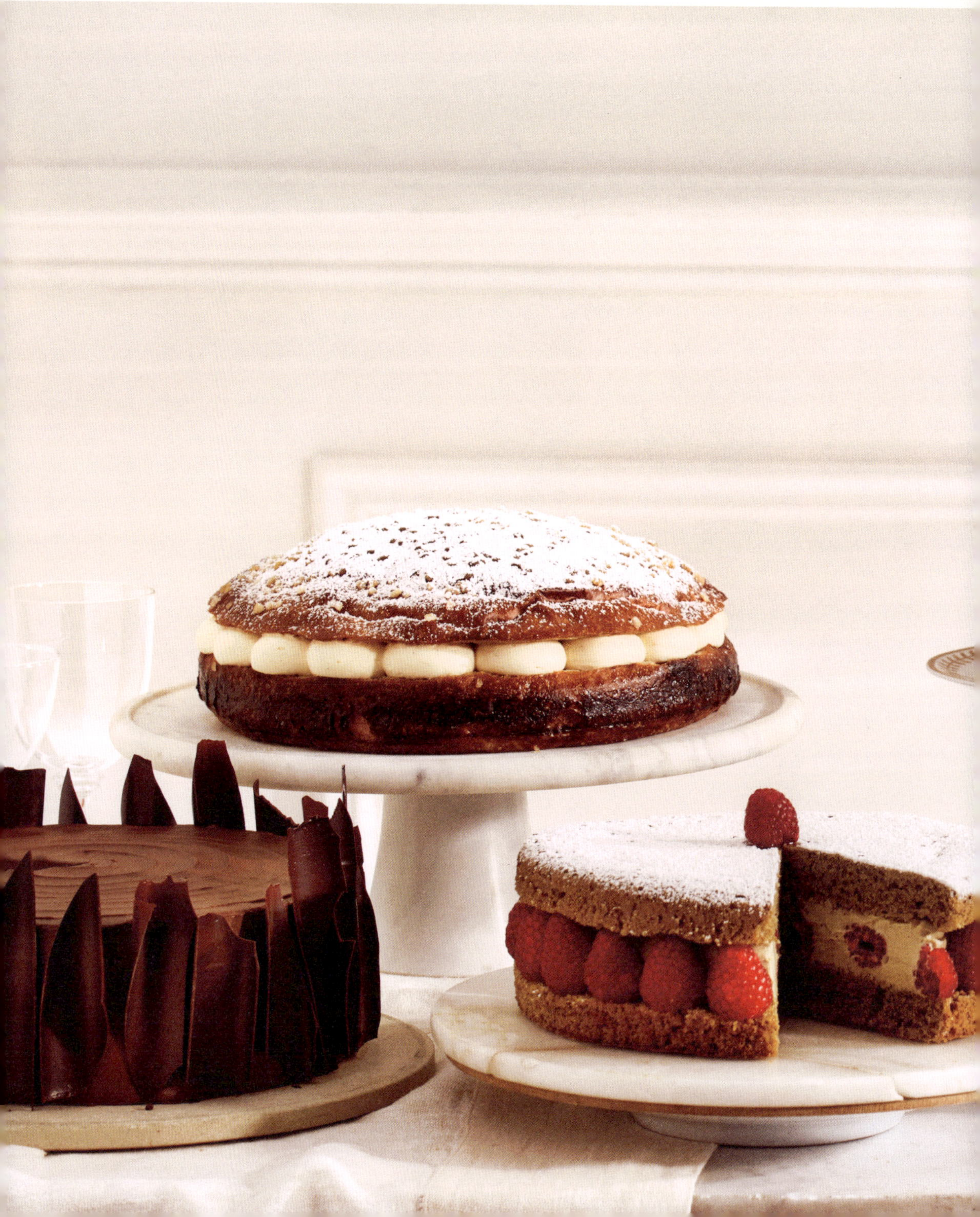

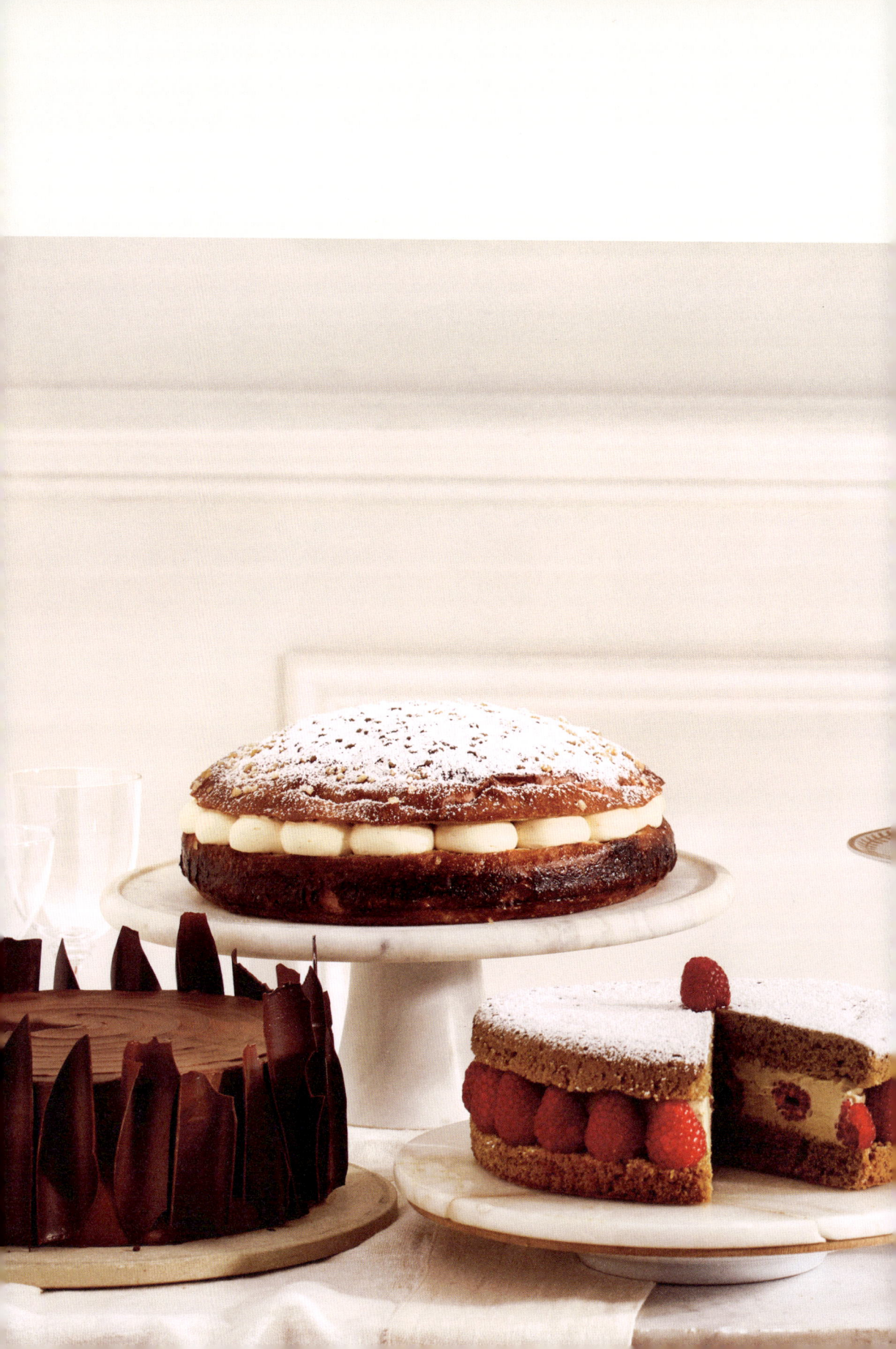

4 CAKE FOR A SPECTACLE

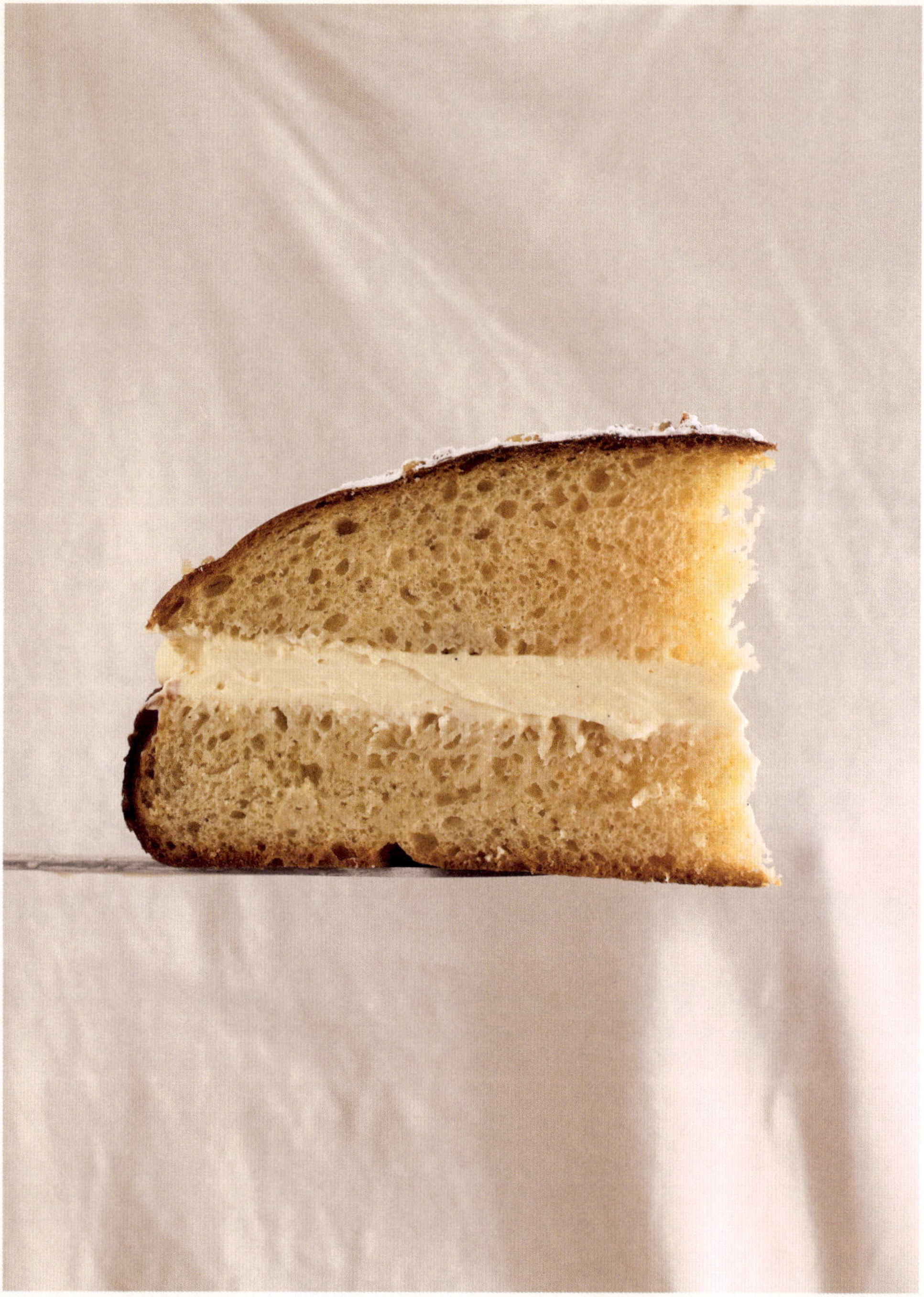

CLASSICS
REINVENTED

In this chapter, we take the foundational elements of simple cakes and build on them – layering in luscious fillings, whipped creams and striking textures to create bakes that not only taste incredible but look extraordinary, too. These are cakes designed to turn heads, to celebrate, to share.

One of the highlights here is a series of creams made from nuts and cocoa butter, blended until smooth, then chilled and whipped into something truly special. They set into light, clean and rich textures, reminiscent of a whipped ganache or crème Chantilly, but with the natural depth of roasted nuts or cacao at their core. They bring richness without heaviness, and elegance without dairy.

These showstoppers are as much about texture as they are about flavour. One of my greatest inspirations is Pierre Hermé, who describes flavour in terms of structure – what he calls the 'architecture of taste'. His philosophy is simple but powerful: the lightest textures reveal their flavours first, followed by creams and fillings, then sponges and crunches, which take longer to chew and release their character more slowly. I think about this every time I build a cake – how each layer can reveal something new and how, together, they create an experience greater than the sum of its parts.

STRAWBERRY AND CREAM BASKET CAKE

Makes 1 × 20 cm (8 in) cake

Imagine a sponge cake that rises beautifully in the oven, only to collapse upon cooling – but intentionally. This recipe creates a naturally sunken centre, forming a delicate basket for silky crème pâtissière, fresh strawberries and a glossy clear glaze. The edges remain slightly crisp, while the interior stays tender and dense, making for a unique yet elegant dessert.

COLLAPSED ALMOND SPONGE

1. Preheat the oven to 180°C fan (400°F).
2. Lightly grease the base and sides of a 20 cm (8 in) springform cake tin (pan) and line the base with baking parchment.
3. Pulse the almonds, sugar and flour in a food processor or high-powered blender until fine and powdery.
4. Add the milk, olive oil, baking powder, bicarbonate of soda and salt, then pulse again until fully combined. The batter should be smooth and creamy.
5. Using a silicone spatula, scrape the batter into the prepared tin, smoothing the surface evenly.
6. Bake in the oven for 15–17 minutes, or until the cake rises and domes in the centre.
7. Remove the cake from the oven and leave to cool completely in the tin – the centre will gradually collapse as it cools, forming a natural indentation.
8. Once completely cool, carefully release the cake from the tin and transfer it to a serving plate.

raw almonds	175 g	6.2 oz
caster (superfine) sugar	116 g	4.1 oz
plant-based milk	120 g	4.2 oz
extra virgin olive oil, plus extra for greasing	12 g	0.4 oz
plain (all-purpose) flour	40 g	1.4 oz
baking powder	5 g	1 tsp
bicarbonate of soda (baking soda)	2 g	½ tsp
fine sea salt	1 g	¼ tsp

TO ASSEMBLE

9. Briefly whisk the crème pâtissière until soft and smooth.
10. Trim the strawberries and cut larger ones into quarters and smaller ones in half. Cut the raspberries in half. Set aside on a clean paper towel to remove excess moisture.
11. Warm the exotic clear glaze in a small saucepan over a low heat, stirring until it becomes fluid and smooth.
12. Using an offset spatula, spread the chilled crème pâtissière evenly into the sunken centre of the sponge, filling it completely. Dust the edges of the sponge with icing sugar.
13. Arrange the strawberry and raspberry pieces in concentric circles over the crème pâtissière, starting from the outer edge and working inwards.
14. Using a pastry brush, gently coat the berries with the glaze to give them a glossy finish and to help preserve freshness. Refrigerate the cake for at least 30 minutes before serving to allow the flavours to meld. Decorate with a few edible flower petals, if desired.
15. This cake is best served on the day it is made from the refrigerator.

Crème Pâtissière (page 239), chilled	200 g	7 oz
strawberries and raspberries, washed	250 g	8.8 oz
Exotic Clear Glaze (page 242)	50 g	1.8 oz
icing (powered) sugar		for dusting
edible flowers (optional)		for decorating

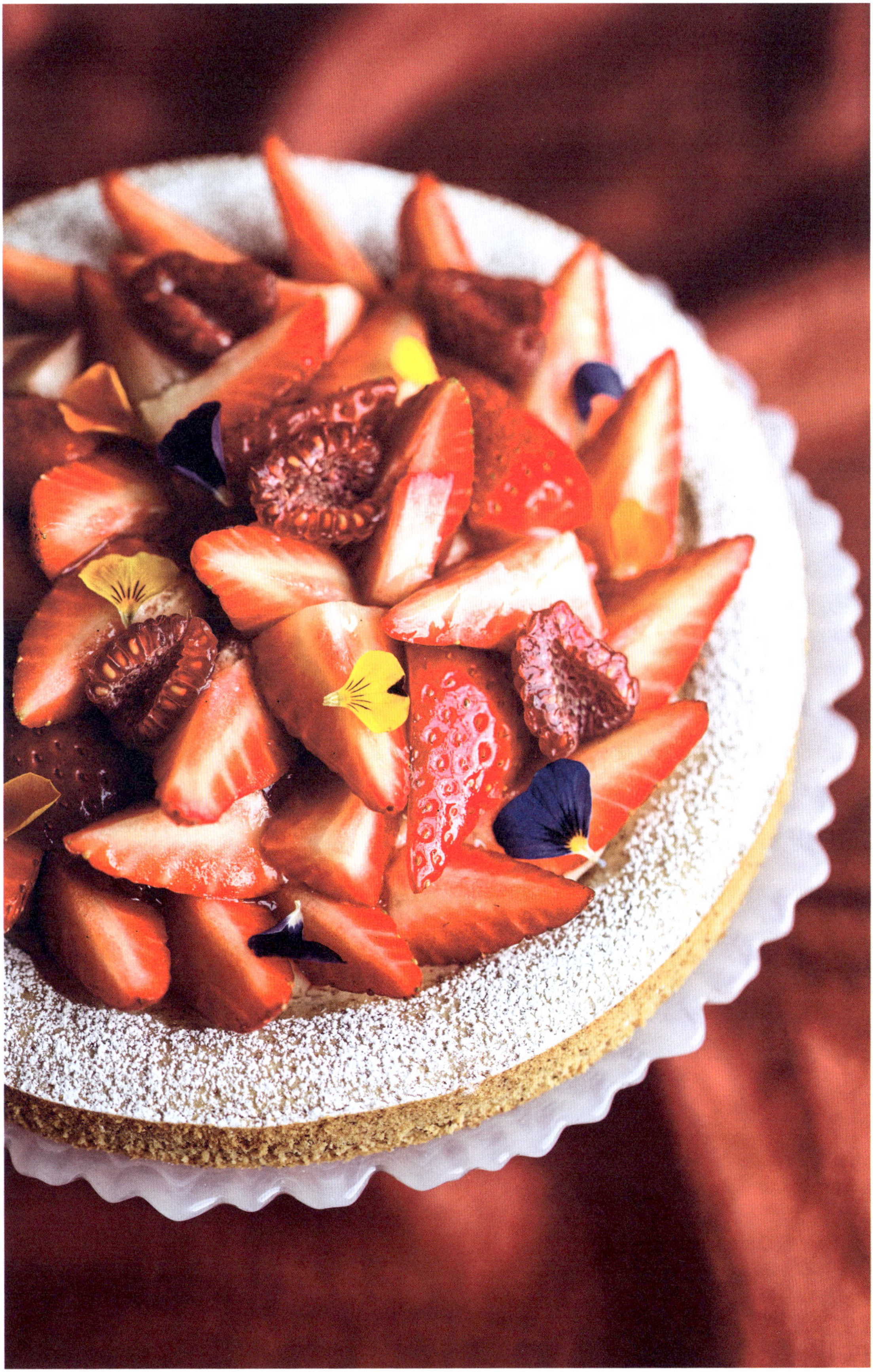

PECAN AND MUSCOVADO MEDOVIK CAKE

Makes 1 x tall 20 cm (8 in) cake

This cake is based on the classic Medovik honey cake, but instead of honey, deep muscovado sugar brings its dark caramel and treacle (molasses) notes, giving the biscuit layers a rich complexity. The pecan Chantilly is made by puréeing milk with roasted nuts, extracting their natural fats to create a smooth, full-bodied cream that carries their warmth and depth through every layer. As the cake rests overnight, the crisp layers soften, absorbing the pecan-infused cream and transforming it into a cake that's both luxuriously light *and* rich at the same time, each bite melting away with nutty, caramelised richness.

MUSCOVADO SYRUP

1. Put the sugar and water into a large, wide saucepan and bring to a simmer over a medium heat, stirring until the sugar has completely dissolved. Remove from the heat.

muscovado or dark brown sugar	250 g	8.8 oz
water	250 g	8.8 oz

MUSCOVADO BISCUIT

2. Whisk the sugar and hot water together in a bowl until the sugar has completely dissolved. Stir in the vinegar and olive oil.

3. In a separate bowl, whisk together the flour, bicarbonate of soda and salt.

4. Gradually add the dry ingredients to the wet ingredients, stirring with a spatula until a dough forms. Lightly knead in the bowl until smooth. Divide the dough into 9–10 equal portions and place on a work surface, then cover with a damp cloth and set aside to rest for 15 minutes.

5. Once rested, lightly flour a work surface and roll out one portion of the dough to 2 mm ($1/16$ in) thickness. Using a 20 cm (8 in) cake tin (pan) as a guide, trim the dough into a disc. Prick the surface with a fork or pastry docker to prevent air bubbles. Repeat with the remaining portions of dough.

6. Preheat the oven to 180°C fan (400°F). Line a baking tray (pan) with baking parchment and bake each round for 6–8 minutes, or until lightly golden and firm. As each disc comes out of the oven, dip it into the saucepan of muscovado syrup for 2 seconds, then remove it.

7. Bake any remaining offcuts of dough for 10–12 minutes, then remove from the oven and allow to cool. Once fully cooled, blend them in a food processor to a crumb and reserve them for coating.

muscovado or dark brown sugar	250 g	8.8 oz
hot water	180 g	6.3 oz
apple cider vinegar	10 g	2 tsp
olive oil	60 g	2 oz
plain (all-purpose) flour, plus extra for dusting	645 g	1 lb 7 oz
bicarbonate of soda (baking soda)	15 g	1½ tsp
fine sea salt	3 g	¾ tsp

PECAN CHANTILLY

8. Preheat the oven to 160°C fan (350°F) and line a baking tray (pan) with baking parchment.

9. Spread the pecans over the prepared baking tray and roast in the oven for 10–12 minutes. I find pecans just need to be 'refreshed' until smelling nutty, as they do burn quite easily. Remove from the oven and leave to cool slightly.

10. Put the roasted pecans into a food processor or high-powered blender along with the remaining ingredients and blend until completely smooth – the mixture should warm up from the friction, to about 45°C (115°F), to melt and fully emulsify the cocoa butter into the mixture. To check the emulsion, dip a spoon into the mixture and hold it up to the light. It should have an even shine with no oily streaks at all. Once emulsified, pour the mixture into a shallow dish and place a layer of cling film (plastic wrap) on the surface to prevent a skin forming. Chill in the refrigerator for at least 4 hours.

11. Once chilled, transfer mixture to the chilled bowl of a stand mixer fitted with the whisk attachment and whip to medium peaks.

TO ASSEMBLE

12. Place one soaked biscuit onto a serving plate. Spread 90–100 g (3.2–3.5 oz) of the pecan Chantilly evenly over the surface, making sure to reach the edges.

13. Repeat the layering process, ensuring each biscuit is well covered with cream. Reserve a small amount to spread a thin layer over the top and sides of the cake.

14. Cover the assembled cake and refrigerate for 10–12 hours to allow the flavours to meld and the biscuits to soften fully.

15. To finish the cake, spread the reserved Chantilly in a thin layer on the top and sides, and gently press fistfulls of the leftover dried crumb to coat the sides, and sprinkle some on the top.

16. This cake is best served the next day, allowing time for the biscuits to absorb moisture and become tender. Store in the refrigerator for up to 3 days. The cake can also be frozen for up to 1 month and defrosted overnight in the refrigerator before serving.

pecans	140 g	4.9 oz
muscovado or dark brown sugar	150 g	5.3 oz
caster (superfine) sugar	50 g	1.8 oz
xanthan gum (optional)	0.5 g	⅛ tsp
soya milk	700 g	1 lb 9 oz
cocoa butter, deodorised	180 g	6.3 oz
fine sea salt	2 g	½ tsp
vanilla pod (bean)	1	

TIP
This quantity can be split between two batches in the larger NutriBullet jug.

WHIPPING CREAM TIPS

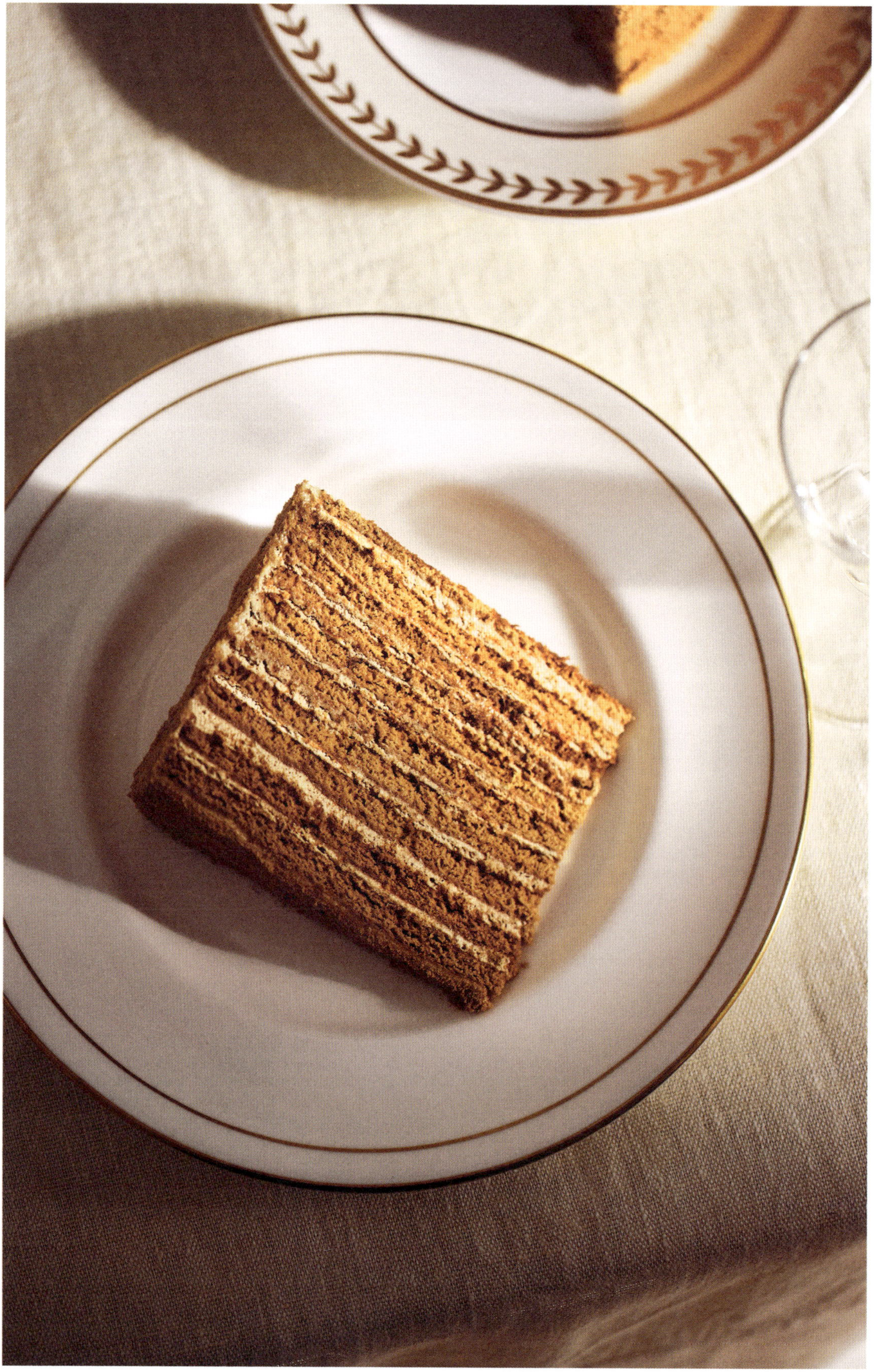

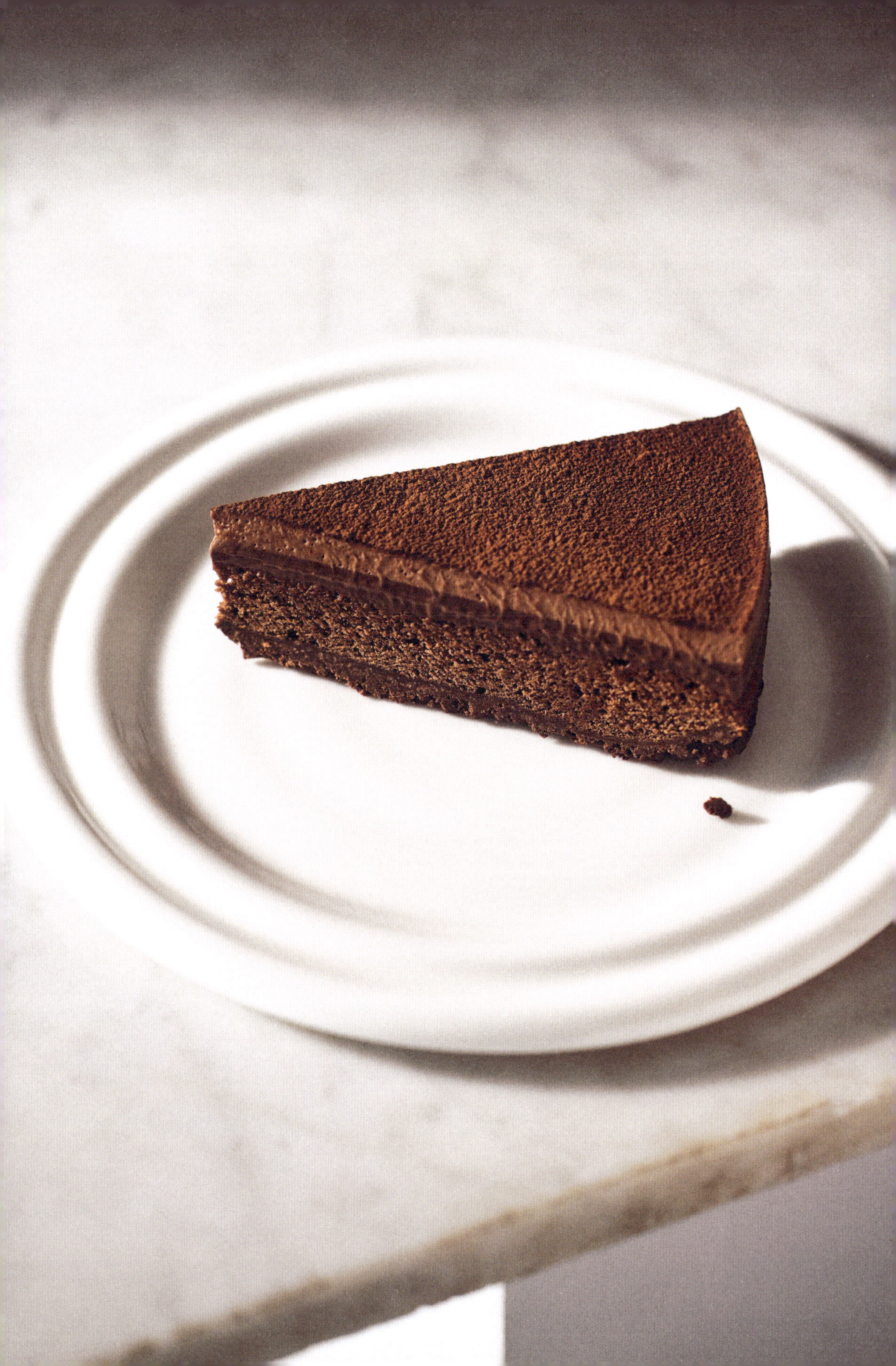

PURE CHOCOLATE DELICE

Makes 1 × 23 cm (9 in) cake

This layered chocolate mousse cake is a balance of textures and deep chocolate flavour – starting with a tender chocolate moelleux, a crisp cocoa crumble base, a rich chocolate custard, and finishing with an airy whipped chocolate mousse. Flipping the crumble layer to the base ensures a delicate crunch with every bite. This cake needs at least 4 hours to chill before serving.

CHOCOLATE MOUSSE

1. Heat the milk (1) and sugar in a saucepan over a medium heat until it just reaches a simmer.
2. Chop the chocolate and place it in a heatproof bowl or jug (pitcher). Pour the hot milk mixture over the chocolate and blend with a hand-held blender until completely smooth.
3. Add the chilled milk (2) and blend again until the mixture is glossy and fully emulsified. The ganache should reflect light, with no oily streaks.
4. Pour into a shallow dish and place a layer of cling film (plastic wrap) on the surface to prevent a skin forming. Chill in the refrigerator for 3–4 hours until firm but spreadable.

plant-based milk (1)	125 g	4.4 oz
caster (superfine) sugar	25 g	0.9 oz
dark chocolate with at least 65% cocoa solids	125 g	4.4 oz
plant-based milk (2), chilled	100 g	3.5 oz

COCOA CRUMBLE

5. Preheat the oven to 160°C fan (350°F) and line a baking tray (pan) with baking parchment. Pulse the sugar, coconut oil, flour, cocoa powder and salt in a food processor until fine crumbs form.
6. Add the water and continue pulsing until the mixture resembles coarse sand with small clumps.
7. Spread the crumble mixture onto the prepared baking tray in an even layer. Bake in the oven for 14–18 minutes, stirring halfway through, until crisp. Remove from the oven and leave to cool completely before using.

caster (superfine) sugar	32 g	1.1 oz
coconut oil	32 g	1.1 oz
plain (all-purpose) flour	120 g	4.2 oz
cocoa (unsweetened) powder	20 g	0.7 oz
fine sea salt	0.5 g	⅛ tsp
water	30 g	2 tbsp

CHOCOLATE CAKE LAYER

8. Preheat the oven to 160°C fan (350°F). Line the base of a 23 cm (9 in) springform cake tin (pan) with baking parchment.
9. Heat the milk in a saucepan over a medium heat until it reaches a gentle simmer.
10. Chop the chocolate and place it in a heatproof bowl. Pour over the hot milk and let it sit for 30 seconds, then whisk until smooth. Add the olive oil and whisk well.
11. In a separate bowl, whisk together the flour, cocoa powder, sugar, baking powder and salt. Pour the wet ingredients into the dry ingredients and fold gently with a spatula until fully combined. Do not overmix.
12. Pour the batter into the prepared tin and bake for 18–22 minutes, or until the top is slightly domed and springs back when lightly pressed.

plant-based milk	170 g	6 oz
dark chocolate with at least 66% cocoa solids	75 g	2.6 oz
olive oil	20 g	0.7 oz
plain (all-purpose) flour	37 g	1.3 oz
cocoa (unsweetened) powder	7 g	½ tbsp
caster (superfine) sugar	50 g	1.8 oz
baking powder	1 g	¼ tsp
fine sea salt	1 g	¼ tsp

13. Remove from the oven and leave to cool in the tin for 10 minutes, then remove and transfer to a wire rack to cool completely.

COCOA CRUMBLE BASE

14. Break the cooled cocoa crumble into small, coarse crumbs and place in a bowl.

15. Melt the dark chocolate in a heatproof bowl over a saucepan of gently simmering water, stirring until smooth. Remove from heat and whisk in the olive oil.

16. Pour the melted chocolate mixture over the crumble and toss quickly to coat, ensuring an even distribution.

17. Spread the cocoa crumble mixture evenly over the cooled chocolate cake layer, pressing gently to adhere.

18. Flip the entire cake over so that the crumble layer is now on the bottom, forming the base of the cake. Return to the cake tin.

cocoa crumble (see above)	160 g	5.6 oz
dark chocolate with at least 70% cocoa solids	36 g	1.3 oz
olive oil	8 g	1½ tsp

CHOCOLATE CRÈMEUX

19. Pour the milk (1) into a high-sided saucepan, then add the sugar and cocoa powder, whisking to combine. Bring to a gentle simmer over a medium heat.

20. In a small bowl, mix the cornflour and milk (2) to form a smooth slurry. Once the milk mixture is simmering, turn the heat to low, then pour in the cornflour mixture while stirring. The custard will immediately thicken.

21. Continue stirring until it begins to bubble, then remove from the heat. Chop the dark chocolate and stir into the hot custard until melted and fully incorporated. The custard should be smooth, glossy and thick enough to cling to the spatula.

22. Allow to cool slightly, then spread the custard evenly over the cake layer inside the tin. Refrigerate the cake for 30 minutes.

plant-based milk (1)	115 g	4 oz
caster (superfine) sugar	45 g	1.6 oz
cocoa (unsweetened) powder	6.5 g	½ tbsp
cornflour (cornstarch)	6.5 g	½ tbsp
plant-based milk (2)	15 g	0.5 oz
dark chocolate with at least 70% cocoa solids	65 g	2.3 oz

TO ASSEMBLE

23. Once chilled, whisk the mousse by hand or in a stand mixer fitted with the whisk attachment until light and airy.

24. Spread the mousse over the chilled chocolate custard layer, smoothing it with a small offset spatula. Refrigerate for at least 3 hours, or overnight. Before serving, dust the top with cocoa powder.

25. To serve, use a sharp knife dipped in hot water, wiping it clean between slices for clean edges.

26. This cake can be stored in the refrigerator for up to 3 days. Allow it to sit at room temperature for 10–15 minutes before serving for the best texture. The cake can also be frozen for up to 1 month and defrosted overnight in the refrigerator before eating.

cocoa (unsweetened) powder	for dusting

TARTE TROPÉZIENNE

Makes 1 × 23 cm (9 in) two-layer cake

A celebration of texture and contrast, this southern French pastry layers rich brioche with a light, aromatic orange blossom syrup and a thick, silky crème diplomat. Crunchy nibbed (pearl) sugar on top adds texture, while a final dusting of icing (powdered) sugar completes the finish. I love this dessert because it tastes familiar, as orange blossom is very Mediterranean and a flavour you'd expect anywhere from the South of France, to Spain, southern Italy and the Levant. It certainly features heavily in my favourite Lebanese desserts. Make sure to use up all the soaking syrup for the most decadent eating experience.

ORANGE BLOSSOM SYRUP

1. Combine the water and sugar in a small saucepan over a medium heat and bring to a simmer, stirring until the sugar has completely dissolved. Remove from the heat and stir in the orange blossom water. Set aside to cool.

water	150 g	5.3 oz
caster (superfine) sugar	120 g	4.2 oz
orange blossom water	10 g	0.4 oz

CRÈME DIPLOMAT

2. Whip the chilled crème pâtissière in a bowl with a balloon whisk until just smooth.

3. In a separate bowl, whip the cream to soft peaks using a hand mixer or whisk. Gently fold it into the crème pâtissière in two stages, being careful not to knock out too much air. Transfer to a piping (pastry) bag fitted with a large, plain 1 cm (½ in) nozzle (tip). Chill until ready to use.

Crème Pâtissière (page 239)	400 g	14.1 oz
Whipping Cream (page 238)	200 g	7 oz

TO ASSEMBLE AND BAKE

4. Lightly grease a 23 cm (9 in) springform cake tin (pan), then gently press the risen and shaped vrioche dough into the tin. Cover loosely with a clean dish towel and leave to prove at room temperature until doubled in size and airy and pillowy to the touch – this may take 1–1½ hours depending on the room temperature.

5. Preheat the oven to 170°C fan (375°F).

6. Once fully proved, brush the surface of the dough gently with the baking glaze. Sprinkle generously with nibbed sugar.

7. Bake in the oven for 22–25 minutes, or until the top is deep golden and the sides begin to pull away from the tin slightly. Remove from the oven and leave to cool in the tin for 10 minutes, then transfer to a wire rack to cool completely.

8. Once cool, use a serrated knife to carefully slice the vrioche horizontally into two layers. Spoon or brush the cooled orange blossom syrup generously over both cut sides.

9. Pipe or spoon the chilled crème diplomat over the bottom half, spreading it all the way to the edges. Gently place the top half back on. Dust with icing sugar to serve. Tarte Tropézienne is best served on the day it is assembled, but can be stored in the refrigerator for up to 24 hours. Allow to sit at room temperature for 15–20 minutes before serving to soften the crumb slightly.

neutral oil	for greasing
Vrioche dough (page 56)	450 g 1 lb
Baking Glaze (page 242)	for brushing
nibbed (pearl) sugar	for topping
icing (powdered) sugar	for dusting

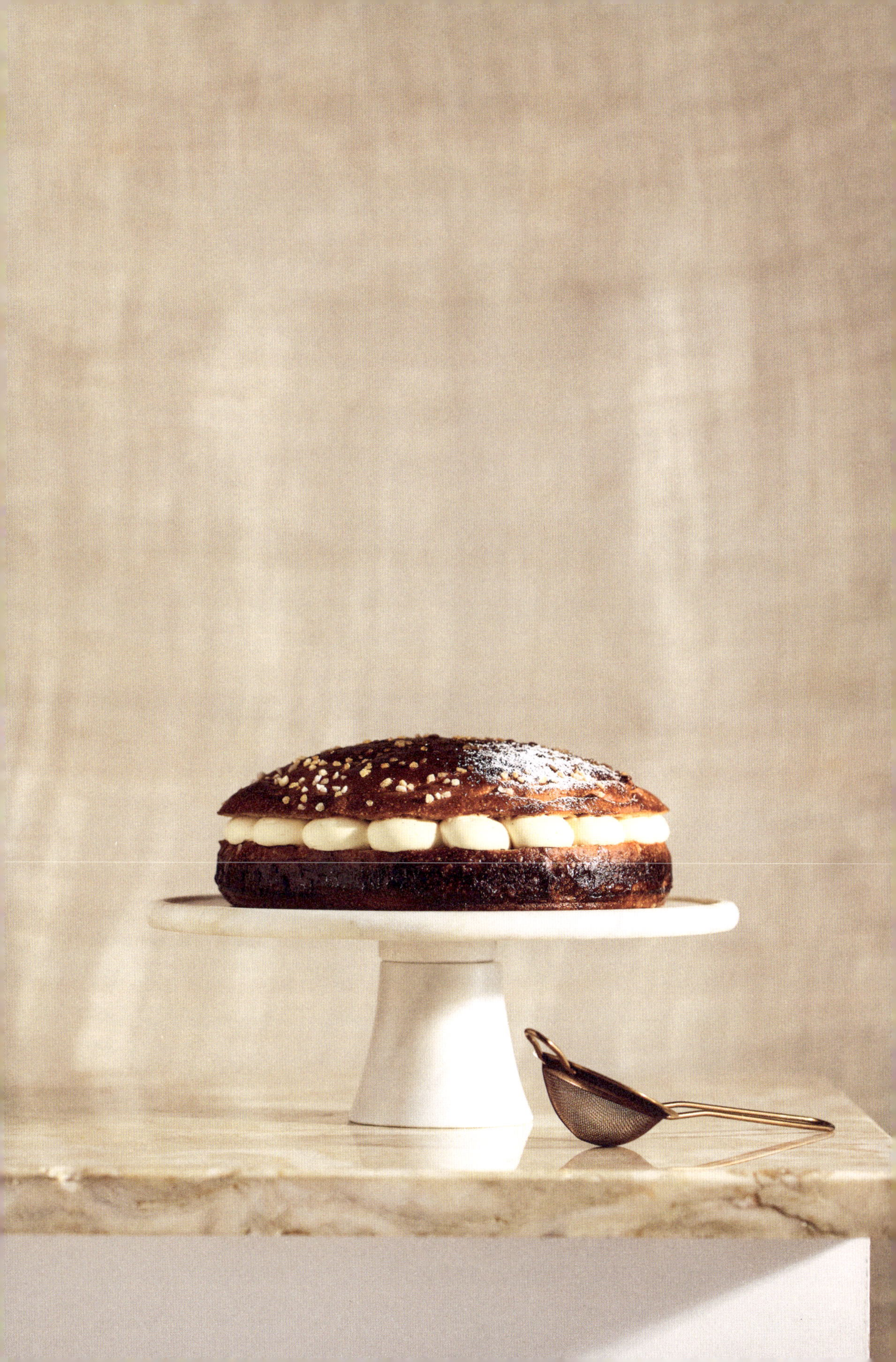

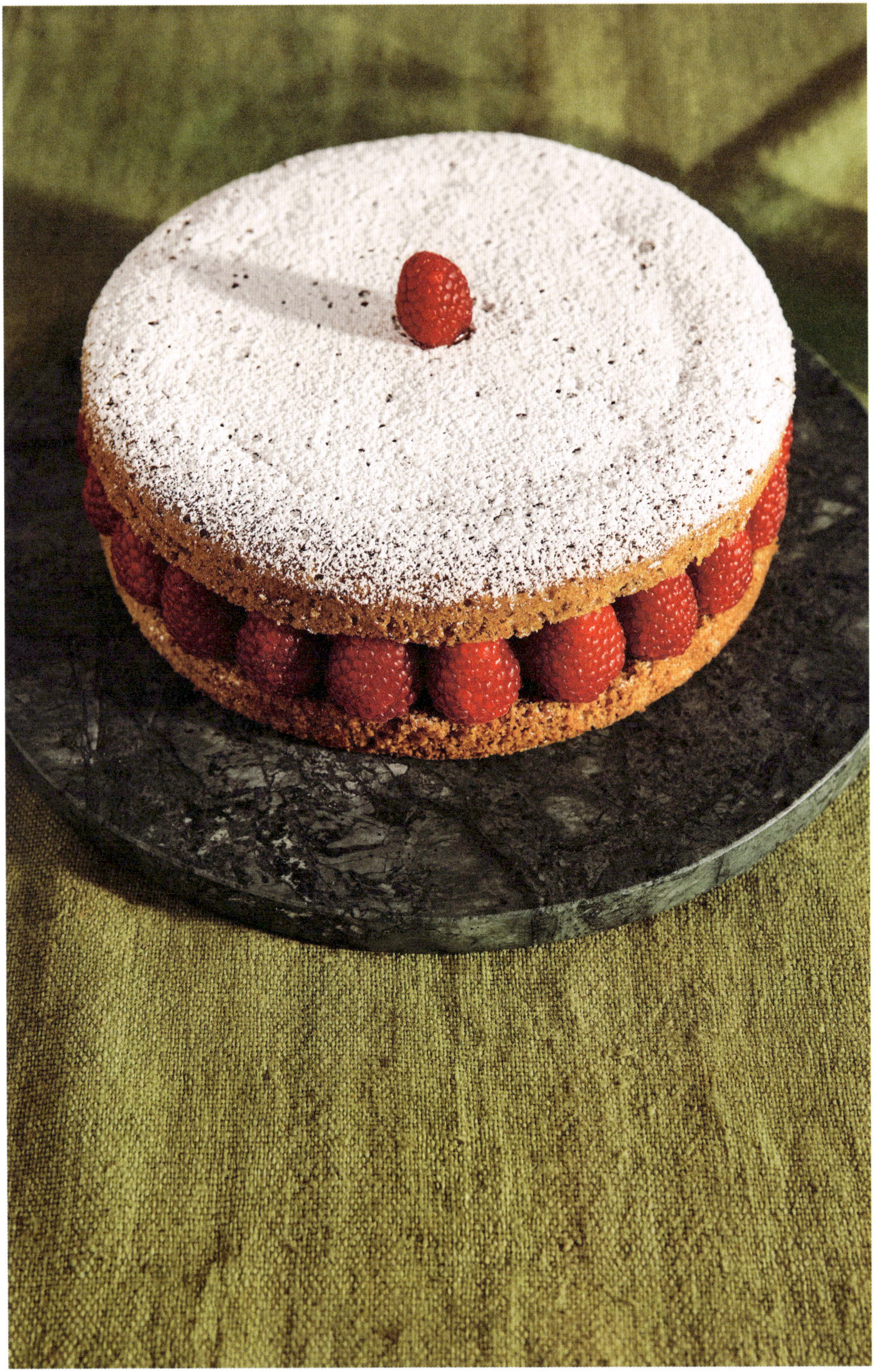

PISTACHIO AND RASPBERRY CREAM DREAM

Makes 1 × 20 cm (8 in) cake

This light but flavourful pistachio sponge takes inspiration from nut-based cakes, where the natural oils in the nuts create a rich yet delicate crumb. The cake is filled with fresh raspberries and a smooth pistachio mousse, offering both structure and freshness. This cake must be fully chilled before slicing, allowing the cream to set properly.

PISTACHIO SPONGE

1. Preheat the oven to 170°C fan (375°F). Line the base of a 20 cm (8 in) springform cake tin (pan) with baking parchment.

2. Spread the pistachios over a baking tray and roast in the oven for 10–12 minutes, or until lightly golden and fragrant. Remove from the oven and leave to cool completely. Keep the oven on.

3. In a food processor or high-powered blender, blend the roasted pistachios until finely ground. Be careful not to over-process or they may become oily.

4. In a large bowl, whisk together the ground pistachios, flour, sugar, baking powder, bicarbonate of soda and salt until evenly combined.

5. In a separate jug (pitcher), mix the warm soya milk with the vinegar and vanilla extract. Let it sit for 5 minutes to slightly curdle.

6. Pour the wet ingredients into the dry ingredients and whisk until fully combined. Slowly drizzle in the olive oil, folding gently until smooth.

7. Pour the batter into the prepared tin and bake in the oven for 30–35 minutes, or until a skewer inserted into the centre comes out clean. Remove from the oven and leave to cool in the tin for 10 minutes, then transfer to a wire rack to cool completely.

pistachios	90 g	3.2 oz
plain (all-purpose) flour	150 g	5.3 oz
caster (superfine) sugar	130 g	4.6 oz
baking powder	6 g	1½ tsp
bicarbonate of soda (baking soda)	4 g	1 tsp
fine sea salt	3 g	¾ tsp
soya milk, warmed	200 g	7 oz
apple cider vinegar	8 g	2 tsp
vanilla extract	4 g	1 tsp
olive oil	60 g	2 oz

PISTACHIO MOUSSE

8. Put the pistachios, sugar, xanthan gum (if using), soya milk, unmelted cocoa butter and salt into a high-powered blender. Blend until completely smooth and warm – it should warm up to 35°C (95°F) from the friction of the blending, which will melt and emulsify the cocoa butter.

9. Pour into a shallow dish, cover and chill in the refrigerator for 3–4 hours until fully chilled and set.

10. Once chilled, transfer the mixture to a stand mixer or use a hand mixer to whip it until light and airy. The texture should be smooth and spreadable.

pistachios	45 g	1.6 oz
caster (superfine) sugar	50 g	1.8 oz
xanthan gum (optional)	0.2 g	
soya milk	220 g	7.8 oz
cocoa butter (deodorised)	70 g	2.5 oz
fine sea salt	0.5 g	⅛ tsp

TO ASSEMBLE

raspberries	250 g	8.8 oz
icing (powdered) sugar		for dusting

11 Place the cooled pistachio sponge on a stable work surface.

12 To trim it into two even layers, take a long, serrated bread knife and hold it level at the midpoint of the cake. Using your non-cutting hand, place your fingertips gently on top of the cake to steady it without pressing down.

13 Position the knife against the edge of the cake and begin cutting by making gentle back-and-forth sawing motions, while slowly rotating the cake with your other hand. The aim is to create a shallow guideline all around the edge.

14 Continue rotating and cutting deeper along the guide with light, even pressure, letting the knife do the work. Once the blade reaches the centre, gently separate the two layers. Use a large flat spatula or cake lifter to carefully transfer the top layer onto a plate.

15 Line the sides of the tin you baked the cake in (clean it if necessary) with baking parchment, then place the bottom cake layer back into the tin.

16 Arrange the whole raspberries around the edge of the cake. Spread the whipped pistachio mousse evenly over the base. Press two concentric rings of raspberries into the filling.

17 Place the second layer of sponge on top, pressing down lightly to secure. Remove the springform ring and baking parchment, then dust the top with icing sugar and place a single raspberry in the centre.

18 Chill the cake in the refrigerator for at least 2 hours before slicing. This cake is best served within 24 hours for optimal texture but can be stored in the refrigerator for up to 3 days, keeping it covered to prevent it drying out. Allow to sit at room temperature for 15 minutes before serving for the best flavour.

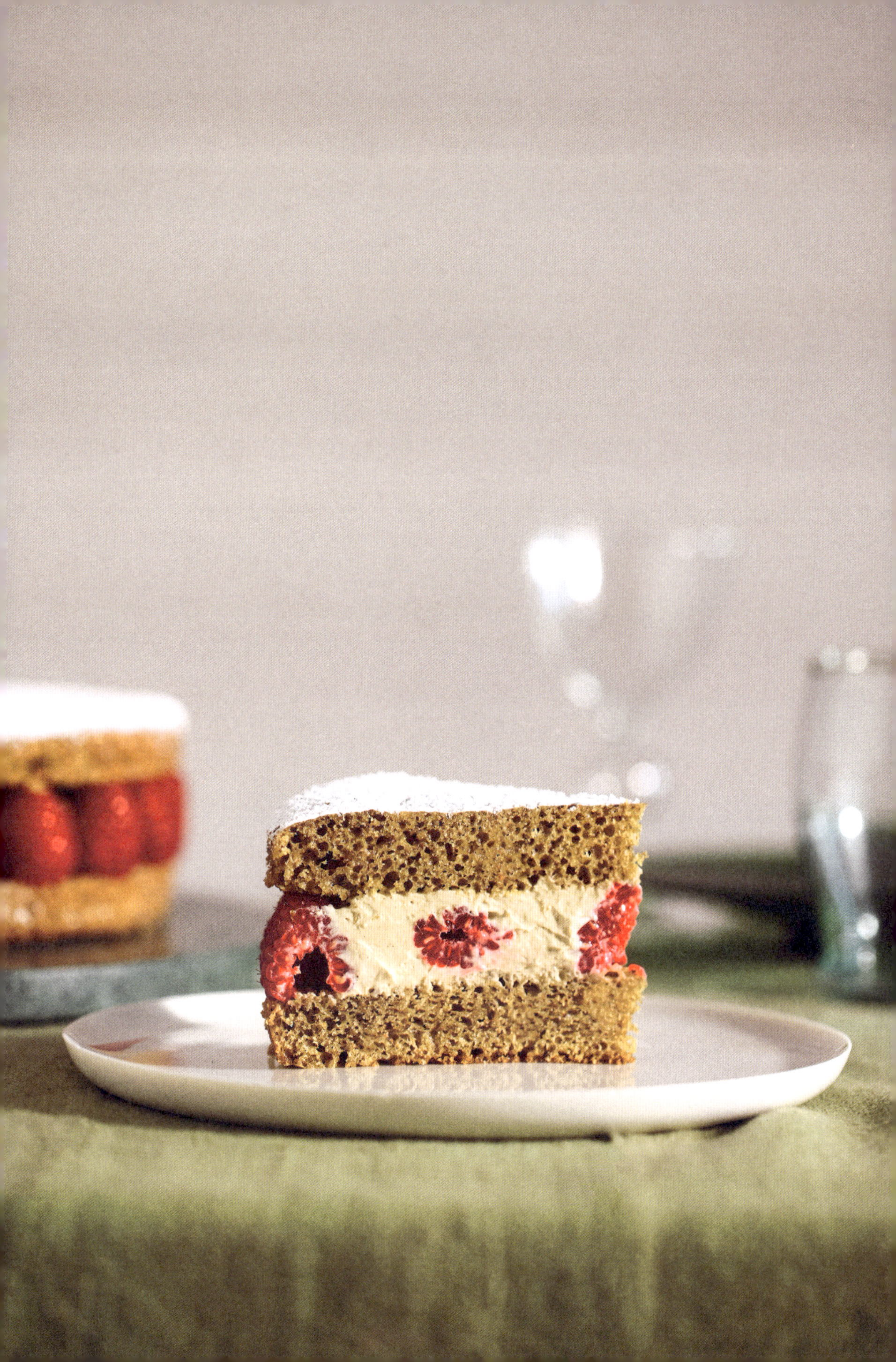

COCONUT MILLEFEUILLE

Serves 6–8

Millefeuille, meaning 'a thousand leaves', is a classic pastry known for its delicate, caramelised layers of puff pastry filled with crème pâtissière. My version is filled with a light, silky coconut mousseline cream. Achieving the right texture relies on properly baking the pastry, so below I share a method of more safely caramelising it. The offcuts of pastry are also finely crumbled and used to coat the sides for an elegant finish.

CARAMELISED PUFF PASTRY

Puff Pastry (page 195)	1 quantity
icing (powdered) sugar	for caramelisation and dusting

1. Place the chilled pastry dough on a lightly floured surface and use a rolling pin to roll it out evenly to 2 mm (⅛ in) thickness, aiming for a 20 × 40 cm (8 × 16 in) rectangle. To ensure an even thickness, roll in one direction at a time, rotating the pastry 90 degrees after every few rolls. Lightly lift the pastry off the surface occasionally to prevent it from sticking, adding a little extra flour if necessary.

2. Preheat the oven to 180°C fan (400°F).

3. Check the final dimensions of the pastry rectangle with a ruler. If it has shrunk back, leave it to rest for 5–10 minutes before rolling again to reach the correct size.

4. Line a 30 × 40 cm (12 × 16 in) baking tray (pan) with baking parchment and transfer the pastry rectangle onto it. Dock the entire surface of the pastry by pricking it all over with a fork or pastry docker. This prevents excessive puffing while baking.

5. Use a fine sieve (strainer) to dust an even layer of icing sugar over the surface. Place another sheet of baking parchment on top, followed by a second baking tray of the same size to weigh the pastry down. This ensures the pastry bakes flat and caramelises evenly.

6. Bake the pastry in the oven for 20 minutes. Carefully remove the top baking tray and layer of baking parchment and return the pastry to the oven for a further 5–8 minutes until it is golden brown, evenly caramelised and crisp all over. Transfer the baked pastry to a wire rack and leave to cool completely.

7. Once cool, use a sharp serrated knife and a gentle sawing motion to trim the edges to neaten them, then cut the sheet of pastry into three equal 12 × 18 cm (4¾ x 7 in) rectangles. Keep the offcuts and finely crumble them into small, even pieces, then set aside for later.

COCONUT MOUSSELINE CREAM

8. Gently melt the butter or coconut oil in a small saucepan over a low heat until it reaches 50°C (122°F) on a thermometer. It should be fully liquid but not boiling.

9. Transfer the chilled crème pâtissière to a stand mixer fitted with the whisk attachment. Begin whipping at medium speed. Slowly drizzle in the melted butter or oil, allowing it to incorporate gradually. Once all the butter or oil has been added, increase the speed to high and whip for 2–3 minutes until the mixture becomes light, fluffy and glossy.

10. If the mixture appears slightly grainy, warm the sides of the bowl using a hairdryer, or briefly dip the bottom of the bowl in a sink of hot water for a few seconds at a time. Continue mixing until the texture becomes completely smooth and aerated. If at this stage it warms up too much and goes soft, place the bowl in the refrigerator for 20 minutes, scrape down the sides and whip again, gently applying the slightest amount of heat to make it smooth.

11. Transfer the mousseline cream to a piping (pastry) bag fitted with a plain nozzle (tip) and refrigerate until needed.

shop-bought block butter, or coconut oil	120 g	4.2 oz
Crème Pâtissière prepared with coconut milk in place of soya milk (page 239, chilled	400 g	14.1 oz

TO ASSEMBLE

12. Place one pastry rectangle onto a flat serving board or tray. Hold the piping bag vertically and pipe even rows of coconut mousseline cream across the entire surface, ensuring the cream extends to the edges.

13. Gently place the second pastry rectangle on top of the cream. Lightly press down with your fingertips to secure the layer without crushing the cream.

14. Pipe a second, even layer of coconut mousseline cream over this layer, ensuring even coverage. Carefully place the final pastry rectangle on top, ensuring it is aligned neatly with the layers below. Using a small offset spatula, spread a thin layer of the remaining mousseline cream around the sides of the millefeuille if needed.

15. Press the reserved pastry crumbs onto the sides to coat them evenly, creating a textural contrast.

16. Lightly dust the top layer with icing sugar using a fine sieve (strainer). Refrigerate for at least 1 hour before slicing to allow the layers to set, making slicing easier. Press down gently rather than sawing through the layers to avoid crushing the pastry.

17. Millefeuille is best served chilled and should be eaten within 24 hours for optimal texture.

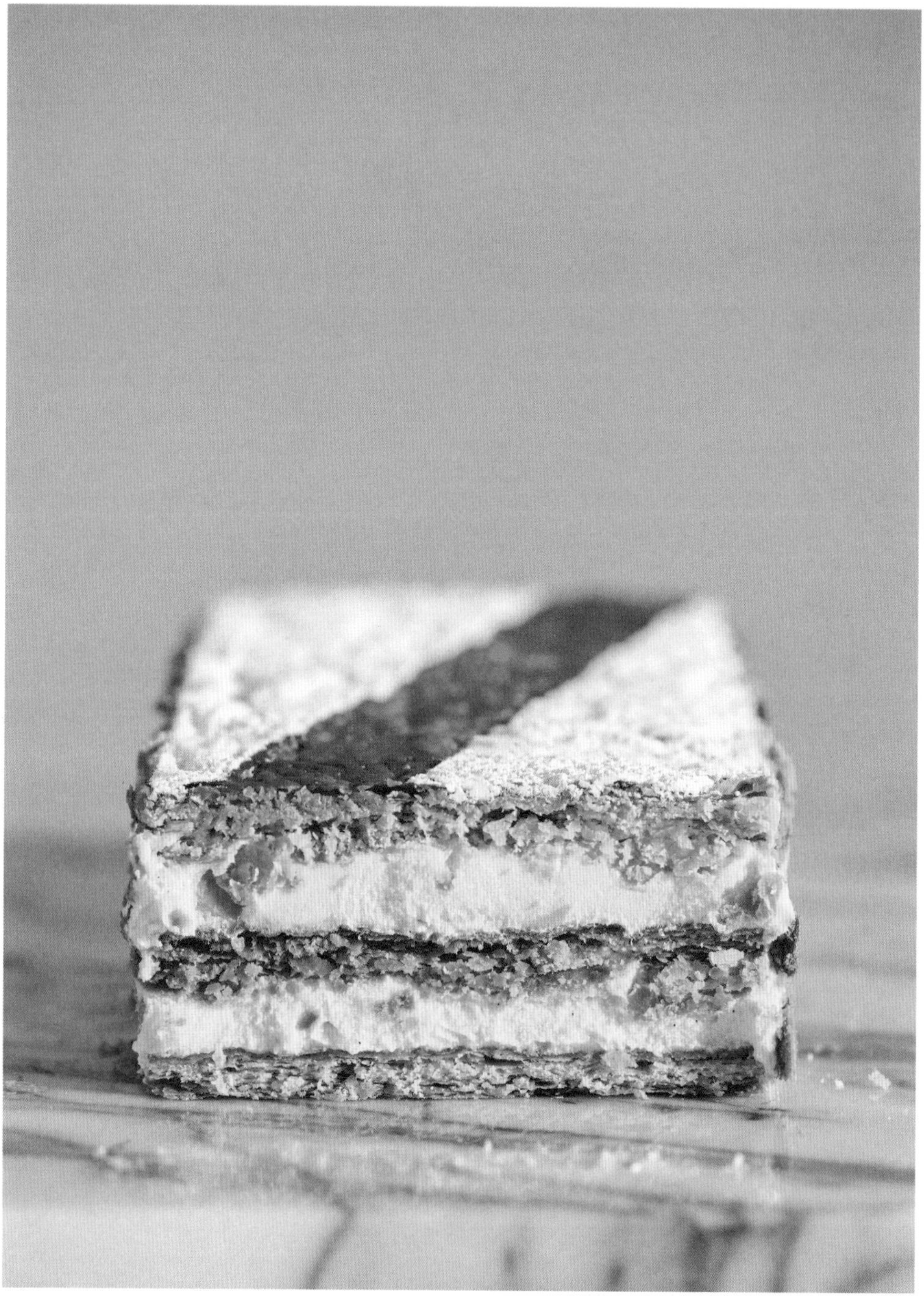

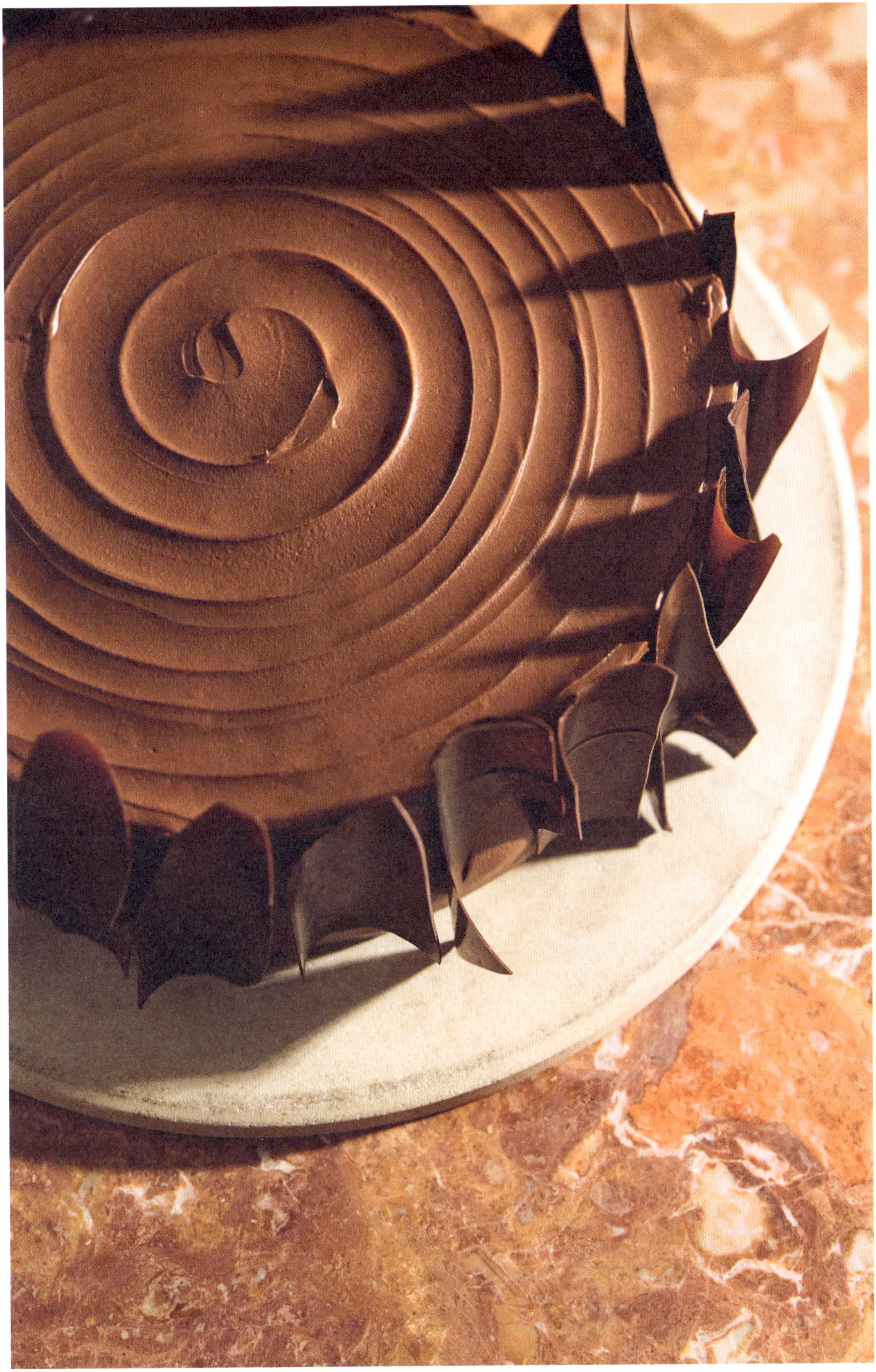

BLACK FOREST CAKE

Makes 1 × 20 cm (8 in) cake

This is a refined take on the classic Black Forest cake, which balances light chocolate sponge, smooth cherry compôte infused with bitter almond, a delicate crème diplomat and a lighter chocolate ganache for masking. The interplay of chocolate, cherries and cream makes this an elegant and nostalgic dessert.

CHOCOLATE SPONGE CAKE

1. Preheat the oven to 175°C fan (350°F). Grease and line two 20 cm (8 in) round cake tins (pans) with baking parchment.
2. Whisk together the flour, cocoa powder, baking powder and salt in a large bowl until evenly combined.
3. In a separate bowl, whisk together the milk, oil and sugar until smooth.
4. Gradually pour the wet ingredients into the dry ingredients, whisking gently until just combined. Do not overmix.
5. Divide the batter evenly between the prepared tins and smooth the tops.
6. Bake in the oven for 20–25 minutes, or until a skewer inserted into the centre comes out clean.
7. Remove from the oven and leave the sponges to cool in the tins for 10 minutes, then turn them out onto a wire rack to cool completely.

plain (all-purpose) flour	224 g	7.9 oz
cocoa (unsweetened) powder	19 g	0.7 oz
baking powder	8 g	1½ tsp
fine sea salt	1.6 g	¼ tsp
plant-based milk	192 g	6.8 oz
groundnut (peanut) oil	64 g	2.3 oz
caster (superfine) sugar	200 g	7 oz

CHERRY COMPÔTE

8. Whisk together the cherry juice, sugar and cornflour in a small saucepan until smooth.
9. Place over a medium heat, stirring constantly until the mixture thickens and turns glossy.
10. Remove from the heat and stir in the bitter almond extract.
11. Pour the compôte into a shallow dish and place a layer of cling film (plastic wrap) on the surface, then refrigerate until fully chilled.
12. Once cold, whisk the compôte until smooth, then stir in the strained cherries.

tinned pitted black cherries	240 g	14 oz
cherry juice (from the tin)	180 g	6.3 oz
caster (superfine) sugar	40 g	1.4 oz
cornflour (cornstarch)	20 g	0.7 oz
bitter almond extract	3–4 drops	

CRÈME DIPLOMAT

13. Combine the milk and vanilla in a small saucepan over a low heat and heat until steaming. Remove from the heat and leave to infuse for 10 minutes.
14. Meanwhile, whisk together the sugar, cornflour and custard powder in a bowl.
15. Gradually whisk the warm milk into the dry ingredients, then return everything to the saucepan.

plant-based milk	200 g	7.1 oz
vanilla pod (bean), split, or vanilla paste	½ pod / ½ tsp	
caster (superfine) sugar	50 g	1.8 oz
cornflour (cornstarch)	20 g	0.7 oz
custard powder	8 g	0.3 oz
coconut oil (deodorised)	24 g	0.8 oz
Whipping Cream (page 238)	120 g	4.2 oz

16 Cook over a medium heat, whisking constantly, until the mixture thickens and coats the back of a spoon.

17 Remove the pan from the heat and whisk in the coconut oil until fully incorporated.

18 Transfer the mixture to a shallow dish and place a layer of cling film (plastic wrap) on the surface to prevent a skin forming, then refrigerate until completely chilled.

19 Once cold, whip the whipping cream to soft peaks.

20 Gently fold the whipped cream into the chilled crème pâtissière in three stages, keeping the mixture light and airy. Refrigerate until needed.

CHOCOLATE GANACHE

21 Combine the milk (1) and sugar in a small saucepan over a medium heat and bring to a gentle simmer, stirring occasionally until the sugar completely dissolves.

22 Chop the dark chocolate and place it in a heatproof jug (pitcher) or bowl. Pour the hot milk mixture over the chocolate and blend immediately using a hand-held blender until the ganache is smooth and fully emulsified.

23 Add the chilled milk (2) and blend again until the ganache is glossy, smooth and free of oily streaks.

24 Pour it into a shallow dish and place a layer of cling film (plastic wrap) on the surface to prevent a skin forming, then refrigerate for 1 hour. Before using, allow to sit at room temperature for 45 minutes to reach a spreadable consistency.

plant-based milk (1)	127 g	4.5 oz
muscovado sugar	50 g	1.8 oz
dark chocolate min. 65% cocoa solids	200 g	7 oz
plant-based milk (2), chilled	127 g	4.5 oz
dark chocolate curls	to decorate	

TO ASSEMBLE

25 Place one chocolate sponge layer on a serving plate or cake board.

26 Spread the cherry compôte evenly over the sponge, ensuring it reaches the edges.

27 Pipe or spread the crème diplomat evenly over the cherry layer, using an offset spatula to smooth.

28 Place the second sponge layer on top, pressing down gently. Refrigerate the cake for 1 hour to set the layers.

29 Using a palette knife, spread the chocolate ganache over the top and sides of the cake, smoothing the surface evenly. Decorate the sides with the chocolate curls.

30 Refrigerate for at least 30 minutes before slicing.

31 The cake is best enjoyed chilled, allowing the flavours to meld together, but can be stored in the refrigerator for up to 2 days. Allow to sit at room temperature for 15 minutes before serving for the best texture.

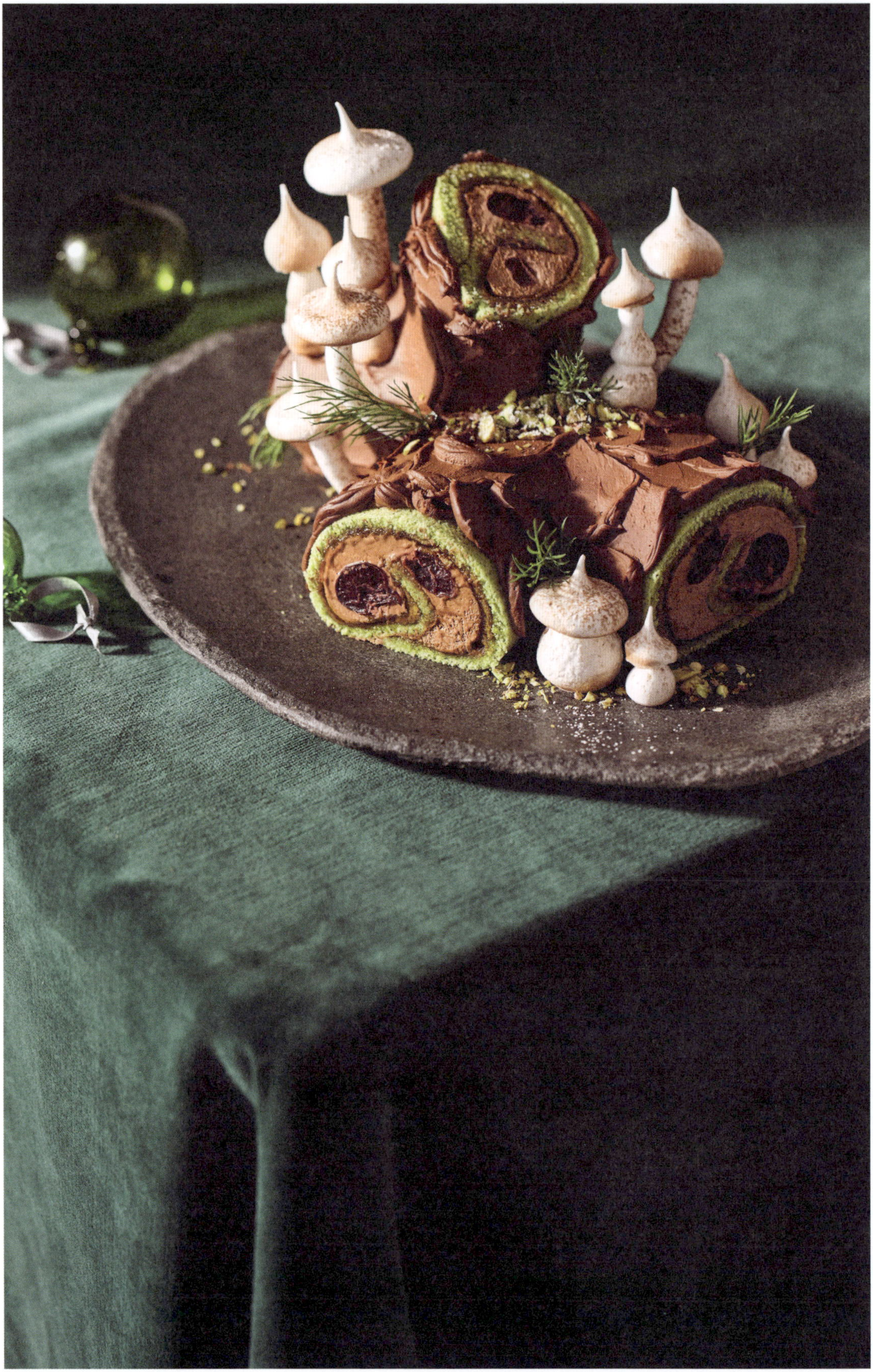

PISTACHIO YULE LOG

Serves 8–10

I love a Yule log, also known as a *bûche de Noël*. They are one of the remnants of Lebanon being a French colony that lingers to the modern day, and they are popular in Lebanese bakeries and pâtisseries in the seasonal period, often decorated with small figurines, plastic holly leaves and festive messages. It was these decorations and the *trompe-l'oeil* nature of this treat that enchanted me as a child. I wanted to bring back some enchantment with this take on a woodland yule log.

CHOCOLATE CHANTILLY MOUSSE

1. Heat the milk (1) in a saucepan over a medium heat until it reaches a gentle simmer.
2. Meanwhile, chop the chocolate and place it in a heatproof bowl.
3. Pour the hot milk over the chocolate and blend with a hand-held blender until completely smooth.
4. Add the chilled milk (2) and blend again until the ganache is glossy and smooth, with no visible streaks. If streaks appear, blend further, scraping down the sides to ensure a proper emulsion.
5. Pour it into a shallow dish and place a layer of cling film (plastic wrap) on the surface to prevent a skin forming, then refrigerate for at least 2 hours.
6. Once chilled, transfer to the chilled bowl of a stand mixer fitted with the whisk attachment. Whip until light and fluffy with stable peaks. Chilling the bowl before whipping helps speed up the process. Refrigerate until needed.

plant-based milk (1)	90 g	3.2 oz
dark chocolate min. 65% cocoa solids	120 g	4.2 oz
plant-based milk (2), chilled	100 g	3.5 oz

CHOCOLATE GANACHE

7. Combine the milk (1) and sugar in a saucepan over a medium heat and heat until just simmering.
8. Meanwhile, chop the chocolate and plate it in a heatproof bowl.
9. Pour the hot milk mixture over the chocolate and blend with a hand-held blender until completely smooth.
10. Add the chilled milk (2) and blend again until completely emulsified.
11. Pour it into a shallow dish and place a layer of cling film (plastic wrap) on the surface to prevent a skin forming, then refrigerate for at least 4 hours.

plant-based milk (1)	100 g	3.5 oz
muscovado or dark brown sugar	50 g	1.8 oz
dark chocolate min. 65% cocoa solids	150 g	5.3 oz
plant-based milk (2), chilled	100 g	3.5 oz

PISTACHIO PRALINE

12. Preheat the oven to 170°C fan (375°F).
13. Spread the pistachios over a baking tray (pan) and lightly roast in the oven for 8 minutes, then remove and leave to cool completely.

shelled pistachios	200 g	7 oz
icing (powdered) sugar	100 g	3.5 oz
fine sea salt	1 g	¼ tsp

14. Pulse the roasted pistachios, icing sugar and salt in a food processor or high-powered blender. The mixture will turn into a fine powder and then a thick paste as the oils from the nuts are released.

15. Stop blending and scrape down the sides whenever the paste starts catching. Continue blending until completely smooth.

16. Set aside until needed. Any leftover praline can be stored in a sealed jar at room temperature for up to 2 weeks.

AQUAFABA MERINGUE MUSHROOMS

17. Preheat the oven to 100°C (210°F) and line a baking tray (pan) with baking parchment. For meringues, it is best to use the static oven setting rather than fan.

18. Pour the aquafaba into a stand mixer fitted with the whisk attachment and whisk until soft peaks form. Add the cream of tartar and whisk again, then continue whisking while gradually adding the sugar. Beat until the meringue forms stiff, glossy peaks.

19. Transfer the meringue mixture to a piping (pastry) bag and pipe small domes for mushroom caps and thin cylinders for stems onto the tray. Dust the caps lightly with cocoa powder.

20. Bake for 1½ hours, then turn off the oven and leave the meringues to cool inside with the oven door slightly open.

21. Once cooled, attach the stems to the caps by dipping the top of the stem in a little melted dark chocolate and attaching it to the top. Leave to set.

aquafaba (page 244)	75 g	2.6 oz
cream of tartar	1 g	¼ tsp
caster (superfine) sugar	150 g	5.3 oz
cocoa (unsweetened) powder	for dusting	
melted dark chocolate	for dipping	

PISTACHIO SPONGE

22. Preheat the oven to 150°C fan (350°F). Spread the pistachios over a baking tray (pan) and lightly roast in the oven for 15 minutes, then remove and leave to cool completely.

23. Increase the oven temperature to 220°C fan (460°F). Spray a large baking sheet with oil, then line with baking parchment. Blend the pistachios, flour, sugar, baking powder, bicarbonate of soda and salt in a food processor until finely ground, then transfer to a large bowl.

24. Warm the soya milk in a saucepan until it reaches 40°C (104°F) on a thermometer.

25. Whisk together the warm soya milk, vanilla extract and apple cider vinegar in a bowl.

26. Pour the wet ingredients over the dry ingredients and whisk until just combined.

27. Spread the batter evenly onto the prepared baking sheet and bake for 6 minutes. The sponge should spring back when lightly touched.

28. Remove from the oven and immediately place a sheet of baking parchment on top, weighing it down with a dish towel to keep it flexible for rolling.

shelled pistachios	60 g	2 oz
vegetable oil	for greasing	
plain (all-purpose) flour	105 g	3.7 oz
caster (superfine) sugar	100 g	3.5 oz
baking powder	3 g	¾ tsp
bicarbonate of soda (baking soda)	1.5 g	¼ tsp
fine sea salt	1 g	¼ tsp
soya milk	135 g	4.8 oz
vanilla extract	3 g	¾ tsp
apple cider vinegar	6 g	1½ tsp

TO ASSEMBLE AND DECORATE

29 Flip the sponge over and gently peel away the baking parchment. Place onto a clean sheet of baking parchment.

30 Spread 150 g (5.3 oz) of the pistachio praline evenly over the sponge, leaving a 1 cm (½ in) border along the edges.

31 Spread a thin layer of chocolate Chantilly mousse over the praline, then arrange the drained cherries in two rows along the long edge.

32 Using the parchment paper, roll the sponge tightly into a log, keeping tension as you go. Secure with parchment paper and chill in the refrigerator for 1 hour.

33 Once chilled, trim one end diagonally, then cut off a third of the log at a 45-degree angle. Attach it as a branch.

34 Spread the chocolate ganache in streaks over the log to mimic bark. Dust with icing sugar, then decorate with glacé cherries, dill fronds and meringue mushrooms.

35 Refrigerate for up to 2 days. Allow to sit at room temperature for 20 minutes before serving.

Amarena cherries (or tinned cherries in syrup)	350 g (12 oz) jar
dill	1 sprig
icing (powdered) sugar	for dusting

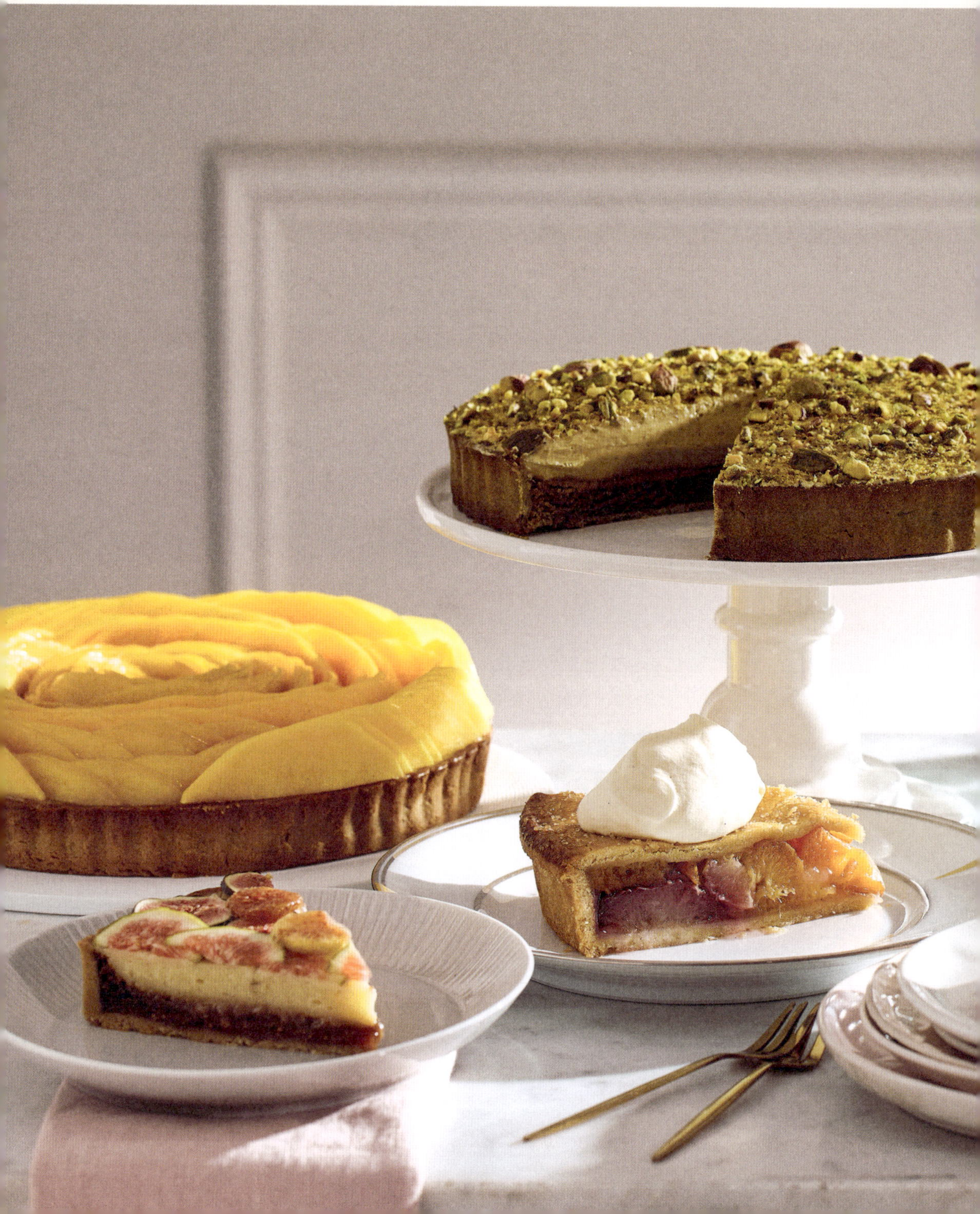

5 SWEET AS PIE

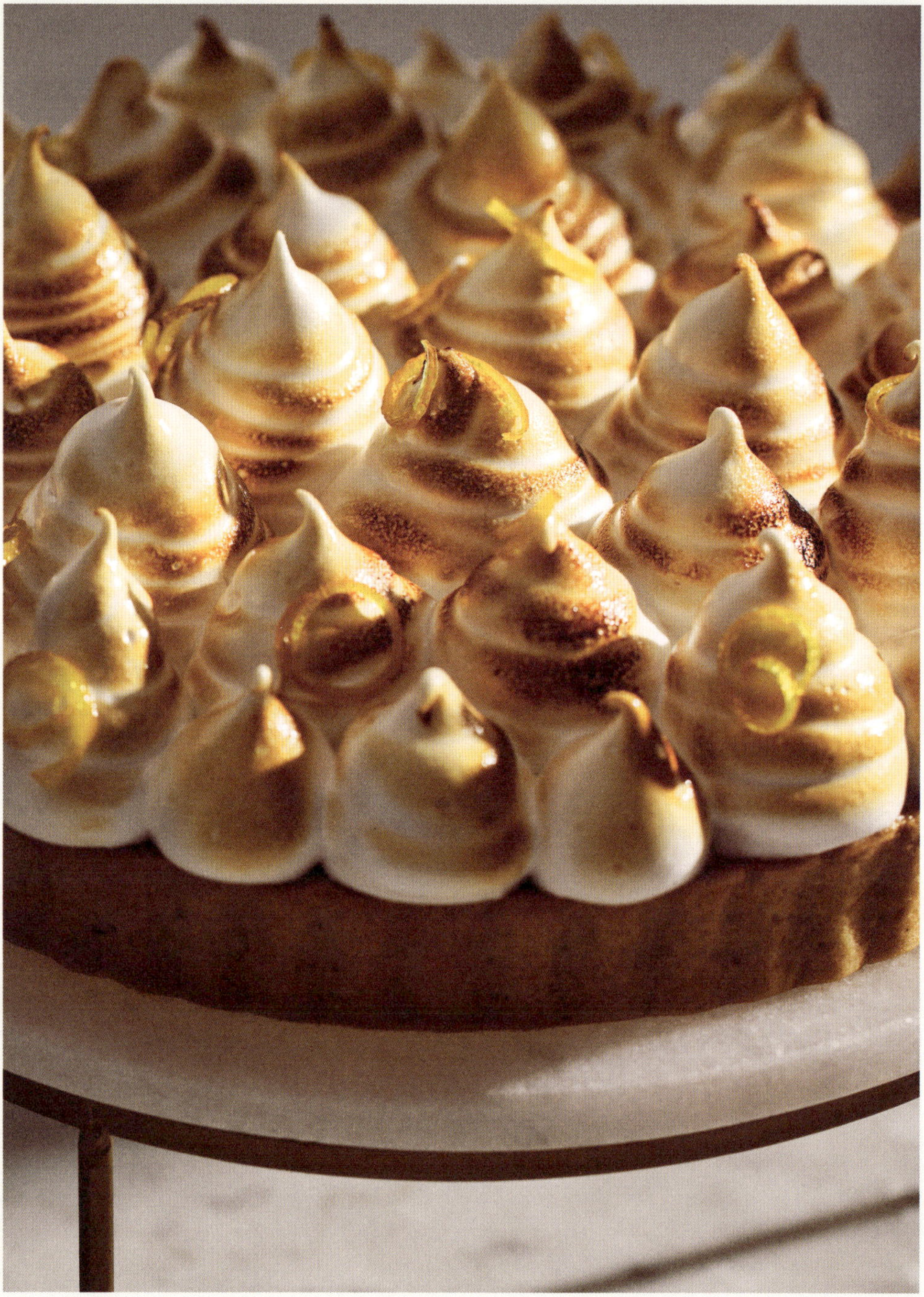

PLANT-BASED
PÂTISSERIE PERFECTED

Trying to define the difference between a tart and a pie is nearly impossible. Ask five people from five different countries and you'll get five different answers. Some say a tart becomes a pie the moment it can be removed from the tin (pan), while others insist that anything with a base and filling is automatically a pie. Then there are those who swear it's all about the crust: tarts are thick and crisp, pies are thinner and more tender. Honestly? I don't mind what you call them – as long as you enjoy making and eating them.

What matters more is that these are vessels for flavour and texture. Whether rustic or refined, filled with fruit, custard, nuts or chocolate, every tart or pie in this chapter is designed to showcase contrast – crisp pastry against smooth cream, sharp compôte under buttery crumble, silky ganache on a sturdy base. I prefer to remove mine from the tin before serving (the pâtissier in me can't resist a clean slice), but feel free to serve them straight from the dish if that's your style.

There are three types of pastry used throughout this chapter, and each one made me question what I thought I knew about how pastry works.

The first – and most commonly used – is a short, sweet pastry that borrows the syrup method I developed while working on the cookie chapter. By whisking oil, water (or plant-based milk) and sugar into a thick emulsion before adding it to the dry ingredients, you get a dough that's softer than traditional butter-based shortcrust pastry, but incredibly forgiving. It can be patched together easily, doesn't require blind baking, and can be rolled out cleanly between two sheets of baking parchment, making it ideal for beginners and pros alike.

The second is a flaky pastry that challenged my assumptions about lamination. I used to believe you needed solid butter to create layers, but it turns out that you can achieve a beautifully flaky texture with oil. Rubbing flour with oil inhibits gluten development, while adding water separately introduces friction. The result is a subtle tension in the dough – a tug-of-war between oil and water – that forms delicate, natural layers and bakes into a pastry that's short, tender and satisfyingly flaky.

The third is my take on classic puff pastry, reimagined with a homemade plant-based butter made from olive oil and cocoa butter. It performs like dairy butter in lamination and creates those dramatic, crisp layers you'd expect from traditional puff. You can absolutely use a high-quality plant-based block butter if that's easier, but if you're up for it, I truly encourage you to try making your own. The results are well worth the effort.

FLAKY PASTRY

This pastry dispels a number of commonly held beliefs. The results and ways of working with it made me completely rethink the way I thought that butter and other solid fats work in traditional pastry. It appears to me that liquid fat stops the dough from wanting to form, while moisture does the opposite and simultaneously binds the dough through its interaction with the gluten. This paradox creates layers and a dough that doesn't want to combine, but rolling it between two sheets of baking parchment makes easy work of this. This pastry can be baked on its own without baking beans (pie weights) if the tart tin (pan) has gently sloping sides, but if it has sharp sides, then do blind bake it. This flaky pastry works great for pies with and without lids, as well as any tart with a rich filling (I always bake mine first before adding the filling, even if it needs to be baked again). Oil-wise, feel free to use any kind – I love using extra virgin olive oil for all my tart cases (shells).

1. Mix the flour, salt and sugar together in a large bowl. Add the oil and use a silicone spatula or your hands to mix it into the flour. The oil should coat all the flour.

2. Add the sweet potato and massage it in until there are no lumps.

3. Add the cold water and mix until the dough just comes together. Don't overmix because the dough will start to separate and become more difficult to handle.

4. Place the dough between two sheets of baking parchment and roll it out until it is 3–4 mm (⅛ in) thick.

5. Line your chosen tart tin (pan) by removing the top sheet of baking parchment from the pastry and gently placing the tart tin on top of the pastry as a guide. Use a paring knife to trim the pastry around the tin, making sure there are a few extra centimetres (inches), then remove the tart tin. Use the bottom sheet of baking parchment to help flip the pastry gently into the tin, then carefully ease it into the shape of the tin with your fingertips.

6. Leave to chill in the refrigerator for 15 minutes, then use the tip of a paring knife to 'dock' the base with a few pricks, about 2 cm (¾ in) apart, to stop the base from puffing up.

7. This pastry can be blind baked. To do so, preheat the oven to 170°C fan (375°F). Scrunch up some baking parchment, then unfurl it, press it into the tart case (shell) and fill it with rice or baking beans (pie weights). Bake for 12 minutes for individual or small tart cases, adding 2 minutes at a time (up to 18 minutes total) for larger tarts until nicely golden. I always fully bake my bases because once they are filled, they don't take on a whole lot of colour. If the edge is browning too quickly, cover it with foil.

Makes 450 g (15.9 oz) or enough for 1 × 23 cm (9 in) pie base or 10 individual tartlets

plain (all-purpose) flour	250 g	8.8 oz
fine sea salt	3 g	¾ tsp
caster (superfine) sugar	40 g	1.4 oz
cold-pressed oil	100 g	3.5 oz
cooked and cooled sweet potato (page 44)	20 g	0.7 oz
cold water	40 g	1.4 oz

Makes 750 g (1 lb 10 oz), or enough for 1 × 23 cm (9 in) pie and lid

plain (all-purpose) flour	450 g	15.9 oz
fine sea salt	5 g	1 tsp
caster (superfine) sugar	70 g	2.5 oz
cold-pressed oil	180 g	6.3 oz
cooked and cooled sweet potato (page 44)	30 g	1 oz
cold water	75 g	2.6 oz

TIPS

I always prefer to blind bake my tart cases (shells) to prevent a soggy bottom. They also tend to last longer and develop more flavour.

I always cook my sweet potato in advance and keep it in a sealed container in the freezer for up to 3 months (page 44).

SHORT SWEET PASTRY

Makes 550 g (1 lb 3 oz), or enough for 2 × 23 cm (9 in) tarts or 12 individual tartlets

A fundamental pastry foundation that produces a crisp, short pastry, perfect for any size tart case (shell). This pastry doesn't shrink and can be flavoured in as many ways as you can think of.

1. First, make a syrup by whisking the soya milk, sugars and olive oil together in a jug (pitcher) until the mixture is glossy and uniform in colour.

2. Put the flour, vanilla seeds, lemon zest and salt into a large bowl, then pour in the syrup and use a silicone spatula or wooden spoon to combine the mixture together into an even dough.

3. Turn out the dough onto a work surface and press it into a 2 cm (¾ in) thick disc if rolling a round shape or square if you want to roll it into a square shape.

4. Lightly sprinkle some flour over the dough, then place it between two sheets of baking parchment and roll it out to the desired thickness: 3 mm (⅛ in) for small tarts and 4 mm (⅙ in) for large ones. You don't need to chill this dough before rolling it.

5. Line your chosen tart tin (pan) by removing the top sheet of baking parchment from the pastry and gently placing the tart tin on top of the pastry as a guide. Use a paring knife to trim the pastry around the tin, making sure there are a few extra centimetres (inches), then remove the tart tin. Use the bottom sheet of baking parchment to help flip the pastry gently into the tin, then carefully ease it into the shape of the tin with your fingertips. Use the side of your finger to press it against the edges (and into the flutes if the tin is fluted). If your pastry breaks, just press pieces together to join them.

6. Before baking, chill in the freezer for 15 minutes, then use the tip of a paring knife to 'dock' the base with a few pricks, about 2 cm (¾ in) apart, to stop the base from puffing up.

7. To blind bake, preheat the oven to 170°C fan (375°F). Bake the chilled pastry in the oven for 9–10 minutes (no baking beans/pie weights required). To fully bake, give it a further 3–5 minutes at 160°C fan (350°F) for a golden colour all the way through.

soya milk	50 g	1.8 oz
caster (superfine) sugar	50 g	1.8 oz
muscovado sugar	50 g	1.8 oz
extra virgin olive oil or oil of your choice	100 g	3.5 oz
plain (all-purpose) flour (gluten-free will also work), plus extra for dusting	300 g	10.6 oz
vanilla pod (bean), seeds scraped	1 pod	
lemon zest	¼ lemon	
fine sea salt	1 g	¼ tsp

VARIATIONS

Cocoa | Replace 45 g (1.6 oz) of the flour with 28 g (1 oz) cocoa (unsweetened) powder and 10 g (0.4 oz) additional sugar and 28 g (1 oz) additional milk.

Nuts | Replace 20 g (0.7 oz) of the oil with 30 g (1 oz) nut paste of your choice. The extra fat in the nut butters make it exceptionally short textured!

Matcha | Replace 10 g (0.4 oz) of the flour with 5 g (1 tsp) matcha powder.

PERFECT PEACH PIE

Makes 1 × 23 cm (9 in) pie

I come from a long line of peach farmers. My earliest childhood memories of visits to my dad's village in the mountains of northern Lebanon involve peaches. In Mrah e Sfireh, in the region of Dunniye, fruit orchards are terraced down the mountain over hundreds of years. A DNA test revealed that, despite my family's migration to Australia, I am native to, rather specifically, northern Lebanon (my mum is from the stunning region of Tannourine). Here's a pie celebrating great summer fruit, picked at its prime and baked in flaky pastry. This peach pie could also be a nectarine pie (they are very closely related!).

peaches	1.2 kg	2 lb 11 oz
caster (superfine) sugar	150 g	5.3 oz
cornflour (cornstarch)	30 g	1 oz
vanilla paste	5 g	1 tsp
lemon zest		½ lemon
lemon juice	15 g	0.5 oz
Flaky Pastry (page 146)		1 quantity
Baking Glaze (page 242) or soya milk		1 tbsp
Demerara sugar		for sprinkling
ice cream or pouring cream		to serve

1. Using a sharp knife, cut the peaches in half, being careful to cut around the stone. If the peach is ripe, it should come away from the stone. If they are not coming away from the stone easily, it may be best to cut them again into quarters and pull the flesh away from the stone.

2. If the fruit is ripe, you can use them as they are. If the fruit is firm, preheat the oven to 190°C fan (400°F). Place the peach pieces in a baking tray (pan) lined with baking parchment and roast for 15 minutes, then remove from the oven and leave to cool so you can peel the skin off.

3. Put the peaches into a large bowl with the sugar, cornflour, vanilla paste, lemon zest and juice and gently toss until everything is well combined. Leave to stand for 20 minutes to macerate – this will draw some moisture out of the fruit.

TO ASSEMBLE AND BAKE

4. Preheat the oven to 180°C fan (400°F) and position a shelf in the bottom quarter of the oven.

5. Roll out two thirds of the pastry between two sheets of baking parchment into a large disc, about 30 cm (12 in) in diameter and 3–4 mm (⅛–⅙ in) thick. Roll out the remaining pastry into a 25 cm (10 in) disc about 3 mm (⅛ in) thick.

6. Remove the top sheet of baking parchment from the larger disc and use the bottom sheet to help flip it over into a 23 cm (9 in) pie or quiche dish with a tiny overhang, then gently press it into the sides of the dish. Leave the paper on top, then fill with baking beans (pie weights). Blind bake for 15 minutes, then remove from the oven and carefully lift out the beans and paper.

7. Arrange the peach halves or quarters on the pastry base, then gently layer some pieces that have been cut into quarters to fill all the gaps. There will be some liquid leftover from the peaches, so stir it to agitate any settled cornflour, then drizzle it slowly over the fruit. You can push the peaches into a slight domed shape.

8. Brush the overhanging edge of the pie crust with water, then place the top disc of pastry over the top and press the edges together. Trim and crimp the edges as you like.

9   Brush the baking glaze or soya milk across the top of the pastry and sprinkle some Demerara sugar on top for a tantalising crunch.

10 Using a sharp knife, poke a steam hole in the middle of the pie. Bake in the oven for 20 minutes, then rotate and bake for a further 20–25 minutes until golden all over.

11 Remove from the oven and leave to stand for at least 25 minutes. Serve warm with a scoop of ice cream or pouring cream. It keeps well in a sealed container in the refrigerator for up to 4 days. I like to slice mine once cooled completely to get a nice clean cut, then reheat slices in the oven or microwave.

TIPS

I always recommend using metal pie dishes because they conduct heat much faster than ceramic or glass ones. This ensures the pastry is baked through and avoids the dreaded soggy bottom.

If you don't have baking beans (pie weights), use you can use beans or rice – these can be kept in a jar once cool for blind baking in future.

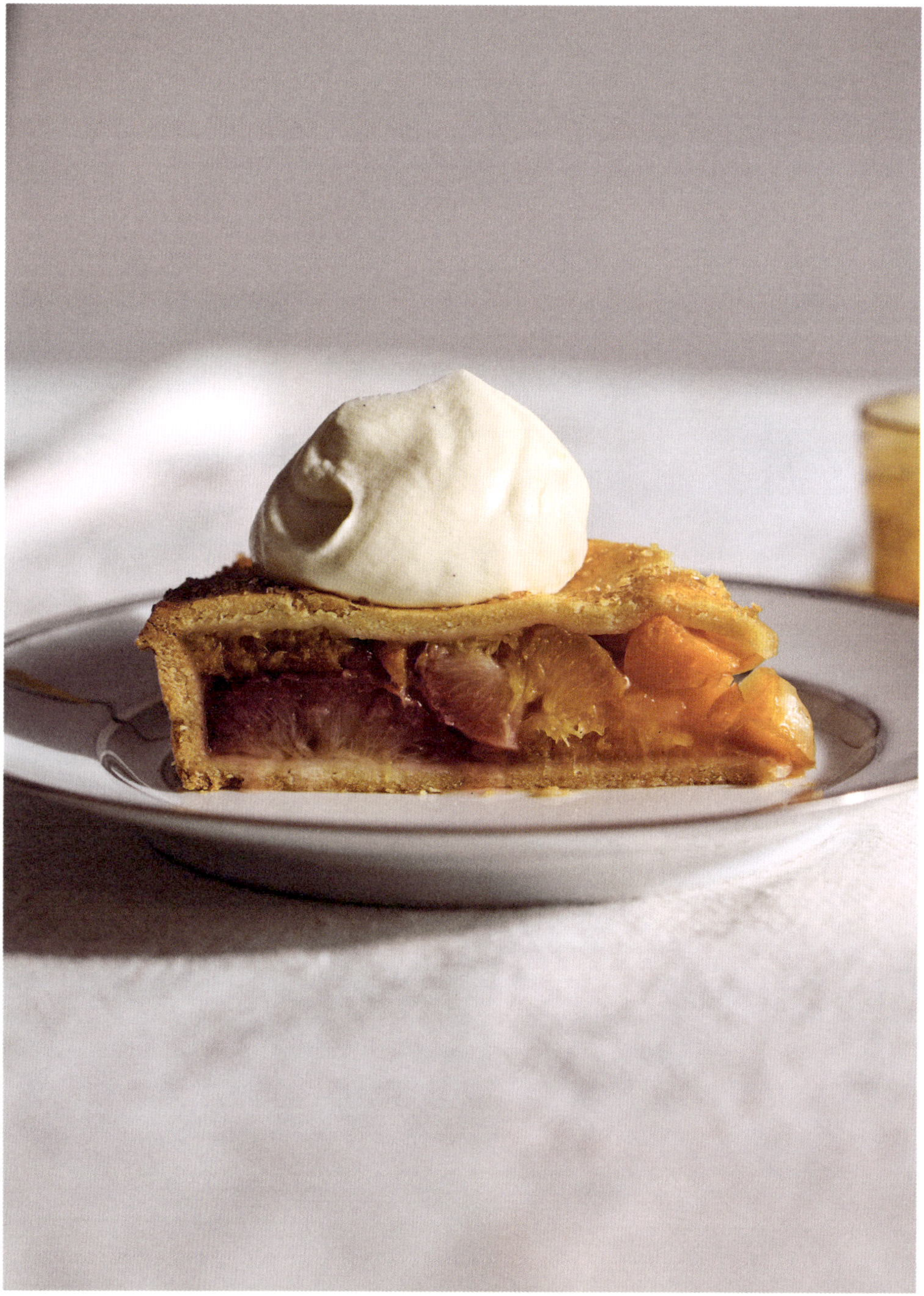

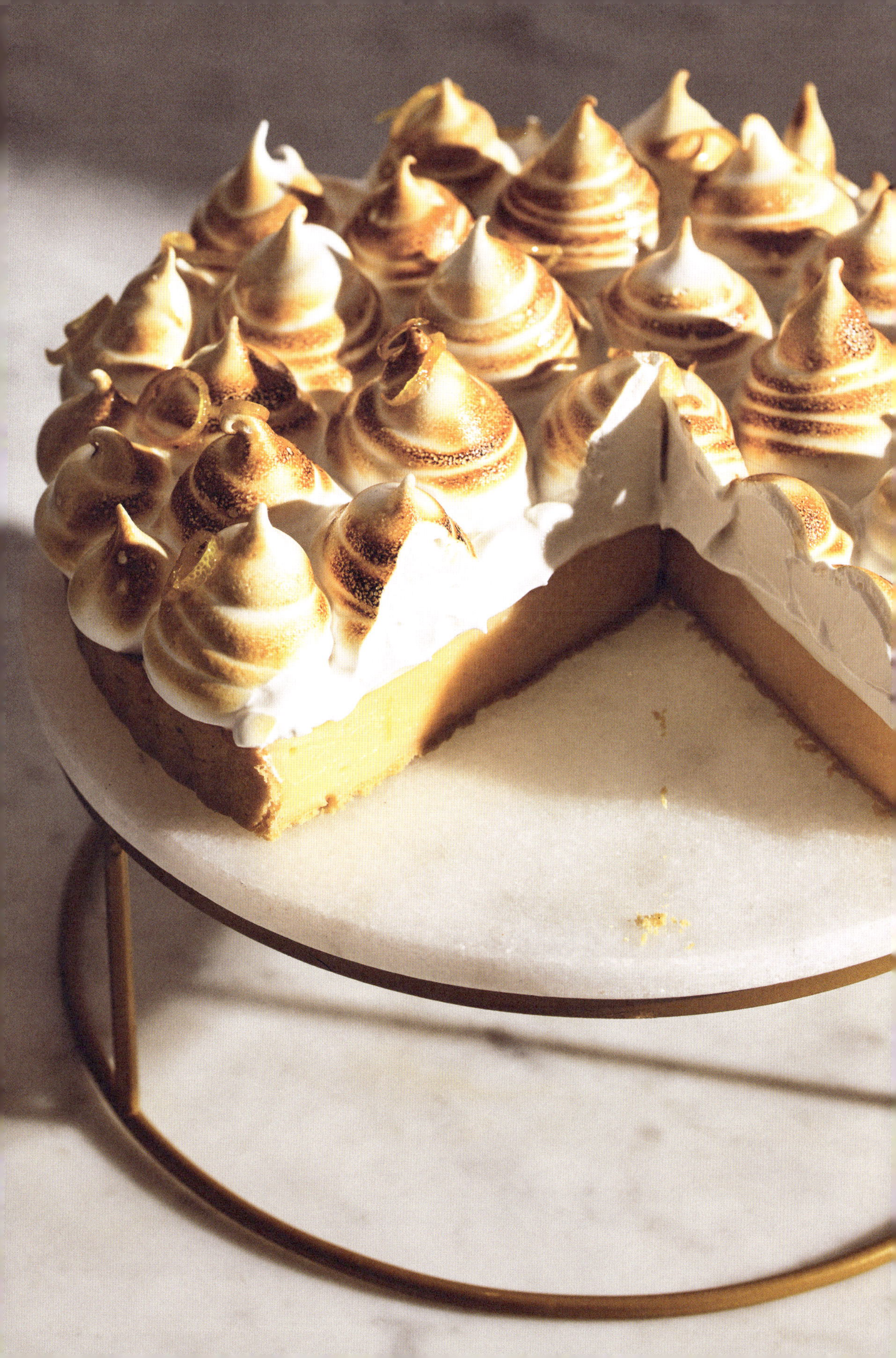

YUZU MERINGUE PIE

Makes 1 × 23 cm (9 in) pie

This lemon and yuzu meringue pie is all about balance – bright, citrusy sharpness mellowed by a delicate sweetness. Yuzu, the incredibly fragrant Japanese citrus, brings a depth of flavour that goes beyond just tartness, offering floral and almost spicy notes that make this pie stand out from a classic lemon tart. The filling is silky and vibrant, nestled in a crisp pastry case (shell) and topped with a light, billowy aquafaba meringue. Since we're using aquafaba here, you'll also find my recipe for it on page 244 – right alongside my hummus recipe. If yuzu juice is not available, it can be replaced with more lemon juice to make the classic lemon meringue pie.

YUZU AND LEMON CURD

1. Put the milk, lemon juice, yuzu juice and sugar into a high-sided saucepan and bring to a simmer. The acidity of the juices will make the milk curdle, but it will come back together.

2. Whisk the water and cornflour together in a medium bowl until smooth, then pour it into the pan in one go, whisking constantly. The mixture will thicken quickly.

3. Add the coconut oil and, using a hand-held blender, blend the mixture. Something slightly magical will happen – the colour will lighten and the texture will become silky and smooth. Be careful not to over-blend. Leaving out this last step will result in a set texture that's far less pleasurable to eat! Pour it into a shallow dish and place a layer of cling film (plastic wrap) on the surface to prevent a skin forming, then chill in the refrigerator for 1 hour.

4. Transfer the chilled curd to a large bowl and whisk it with a balloon whisk until smooth and creamy, then pour it into the pre-baked tart case (shell) and smooth the top.

plant-based milk	245 g	8.6 oz
lemon juice	245 g	8.6 oz
yuzu juice	60 g	2 oz
caster (superfine) sugar	210 g	7.4 oz
water	75 g	2.6 oz
cornflour (cornstarch)	53 g	1.8 oz
custard powder	28 g	1 oz
coconut oil (deodorised)	56 g	2 oz
pre-baked 23 cm (9 in) Short Sweet Pastry tart case (page 147)	1	

CANDIED LEMON STRIPS

5. Finely peel the skin from the lemon and then slice it into 1 mm (1/16 in) thin strips.

6. Place in a saucepan with the sugar and water and bring to a simmer for 2 minutes. Strain before using.

lemon	1	
caster (superfine) sugar	230 g	8.1 oz
water	240 g	8.5 oz

AQUAFABA MERINGUE

7. Up to 1 hour before you want to serve the pie, make the meringue and decorate the pie (any more than this and it can start to lose its structure).

8. Place the aquafaba into the clean bowl of a stand mixer along with the sugar and cream of tartar. Use the whisk attachment to whip the mixture for 4–5 minutes until you have a stable, fluffy meringue with firm peaks.

9. Transfer the meringue to a piping (pastry) bag fitted with a large, plain nozzle (tip). Pipe peaks over the yuzu and lemon curd to decorate the pie. (Alternatively, you can use a spatula to decorate it in a free-form way.) You may use a kitchen blowtorch to blowtorch the meringue if you fancy, otherwise simply leave it as angelic white.

10. Decorate with the candied lemon strips.

aquafaba (page 244)	150 g	5.3 oz
caster (superfine) sugar	150 g	5.3 oz
cream of tartar	3 g	¾ tsp

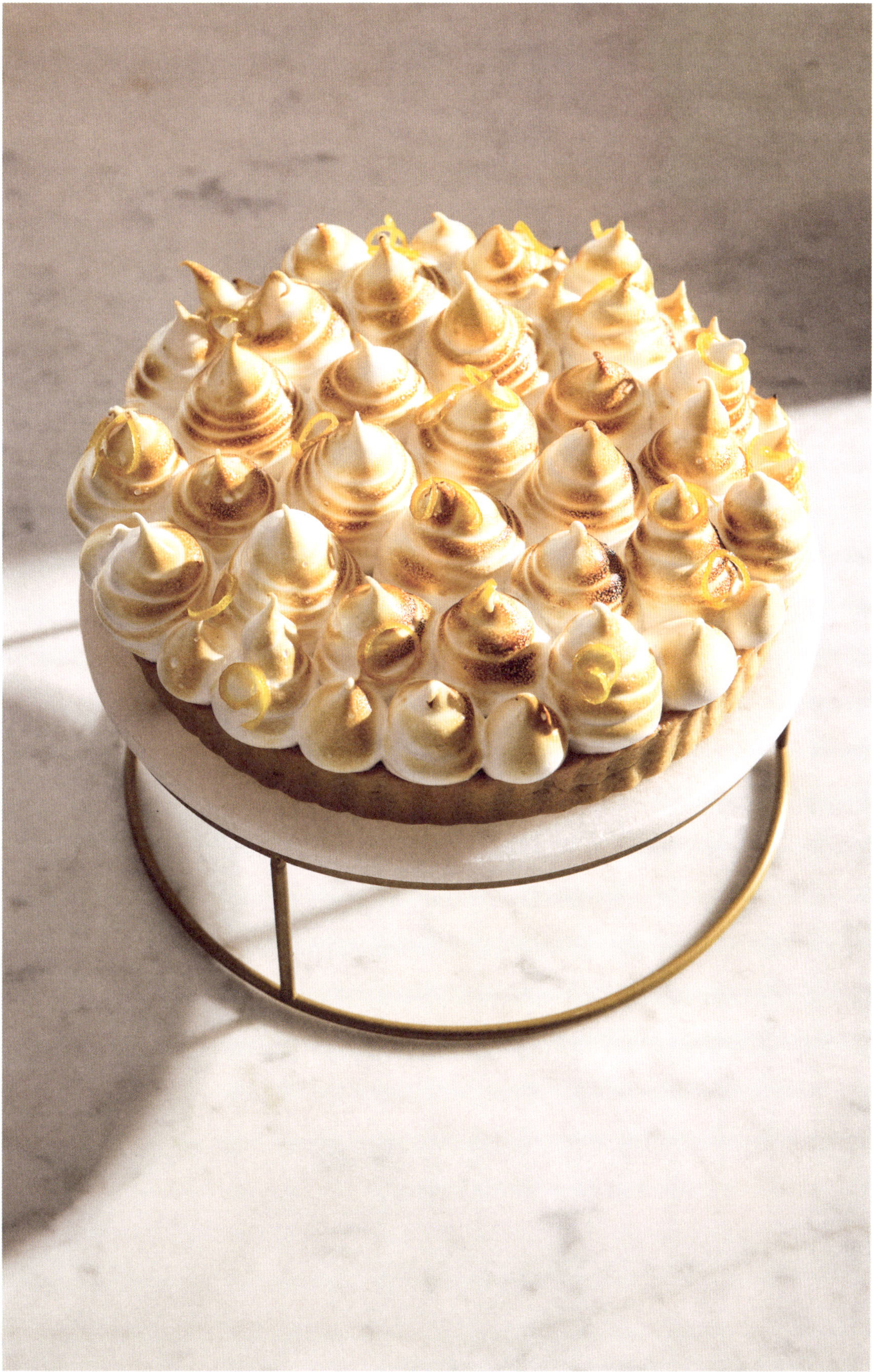

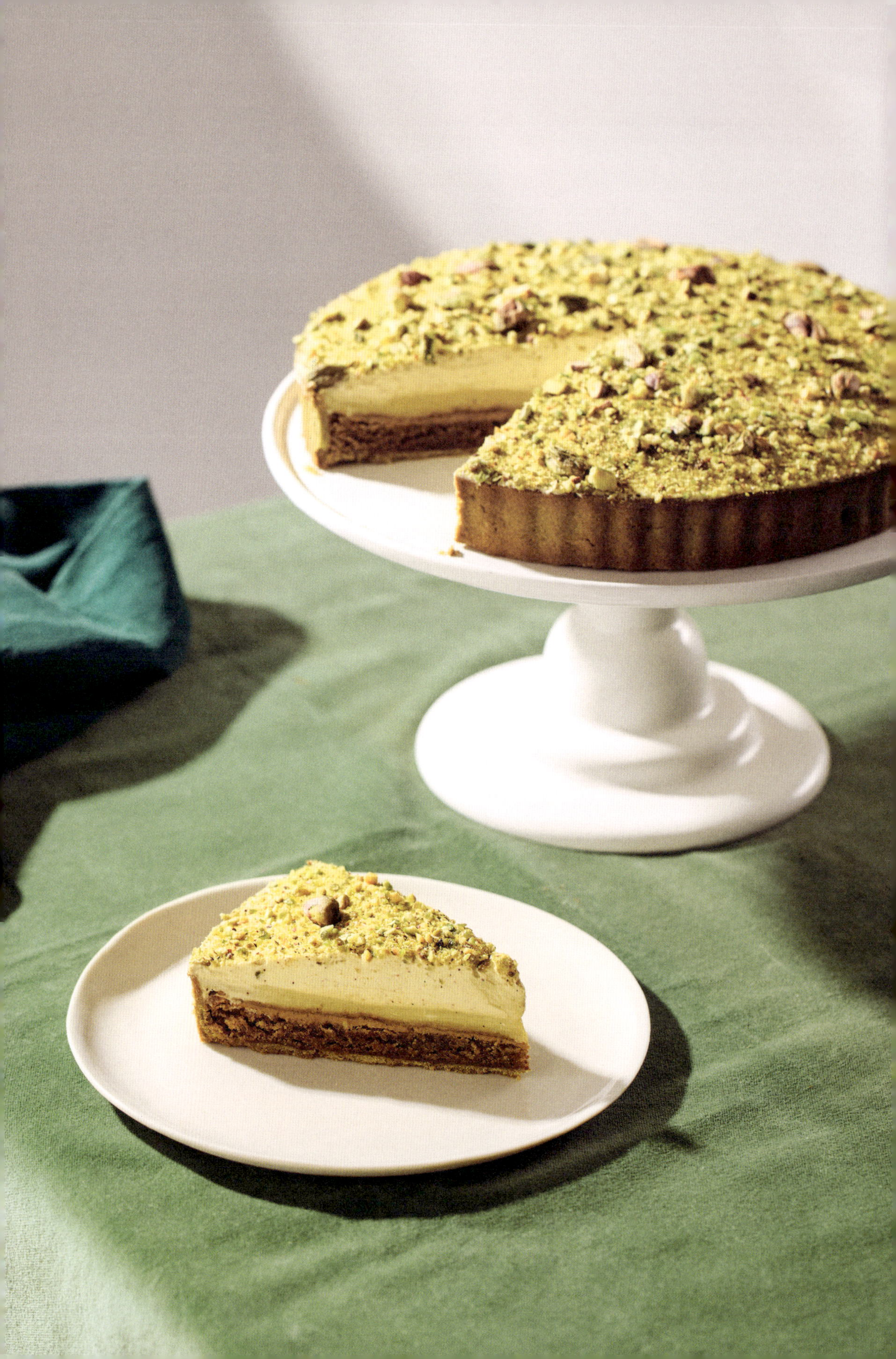

PURE PISTACHIO TART

Makes 1 × 23 cm (9 in) tart

Ever since the wider public rediscovered the true flavour of pistachio – a prized, naturally sweet nut far removed from the artificially coloured pastes flavoured with bitter almond oil – it has become an undeniable smash hit of a flavour. This tart celebrates pistachio in its purest form, layered in a spectrum of natural green tones: matcha-infused pastry, luxurious pistachio frangipane, silky pistachio praline, smooth pistachio custard and airy pistachio crème diplomat.

MATCHA SWEET PASTRY

1. First, make a syrup by whisking the soya milk, sugar, olive oil and matcha powder together in a bowl until the mixture is glossy and uniform in colour.

2. Add the flour and salt to the bowl and use a silicone spatula or wooden spoon to combine the mixture together until an even dough forms.

3. Turn out the dough onto a work surface and press it into a 2 cm (¾ in) thick disc if rolling a round shape or square if you want to roll it into a square shape.

4. Lightly sprinkle some flour over the dough, then place it between two sheets of baking parchment and roll it out to the desired thickness: 3 mm (⅛ in) for small tarts and 4 mm (⅙ in) for large ones. You don't need to chill this dough before rolling.

5. Line a 23 cm (9 in) tart tin (pan) by removing the top sheet of baking parchment from the pastry and gently placing the tart tin on top of the pastry as a guide. Use a paring knife to trim the pastry around the tin, making sure there are a few extra centimetres (inches), then remove the tart tin. Use the bottom sheet of baking parchment to help flip the pastry gently into the tin, then carefully ease it into the shape of the tin with your fingertips. Use the side of your finger to press it against the edges (and into the flutes if the tin is fluted).

6. Chill in the freezer for 10 minutes, then use the tip of a paring knife or fork to 'dock' the base with a few pricks, about 2 cm (¾ in) apart, to stop the base from puffing up.

7. To blind bake, preheat the oven to 170°C fan (375°F). Bake the chilled pastry in the oven for 8–10 minutes (no baking beans/pie weights required) until light golden on the top and paler in colour. Remove from the oven and leave the oven on.

soya milk	35 g	1.3 oz
caster (superfine) sugar	50 g	1.8 oz
extra virgin olive oil or oil of your choice	50 g	1.8 oz
matcha powder	3 g	2 tsp
plain (all-purpose) flour (gluten-free will also work), plus extra for dusting	140 g	5 oz
fine sea salt	1 g	¼ tsp

PISTACHIO FRANGIPANE

8. Meanwhile, make the frangipane. Pulse the pistachios, almonds, sugar and cornflour in a food processor or high-powered blender. Add the remaining ingredients and pulse to combine – it will have a creamy texture.

9. Use a silicone spatula to scrape the pistachio frangipane into the tart case (shell), then bake in the oven for 12–15 minutes until the top domes. Remove the tart from the oven and allow it to cool fully – it will deflate slightly.

shelled pistachios	100 g	3.5 oz
blanched almonds	50 g	1.8 oz
caster (superfine) sugar	100 g	3.5 oz
cornflour (cornstarch)	20 g	0.7 oz
plant-based milk	90 g	3.2 oz
extra virgin olive oil	20 g	0.7 oz
plain (all-purpose) flour	10 g	0.4 oz
baking powder	4 g	1 tsp
fine sea salt	1 g	¼ tsp

SWEET AS PIE

PISTACHIO 'COLD' PRALINE

10. Place the nuts on a baking tray (pan) and roast them in the oven for 8 minutes, then remove and leave to cool completely.

11. In a small, powerful blender like a Nutribullet, blend the nuts with the sugar and salt – at first, the mixture will turn to a powder, then it will start to catch on the sides of the jug or bowl as the nuts become pulverised and the natural oils are released. Each time the mixture catches on the sides, stop the blender and scrape down the sides with a spatula. This will happen a few times before the mixture is totally smooth.

12. Reserve 90 g (3.2 oz) for the pistachio crème, then pipe the rest on top of the cooled frangipane.

shelled pistachios	200 g	7 oz
icing (powdered) sugar	100 g	3.5 oz
flaky sea salt	1 g	¼ tsp

PISTACHIO CRÈME

13. Put all the ingredients except the pistachio paste and coconut oil into a high-sided saucepan and whisk well to combine, then place over a medium heat and continue stirring with a silicone spatula until the mixture starts to thicken and come to the boil – keep stirring to avoid it catching on the bottom, then remove from the heat.

14. Add the pistachio paste and coconut oil and mix until fully incorporated.

15. Pour the hot mixture into a shallow dish and place a layer of cling film (plastic wrap) on the surface to prevent a skin forming. Refrigerate until firm and set.

16. To use, tip the set custard into a bowl and use a balloon whisk to whisk until smooth and creamy.

17. Spread 300 g (10.6 oz) of the pistachio crème onto the pistachio praline layer that has been spread over the cooled frangipane.

plant-based milk	320 g	11.3 oz
caster (superfine) sugar	100 g	3.5 oz
vanilla bean paste	5 g	1 tsp
cornflour (cornstarch)	45 g	1.6 oz
flaky sea salt	1 g	¼ tsp, plus a pinch
pistachio praline (see above)	100 g	3.5 oz
coconut oil (deodorised)	35 g	1.2 oz

TO ASSEMBLE

18. Whip the cream until fluffy, stable peaks form, then add a third of the remaining whisked pistachio crème at a time and fold together until combined. Spoon this on top of the pistachio crème layer in the tart. Spread with a spatula to create a dome in the middle.

19. Chop the pistachios and sprinkle them all over to cover the tart. This tart can be stored in the refrigerator for up to 2 days, so can be prepared a day in advance. To serve, push the loose base upwards from beneath to remove the tart from the tart tin, then transfer to a large flat serving dish.

Whipping Cream (page 238)	150 g	5.3 oz
pistachio crème (see above)	300 g	10.6 oz
shelled pistachios	50 g	1.8 oz

WHIPPING CREAM TIPS

FIGWELL TART

Makes 1 × 23 cm (9 in) tart

Summers in my dad's village in Lebanon smelled like figs – their leaves warming under the sun, releasing a soft, green perfume that filled the air as we played nearby. That same fragrance radiates through the layers of this tart, where figs take centre stage in every form. A smooth fig leaf-infused custard carries their delicate aroma, but if you can't source fresh leaves, a classic crème pâtissière works just as well – just skip the leaf infusion. It is then topped with fresh figs, their honeyed sweetness balancing the crisp pastry, sweet fig jam and coarse walnut frangipane. This tart is a tribute to those sun-drenched days and the scent that still lingers in my memory.

WALNUT FRANGIPANE

1. Preheat the oven to 160°C fan (350°F).
2. Spread the walnuts on a baking tray (pan) and roast for 8–10 minutes until fragrant and slightly darker in colour. Remove from the oven and leave to cool slightly.
3. In a food processor, pulse the roasted walnuts with all the remaining ingredients until combined. Often when making frangipanes I would grind the nuts fully first, but for this I want the walnuts to be chopped and retain some texture. Scrape down the sides of the food processor to ensure everything is evenly mixed. Pour the walnut frangipane into the tart case (shell), spreading it out evenly.
4. Bake in the oven for 12–15 minutes until the frangipane rises and domes slightly. It should feel firm to the touch but will deflate slightly as it cools.
5. Remove from the oven and let the tart cool completely.

walnuts	150 g	5.3 oz
caster (superfine) sugar	100 g	3.5 oz
cornflour (cornstarch)	20 g	0.7 oz
plain (all-purpose) flour	20 g	0.7 oz
baking powder	4 g	1 tsp
fine sea salt	1 g	¼ tsp
soya milk	90 g	3.2 oz
extra virgin olive oil	10 g	0.4 oz
orange blossom water	5 g	1 tsp
pre-baked 23 cm (9 in) Sweet Shortcrust Pastry tart case (page 147)	1	

FIG JAM

6. Roughly chop the dried figs and place them in a small blender, then blend to a smooth, jam-like consistency. If too thick, add a teaspoon of water at a time until spreadable.
7. Spread the fig jam in an even 5 mm (¼ inch) thick layer over the baked frangipane in the tart.

dried figs	150 g	5.3 oz
water	50 g	1.8 oz

FIG LEAF CRÈME PÂTISSIÈRE

8. Wash the fig leaf well and then cut into four pieces and lay it flat in a saucepan. Pour over the milk (1) and bring it to a simmer, then remove from heat and leave to infuse for 1 hour.
9. After 1 hour, lift the leaves out and mix in the sugar and vanilla. Return the pan to the heat and bring to a simmer over a medium heat.
10. In a small bowl, prepare the slurry by mixing the cornflour with the milk (2), then add it to the simmering infused milk in the saucepan and stir with a silicone spatula until it thickens and the mixture comes to the boil.

fig leaf	1	
plant-based milk (1)	290 g	10.2 oz
caster (superfine) sugar	90 g	3.2 oz
vanilla paste	5 g	1 tsp
cornflour (cornstarch)	43 g	1.5 oz
plant-based milk (2)	40 g	1.4 oz
coconut oil (deodorised)	30 g	1 oz

11. Add the coconut oil and let it melt into the mixture, then start to slowly whisk with a small balloon whisk or spatula (so the melting oil doesn't splash) and continue whisking until it is fully incorporated and the mixture clings to the sides of the pan. Pour into a shallow dish and place a layer of cling film (plastic wrap) on the surface to prevent a skin forming. Chill in the refrigerator until set and cold.
12. Once cold, whisk with a small balloon whisk until smooth and creamy, then spread evenly over the fig jam layer, smoothing it with a spatula.

TO ASSEMBLE

13. Wash and dry the figs. Trim the stems, then slice into thin rounds, widthways.
14. Arrange the fig slices in concentric circles over the crème pâtissière, ensuring they fully cover the surface. Slightly overlap each slice for a neat and decorative look. You can trim the skins, especially if they are thick, with small round pastry cutters.
15. Warm the exotic clear glaze in a small heatproof jar in the microwave or in a saucepan.
16. Using a pastry brush, lightly glaze the fig slices to give them a glossy finish. This helps preserve their freshness and enhances their appearance.
17. Serve at room temperature or slightly chilled. It is best enjoyed on the day it is made but can be stored in an airtight container in the refrigerator for up to 2 days.

figs	6–8 (about 300 g/10.6 oz)
Exotic Clear Glaze (page 242)	for brushing

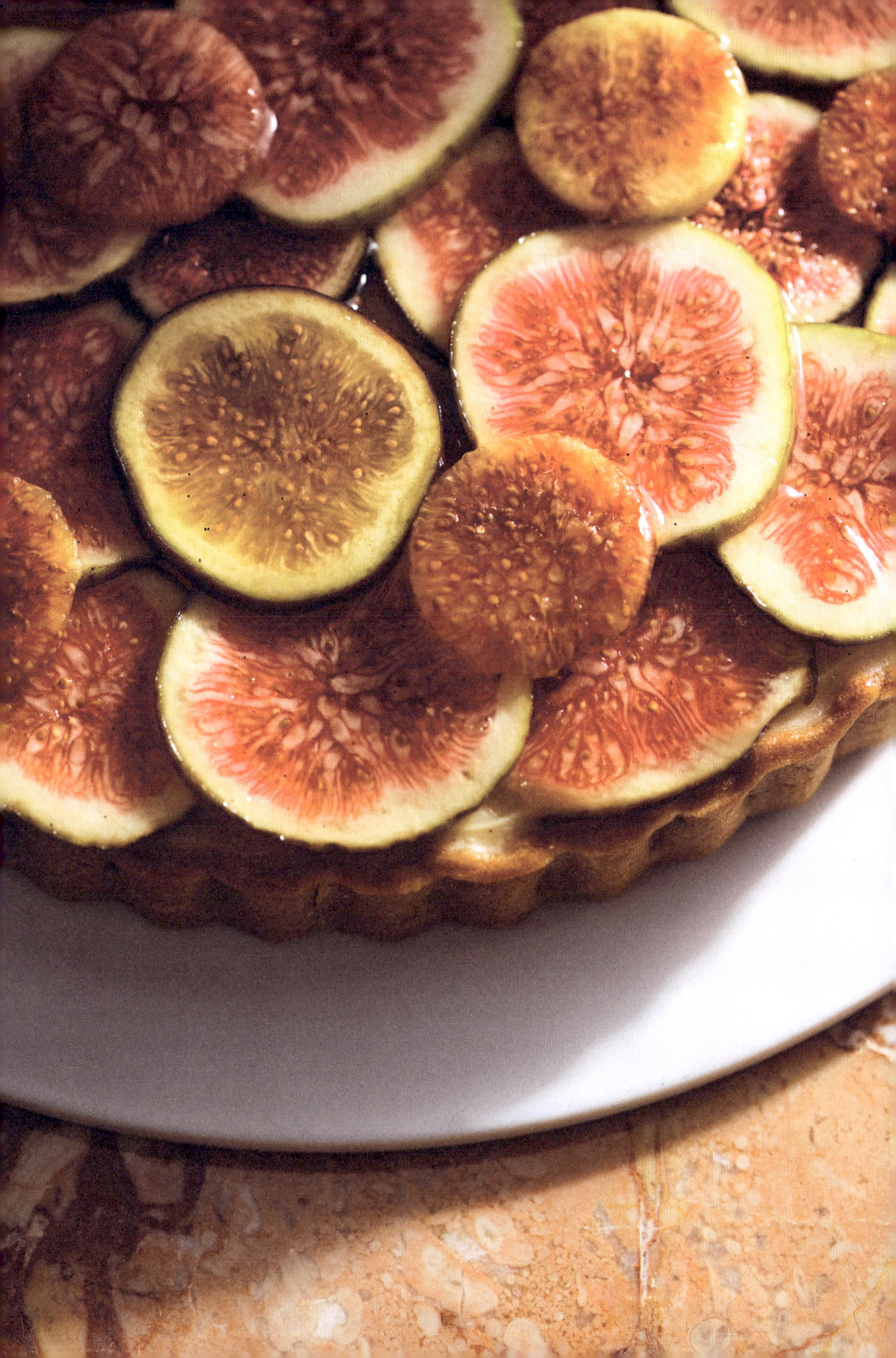

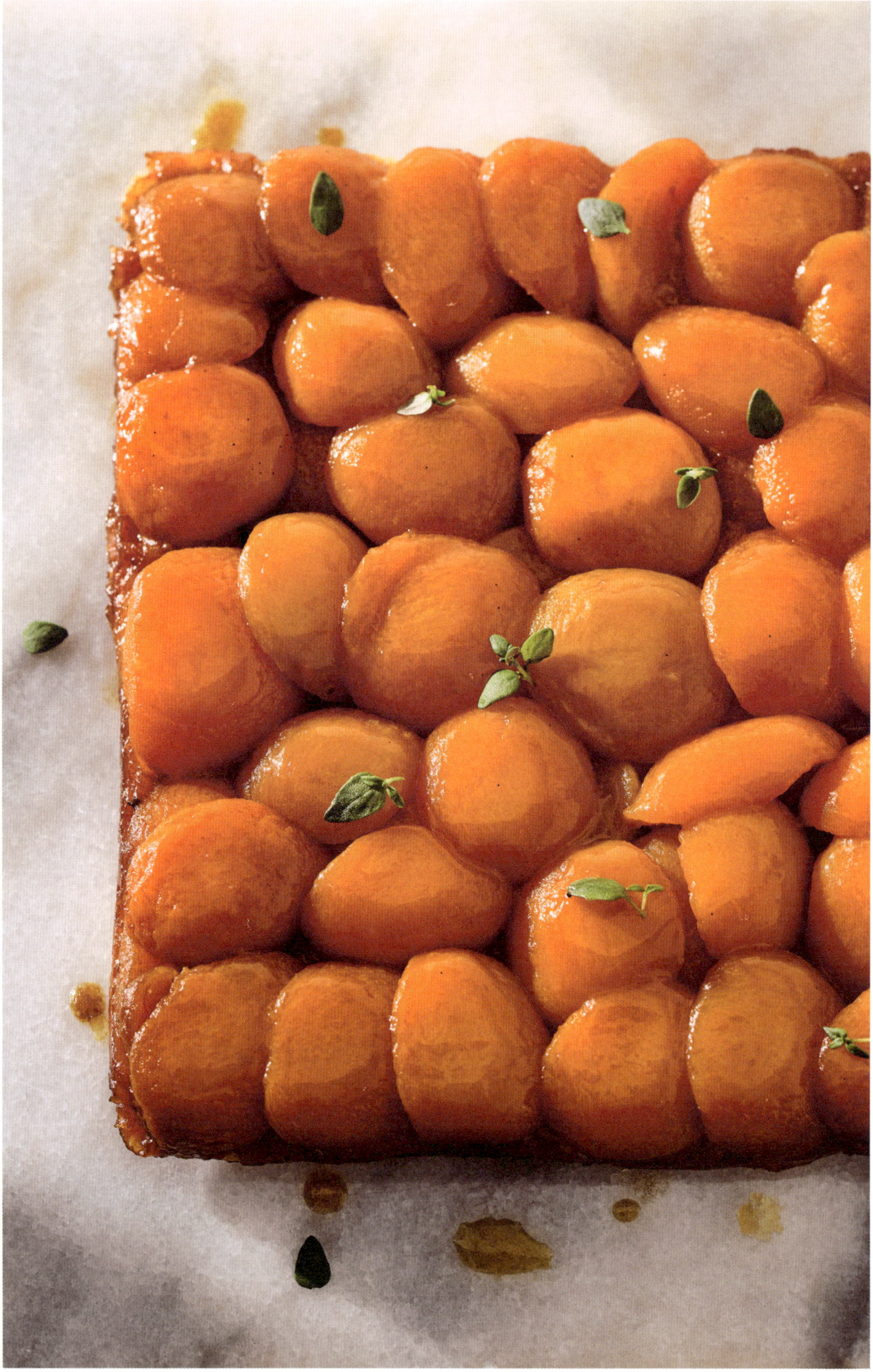

APRICOT TARTE TATIN

Makes 1 × 20 cm (8 in) tart

There's something magical about the way apricots caramelise, turning golden and intensely fragrant. This tarte tatin captures that magic, whether using fresh fruit or tinned when out of season. Nestled in a thyme-scented caramel, the apricots' tartness balances the rich, crisp pastry beneath. Once flipped, their glossy, syrupy juices soak into the layers, creating a dessert that's simple, stunning and effortlessly elegant, year-round.

caster (superfine) sugar	100 g	3.5 oz
coconut oil	30 g	1 oz
soya milk	20 g	0.7 oz
sprigs of thyme, plus extra to serve	4–5	
1 x quantity Puff Pastry (page 195)	200 g	7 oz
apricots (or fresh equivalent)	2 x 400 g tins	2 x 14 oz tins
Whipping Cream (page 238) or vanilla ice cream	to serve	

1. Preheat the oven to 180°C fan (400°F).

2. Place the sugar in a small, heavy-based saucepan over a medium heat. Leave it to melt, undisturbed, until it starts to turn golden. Swirl the pan gently but do not stir. Once the sugar has melted completely and is a deep amber colour, carefully add the coconut oil and stir it in.

3. Remove the pan from the heat and whisk in the soya milk. The caramel will bubble up – stir continuously until smooth. Pour the caramel into the base of a 20 cm (8 in) square cake tin (pan), tilting the tin slightly to spread it out evenly. Scatter the thyme sprigs over the caramel while it is still warm.

4. If using tinned apricots, drain them well and pat dry with a clean cloth to remove excess liquid. If using fresh apricots, halve and remove the stones.

5. Arrange the apricot halves, cut-sides-down, on top of the caramel in a snug, even layer – they should almost stand up, overlapping.

6. Roll out the puff pastry to a slightly larger size than the tin (about 22 cm/8½ in to allow for slight shrinkage).

7. Drape the pastry over the apricots and gently tuck in the edges around the fruit. This creates a neat shape when the tart is flipped after baking.

8. Prick the pastry a few times with a fork to allow steam to escape during baking.

9. Bake in the oven for 25–30 minutes, or until the pastry is golden brown and crisp.

10. Remove from the oven and leave to rest for about 15 minutes – this allows the caramel to settle slightly. Place a serving plate upside down over the tin. Using oven gloves, carefully and swiftly flip the tart onto the plate. Allow gravity to help release it from the tin. Remove the tin and let any excess caramel drizzle over the tart.

11. Garnish with additional fresh thyme sprigs if desired. Serve warm, ideally with some fresh whipping cream or vanilla ice cream.

MANGO LEMONGRASS TART

Makes 1 × 23 cm (9 in) tart

This tart is all about mango – layered, infused and celebrated in every bite. It starts with a crisp tart shell, which is filled with a delicate vanilla frangipane that bakes around sweet mango offcuts, intensifying their flavour. Then comes the star: a silky mango and lemongrass-infused custard, fragrant and bright, bringing a citrusy lift to the fruit's natural sweetness. To finish, fresh mango is arranged in a mesmerising swirl, catching the light and making it almost too beautiful to eat ... almost.

ALMOND FRANGIPANE AND MANGO LAYER

1. Preheat the oven to 180°C fan (400°F).

2. Pulse the almonds, sugar and cornflour in a food processor or high-powered blender. Add the remaining ingredients except the mangoes and pulse to combine – it will have a creamy texture.

3. Peel the mangoes and slice off the two 'cheeks' from either side of the stone, then trim around the stones. Reserve the cheeks and offcuts separately.

4. Use a silicone spatula to scrape the pistachio frangipane into the tart case (shell), then place the mango offcuts on top. Bake in the oven for 12–15 minutes until the top domes, then remove from the oven and leave to cool completely – it will deflate slightly.

blanched almonds	120 g	4.2 oz
caster (superfine) sugar	80 g	2.8 oz
cornflour (cornstarch)	16 g	0.7 oz
plant-based milk	72 g	2.5 oz
extra virgin olive oil	16 g	0.7 oz
plain (all-purpose) flour	8 g	2 tsp
baking powder	3 g	¾ tsp
fine sea salt	0.5 g	⅛ tsp
large, ripe but firm mangoes	2–3	
pre-baked 23 cm (9 in) Short Sweet Pastry tart case (page 147)	1	

MANGO LEMONGRASS CUSTARD

5. Chop the lemongrass into 2 cm (¾ in) pieces, then place in a powerful blender with all the remaining ingredients except the coconut oil and blend well.

6. Pour the mixture through a sieve (fine-mesh strainer) into a saucepan to remove all the fibres from the lemongrass.

7. Heat the mixture over a medium heat while constantly stirring until it begins to simmer and thicken. It should start to boil and thicken all the way through. Add the coconut oil and stir gently so the melting coconut oil doesn't splash. Stir until the mixture clings to the side of the pan. Pour into a shallow dish and place a layer of cling film (plastic wrap) on the surface to prevent a skin forming.

8. Use a balloon whisk to whisk until smooth and creamy, then spread the mango custard evenly over the frangipane layer.

lemongrass stalks	2	
plant-based milk	160 g	5.6 oz
mango, chopped	85 g	3 oz
caster (superfine) sugar	75 g	2.6 oz
vanilla paste	5 g	1 tsp
cornflour (cornstarch)	35 g	1.2 oz
coconut oil (deodorised)	34 g	1.2 oz

TO ASSEMBLE

9. Place the mango cheeks flat-side down on a cutting board and use a sharp knife to slice them into 1–2 mm (1/16 in) thick slices while keeping the shape intact. Hold the knife almost vertically and draw the tip through the mango cheeks so they stay in place – cutting with a horizontal slicing motion will move the pieces out of place and make this task difficult. Placed a hand on each side of a cheek, perpendicular to the direction of the cuts, and push in opposite directions to fan out the pieces. Arrange the thin slices of fresh mango on top of the custard, spiralling to form a rose (start from the centre and add layers spiralling outwards).

10. Warm the exotic clear glaze in a small heatproof jar in the microwave or in a saucepan. Using a pastry brush, lightly glaze the mango slices to give them a glossy finish. Serve at room temperature or slightly chilled. This tart is best enjoyed on the day it is made but can be stored in an airtight container in the refrigerator for up to 2 days.

Exotic Clear Glaze (page 242) — for brushing

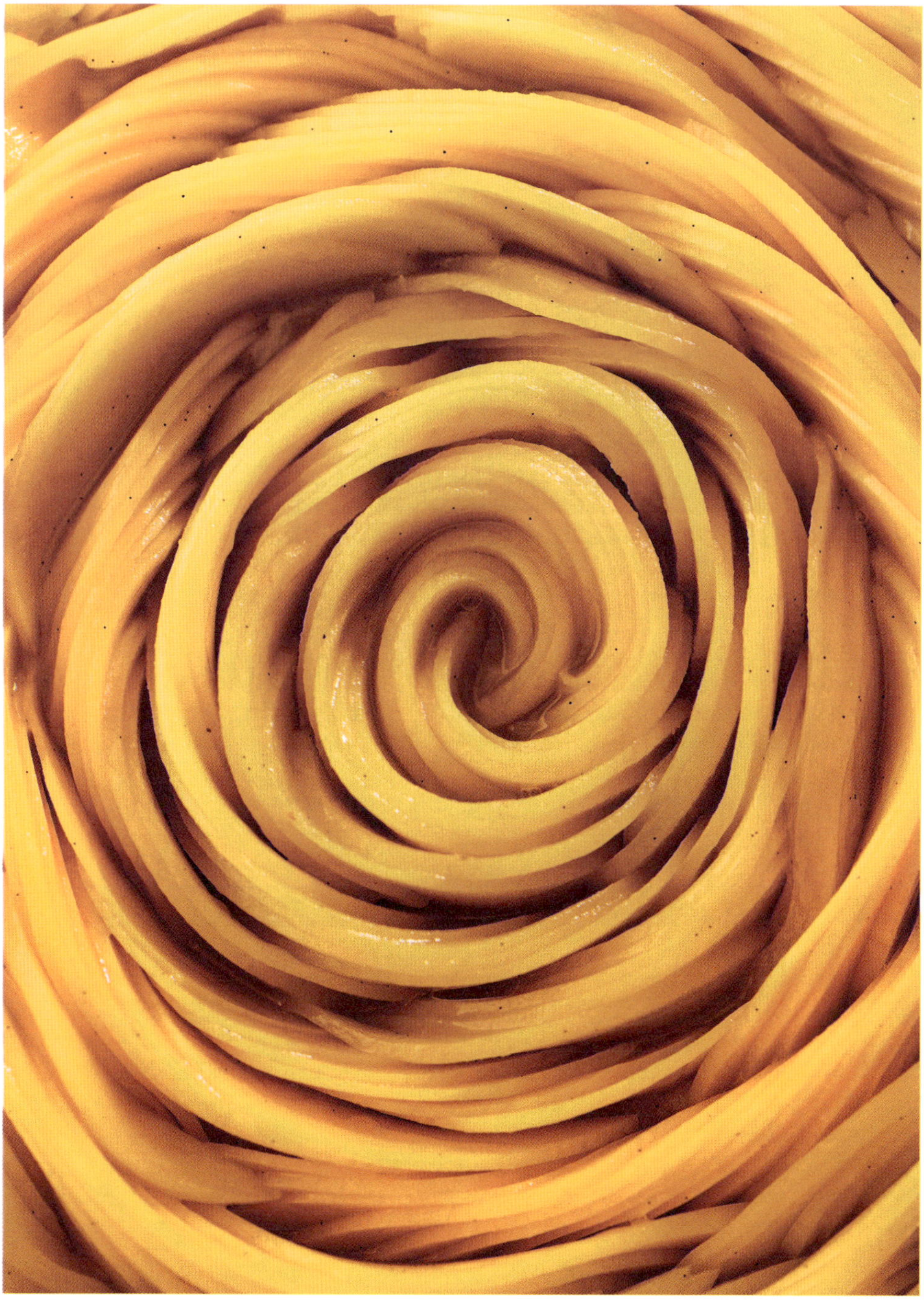

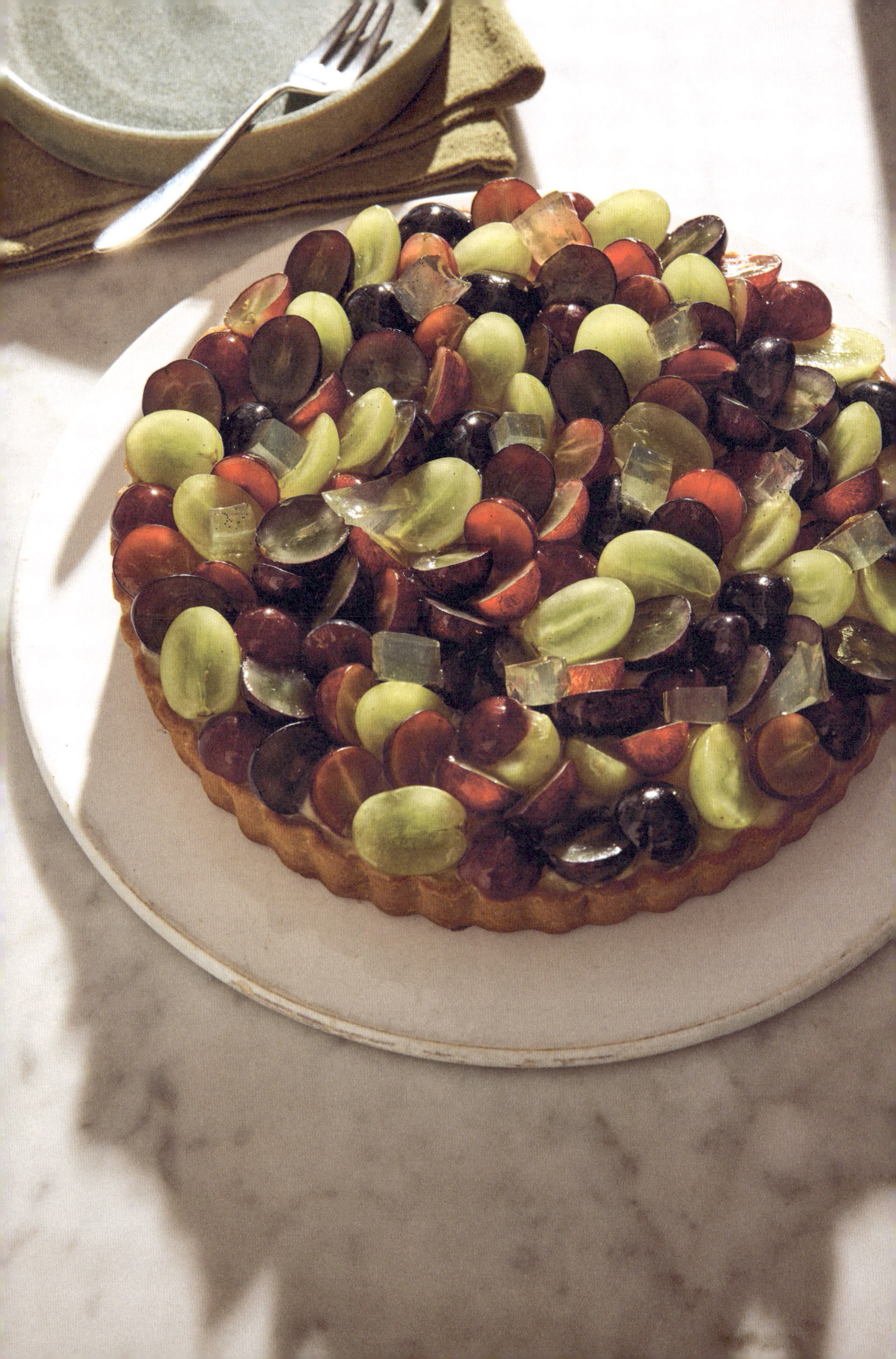

GRAPE TART

Makes 1 × 23 cm (9 in) tart

As I was finishing my apprenticeship at a Sydney hotel, I once made the mistake of placing half a grape on a classic mini fruit tart – only to be swiftly berated by the executive pastry chef: 'Chef, I have never seen a grape on a fruit tart! When you're head chef, you can put grapes on your fruit tart. Start again!' Well, now I can – and I do. I love the bright, juicy crunch of table grapes, so I developed a tart where they take centre stage, piled over a silky custard for a refreshing twist on tradition.

ALMOND AND PECAN FRANGIPANE

1. Preheat the oven to 170°C fan (375°F).
2. Pulse the almonds, pecans, sugar and cornflour in a food processor or high-powered blender. Add the milk, oil, flour, baking powder and salt and pulse to combine – it will have a creamy texture.
3. Use a silicone spatula to scrape the frangipane into the tart case (shell) and spread it out to smooth the top.
4. Slice the grapes in half and press the halves into the frangipane. Bake in the oven for 12–15 minutes until the top domes, then remove from the oven and leave to cool fully – it will deflate slightly.

raw almonds	75 g	2.6 oz
pecans	75 g	2.6 oz
caster (superfine) sugar	100 g	3.5 oz
cornflour (cornstarch)	20 g	0.7 oz
plant-based milk	90 g	3.2 oz
extra virgin olive oil	10 g	0.4 oz
plain (all-purpose) flour	10 g	2 tsp
baking powder	4 g	1 tsp
fine sea salt	1 g	¼ tsp
pre-baked 23 cm (9 in) Short Sweet Pastry tart case (page 147)	1 quantity	
seedless grapes	5	

SAUTERNES CUSTARD

5. Combine the Sauternes, milk (1), sugar and vanilla paste in a high-sided saucepan. Whisk to combine, then place over a medium heat and bring just to the edge of a simmer.
6. In a small bowl, whisk the cornflour with milk (2) to form a smooth slurry. Once the liquid in the pan is warm, slowly pour in the slurry while stirring continuously with a silicone spatula. Continue stirring for a few minutes until the mixture thickens and comes to a gentle boil – make sure to scrape the bottom and sides of the pan to avoid catching. Remove the pan from the heat as soon as it thickens.
7. Add the coconut oil and gently whisk (to avoid splashing the melting oil) until the mixture clings to the sides of the pan and there are no oily streaks.
8. Pour the hot custard into a shallow dish and press a layer of cling film (plastic wrap) onto the surface to prevent a skin forming. Refrigerate until completely cool and set.
9. To use, transfer the set custard to a bowl and whisk with a balloon whisk until smooth and creamy, then spread over the cooled tart base filled with the frangipane.

Sauternes dessert wine	60 g	2 oz
plant-based milk (1)	120 g	4.2 oz
caster (superfine) sugar	60 g	2 oz
vanilla paste	5 g	1 tsp
cornflour (cornstarch)	32 g	1.1 oz
plant-based milk (2)	35 g	1.2 oz
coconut oil (deodorised)	20 g	0.7 oz

TO ASSEMBLE

10 Melt the glaze in short bursts in the microwave or in a small saucepan over a medium heat, then set aside.

11 Cut the grapes in half and place them around the edges of the tart first, then fill inwards to cover all the custard.

12 With a pastry brush, generously dab the hot melted glaze to cover the fruit well, then chill in the refrigerator for 15 minutes.

13 Serve at room temperature or slightly chilled. This is best enjoyed on the day it is made but can be stored in an airtight container in the refrigerator for up to 2 days.

14 To slice, use a sharp knife and a gentle sawing motion to cut through the grapes, then press down to cut into the pastry. Wipe down the knife with a dish towel between cuts for the neatest slices.

Exotic Clear Glaze (page 242)	55 g	2 oz
mixed colour seedless grapes		1 bunch each

ANZAC MUSCOVADO CUSTARD PIE

Makes 1 × 23 cm (9 in) tart

A base of crumbled Anzac biscuits (you can buy them or make your own using the recipe from my book *A New Way to Bake*) forms a buttery, toasty foundation, perfectly complementing the custard that follows. If you can't find Anzac biscuits, replace them with 250 g (8.8 oz) oat biscuits and 50 g (1.8 oz) desiccated (dried shredded) coconut, pulsed together in a food processor.

The custard itself is a dream, it's velvety, rich and packed with the deep, complex notes of black treacle (molasses). When poured over the biscuit base and left to set, the result is something effortlessly elegant yet deeply comforting.

BISCUIT BASE

1. Blend the biscuits in a food processor until they form fine crumbs.
2. Melt the coconut oil in a small saucepan over a low heat, then pour the coconut oil into the biscuit crumbs and blend until well combined.
3. Press the biscuit mixture into the base of a 23 cm (9 in) pie dish, ensuring an even layer across the bottom and spreading it slightly up the sides. Place in the refrigerator to chill for at least 1 hour.

Anzac biscuits (cookies)	300 g	10.6 oz
coconut oil	80 g	2.8 oz

MUSCOVADO CUSTARD

4. Pour the milk (1) into a high-sided saucepan along with the muscovado sugar and vanilla paste. Stir with a whisk to combine. Bring the mixture to a simmer over a medium heat.
5. In a small bowl, combine the cornflour with the milk (2) and fine sea salt. Mix until the cornflour is completely dissolved and no lumps remain.
6. When the milk mixture in the saucepan comes to a simmer, reduce the heat to low. Pour in the cornflour mixture, stirring continuously. The mixture will thicken immediately. Continue stirring until the mixture comes to the boil and starts to bubble, then remove from the heat.
7. Pour the custard into a stand mixer fitted with the paddle attachment, add the coconut oil and mix on low speed until it cools to 35°C (95°F) – this will ensure a silky, just-set texture.
8. Pour the warm, smooth custard onto the prepared Anzac base, trying to do this in one movement by pouring it into the centre of the base to avoid needing to smooth it.
9. Place the pie in the refrigerator for at least 2 hours to chill.

plant-based milk (1)	550 g	19.4 oz
muscovado sugar	200 g	7 oz
vanilla paste	5 g	1 tsp
cornflour (cornstarch)	70 g	2.5 oz
plant-based milk (2)	75 g	2.6 oz
fine sea salt	1 g	¼ tsp
coconut oil (deodorised)	70 g	2.5 oz

TO SERVE

10. Once the pie is fully set, slice. The best way to do this is with a knife dipped in a jug (pitcher) of hot water or warmed gently with a blowtorch – wipe down between cuts for a flawless cut. Serve with a dollop of freshly whipped cream.

Whipping Cream (page 238), lightly whipped	to serve

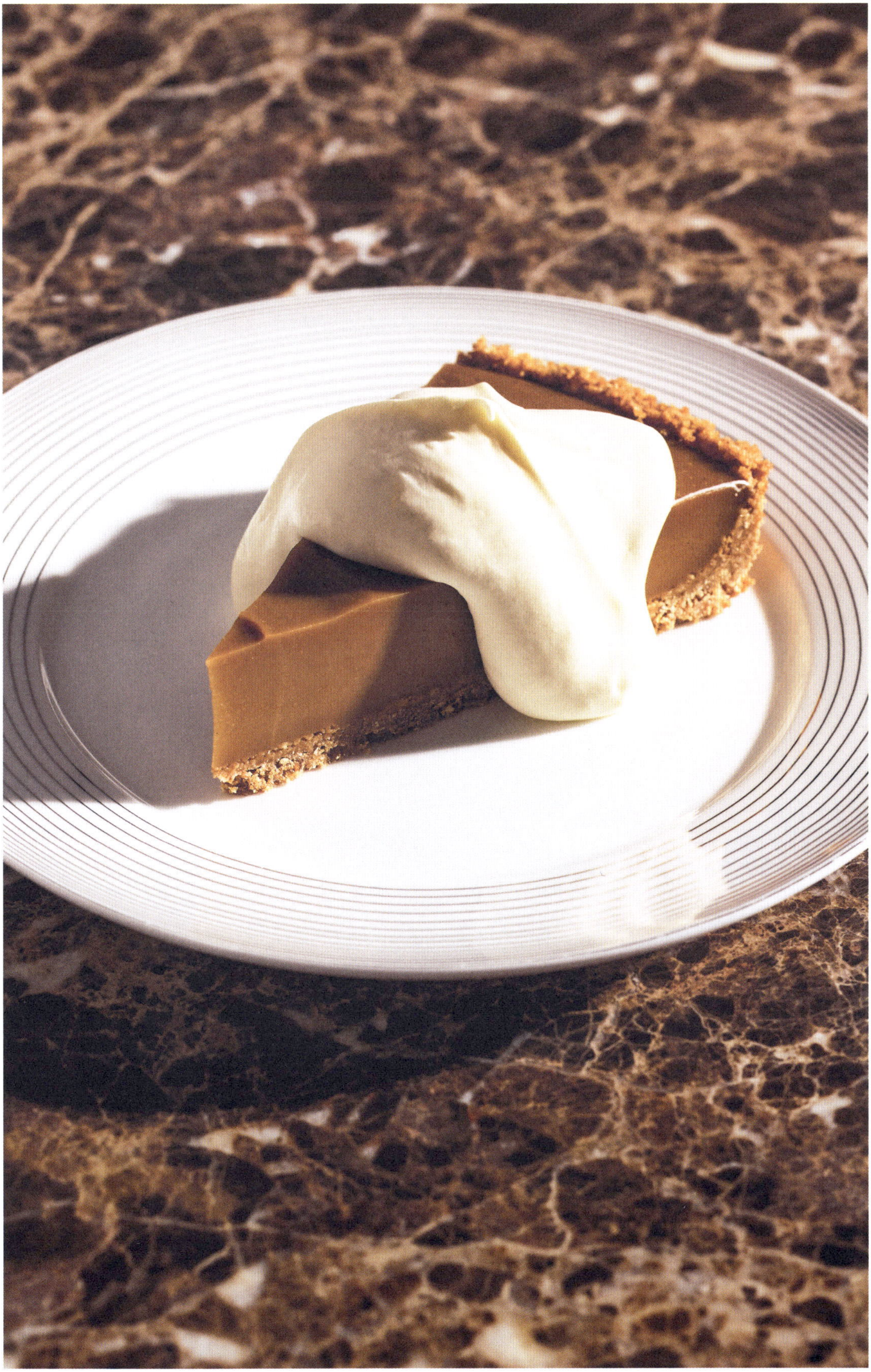

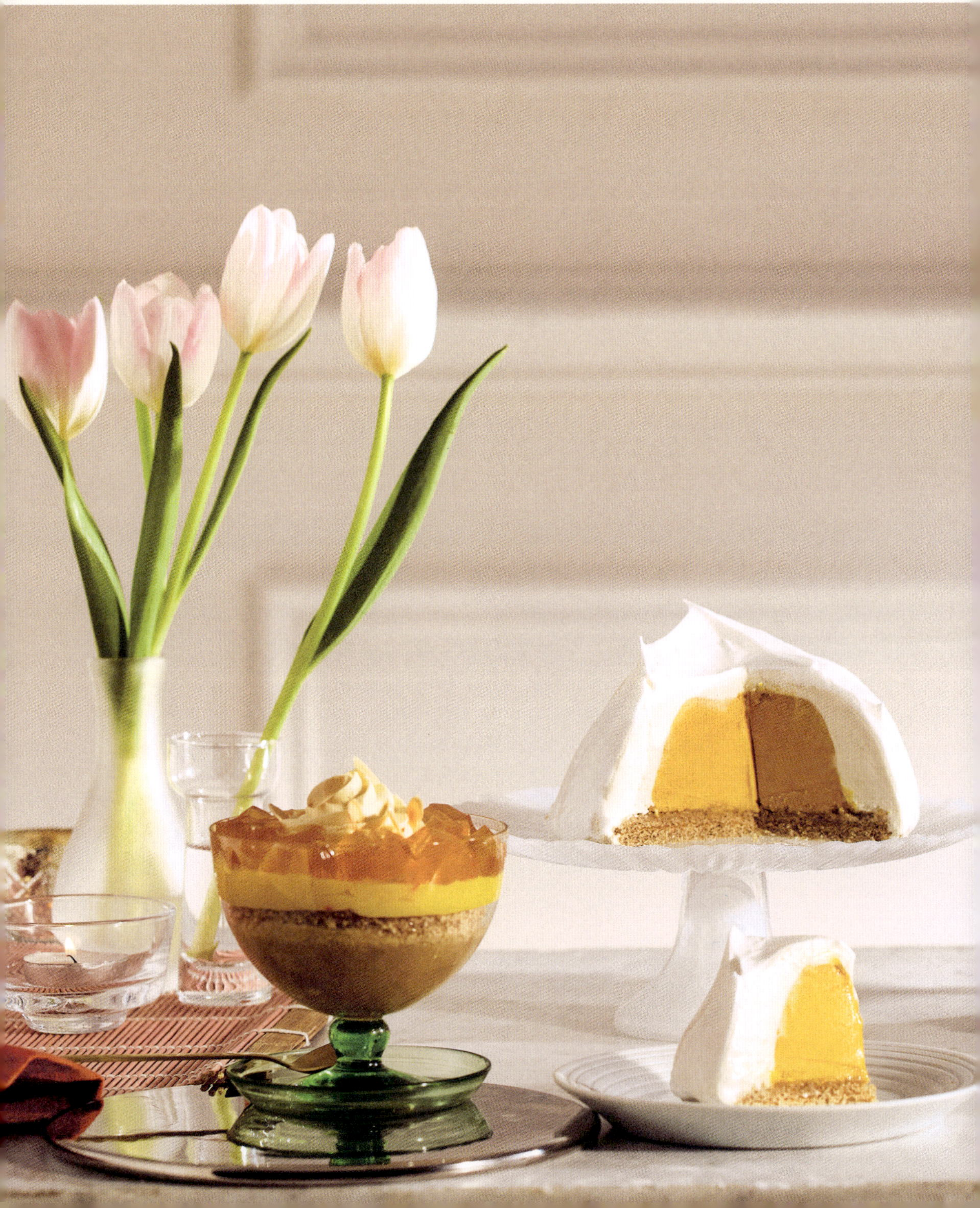

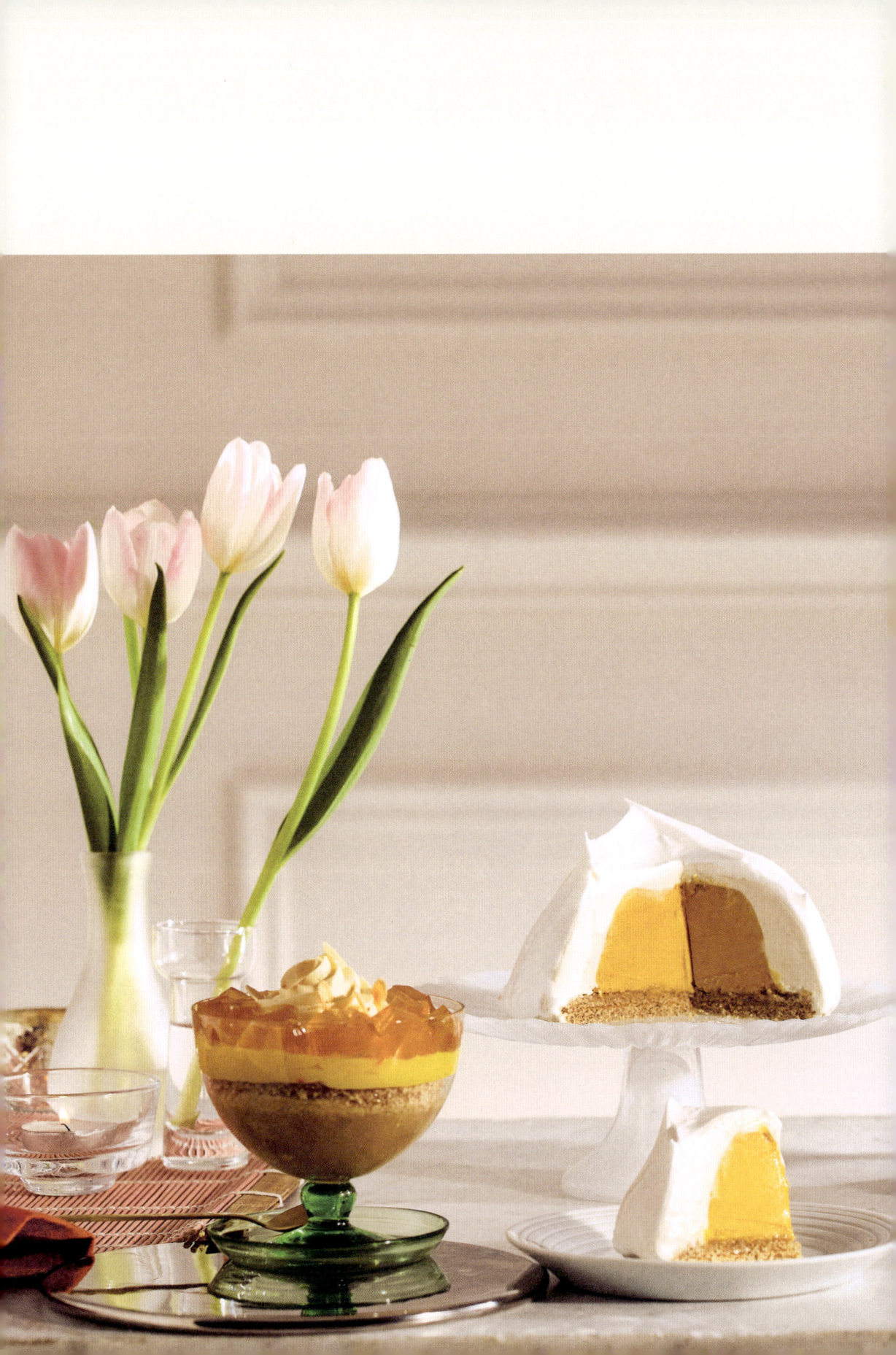

6 SOME ROOM FOR DESSERT

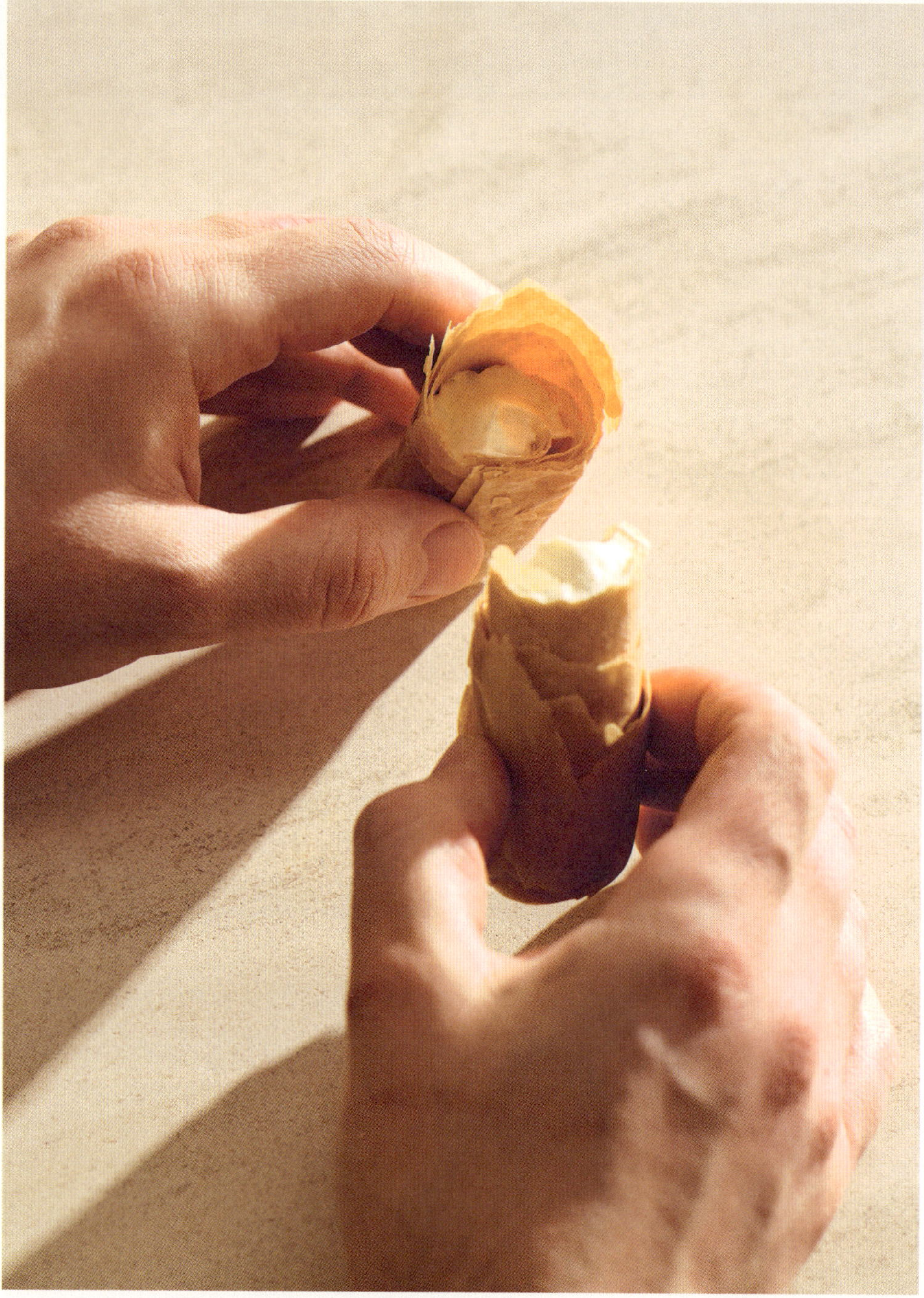

NOSTALGIC
INDULGENCE

There's a special kind of joy in a dessert that feels effortless – light, refreshing and just the right note to end a meal on. This chapter is a celebration of those final bites you always have space for. These recipes are designed to be satisfying without heaviness, refined without fuss, and deeply flavourful without being overwhelming.

Here, I reimagine mousse three ways, using principles borrowed from classic pastry but interpreted through a plant-based lens. There's a playful twist on baklava, layered with crisp pastry, and a modern trifle that balances nostalgia with clarity. You'll also find a new take on bombe Alaska.

At the heart of this chapter is a dessert that, to me, captures the essence of summer: a simple, striking composition that's as versatile as it is pure. In this version, I share an expression of the fig – a fruit close to my heart and a symbol of slow, sun-drenched sweetness. These are the kinds of desserts that stay with you – light, memorable and always welcome, no matter how full you thought you were.

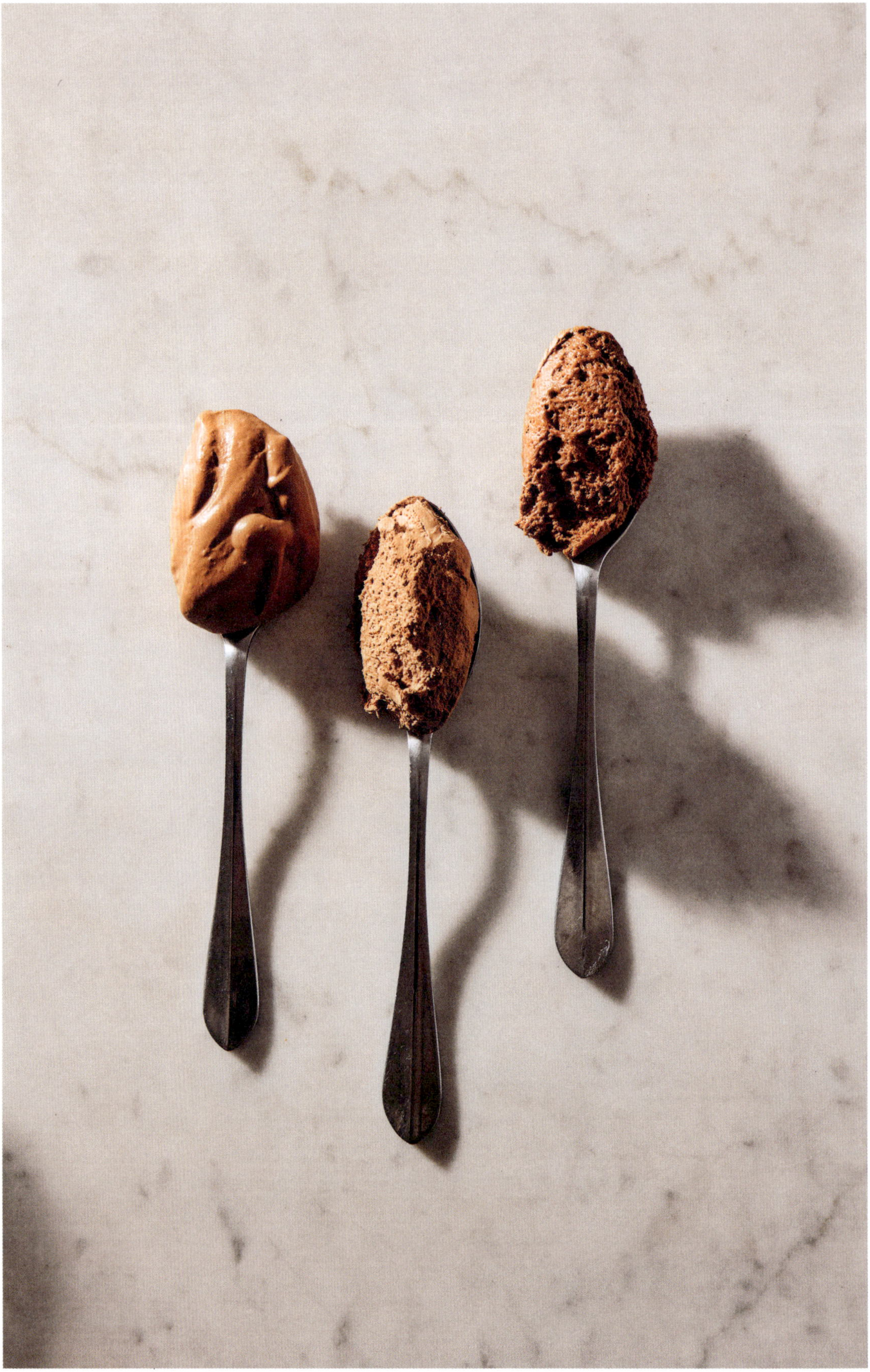

CHOCOLATE MOUSSE THREE WAYS

Serves 4–6

Mousse au chocolat is one of the most exquisite ways to enjoy chocolate – so here are three recipes that offer it in different textures and levels of chocolate intensity. Each one works beautifully with dark chocolate containing 65–80 per cent cocoa solids. Choose one you love the flavour of. Blends with no specific origin can be further rounded out with 1 teaspoon vanilla paste or the seeds from a vanilla pod (bean). The soya milk in these recipes (although any plant-based milk can be used) can also be infused with tea, coffee, spices or citrus zest for more adventurous flavours (see overleaf). Once the mousses have been prepared, they can be frozen and gently defrosted in the refrigerator. Top with chocolate shavings, cocoa nibs or a dusting of cocoa (unsweetened) powder for texture and contrast.

RICH AND DENSE: WHIPPED GANACHE BASE

A rich and pure-tasting mousse that whips directly from a blended chocolate ganache, this is the densest of the three and has a luxurious, truffle-like texture.

1   Heat the milk (1) in a small saucepan over a medium heat until just steaming.
2   Chop the chocolate and place it into a heatproof jug (pitcher). Pour the hot milk over the chocolate and let it sit for 1 minute.
3   Blend with a hand-held blender, scraping down the sides of the jug if needed, until completely smooth.
4   Add the chilled milk (2) and blend again until glossy and emulsified.
5   Pour into a container, place a layer of cling film (plastic wrap) on the surface, and chill for at least 4 hours.
6   Once chilled, transfer the ganache to the chilled bowl of a stand mixer fitted with the whisk attachment and whip for 2–4 minutes until light and aerated.
7   Spoon or pipe the mousse into bowls or glasses and chill in the refrigerator for 20 minutes, or up to 1 day, before serving.

soya milk (1)	200 g	7 oz
dark chocolate min. 65% cocoa solids	250 g	8.8 oz
soya milk (2), chilled	250 g	8.8 oz

FLUFFY: AQUAFABA MERINGUE BASE

Light and airy, with a bubbly texture from the whipped aquafaba, this is the lightest mousse in texture, with a clean, melt-in-the-mouth finish.

1   Heat the milk in a saucepan until steaming.
2   Chop the chocolate and place it in a heatproof bowl. Pour the hot milk over the chocolate and let it sit for 1 minute, then whisk until smooth. Cover with a layer of cling film (plastic wrap), then leave to cool slightly. It is best to fold the meringue into the ganache when it is lukewarm or at room temperature, but not cold.

soya milk	140 g	4.9 oz
dark chocolate min. 65% cocoa solids	210 g	7.3 oz
aquafaba (page 244)	100 g	3.5 oz
caster (superfine) sugar	100 g	3.5 oz
cream of tartar	0.7 g	¼ tsp

3   Place the aquafaba, sugar and cream of tartar in a stand mixer fitted with the whisk attachment. Whisk on high speed until the meringue forms stiff, glossy peaks – this may take 6–8 minutes.

4   Ensure the chocolate ganache base is no longer warm, then fold in one-third of the meringue to lighten it. Fold in the remaining meringue in two additions, keeping as much air in the mixture as possible.

5   Spoon or pipe the mousse into bowls or glasses and chill in the refrigerator for at least 1 hour, or up to 1 day, before serving.

CREAMY: CUSTARD BASE WITH WHIPPED CREAM

This version has a creamy, velvety texture with a clean finish. It's soft, rich and elegant – the most mousse-like in a classical sense.

1   Combine the milk, sugar and tapioca starch in a saucepan and whisk until smooth. Place over a medium heat and stir constantly for a couple of minutes until the mixture just begins to bubble and thickens enough to coat a spatula.

2   Chop the chocolate and place it in a heatproof bowl. Pour the custard mixture over the chocolate and let it sit for 1 minute, then whisk until glossy. Place a layer of cling film (plastic wrap) on the surface and leave to cool to room temperature.

3   In the chilled bowl of a stand mixer, whip the whipping cream for 3–4 minutes until medium peaks form.

4   Fold one-third of the cream into the cooled chocolate custard to loosen it, then fold in the rest in two additions until fully incorporated and there are no streaks.

5   Spoon or pipe into bowls or glasses and chill in the refrigerator for at least 1 hour, or up to 1 day, before serving.

soya milk	200 g	7 oz
caster (superfine) sugar	35 g	1.2 oz
tapioca starch	5 g	1 tsp
dark chocolate min. 65% cocoa solids	150 g	5.3 oz
Whipping Cream (page 238)	150 g	5.3 oz

FLAVOUR VARIATIONS

Vanilla paste | Add 1 teaspoon to any ganache or custard base.

Orange zest | Infuse 1 teaspoon zest in the hot milk, then strain before using as directed.

Espresso powder | Dissolve 1 teaspoon in the hot milk for a mocha version.

Chilli flakes | Infuse ½ teaspoon in the hot milk, then strain for a warm, spicy note.

Cardamom pods | Lightly crush 3 pods and steep in the hot milk for 5 minutes, then strain before use.

Cinnamon stick | Simmer ½ stick in the milk, then remove before using.

Whisky | Add 1 tablespoon to the finished ganache or custard once cooled.

Sea salt flakes | Sprinkle on top before serving for a refined finish.

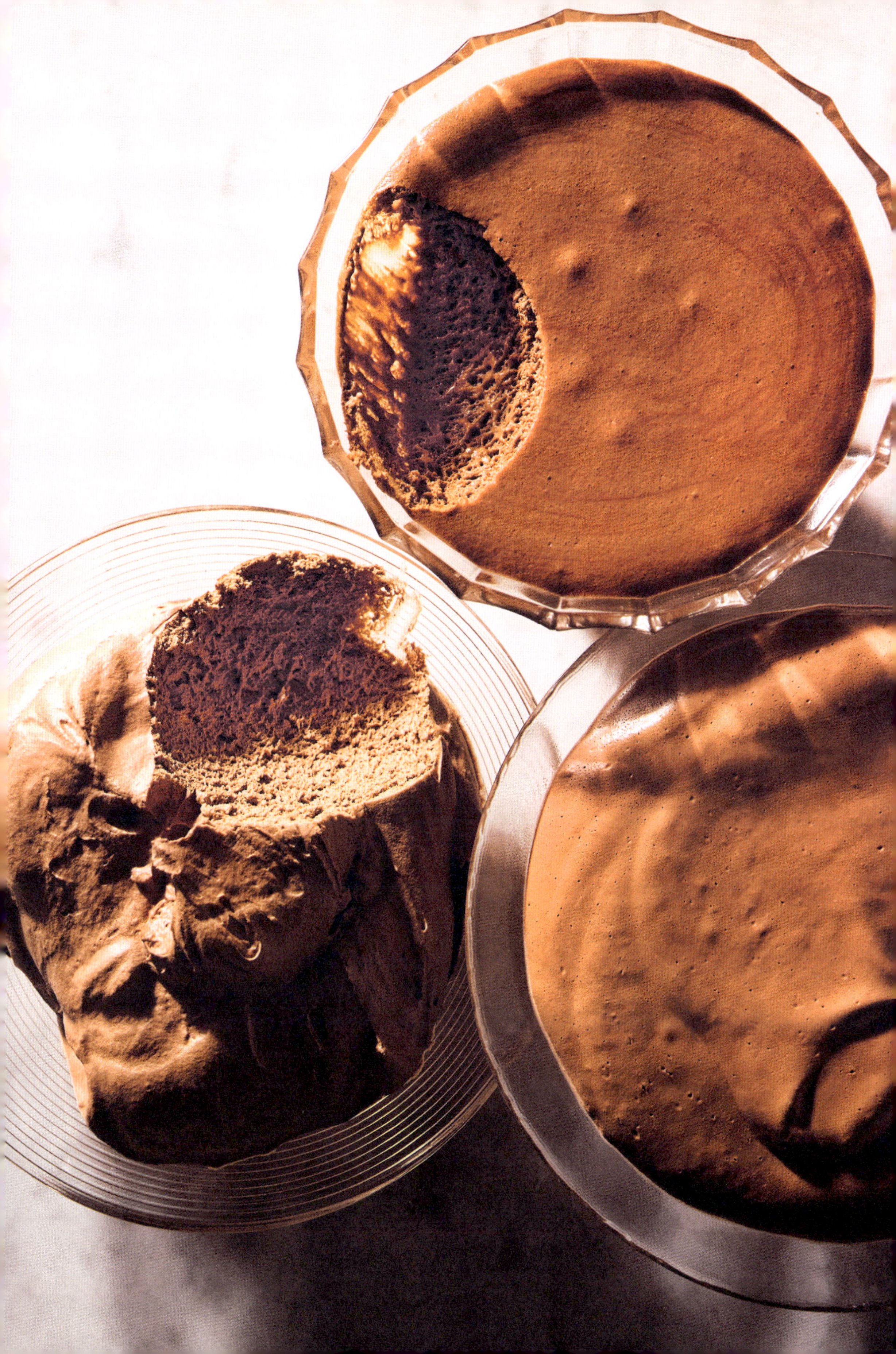

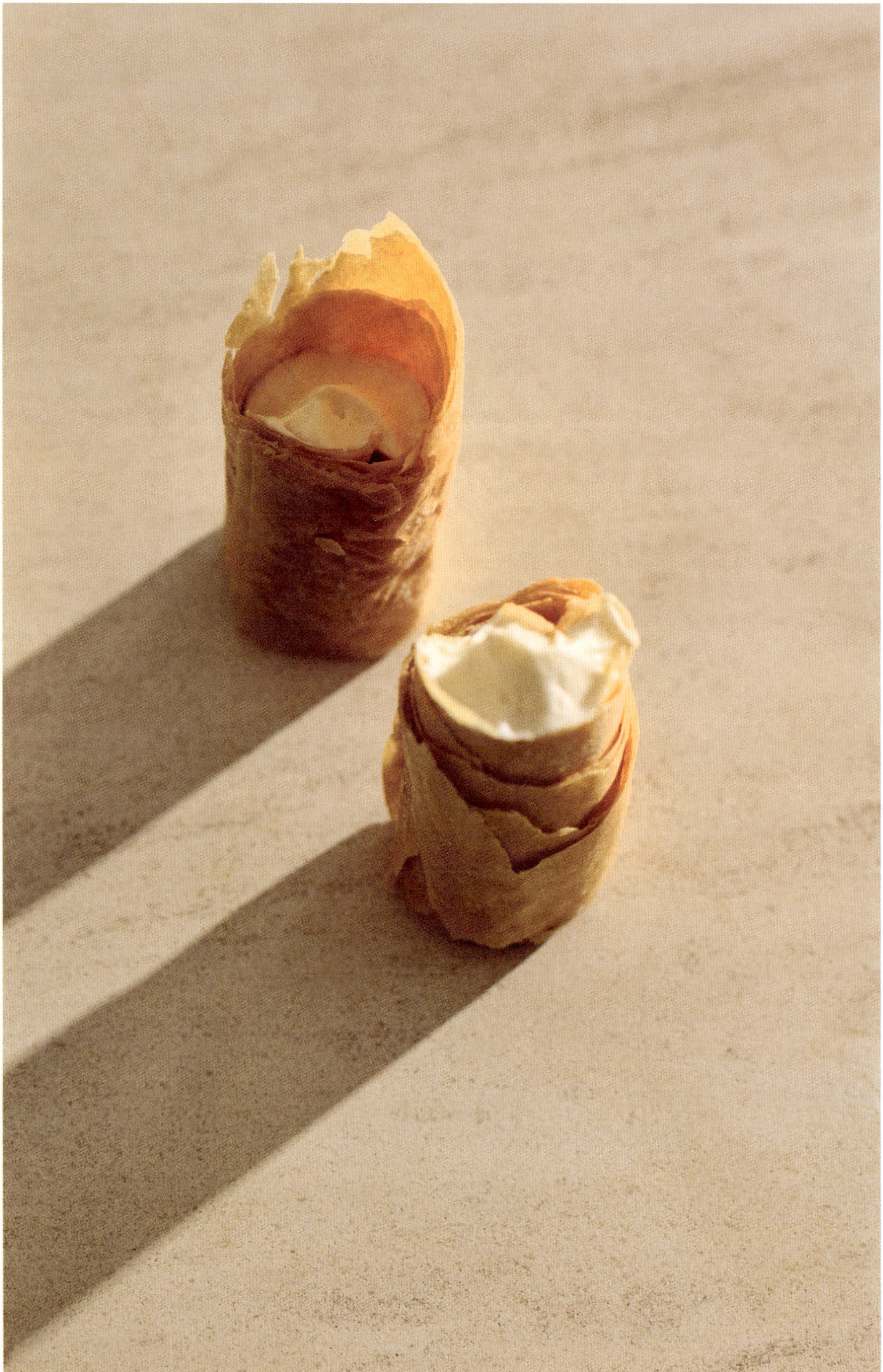

BAKLAVA PARFAIT ROLL

Serves 12

This dessert was inspired by a trip to Greece. It was 40°C (104°F) and I spotted a sweet shop selling a frozen treat that looked like a baklava cigar. I assumed the filo would be soggy but was surprised to bite into perfect shards of delicate crunch around frozen cream. I've recreated the magic here by adapting my no-churn ice cream and using orange blossom water to complement the pistachio. It is then piped into golden, baked filo rolls.

FILO ROLLS

1. Preheat the oven to 160°C fan (350°F) and position a shelf in the middle of the oven. Wrap 12 cannoli tube moulds in a strip of baking parchment – this is so the melting sugar doesn't stick to the stainless steel and make it impossible to remove the delicate baked filo.

2. Take a single sheet of filo pastry and lay it on a clean work surface. Keep the remaining sheets covered with cling film (plastic wrap) and a damp dish cloth to prevent them drying out.

3. Lightly brush the filo sheet with olive oil, then flip it over and brush the other side.

4. Cut the sheet into strips measuring 11 cm (4¼ in) wide, or 5 mm (¼ in) shorter than your cannoli tubes.

5. Place a tube at one end of the filo rectangle and roll it up, then place it seam-side down on a large baking tray (pan). Repeat with the remaining filo to make 12 rolls, leaving 2–3 cm (¾–1¼ in) between them.

6. Bake in the oven for 12–15 minutes, or until golden and crisp. Remove from the oven and carefully slide the filo rolls off the tubes while warm. Transfer to a wire rack to cool completely.

filo pastry sheets	6 sheets
olive oil	for brushing
icing (powdered) sugar	for dusting

ORANGE BLOSSOM NO-CHURN PARFAIT

7. Melt the coconut oil in a small saucepan over a medium heat or in a microwave-safe bowl in the microwave, then leave to cool slightly.

8. Combine the milk, liquid glucose, sugar, vanilla paste, orange blossom water and salt in a blender. Blend for 20 seconds.

9. Add the melted coconut oil and blend for 1 minute until smooth and glossy. If any oily streaks remain, blend a little longer. It should warm up to at least 35°C (95°F).

10. Pour it into a shallow dish and place a layer of cling film (plastic wrap) on the surface to prevent a skin forming, then refrigerate for 4 hours, or until chilled to 5°C (41°F).

11. Whip the chilled mixture in a stand mixer fitted with the whisk attachment for 4–6 minutes until fluffy and thick.

12. Transfer to a piping (pastry) bag and pipe into the cooled filo rolls.

coconut oil (deodorised)	180 g	6.4 oz
soya milk	290 g	10.2 oz
liquid glucose or light corn syrup	112 g	4 oz
vanilla paste	4 g	1 tsp
orange blossom water	2 g	½ tsp
flaky sea salt	1.5 g	⅓ tsp

TIP

You can also serve these fresh with the chilled and whipped ice cream base and forgo freezing.

MANGO AND VANILLA BOMBE ALASKA

Serves 8–10

Growing up in Australia, one of the best-ever ice cream bars you could buy was the mango and macadamia Weis bar – a memory that inspired this bombe Alaska. Layers of vibrant mango sorbet and creamy vanilla–macadamia gelato sit over a soft coconut sponge, all sealed under peaks of aquafaba meringue. Built in nested bowls and frozen ahead, it's a nostalgic tribute with a dramatic reveal.

COCONUT SPONGE

1. Preheat the oven to 180°C fan (400°F). Line the base of a 20 cm (8 in) springform cake tin (pan) with baking parchment.
2. Blend the flour, desiccated coconut and baking powder in a small food processor until very fine and slightly clumping.
3. In a large bowl, whisk together the milk, sugar, oil and vanilla. Add the dry ingredients and whisk gently until just combined. Pour into the prepared tin and smooth the top.
4. Bake in the oven for 10–12 minutes until golden and springy. Remove from the oven and leave to cool completely in the tin.

plain (all-purpose) flour	105 g	3.7 oz
desiccated (dried shredded) coconut	31 g	1.1 oz
baking powder	4.2 g	1 tsp
soya milk	105 g	3.7 oz
caster (superfine) sugar	96 g	3.4 oz
groundnut (peanut) oil	21 g	0.7 oz
vanilla extract	3 g	¾ tsp

MANGO SORBET

5. Blend the mango and sugar together in a blender until smooth. Scrape into a container and chill in the refrigerator for 1 hour.
6. Churn in an ice-cream machine according to the manufacturer's instructions.
7. Meanwhile, line a 14–15 cm (5½–6 in) bowl that is 8–9 cm (3–3½ in) deep with cling film (plastic wrap) or scrunched baking parchment.
8. Press the churned sorbet into the bowl, smoothing the top.
9. Freeze until solid, then remove and unwrap. Keep frozen.

ripe mango flesh	400 g	14.1 oz
caster (superfine) sugar	100 g	3.5 oz

MACADAMIA–VANILLA GELATO

10. Preheat the oven to 150°C fan (300°F).
11. Spread out the macadamia nuts on a baking tray (pan) and roast in the oven for 15 minutes. Remove from the oven and leave to cool.
12. Put the cooled nuts into a food processor or high-powered blender along with all the remaining ingredients and blend for about 1 minute until smooth.
13. Strain through a nut milk bag or muslin (cheesecloth) into a container and chill in the refrigerator for 3 hours.
14. Once chilled, churn in an ice-cream machine according to the manufacturer's instructions.

macadamias	150 g	5.3 oz
plant-based milk or water	490 g	1 lb 1.7 oz
caster (superfine) sugar	120 g	4.2 oz
fine sea salt	1 g	¼ tsp
vanilla paste or seeds from 1 scraped pod (bean)	3 g	¾ tsp

15 Line a 20–22 cm (8–8½ in) bowl that is 8–10 cm (3–4 in) deep with cling film or scrunched baking parchment.

16 Spoon the churned gelato into the bowl, spreading it along the base and up the sides.

17 Press the frozen mango sorbet dome into the centre and cover with more gelato to encase the sorbet.

18 Trim the coconut sponge into a round that fits the diameter of the bowl and press onto the top to seal.

19 Wrap and freeze for at least 1 hour, or up to 1 month.

AQUAFABA MERINGUE

20 Place the aquafaba in a stand mixer fitted with the whisk attachment and whisk until frothy.

21 Add the cream of tartar, then slowly incorporate the sugar.

22 Continue whisking for about 10 minutes until stiff, glossy peaks form. Use immediately.

aquafaba (page 244)	150 g	5.3 oz
cream of tartar	1.5 g	½ tsp
caster (superfine) sugar	250 g	8.8 oz

TO ASSEMBLE

23 Remove the frozen bombe from the freezer. Dip the base of the bowl briefly into warm water if needed.

24 Lift out the bombe using the overhanging wrap and remove the lining.

25 Insert a large fork into the base of the sponge to hold the dome.

26 Dip the dome into the bowl of meringue to coat it completely, letting the effect of suction form natural peaks. Re-dip once or twice for a dramatic finish.

27 Optional: lightly torch the meringue for colour and flavour.

28 Place on a chilled serving plate and return to the freezer until ready to serve.

29 Slice with a hot, clean knife. Serve immediately.

30 If making ahead, the ice cream bases will last for up to 3 months in the freezer, and the meringue will last for a couple of hours in the freezer.

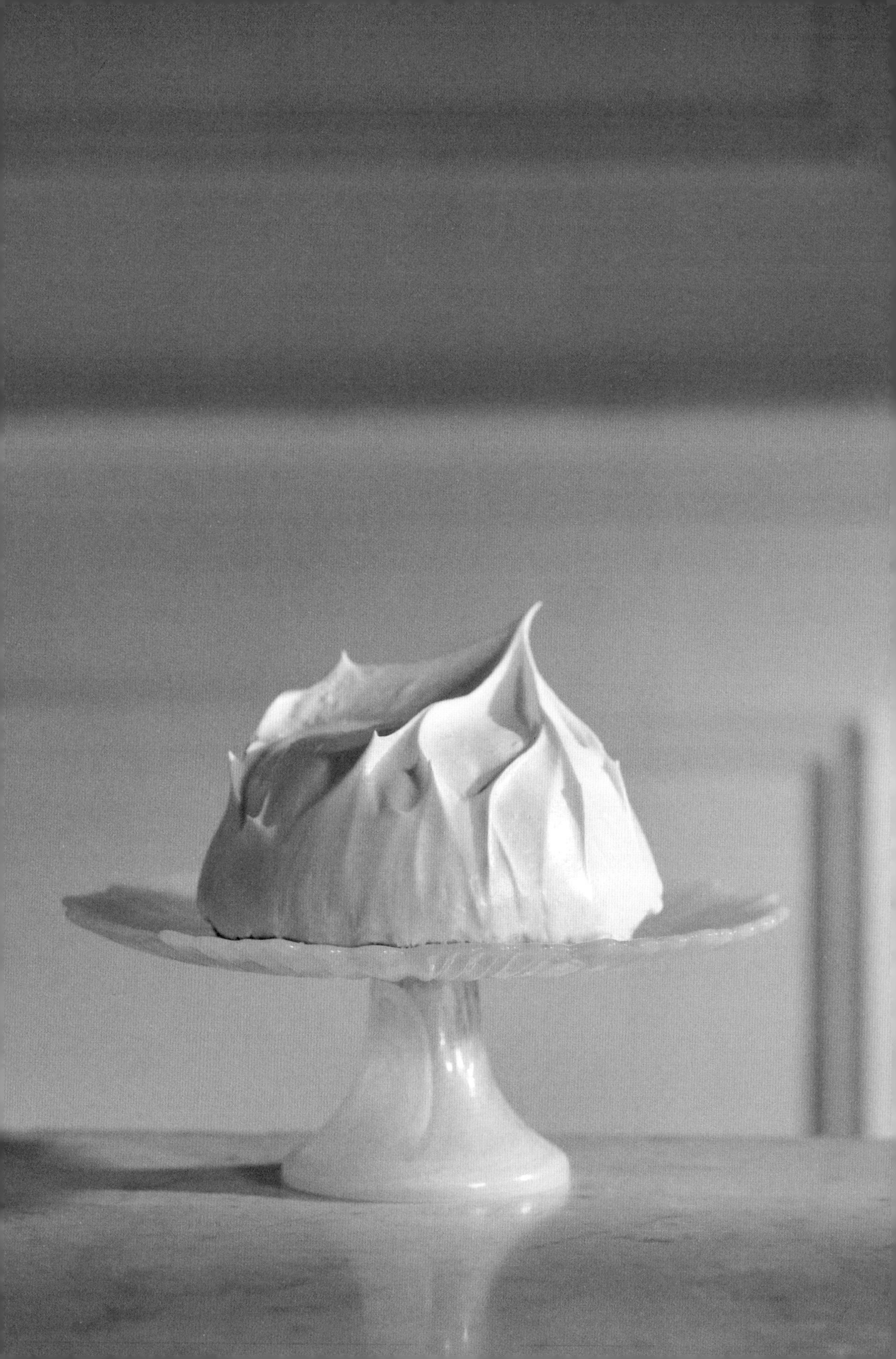

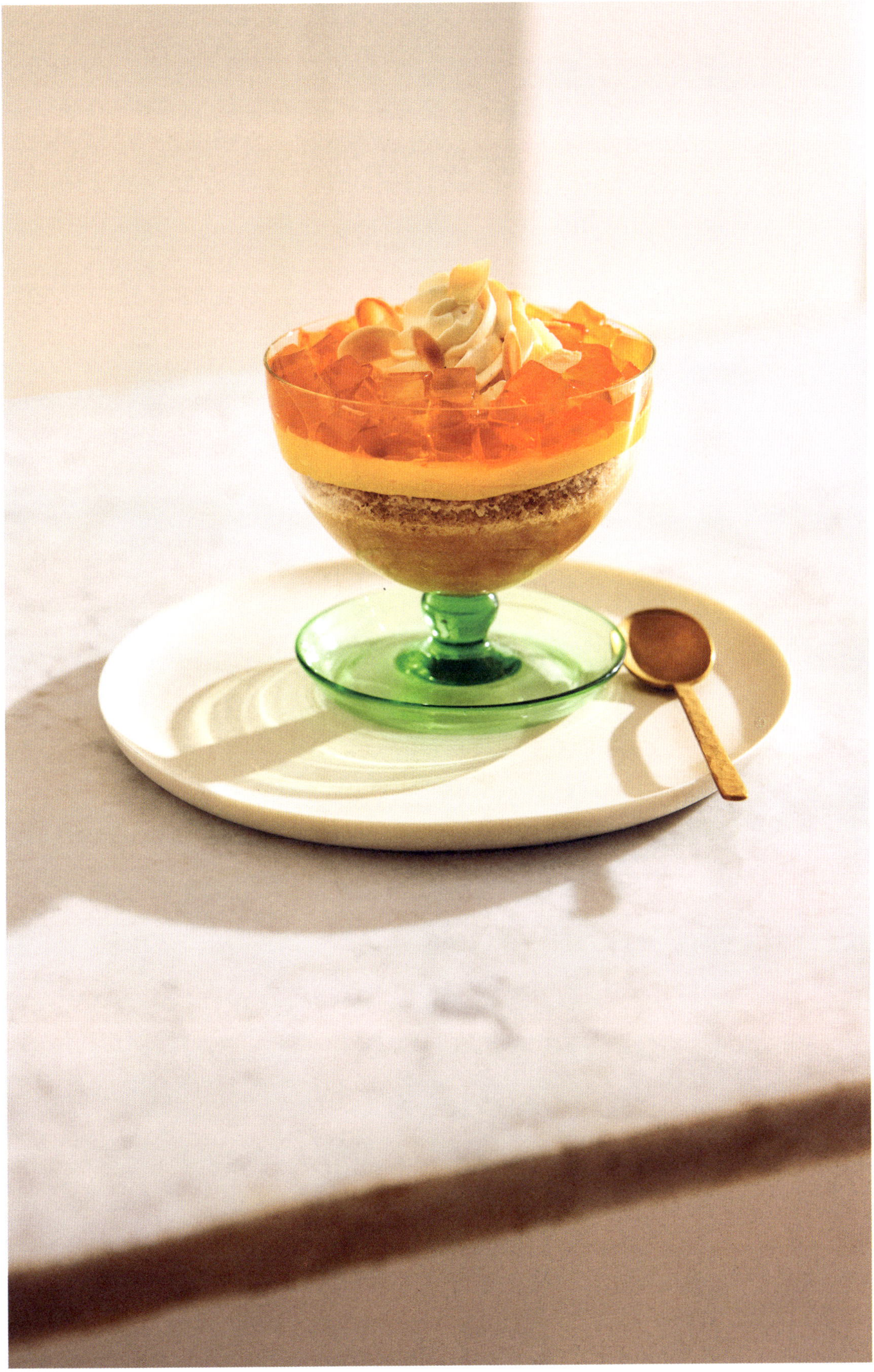

ROASTED ALMOND, PEAR AND SAFFRON TRIFLE

Makes 1 large or individual trifles to serve 6–8

This elegant trifle layers a variety of light, smooth and delicate elements: saffron-infused crème pâtissière, whipped roasted almond cream, a soft roasted almond sponge, light pear compôte and softly set caramel jelly cubes. The inspiration came from my father's village in the mountains of northern Lebanon, where at the end of summer, they preserve pears from their orchards in syrup. The pears are stuffed or surrounded with roasted almonds, so the fruits slowly take on caramel flavours as they cook. That memory is carried through here, paired with saffron for its earthy floral note and brilliant golden hue.

ROASTED ALMOND SPONGE

1. Preheat the oven to 160°C fan (350°F). Lightly oil the base of a 20 cm (8 in) springform cake tin (pan) and line with baking parchment, smoothing it flat.
2. Spread out the almonds on a baking tray (pan) and roast in the oven for 15–18 minutes until golden in the middle when broken in half. Remove from the oven and leave to cool. Increase the oven temperature to 180°C fan (400°F).
3. Pulse the flour, cooled almonds and baking powder in a small food processor until fine and well combined.
4. In a large bowl, whisk together the milk, sugar and oil until smooth.
5. Add the dry ingredients to the wet ingredients and whisk gently until just combined.
6. Pour into the prepared tin and level with a spatula. Bake in the oven for 12–15 minutes, or until golden and springy.
7. Remove from the oven and leave to cool in the tin.
8. If preparing individual trifles, cut out rounds using a plain round cutter to match your glass size (about 6–7 cm/ 2¼–2¾ in) – the sponge layer will sit about a third of the way from the bottom. Set aside.

raw almonds	35 g	1.2 oz
plain (all-purpose) flour	115 g	4.1 oz
baking powder	5 g	1 tsp
soya milk	115 g	4.1 oz
caster (superfine) sugar	105 g	3.7 oz
groundnut (peanut) oil, plus extra for greasing	24 g	0.8 oz

PEAR COMPÔTE

9. Peel, core and dice the pears into 1 cm (½ in) cubes.
10. Heat the sugar in a large saucepan until it melts and turns a golden caramel colour.
11. Carefully add the water (it will bubble) and stir to dissolve. This forms a light syrup at about 25 per cent sugar density.
12. Add the diced pears and simmer gently for 8–10 minutes until the pears are just soft.
13. Drain the pears through a sieve (fine-mesh strainer) set over a bowl to reserve the poaching syrup.
14. Set aside two-thirds of the poached pears, then blend the remaining third in a blender to create a purée.
15. Fold the puréed and diced pears together to form a compôte. Chill until needed.

6–7 Conference or Bosc pears	850–950 g	1 lb 14 oz–2 lb 2 oz
caster (superfine) sugar	180 g	6.3 oz
water	650 g	1 lb 7 oz

SOME ROOM FOR DESSERT

SAFFRON CRÈME PÂTISSIÈRE

16. Crush the saffron in a mortar and pestle, then add a splash of boiling water (just over a tablespoon) and continue grinding – this will help extract the flavour and colour.

17. In a saucepan, heat the milk (1) with the saffron water and sugar over a medium heat until just steaming.

18. In a bowl, whisk together the cornflour, custard powder and milk (2) to form a smooth paste.

19. Gradually whisk a little of the hot milk mixture into the cornflour mixture, then pour it into the pan with the rest of the milk. Cook over a medium heat, whisking constantly, until thickened and bubbling – this should happen quickly.

20. Remove from the heat and whisk in the coconut oil until smooth – slowly at first, so it doesn't splash.

21. Pour it into a shallow dish and place a layer of cling film (plastic wrap) on the surface to prevent a skin forming, then refrigerate until fully chilled.

saffron strands	8	
boiling water	20 g	0.7 oz
plant-based milk (1)	270 g	9.5 oz
caster (superfine) sugar	90 g	3.2 oz
cornflour (cornstarch)	28 g	1.0 oz
custard powder	15 g	0.5 oz
plant-based milk (2)	40 g	1.4 oz
coconut oil (deodorised)	30 g	1 oz

CARAMEL JELLY CUBES

22. Pour the poaching syrup into a saucepan and add the agar-agar. Bring to a rolling simmer and cook for 1 minute, whisking constantly.

23. Pour into a shallow tray to a depth of about 1 cm (½ in), then chill until set (about 1 hour). Cut into 1 cm (½ in) cubes.

24. Sprinkle a little water on the surface and gently separate the cubes using your fingers. Slide a flat scraper or spatula along the base of the tray to release the jelly cubes without breaking them. Set aside.

reserved pear poaching syrup (see left)	750 g	1 lb 10 oz
agar-agar powder	2 g	½ tsp

ROASTED ALMOND CHANTILLY

25. Preheat the oven to 160°C fan (350°F) and line a baking tray (pan) with baking parchment. Spread out the almonds on the prepared baking tray and roast in the oven for 10–12 minutes until golden and fragrant. Remove from the oven and leave to cool completely.

26. Place the cooled roasted nuts in a food processor or high-powered blender along with all the remaining ingredients and blend until silky smooth. The mixture should warm slightly to help emulsify the cocoa butter.

27. Pour it into a shallow dish and place a layer of cling film (plastic wrap) on the surface to prevent a skin forming, then chill for at least 4 hours.

28. Once chilled, transfer the mixture to the chilled bowl of a stand mixer fitted with the whisk attachment and whip for about 5 minutes until medium peaks form.

blanched almonds	84 g	3 oz
caster (superfine) sugar	90 g	3.2 oz
xanthan gum (optional)	0.3 g	⅛ tsp
soya milk	420 g	14.8 oz
cocoa butter (deodorised)	108 g	3.8 oz
fine sea salt	1.2 g	¼ tsp
vanilla pod (bean) or paste	1 pod or 1 tsp	

TO ASSEMBLE

29 Spoon or pipe the pear compôte into individual glasses or one deep 20 cm (8 in) trifle dish.

30 Press a disc of the roasted almond sponge on top of the compôte.

31 Spoon or pipe a layer of saffron crème pâtissière.

32 Arrange the caramel jelly cubes in a ring around the edge, followed by a rosette of roasted almond Chantilly in the middle.

33 Garnish with a few saffron threads, edible flowers or slivered almonds, if desired.

34 Chill until ready to serve. This is best enjoyed within 48 hours.

saffron threads, edible flowers or slivered almonds, to decorate (optional)	84 g	3 oz

A PERFECT SUMMER DESSERT

Serves 6

This is a dessert that celebrates the fleeting joys of summer – a spoonful of contrasting textures and barely there infusions that melt on the tongue almost as soon as you put them in your mouth. Served in a glass, the dessert layers fig leaf-infused custard, olive oil gelato and granita with fresh figs, which provide soft ripeness beneath the chill.

The beauty of this dish is its endless adaptability. You can swap fig leaves for bay leaves or cherry blossom, or for refreshing sencha or jasmine green tea; replace the figs with fresh berries, nectarines or plums; or infuse the milk with jasmine, lemon verbena or toasted green tea. The granita can be spiked with herbal tisanes, shiso or mint; and the ice cream reimagined with nuts like almonds or pistachios. It's a template more than a rule – one that allows summer to speak through every glass.

FIG LEAF OLIVE OIL ICE CREAM

1 Wash the fig leaves and trim them if needed, but don't shred them. Place in a saucepan with the milk and cashews over a medium heat and bring just to a simmer, then remove from the heat, cover and leave to infuse in the refrigerator overnight (8–12 hours).

2 The next day, remove and discard the fig leaves. Pour the infused mixture into a high-powered blender. Add the oil, sugar and vanilla paste, then blend until completely smooth. The mixture should be silky and emulsified.

3 Pour into an ice-cream machine and churn according to the manufacturer's instructions. Alternatively, pour into a shallow tray and freeze, stirring every 30 minutes until the texture becomes thick and smooth, like soft gelato.

fig leaves	4	
soya milk	500 g	1 lb 2 oz
cashews	100 g	3.5 oz
extra virgin olive oil	50 g	1.8 oz
caster (superfine) sugar	120 g	4.2 oz
vanilla paste	5 g	1 tsp

FIG LEAF CUSTARD

4 Wash the fig leaves and trim them if needed, but don't shred them. Place in a saucepan with the milk (1) over a medium heat and bring just to a simmer, then remove from the heat, cover and leave to infuse for at least 1 hour.

5 Once infused, remove and discard the fig leaves. Split open the vanilla pod and scrape the seeds into the milk, then return the saucepan to a medium heat.

6 Meanwhile, whisk the cornflour with the milk (2) to form a smooth slurry.

7 Once the milk begins to steam again, whisk in the sugar, followed by the slurry. Stir constantly with a silicone spatula until the custard thickens and coats the back of the spatula.

8 Remove the pan from the heat, pour the custard mixture into a shallow dish and place a layer of cling film (plastic wrap) on the surface to prevent a skin forming, then leave to cool completely.

9 When ready to use, whisk in a bowl with a balloon whisk until silky smooth.

fig leaves	2	
soya milk (1)	300 g	10.6 oz
vanilla pod (bean)	1	
cornflour (cornstarch)	20 g	0.7 oz
soya milk (2), chilled	2 tbsp	
caster (superfine) sugar	60 g	2 oz

FIG LEAF GRANITA

10 Combine the water and sugar in a saucepan over a low heat. Heat gently, stirring until the sugar has completely dissolved.

11 Wash the fig leaves and add to the pan, then simmer for 5 minutes.

12 Remove the pan from the heat and leave to infuse for 30 minutes.

13 Strain and discard the leaves. Pour the mixture into a shallow tray and transfer to the freezer.

14 For a flakier texture, scrape the surface with a fork every 30–60 minutes as it freezes. For a fluffier texture (which I prefer) let it freeze solid, then rest the tray on a folded dish towel and use a fork to rake from one end to the other, reaching all the way to the base to create fine, feathery crystals.

15 Store in the freezer until needed.

water	500 g	1 lb 2 oz
caster (superfine) sugar	85 g	3 oz
fig leaves	3	

TO ASSEMBLE

16 Slice the figs into quarters or halves, depending on size.

17 Spoon 2 tablespoons of the fig leaf custard into the base of six serving glasses.

18 Add a few pieces of fresh fig on top.

19 Spoon 1–2 tablespoons of granita around the figs and over the custard.

20 Finish with a rocher or small scoop of the fig leaf ice cream in the centre.

21 Serve immediately while the granita is fluffy and the ice cream is firm.

figs	3–4

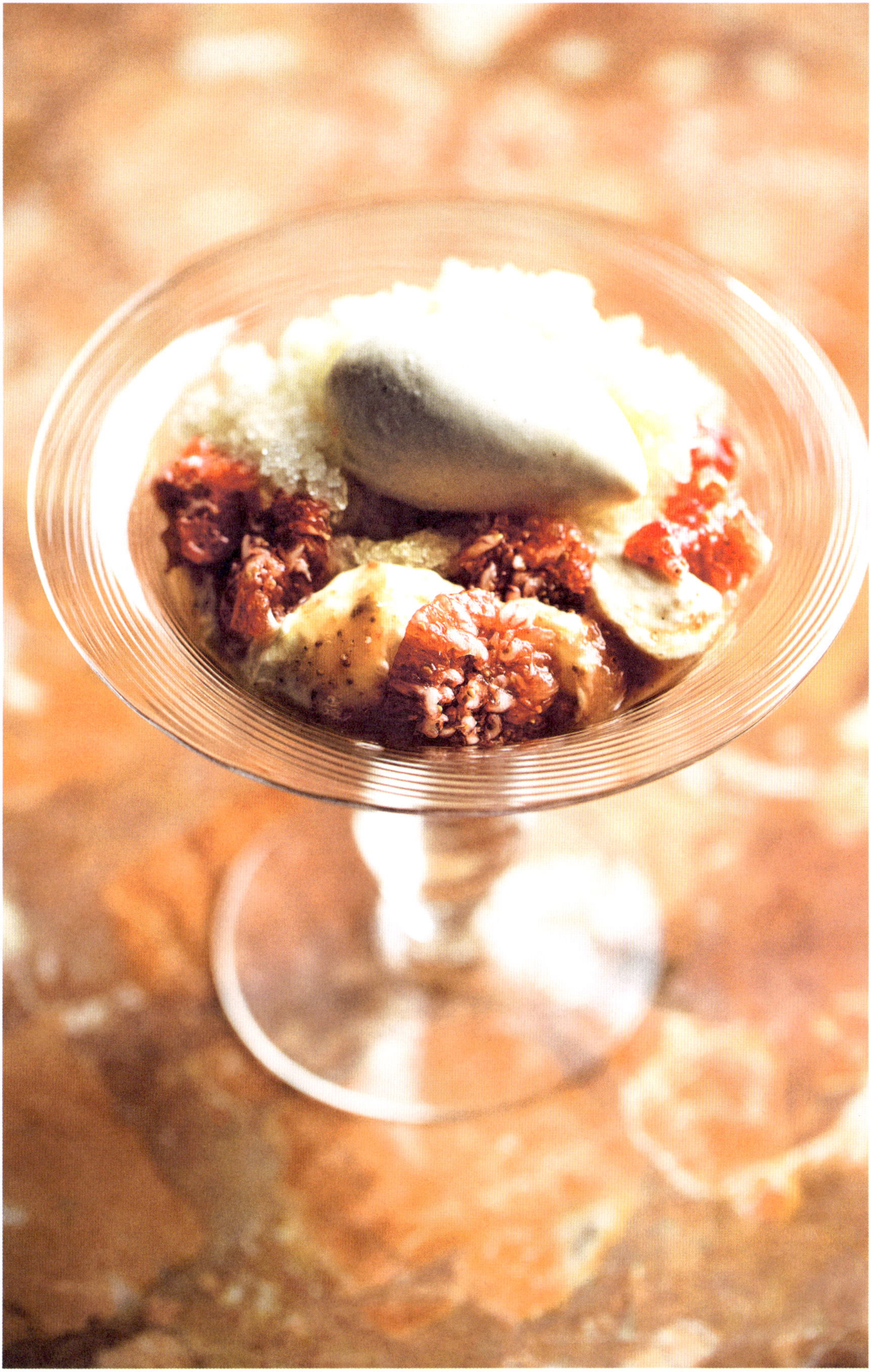

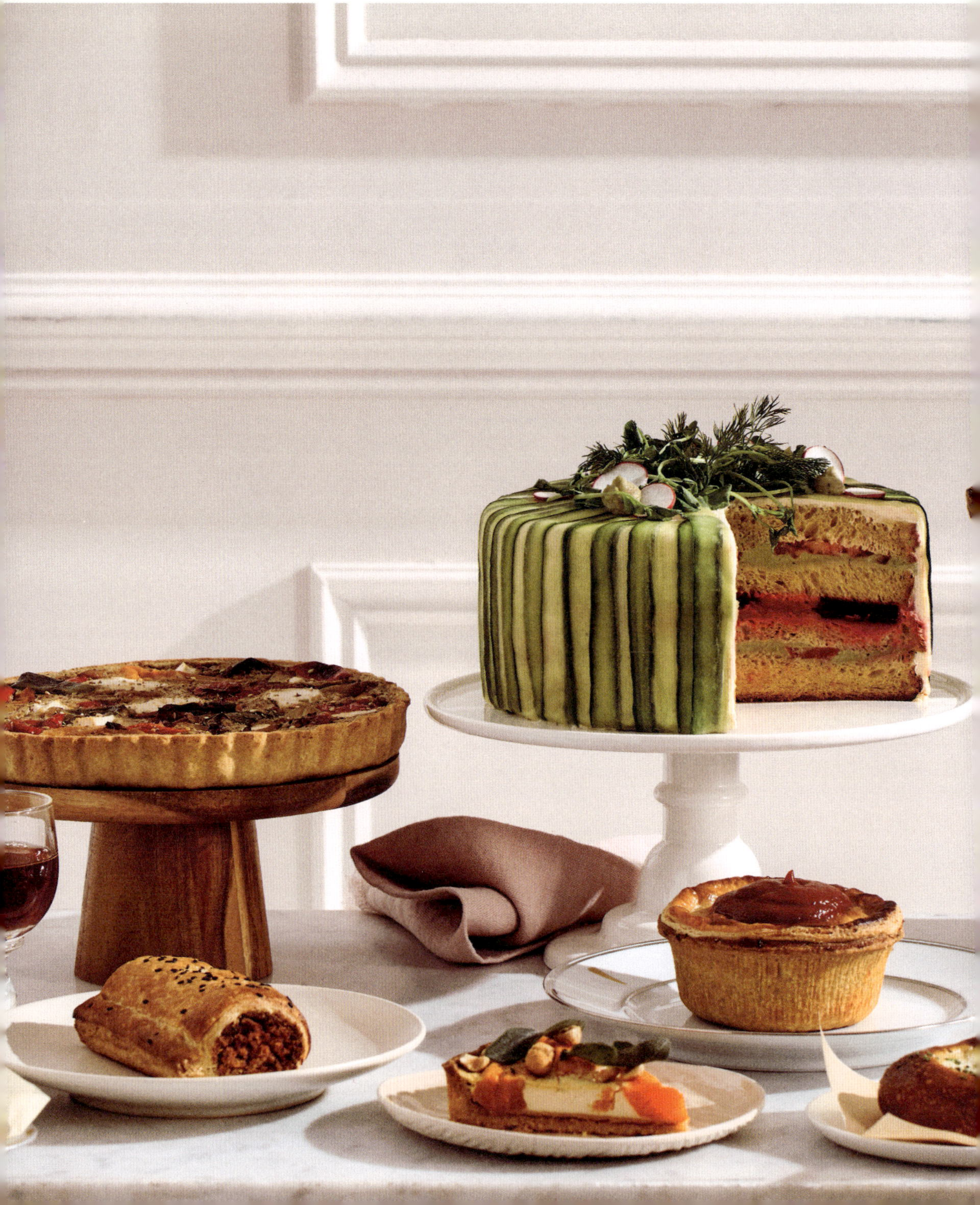

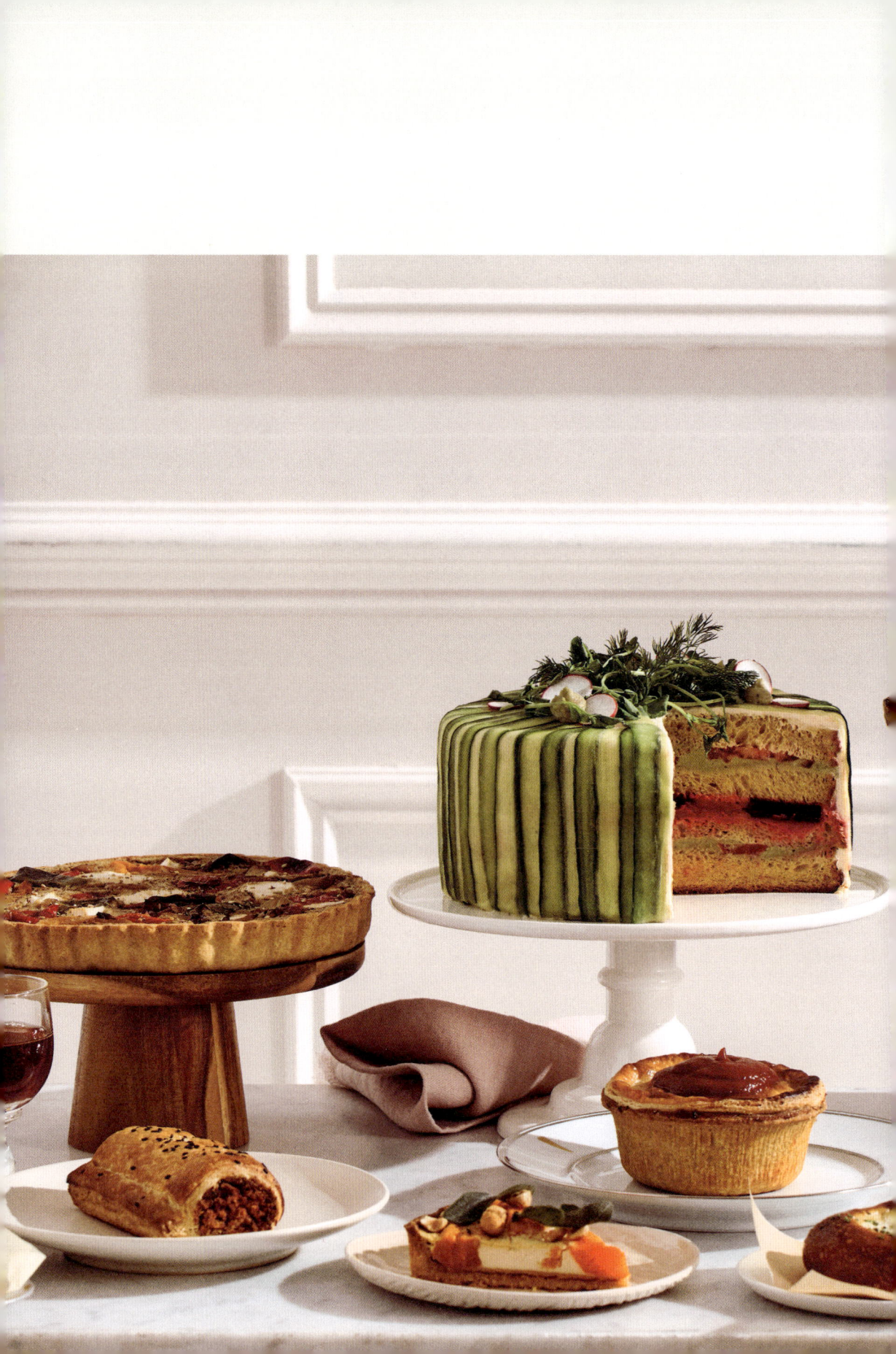

7 A COLLECTION TO SAVOUR

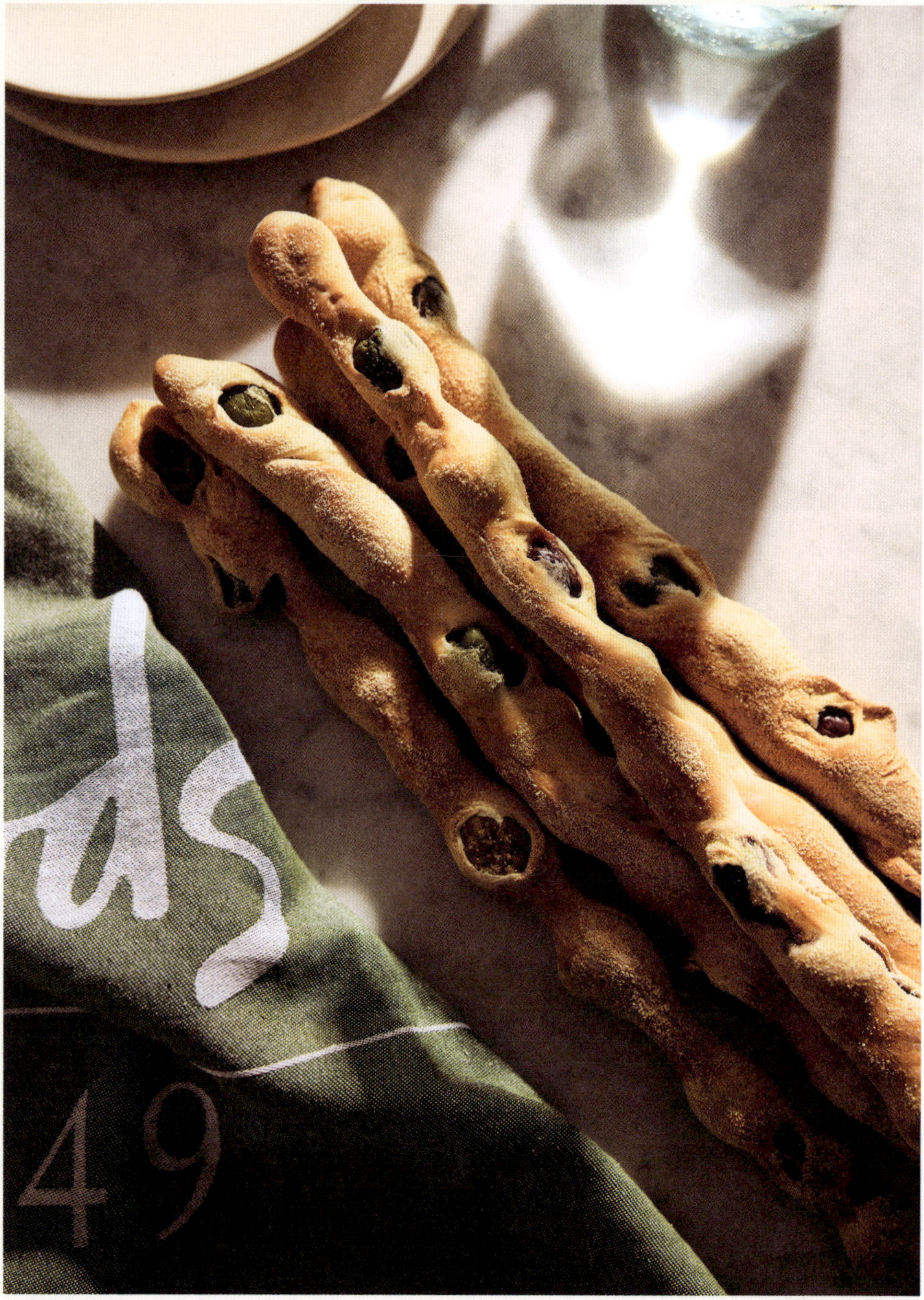
49

SAVOURY EXPLORATIONS: THE PERFECT PUFF AND BEYOND

For most of my life, I have succumbed to eating dessert first. I am a pastry chef because I love sweet things, and there's nothing more satisfying to me than crafting a perfect éclair or a delicate macaron. However, even in the world of confectionery delights, there lies a savoury chapter that holds a special place in my heart. This chapter is dedicated to those moments when a touch of salt, a hint of spice, or a robust flavour is all I need to balance the sweetness that surrounds me, providing a little break before I go back for that second helping of something sweet. As much as I savour a weekend bakery visit for some perfectly executed pastries, sometimes it's a savoury bake that hits the spot.

This chapter also introduces some new innovations in pastry. These recipes may sound or look familiar, as they are certainly inspired by traditional favourites, but they take shape using well-known natural ingredients, combined with new methods and techniques.

I am a huge fan of reducing sweetness in food and drinks – and I am not talking about swapping sugar for a less calorific substitute; I mean reducing the sweetness. This chapter isn't about less sweet, however. It's about the salty side of things – proving that sometimes, the best way to appreciate sweetness is to balance it with a touch of salt.

PUFFY PASTRY

Makes 420 g (14.8 oz) or enough for 6 × 10 cm (4 in) sausage rolls or 1 × 30 cm (12 in) galette

This is a light, versatile short pastry that's perfect for free-form baking – think sausage rolls, spinach parcels and rustic galettes, both sweet and savoury. A simple variation on flaky pastry that is lightened with baking powder, it comes together quickly with no need for extensive mixing, resting or lamination. Just mix, roll and bake. While it's no replacement for a true laminated dough (that recipe follows opposite), it's a reliable shortcut for those moments when time is short but the craving for something savoury and satisfying is not.

1. Whisk together the flour, salt and baking powder in a large bowl to evenly distribute.
2. Drizzle in the oil and use your fingertips to rub it in until the mixture resembles coarse crumbs.
3. Gradually pour in the water, mixing with a spoon or spatula until a rough dough forms.
4. Turn out the dough onto a lightly floured surface and knead it just enough to bring it together, being careful not to overwork it to maintain its flakiness.
5. Roll out as needed for your recipe, then proceed with shaping and baking according to your desired application.

strong white bread flour, plus extra for dusting	250 g	8.8 oz
fine sea salt	4 g	¾ tsp
baking powder	6 g	1 tsp
olive oil	90 g	3.2 oz
cold water	80 g	2.8 oz

TIP

This is an oil-based dough, so it's best made and used in the same session. If you have leftover scraps, they can be wrapped and stored in the refrigerator for up to 2 days. To reuse, add a few drops of water and knead by hand until the crumbly texture comes together into a cohesive dough.

PUFF PASTRY

Makes about 700 g (1 lb 9 oz)

This is the essential version of puff pastry that makes flawless sausage rolls and flaky pie lids. With 75 per cent butter to flour, it gives excellent lift and flavour without being too delicate or prone to melting during lamination. Any extra dough can be rolled out into a sheet, placed on a sheet of cling film (plastic wrap), then rolled up and frozen. To use, simply defrost in the refrigerator overnight.

plain (all-purpose) flour	250 g	8.8 oz
fine sea salt	5 g	1 tsp
olive oil	15 g	0.5 oz
cold water	125 g	4.4 oz
white or apple cider vinegar	5 g	1 tsp
Olive Oil Butter (page 55) or shop-bought block butter, cold	190 g	6.7 oz

1. Combine the flour and salt in a large bowl. Drizzle in the olive oil and mix through with a fork or your fingertips until evenly distributed. Add the cold water and vinegar gradually, mixing until the dough just begins to come together. Use your hands to bring it into a soft but not sticky dough – add a teaspoon of water if it feels very dry. Do not knead much – the dough should be quite firm, to match the texture of cold butter. Shape into a square, wrap and chill in the refrigerator for 20–30 minutes.

2. Meanwhile, if using shop-bought block butter, cut the chilled block in half vertically with a sharp knife and place the two halves side by side between two sheets of baking paper. Use a rolling pin and a firm press and rolling motion to shape it into a 13–15 cm (5–6 in) square, about 1 cm (½ in) thick. Place in the refrigerator while the dough finishes resting. (If you are using olive oil butter, it should already be shaped.)

3. Roll the rested dough into a rectangle approximately 20 × 40 cm (8 × 15¾ in). Place the butter square in the centre of the dough and fold the short edges to meet in the middle. Press the edges gently to seal. I also seal the exposed sides by gently pinching them together with my fingertips. You now have a neat butter package.

4. Roll this out lengthways into a long rectangle, about 20 × 60 cm (8 × 23½ in). Perform a double (book) fold: fold each short end towards the centre so they meet in the middle, then fold the whole thing in half like a book. Wrap and chill in the refrigerator for 30 minutes.

5. Rotate the dough 90 degrees, so you are rolling in the same direction as the folded side, and repeat the same rolling and double fold for a second time. Wrap and chill again for 30–60 minutes, then repeat a third time. At this stage, the block can be stored in the refrigerator for up to 3 days, or frozen for up to 3 months and defrosted in the refrigerator overnight.

6. When ready to use, roll the dough block to the desired size, about 2–3 mm (⅛ in) thick.

7. To freeze excess rolled dough, place on a large piece of cling film (plastic wrap), then roll up and freeze for up to 2 months. Defrost overnight in the refrigerator before using.

TIP

Remember that when laminating pastry, it needs to be rolled with as sharp a right-angle on each corner as you can manage – dough naturally wants to round out as you roll it, so I find that after rolling the dough as square as I can, a gentle tug on the corner with your hand to pull it into shape helps. Always rotate the dough 90 degrees between turns, rest in the refrigerator between folds and use a light dusting of flour to prevent sticking, but brush it off before folding to avoid tough spots.

BLIND-BAKED FLAKY PASTRY

My flaky pastry recipe is the only tart dough that I feel needs blind baking. The goal is to roll it out in a circular shape, starting by pressing it out with a rolling pin from the centre of the dough in both directions to create a strip or oval shape, then rotate it 90 degrees and roll it out again. This is called 'cross pinning' and is good practice to avoid dough that shrinks in one direction. I recommend rolling pastry dough out between two sheets of baking parchment, as it makes it easier and is also cleaner to handle as you don't need flour, which can get everywhere!

	300 g	10.6 oz	400 g	14.1 oz	500 g	1 lb 2 oz	600 g	1 lb 5 oz	700 g	1 lb 9 oz
plain (all-purpose) flour	167 g	5.9 oz	222 g	7.8 oz	278 g	9.8	333 g	11.7 oz	389 g	13.7 oz
fine sea salt	2 g	½ tsp	3 g	¾ tsp	3.5 g	¾ tsp	4 g	¾ tsp	5 g	1 tsp
caster (superfine) sugar	13.5 g	0.5 oz	18 g	0.6 oz	22.5 g	0.8	27 g	1 oz	31.5 g	1 oz
olive oil	67 g	2.4 oz	89 g	3.1 oz	111 g	3.9	133 g	4.7 oz	156 g	5.5 oz
cooked sweet potato (page 44)	13 g	0.5 oz	18 g	0.6 oz	22 g	0.8	27 g	1 oz	31 g	1 oz
cold water	27 g	1 oz	36 g	1.3 oz	44 g	1.6	53 g	1.9 oz	62 g	2.2 oz

1. Preheat the oven to 180°C fan (400°F).

2. Prepare the dough following the instructions on page 146, then roll it out between two large sheets of parchment paper – this makes it much cleaner and easier to handle. Alternatively, roll the dough out on a lightly floured surface the old-fashioned way, until it is large enough to line a 23 cm (9 in) fluted tart tin (pan). Carefully transfer the dough to the tin, pressing it gently into the base and fluted edges. If the pastry tears or breaks apart, simply press it back together with your fingers. Trim away any excess pastry from the top. Prick the base all over with a fork to prevent it from puffing up, then place it in the freezer for 10 minutes to firm up.

3. Take a large sheet of baking parchment, scrunch it up, then open it out – this makes it more flexible. Press it into the chilled pastry case, then fill with baking beans (pie weights), uncooked rice or dried beans to weigh the pastry down. This process is known as blind baking, as there is no filling yet.

4. Bake in the oven for 12–15 minutes. Remove from the oven and carefully lift out the baking parchment by its corners and remove the baking beans (they will be hot, so take care). Once cooled, the beans or other weights can be stored in a container and used again for blind baking.

5. Return the pastry case to the oven and bake for a further 5–10 minutes, or until the base is fully baked and the pastry has taken on a light golden colour. Once filled, the pastry won't gain much more colour, so it's important to ensure it is baked through at this stage for the best flavour and texture.

6. Remove from the oven and leave to cool completely on a wire rack. Empty, cooled tart cases can be wrapped and stored at room temperature for up to 2 weeks.

SAVOURY ROYALE CUSTARD

Makes 350 g (12.5 oz)

This is a simple, one-bowl quiche filling that blends together in seconds but delivers plenty of flavour and structure. Tofu and soya milk provide protein and body, while miso and Dijon mustard add depth and gentle sharpness. A small pinch of kala namak – a sulphurous, mineral-rich black salt used in South Asian cooking – brings an unmistakable eggy aroma (use sparingly!) and gives this quiche filling its familiar savoury character, without relying on eggs at all.

1 Combine all the ingredients in a high-powered blender and blend for 30–60 seconds until silky smooth (taste and check). If it is not totally smooth, continue blending.

soya milk	200 g	7 oz
firm tofu	120 g	4.2 oz
white miso paste	4 g	½ tsp
Dijon mustard	4 g	½ tsp
kala namak (black salt)	1.3 g	¼ tsp
fine sea salt	4 g	¾ tsp
cornflour (cornstarch)	20 g	0.7 oz

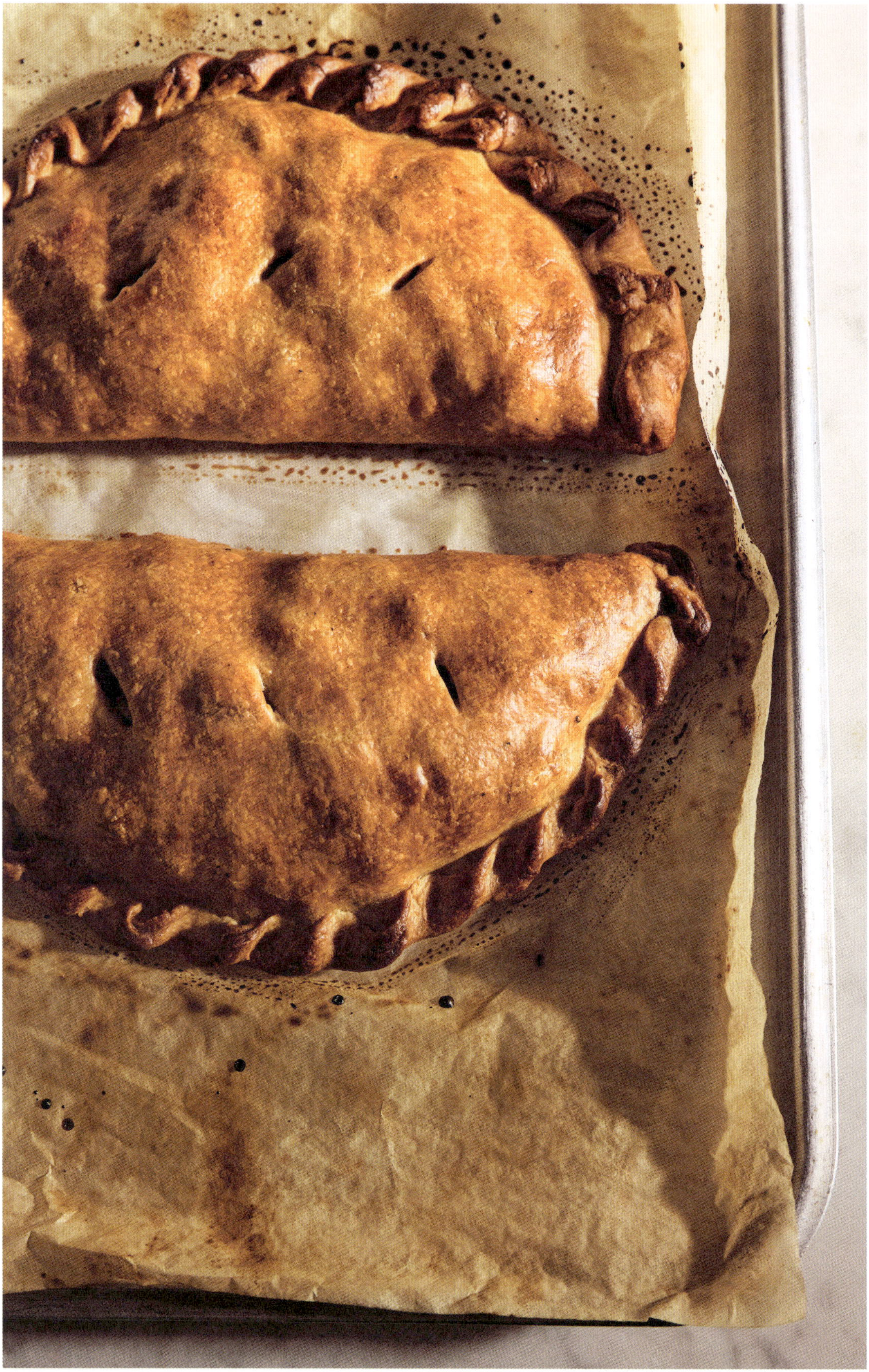

CORN-ISH PASTY

Makes 4 large pasties

Cornish pasties are traditional pastries from Cornwall, England, known for their distinctive semi-circular shape and hearty fillings of skirt (hanger) steak, potato and swede (rutabaga). Originally designed as a convenient meal for miners, their thick crust served as a handle for holding the pastie with soiled hands. This version keeps the spirit of the original but takes a Corn-ish turn with the addition of sweetcorn, which is a natural fit alongside tender potatoes and shiitake mushrooms, which bring a savoury, umami-rich depth in place of the steak. If swede is unavailable, carrots make a great substitute. Be sure to season generously with salt and plenty of black pepper for a proper punch of flavour. Best enjoyed warm, not long from the oven.

SIMPLE OLIVE OIL PASTRY

1. Put the flour, salt and oil into a large bowl and rub together until the mixture resembles breadcrumbs. This can also be done in a stand mixer with the beater attachment.

2. Add the water and continue mixing until a dough forms. Divide the dough into four 200 g (7 oz) balls.

plain (all-purpose) flour	500 g	1 lb 2 oz
fine sea salt	8 g	1½ tsp
olive oil	160 g	5.6 oz
water	160 g	5.6 oz

VEGETABLE FILLING

3. Heat the oil in a frying pan over a medium heat. Thinly slice the mushrooms, then add to the pan. Sauté for 5–8 minutes until browned and reduced in size, then remove the pan from the heat.

4. Quarter the potato and slice into 3 mm (⅛ in) thick pieces. Peel and slice the carrot or swede and slice into 3–4 mm (⅛ in) thick pieces. Finely chop the onion.

5. Add the prepared vegetables to the pan of mushrooms along with the sweetcorn, then add the salt, pepper and flour and toss all the ingredients to combine well. Set aside.

olive oil	40 g	1.4 oz
shiitake or chestnut (cremini) mushrooms	200 g	7 oz
potato	180 g	6.3 oz
carrot or swede (rutabaga)	180 g	6.3 oz
onion	90 g	3.2 oz
sweetcorn kernels (fresh or frozen)	120 g	4.2 oz
flaky sea salt	3 g	¾ tsp
freshly ground black pepper	1 g	¼ tsp
plain (all-purpose) flour	5 g	1 tbsp

TO ASSEMBLE AND BAKE

6. Preheat the oven to 180°C fan (400°F) and line two baking sheets with baking parchment.

7. Roll one piece of dough between two sheets of baking parchment, gently pressing and rolling outwards from the middle to create a longish oval shape. Rotate the dough 90 degrees and roll again, starting in the middle. Roll it out into a circle, 2–3 mm (⅛ in) thick, then remove the top piece of baking parchment (reserve it for rolling out the remaining dough) and place a 23 cm (9 in) cake tin (pan) on top and cut out a disc with a sharp paring knife.

8. Spoon a quarter of the filling mixture (about 150 g/5.3 oz) into the middle of one half of the dough, leaving a 2 cm (¾ in) border around the edge. Brush the edge with a little water.

baking glaze (page 242)		for brushing

9. Fold the dough over to cover the filling and line up the opposite edges as much as you can to seal in the filling. Brush a little water where you'll be crimping so that the 'crimps' stick down. Start from one end of the crescent and crimp the pastry by pinching the corner between a thumb and forefinger and twisting the edge around so it's upside down, then use the forefinger of your opposite hand to press it down and hold the crimp in place. Repeat this at 2 cm (¾ in) increments along the pastry until it is all crimped.

10. Brush the whole top of the pasty and the crimped edges gently with baking glaze, then use a sharp paring knife to make 3 small incisions on top of the pasty to make steam holes.

11. Repeat with the remaining pastry and filling.

12. Place two pasties on each prepared baking sheet and bake in the oven for 40 minutes until golden on top.

13. Remove from the oven and leave to cool slightly before serving.

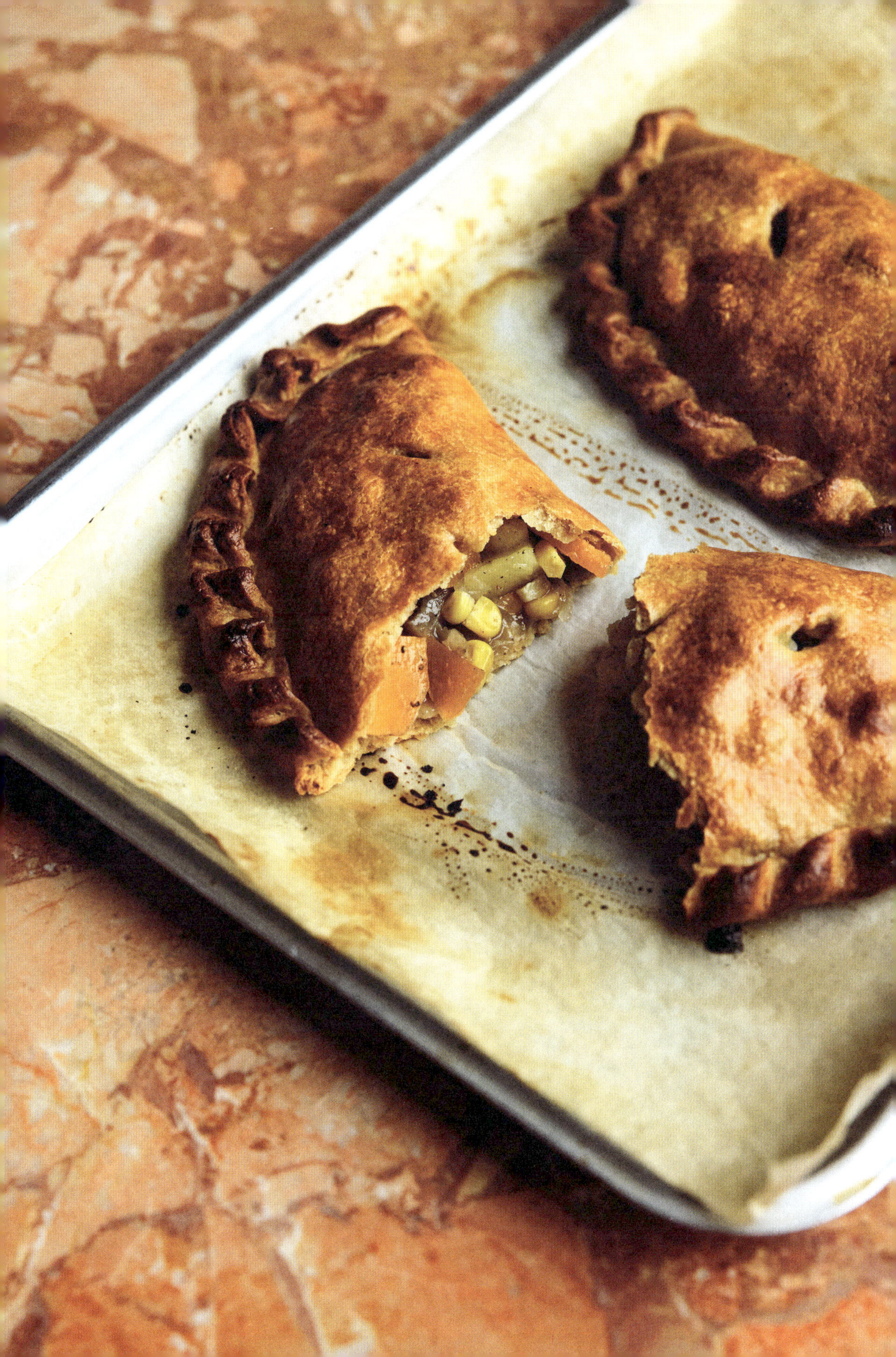

NIGHTSHADE QUICHE

Makes 1 × 23 cm (9 in) quiche or 5 × 10 cm (4 in) individual quiches

Nightshades have had their fair share of controversy in recent years, but for most of us, they remain some of the most flavour-packed ingredients in the kitchen. This quiche is a celebration of their depth and richness – roasted aubergines (eggplants), (bell) peppers and tomatoes, their sweetness intensified in the oven, folded into a silky, savoury filling with briny capers and olives. My favourite way to make quiche is simple: roast the vegetables while preparing a flaky pastry base, then let the still-hot vegetables tumble straight in before pouring over the custard and baking until just set.

Nightshades may have taken a hit on social media, with some claiming that the alkaloids in these flowering vegetables can increase symptoms of arthritis or inflammatory bowel disease, but a regular person would need to consume 7–9 kg (15–20 lb) of potatoes to get anywhere near a dose that would be considered even potentially harmful.

1. Preheat the oven to 180°C fan (400°F) and line a baking tray (pan) with baking parchment.

2. Peel the aubergine and potato and cut into small cubes. Toss them with a drizzle of olive oil and a pinch of salt, then spread them evenly on the prepared baking tray. Add the cherry tomatoes to the tray and then roast in the oven for 20–25 minutes, or until the vegetables are tender and slightly caramelised. Stir halfway through to ensure even roasting. Remove from the oven and set aside.

3. Reduce the oven temperature to 160°C fan (350°F).

4. Pour the custard into the tart case (shell) to fill it two-thirds full. Add the roasted vegetables around the quiche. Top with more spoonfuls of custard to fill the tart, then sprinkle the capers and olives on top.

5. Bake in the oven for 20–25 minutes (12–15 minutes for individual quiches), or until the custard is just set if you wobble the tart case. Another way to test it is with a gentle and quick prod of the custard – it should feel just set and not liquid underneath.

6. Remove from the oven and leave to cool in the tin for 30 minutes before slicing. This resting time helps the filling firm up and makes for cleaner slices.

7. The quiche will keep well in the refrigerator for up to 3 days. Reheat in the oven at 160°C fan (350°F) for 10–15 minutes, or until warmed through. It can also be frozen in individual slices – reheat from frozen at the same temperature for 20–25 minutes.

Ingredient	Metric	Imperial
aubergine (eggplant) (about 1 large)	200 g	7 oz
potato (about 1)	150 g	5.3 oz
cherry tomatoes on the vine	100 g	3.5 oz
Savoury Royale Custard (page 197)	1 quantity	
pre-baked 23 cm (9 in) Flaky Pastry tart case or 10 cm (4 in) individual tartlet cases (page 196)	1 tart case or 5 tartlet cases	
capers	30 g	1 oz
black or green pitted olives	40 g	1.4 oz
olive oil	for drizzling	
flaky sea salt and freshly ground black pepper	to taste	

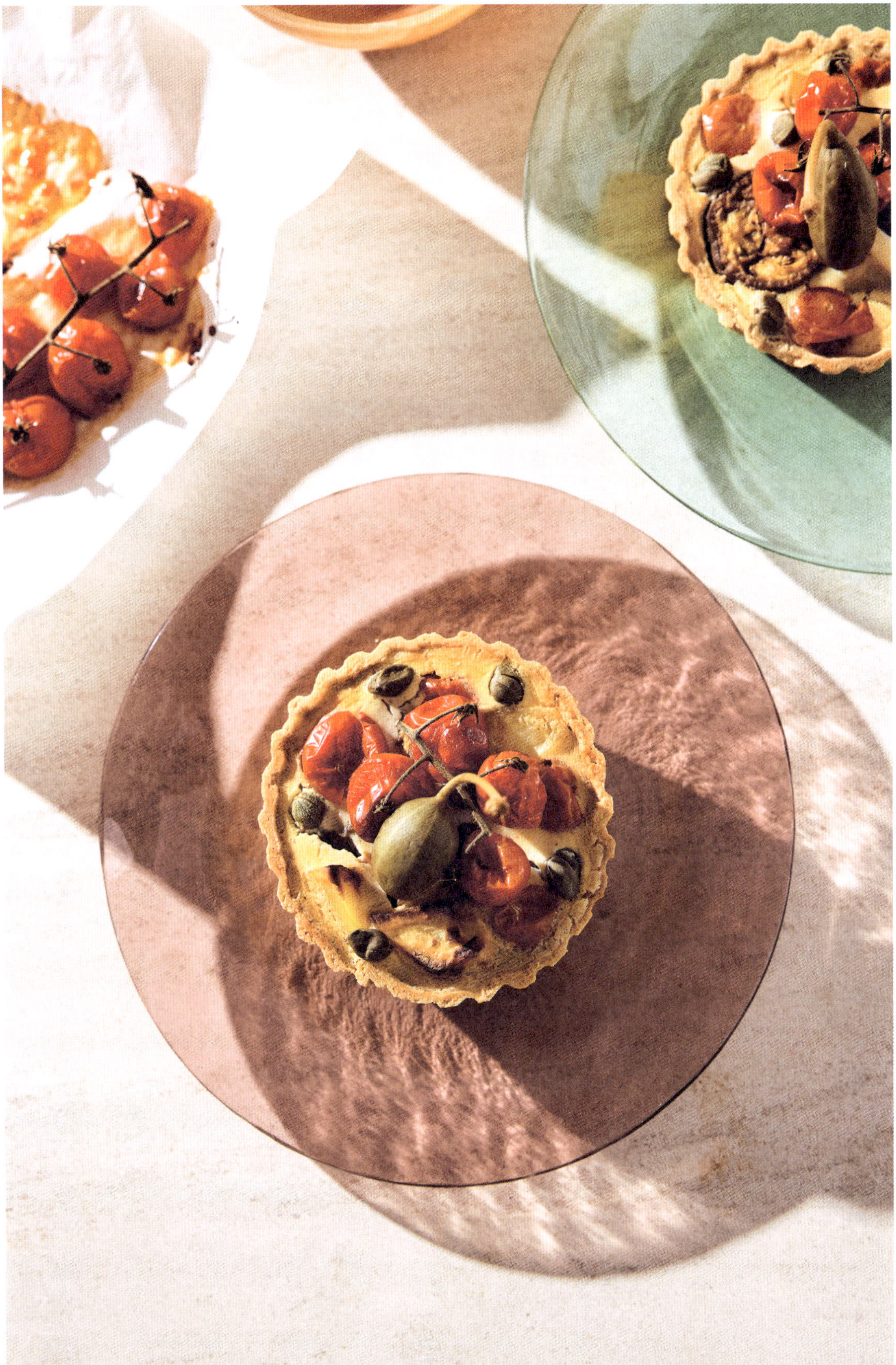

SQUASH, HAZELNUT AND SAGE QUICHE

Makes 1 × 23 cm (9 in) quiche or
5 × 10 cm (4 in) individual quiches

Roasted squash brings natural sweetness and softness to this quiche, balanced by the richness of roasted hazelnuts and the earthy aroma of fresh sage. It's a warmly flavoured combination, with plenty of texture, and works just as well served warm or at room temperature.

butternut squash	1 kg	2 lb 4 oz
hazelnuts	70 g	2.5 oz
sage	5 g	0.2 oz
Savoury Royale Custard (page 197)	1 quantity	
pre-baked 23 cm (9 in) Flaky Pastry tart case or 10 cm (4 in) individual tartlet cases (page 196)	1 tart case or 5 tartlet cases	
toasted pine nuts	30 g	1 oz
olive oil	for drizzling	
flaky sea salt and freshly ground black pepper	to taste	

1. Preheat the oven to 200°C (425°F) and line a baking tray (pan) with baking parchment.

2. Using a sharp knife, cut the butternut squash in half lengthways. Scoop out the seeds with a spoon and discard or save for roasting. Place the squash halves cut-side down on a cutting board and slice them widthways into 2–3 cm (¾–1¼ in) wide strips, keeping the skin on for now.

3. Arrange the squash strips on the prepared baking tray in a single layer. Drizzle with olive oil and season with salt and pepper (you can also add any spices you like at this stage). Toss to coat.

4. Roast in the oven for 25–35 minutes, turning halfway through, until the squash is golden, caramelised and easily pierced with a fork. Remove from the oven and leave to cool a little.

5. Reduce the oven temperature to 160°C fan (350°F) and spread the hazelnuts on a baking tray. Roast in the oven for 16 minutes until golden brown in the middle when split open.

6. Once the squash is cool enough to handle, use a small knife or your fingers to gently remove the softened skin – it should slide off easily. Chop the sage and sprinkle it over the base of the baked pastry case (shell). Pour in the custard to fill halfway, spreading it out evenly. Arrange the pumpkin pieces and half the nuts over the custard, then top with spoonfuls of custard to fill the tart. Sprinkle the remaining hazelnuts and the pine nuts on top.

7. Bake in the oven for 20–25 minutes (12–15 minutes for individual quiches), or until the custard is just set if you wobble the tart case. Another way to test it is with a gentle and quick prod of the custard – it should feel just set and not liquid underneath.

8. Remove from the oven and leave to cool in the tin for 30 minutes before slicing. This resting time helps the filling firm up and makes for cleaner slices.

9. The quiche will keep well in the refrigerator for up to 3 days. Reheat in the oven at 160°C fan (350°F) for 10–15 minutes, or until warmed through. It can also be frozen in individual slices – reheat from frozen at the same temperature for 20–25 minutes.

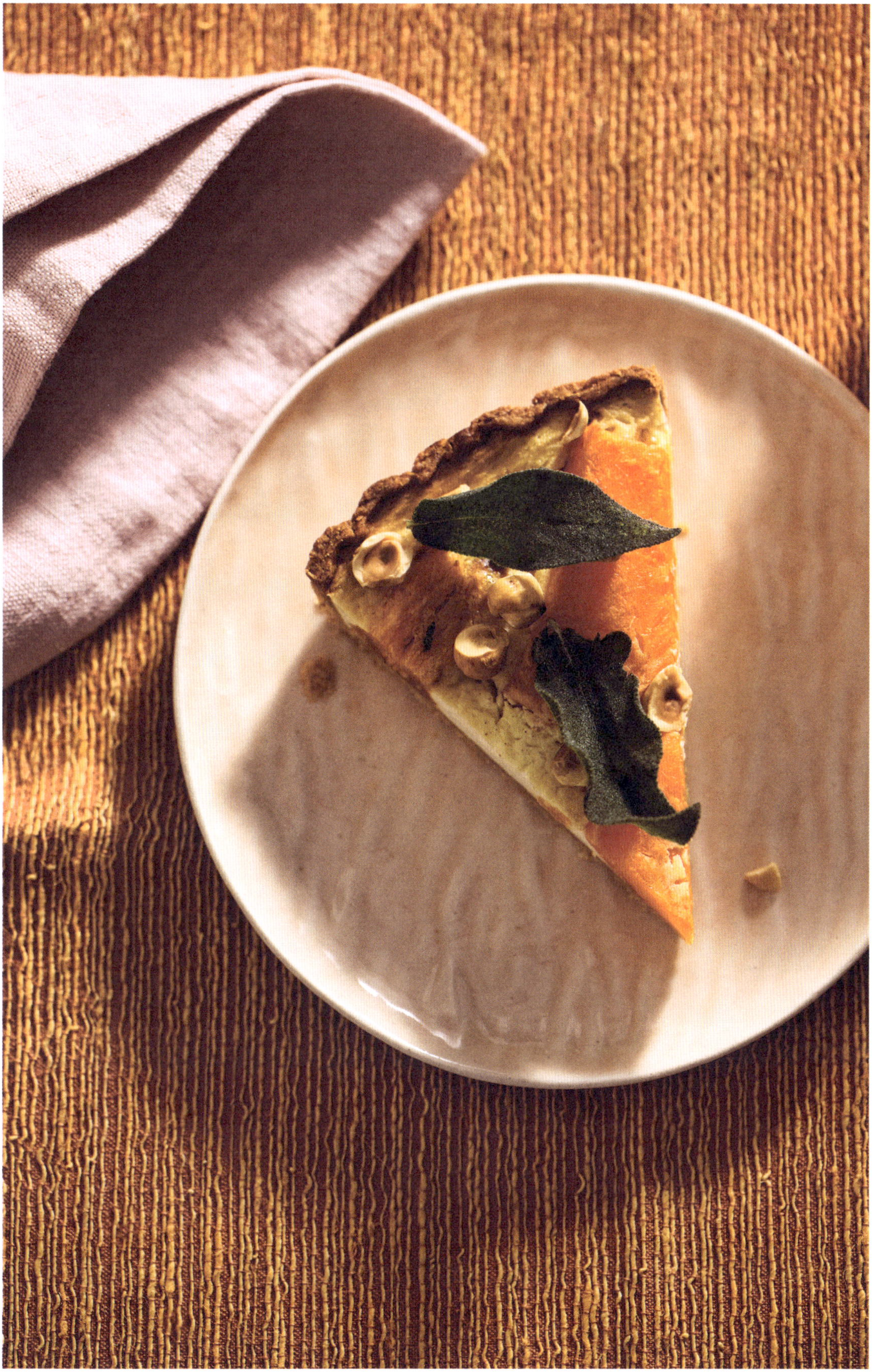

MUSHROOM AND TRUFFLE QUICHE

Makes 1 × 23 cm (9 in) quiche
or 5 × 10 cm (4 in) individual quiches

Earthy, rich and deeply savoury, this quiche leans into the full spectrum of umami. A medley of mushrooms – whatever is freshest or most fragrant in the market – are sautéed until golden, then tossed with truffle paste for added depth. If you're feeling generous, a few shavings of truffle on top take it one quiet step further.

1. Clean and slice the mushrooms into roughly 1 cm (½ in) thick slices. Finely chop the garlic.

2. Heat the oil in a large frying pan over a medium heat. Add the garlic and sauté for 1–2 minutes until fragrant – make sure to stir so it doesn't burn. Add the mushrooms and cook for 5–7 minutes until they release their moisture and start to brown.

3. Stir in the thyme, salt and pepper. Cook for a further 2 minutes.

4. Remove the pan from the heat and stir in the truffle paste. Set the mushroom mixture aside to cool slightly.

5. Preheat the oven to 160°C fan (350°F).

6. Pour the custard into the tart case (shell) to fill it two-thirds full. Add the roasted mushrooms, then top with spoonfuls of custard to fill the tart.

7. Bake in the oven for 20–25 minutes (12–15 minutes for individual quiches), or until the custard is just set if you wobble the tart case. Another way to test it is with a gentle and quick prod of the custard – it should feel just set and not liquid underneath.

8. Remove from the oven and leave to cool in the tin for 30 minutes before slicing. This resting time helps the filling firm up and makes for cleaner slices.

9. The quiche will keep well in the refrigerator for up to 3 days. Reheat in the oven at 160°C fan (350°F) for 10–15 minutes, or until warmed through. It can also be frozen in individual slices – reheat from frozen at the same temperature for 20–25 minutes.

mixed mushrooms (button, chestnut/cremini, shiitake)	800 g	1 lb 12 oz
garlic (2 cloves)	10 g	0.4 oz
olive oil	40 g	1.4 oz
chopped thyme leaves		1 tsp
flaky sea salt	5 g	1 tsp
freshly ground black pepper	1 g	¼ tsp
truffle paste	30 g	1 oz
Savoury Royale Custard (page 197)		1 quantity
pre-baked 23 cm (9 in) Flaky Pastry tart case or 10 cm (4 in) individual tartlet cases (page 196)		1 tart case or 5 tartlet cases

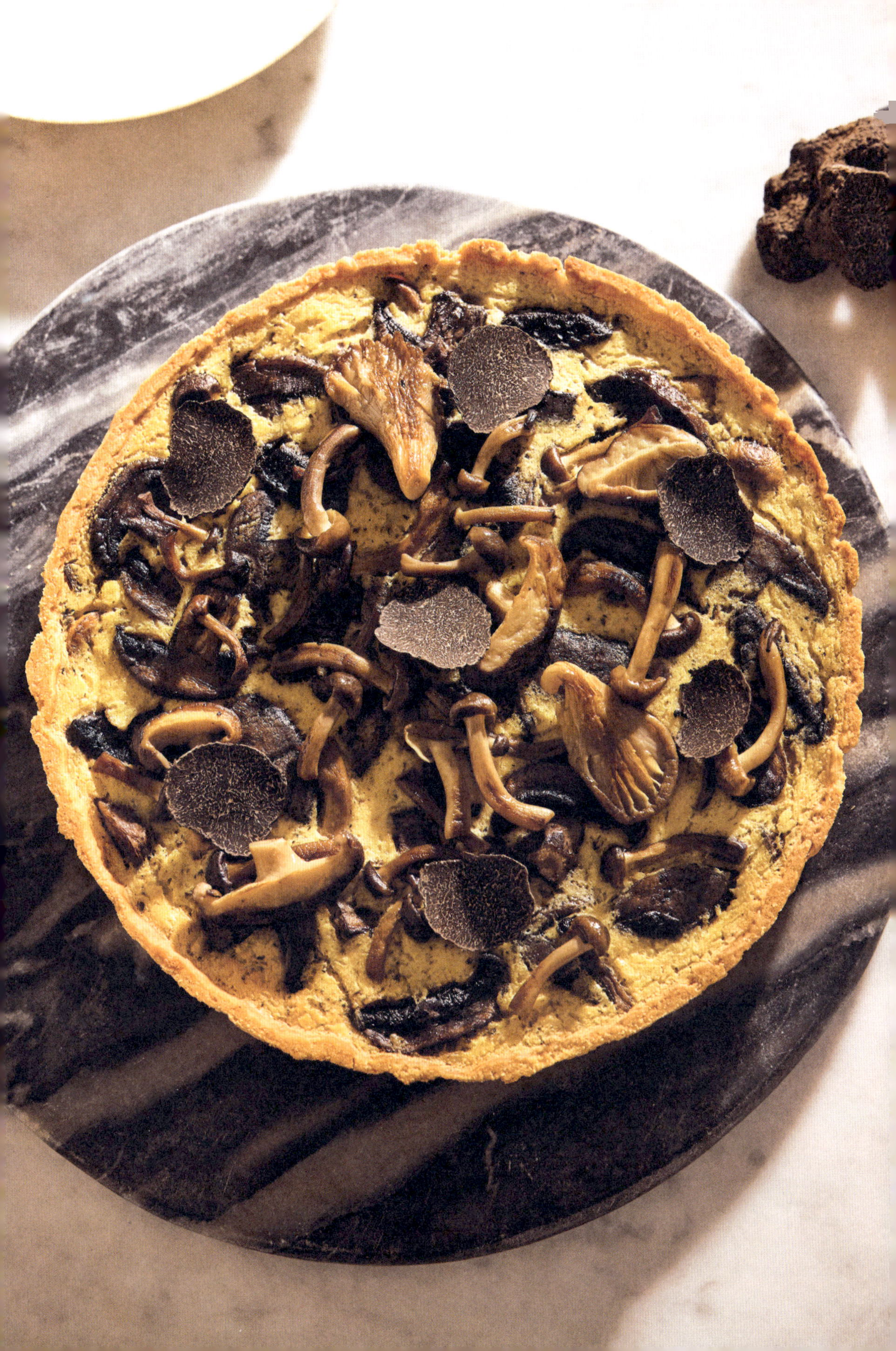

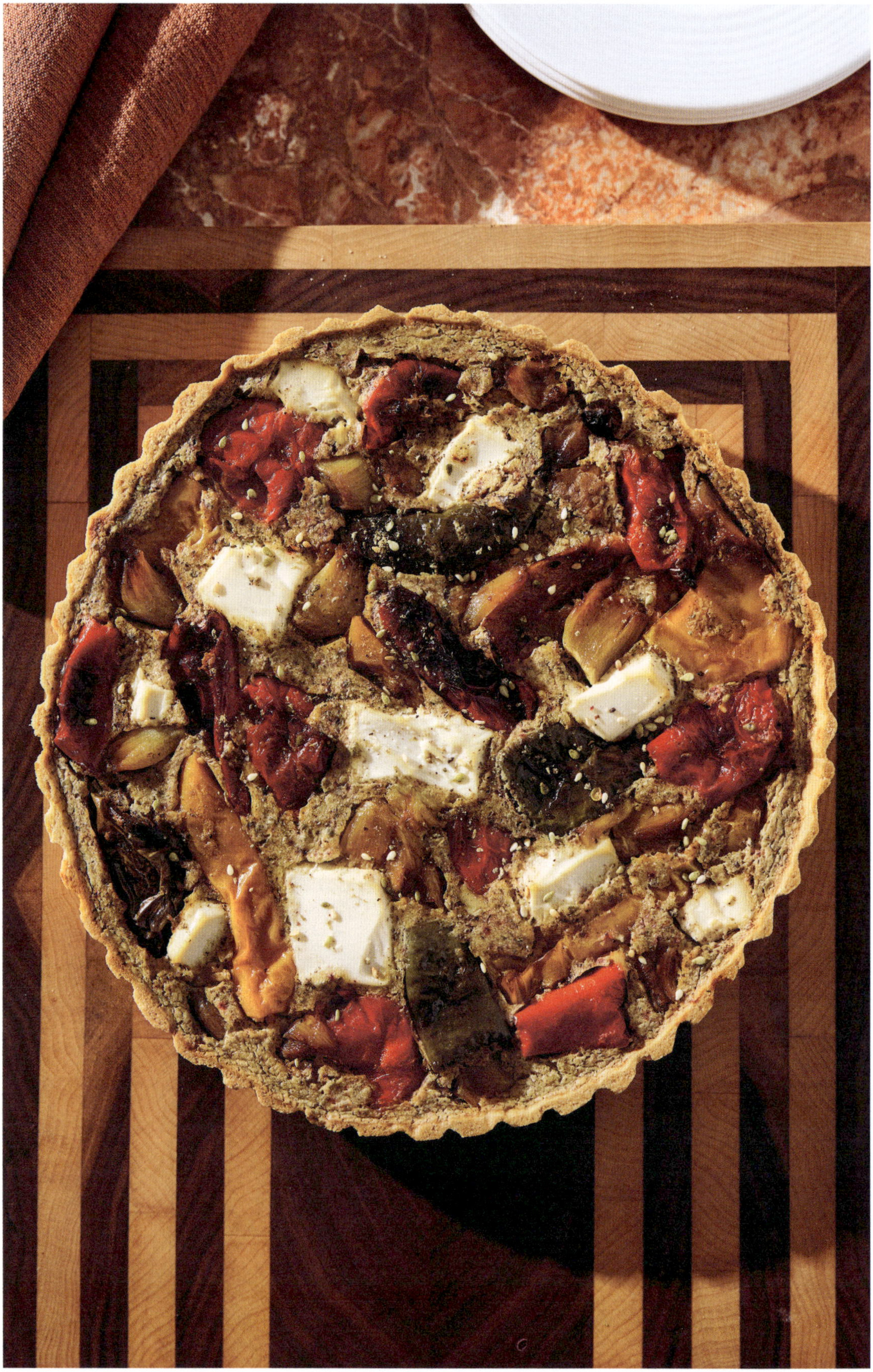

CARAMELISED ONION, PEPPER AND ZA'ATAR QUICHE

Makes 1 × 23 cm (9 in) quiche or 5 × 10 cm (4 in) individual quiches

This quiche brings together deep, slow-cooked flavour and bright, aromatic spice. Caramelised onions add rich sweetness, roasted (bell) peppers bring smoky depth and za'atar ties everything together with its earthy, herbaceous notes. Dollops of silken tofu bake into a creamy, fresh cheese-like topping, giving the quiche a beautifully soft contrast. Wrapped in a crisp, golden pastry, it's the kind of dish that's just as good warm from the oven as it is cold the next day – if there's any left.

1. Preheat the oven to 200°C fan (425°F) and line a large baking tray (pan) with baking parchment.
2. Cut the top off the garlic bulb to expose the cloves. Drizzle with a little olive oil and wrap tightly in a small piece of foil.
3. Peel and halve the onion and place on the prepared baking tray. Halve and deseed the peppers and place them on the tray too.
4. Drizzle the peppers and onions with olive oil and sprinkle with the salt, pepper and za'atar. Add the foil-wrapped garlic to the tray.
5. Roast in the oven for 40–45 minutes, or until the vegetables have softened and started to caramelise. The peppers and onions should be lightly browned at the edges, and the garlic soft enough to squeeze from the skins. Check halfway and turn or toss the vegetables if needed to encourage even roasting.
6. Remove from the oven and leave to cool slightly. Once cooled a little, peel the skins from the peppers and discard. Set the vegetables aside.

TO ASSEMBLE AND BAKE

7. Reduce the oven temperature to 160°C fan (350°F). Arrange the roasted vegetables evenly across the base of the pre-baked tart case (shell). Use your fingers or a spoon to gently spread out the cloves of confit garlic.
8. Pour over the custard to fill the tart case two-thirds full. Spoon the silken tofu on top in six or so evenly spaced spoonfuls – this adds pockets of creaminess and light texture throughout the quiche. Top with more spoonfuls of custard to fill the tart.
9. Bake in the oven for 20–25 minutes (12–15 minutes for individual quiches), or until the custard is just set if you wobble the tart case.
10. Remove from the oven and leave to cool in the tin for 30 minutes before slicing.
11. The quiche will keep well in the refrigerator for up to 3 days. Reheat in the oven at 160°C fan (350°F) for 10–15 minutes, or until warmed through. It can also be frozen in individual slices – reheat from frozen at the same temperature for 20–25 minutes.

garlic bulb	1	
olive oil	40 g	1.4 oz
red onion (about 1)	190 g	6.7 oz
red (bell) peppers (about 3)	220 g	7.8 oz
fine sea salt	3 g	¾ tsp
freshly ground black pepper	2 g	½ tsp
za'atar	13 g	½ tbsp
pre-baked 23 cm (9 in) Flaky Pastry tart case or 10 cm (4 in) individual tartlet cases (page 196)	1 tart case or 5 tartlet cases	
Savoury Royale Custard (page 197)	300 g	10.6 oz
silken tofu	120 g	4.2 oz

SPINACH ROLL

Makes 8

This roll leans into the flavours and textures of *spanakopita*, *börek* and other savoury pastries from across the Mediterranean and Middle East. The filling is a well-seasoned mix of spinach and crumbled tofu, studded generously with toasted pine nuts and gently spiced with nutmeg and black pepper. Wrapped in flaky puff pastry, it's satisfying, crisp and deeply familiar.

SPINACH AND TOFU FILLING

1. If you're using frozen spinach, defrost it and chop it coarsely if it isn't already chopped. Place it in a sieve (fine-mesh strainer) and squeeze out as much excess moisture as you can. If using fresh spinach, heat up a large fry pan and cook the spinach until wilted and then allow it to cool and strain out the excess moisture.
2. Preheat the oven to 170°C fan (375°F). Finely chop the spring onion.
3. Spread the pine nuts on a baking tray (pan) and toast in the oven for 8–11 minutes until nicely golden. Remove from the oven and set aside.
4. Crumble the tofu into a bowl, then add the strained spinach, spring onion, pine nuts and all the remaining ingredients. Mix well until thoroughly combined. Place in a piping (pastry) bag and set aside.

spinach (frozen/fresh)	450 g / 1 kg	15.9 oz / 2.2 lb
spring onion (scallion) (about 1)	20 g	0.7 oz
pine nuts	40 g	1.4 oz
firm or extra-firm silken tofu	300 g	10.6 oz
flaky sea salt	10 g	2 tsp
black pepper	2 g	½ tsp
ground nutmeg	1 g	¼ tsp

TO ASSEMBLE AND BAKE

5. Preheat the oven to 200°C fan (425°F) and line a baking sheet with baking parchment.
6. Roll out the pastry on a lightly floured surface into a rectangle slightly larger than 40 × 24 cm (15¾ × 9½ in), then trim it down to this size with a sharp knife. Cut the rectangle in half lengthways to make two strips, each about 40 × 12 cm (15¾ × 4¾ in).
7. Pipe the filling in a log along one side of each strip, about 2 cm (¾ in) in from the edge. Lightly brush the opposite edge with water. Fold the pastry over the filling and press gently to seal, allowing for a 1.5–2 cm (½–¾ in) overlap. Press the seam to close – and trim the open seam if needed – then crimp gently with a fork. Using a sharp knife, cut each long roll into 3 × 10 cm (4 in) pieces, then brush the tops with baking glaze and sprinkle with sesame seeds. Transfer to the prepared baking sheet, spacing them at least 3 cm (1¼ in) apart.
8. Bake in the oven for 20–25 minutes, or until golden and crisp. Remove from the oven and leave to cool completely on a wire rack. These are best served on the day they are baked, but leftovers can be wrapped and stored in the refrigerator and then gently reheated in the oven at 160°C fan (350°F) for 10–12 minutes to crisp up the pastry. The unbaked rolls can be wrapped well and stored in the freezer for up to 3 months.

Puff Pastry (page 195)	400 g	14.1 oz
plain (all-purpose) flour	for dusting	
Baking Glaze (page 242)	for brushing	
sesame seeds	10 g	1 tbsp

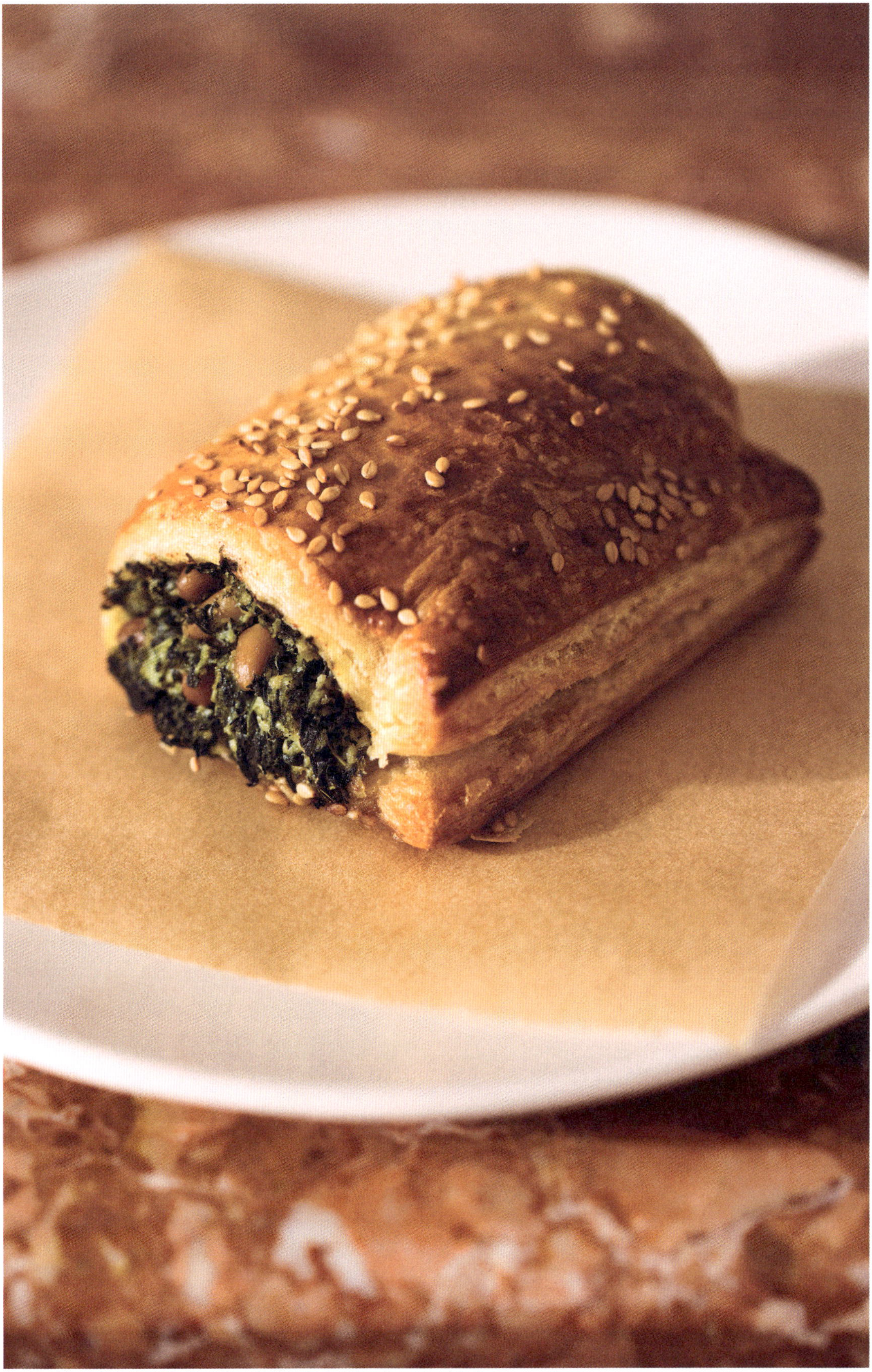

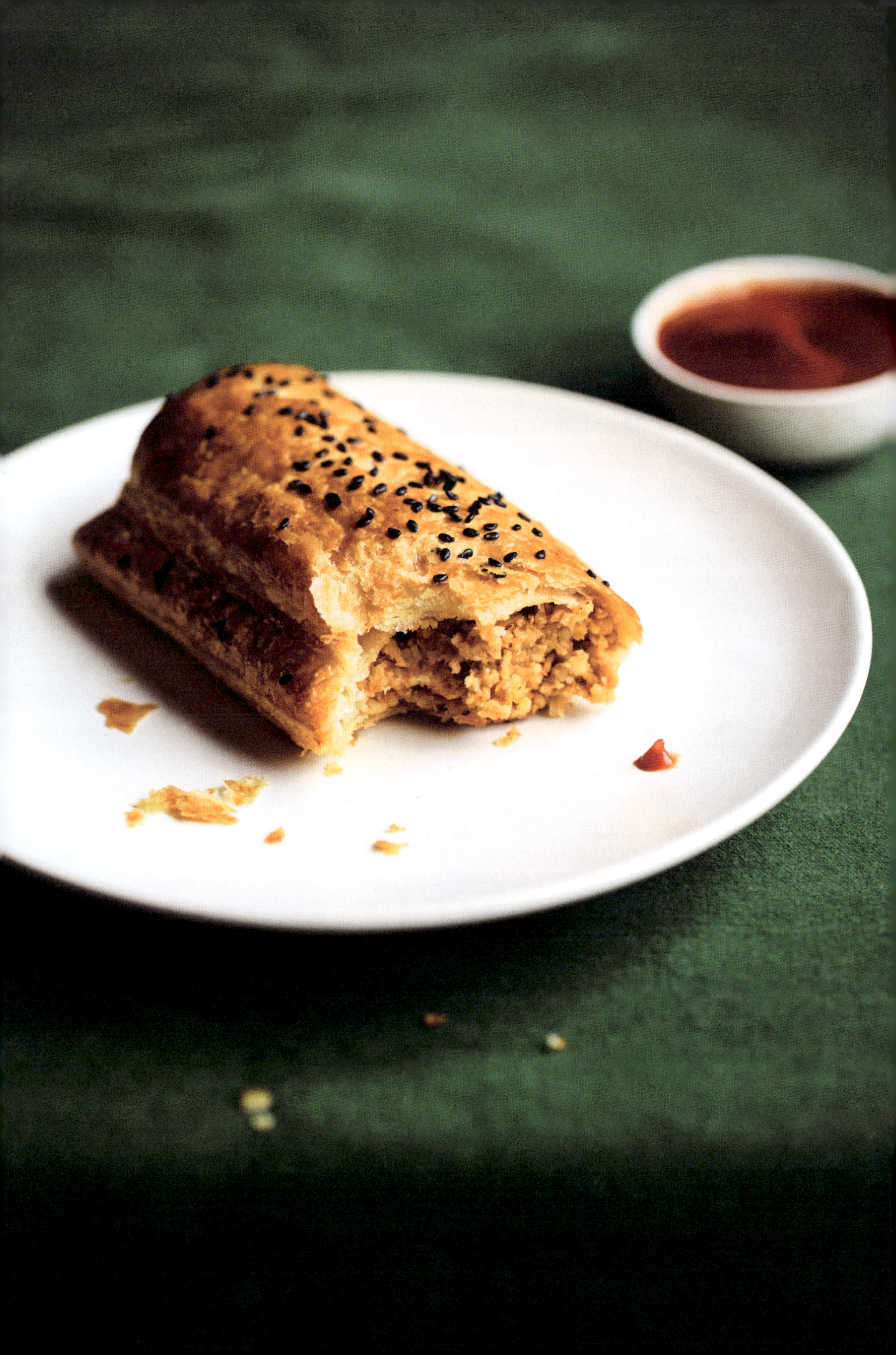

SAUSY ROLL

Makes 8

Although I was born and raised in Australia, where sausage rolls are typically rolled so that the seam sits underneath, I came to appreciate the side fold after I moved to London. In the UK, it's the more common approach, and one that allows the puff pastry to rise freely and turn beautifully crisp. High-street staple Greggs helped spark a cultural shift when they introduced their vegan sausage roll in 2019. These are best eaten warm, with a generous dunk in Tomato Ketchup (page 246).

1. Place the couscous and soya mince in a heatproof bowl. Pour the stock into a saucepan and bring to the boil, then pour it over the mixture. Cover and set aside to swell.

2. Meanwhile, roughly chop the mushrooms. Dice the onion and finely chop the garlic. Heat a frying pan over a medium heat and cook the onion with a splash of oil until soft and translucent. Add the garlic and mushrooms and cook for 10–12 minutes, or until the mushrooms have released their moisture and are starting to brown. Remove from the heat and leave to cool slightly.

3. Once cooled, transfer the mushroom mixture to a food processor, along with the cannellini beans, tomato purée, sage, smoked paprika, black pepper to taste and the liquid smoke (if using). Pulse to form a paste, then add to the soaked couscous and soya mince and massage/mix them together until well combined. Transfer to a piping (pastry) bag fitted with a 2 cm (¾ in) plain nozzle (tip), or use a ziploc bag with the corner snipped off.

4. Roll out the pastry on a lightly floured surface into a rectangle slightly larger than 40 × 24 cm (15¾ × 9½ in), then trim it down to this size with a sharp knife. Cut the rectangle in half lengthways to make two strips, each about 40 × 12 cm (15¾ × 4¾ in).

5. Pipe the filling in a log along one side of each strip, about 2 cm (¾ in) in from the edge. Lightly brush the opposite edge with water. Fold the pastry over the filling and press gently to seal, allowing for a 1.5–2 cm (½–¾ in) overlap. Press the seam to close – and trim the open seam if needed – then crimp gently with a fork. Brush the top with baking glaze and sprinkle with poppy seeds (if using).

6. Using a sharp knife, cut each long roll into 3 × 10 cm (4 in) pieces. Transfer to the prepared baking sheet, spacing them at least 3 cm (1¼ in) apart.

7. Bake in the oven for 20–25 minutes, or until golden and crisp.

8. These are best eaten warm. Leftovers can be stored in an airtight container in the refrigerator for up to 3 days. Reheat in the oven at 180°C fan (400°F) for 10–12 minutes until crisp again. The rolls can also be frozen raw or baked – reheat from frozen at 180°C (400°F) for 20–25 minutes until heated through and golden.

couscous	60 g	2 oz
soya or pea mince (TVP)	70 g	2.5 oz
vegetable or mushroom stock	220 g	7.8 oz
chestnut (cremini) mushrooms	400 g	14.1 oz
onion (about ½)	100 g	3.5 oz
garlic (1 clove)	4 g	0.1 oz
drained 400 g (14 oz) tin of cannellini beans	270 g	9.5 oz
tomato purée (paste)	15 g	0.5 oz
dried sage	1 g	1 tsp
smoked paprika		½ tsp
liquid smoke (optional)	5 g	1 tsp
Puff Pastry (page 195)	400 g	14.1 oz
plain (all-purpose) flour		for dusting
Baking Glaze (page 242)		for brushing
olive oil		for frying
poppy or nigella seeds		for sprinkling (optional)
freshly ground black pepper		to taste

TEMPEH AND MUSHROOM PIE

Makes 1 × 23 cm (9 in) pie or 6 × 10 cm (4 in) individual pies

Inspired by the classic Aussie meat pie, this version is just as rich, hearty and satisfying, only the filling swaps meat for something just as bold. Tempeh and mushrooms bring deep, savoury flavour, lentils add bite and a luscious gravy ties it all together, tucked inside layers of golden, flaky puff pastry. It's the kind of pie that feels like a warm hug, best enjoyed not too long out of the oven with a generous splodge of Tomato Ketchup (page 246). You can replace the impressive puff pastry with shop-bought, or just increase the flaky pastry quantity to use for the lids if you want to keep it simpler.

MUSHROOM AND TEMPEH FILLING

1. Place the sugar in a wide, heavy-based saucepan over a medium heat. Let it start to melt and then caramelise. It will burn quickly, and that is okay – it is mainly here to add a rich caramel colour. Carefully pour in a little vegetable stock at a time – it will bubble up – and stir to deglaze the caramelised sugar from the base of the pan. Add the soy sauce and tomato purée and mix well.

2. Place the soya mince in a heatproof bowl and pour over the hot liquid. Stir well. Cover and set aside for 5 minutes to rehydrate.

3. Prepare the vegetables using a food processor or knife. Finely dice the onion, peel and dice the carrots and finely chop the garlic. Crumble the tempeh and finely chop the mushrooms and place the tempeh and mushrooms in a bowl.

4. Return the pan to a medium heat. Add the olive oil, onion, garlic and carrot. Cook for 5–6 minutes, or until softened and fragrant, then transfer to the bowl with the soya mince.

5. Add the tempeh and mushrooms to the pan, along with a splash of olive oil. Cook for 10–12 minutes until most of the liquid has evaporated and the mixture is starting to brown. Add the thyme, smoked paprika, soaked soya mince and stock and bring to a gentle simmer.

6. In a small bowl, combine the cornflour with the cold water to make a slurry. Stir this into the pan and cook for a further 5–7 minutes, or until the mixture thickens and holds its shape. Season to taste with salt and black pepper. Remove from the heat and leave to cool completely before using.

caster (superfine) sugar	40 g	1.4 oz
vegetable stock	300 g	10.6 fl oz
dark soy sauce	40 g	1.4 oz
tomato purée (paste)	40 g	1.4 oz
soya or pea mince (TVP)	100 g	3.5 oz
onion	150 g	5.3 oz
carrots, peeled	150 g	5.3 oz
garlic (about 3 cloves)	15 g	0.5 oz
olive oil, plus extra as needed	40 g	1.4 oz
tempeh	250 g	8.8 oz
chestnut (cremini) mushrooms	250 g	8.8 oz
chopped thyme leaves	5 g	1 tsp
smoked paprika	2 g	½ tsp
cornflour (cornstarch)	20 g	0.7 oz
cold water	30 g	1 oz
flaky sea salt and freshly ground black pepper	to taste	

TO ASSEMBLE AND BAKE

7 Preheat the oven to 180°C fan (400°F).

8 Roll out the flaky pastry dough on a lightly floured surface. Cut out a circle or circles large enough to line your chosen pie dish or dishes, with some overhang.

9 Line the pie dishes with the circles, pressing them into the sides and base.

10 Fill each pie with the cooled tempeh and mushroom filling, spreading it out evenly.

11 Roll out the puff pastry dough on a lightly floured surface. Cut out a circle or circles large enough to top the pie or pies. Cover the filling with the pastry, press the edges together to seal and trim any excess pastry.

12 Use a fork to crimp the edges, then cut a small slit in the top of each pie to allow steam to escape.

13 Brush the tops of the pies with baking glaze to help them brown.

14 Bake in the oven for 22–25 minutes for individual pies or 30–35 minutes for one large pie, or until the pastry is golden brown and crisp.

15 Remove the pies from the oven and leave to cool slightly before serving.

FOR 6 × 10 CM (4 IN) PIES

Flaky Pastry (page 146)	600 g	1 lb 5 oz
plain (all-purpose) flour	for dusting	
Puff Pastry (page 195)	300 g	10.6 oz

FOR 1 × 23 CM (9 IN) PIE

Flaky Pastry (page 146)	300–350 g	10.6–12.4 oz
plain (all-purpose) flour	for dusting	
Puff Pastry (page 195)	200–250 g	7–8.8 oz
Baking Glaze (page 242)		

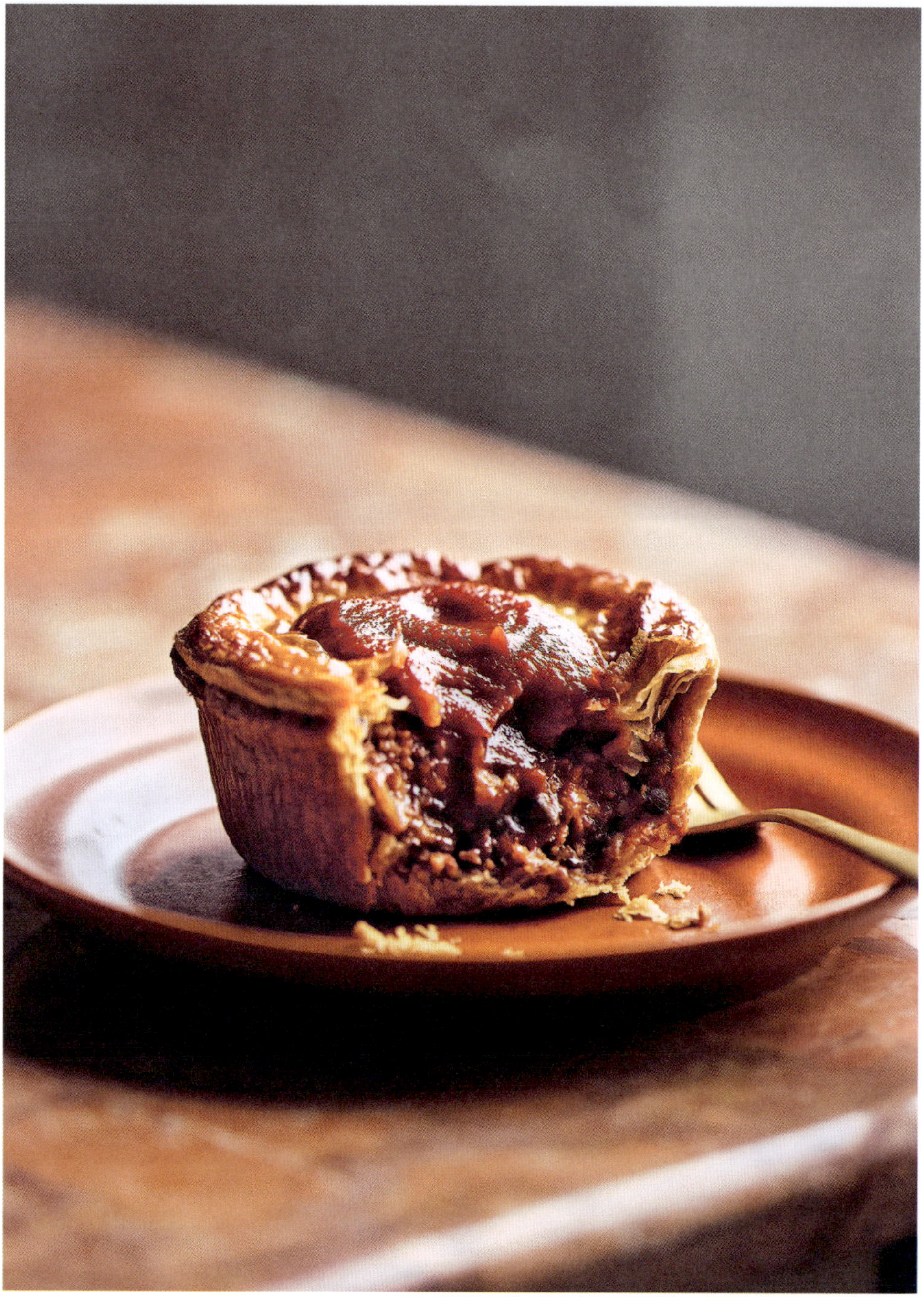

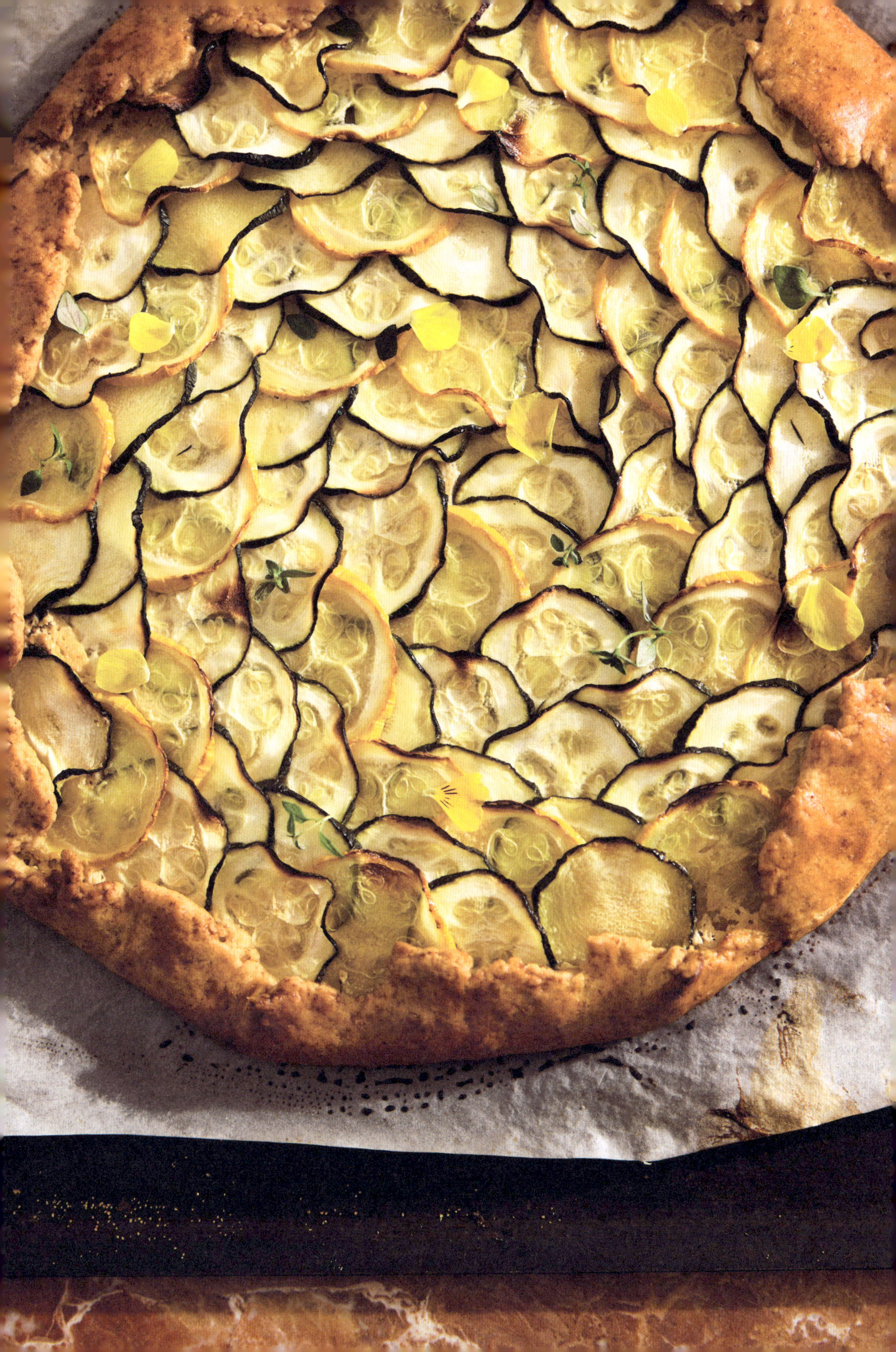

COURGETTE GALETTE

Makes 1 × 30 cm (12 in) galette

This courgette (zucchini) galette is the perfect mix of effortless and elegant – rustic in form, yet mesmerisingly beautiful before and after baking. A flaky pastry base provides the perfect crisp contrast to a creamy layer of whipped garlic and herb tofu, blended into a smooth, flavour-packed spread. On top, thinly sliced courgettes are arranged in a simple spiral, their edges curling and caramelising in the oven. It's the kind of dish that looks like you've spent hours on it but comes together in no time – just roll, spread, layer and bake.

WHIPPED GARLIC AND HERB TOFU

1. Combine all the ingredients in a small food processor or blender and blend to a smooth paste, or blend in a jug (pitcher) with a hand-held blender. If you only have a large food processor, just double this batch and retain half the mixture in an airtight container in the refrigerator for up to 7 days – it makes a great spread for bagels or toast.

silken tofu	340 g	12 oz
lemon juice	30 g	1 oz
spring onion (scallion) (about 1)	20 g	0.7 oz
chives	10 g	0.4 oz
parsley leaves	3 g	0.1 oz
smoked paprika	½ tsp	
flaky sea salt	8 g	1½ tsp
cashews or sunflower seeds	30 g	1 oz

TO ASSEMBLE AND BAKE

2. Preheat the oven to 190°C fan (400°F) and position a shelf in the middle of the oven.

3. Place the disc of pastry dough between two large sheets of baking parchment. From the middle, press and roll gently outwards with a rolling pin to make an oval shape, then turn the dough 90 degrees and roll again, starting in the middle. Roll it into a 34–35 cm (13¼–13¾ in) circle. If the edges fray, it's okay – it's meant to look a little rustic. Remove the top piece of baking parchment but leave the bottom paper in place.

4. Spread the whipped tofu mixture in the middle of the pastry disc, leaving a 3–4 cm (1¼–1½ in) border around the edge.

5. Slice the courgettes into 2 mm (⅛ in) thick slices – a mandoline makes very quick work of this, but make sure to use a guard as you get closer to the end! Starting from the centre, place five courgette slices in a circle, overlapping by half to a third of their width (courgette slices will shrink as they bake). Cover all the whipped tofu mixture with courgettes in this manner, all the way to the edge of the tofu but leaving the pastry border exposed.

Flaky Pastry (page 146)	450 g	15.9 oz
courgettes (zucchini) (about 2)	400 g	14.1 oz
Baking Glaze (page 242)	for brushing	
lemon zest and juice	½ lemon	
olive oil	for drizzling	
flaky sea salt	to taste	
sprig of thyme	1	
edible flowers, such as violas	to serve (optional)	

6   With the help of the bottom sheet of parchment paper, fold over the opposing sides of pastry, pressing them down with the help of the paper. Proceed to fold over the opposite edges until you have a nice border. Brush baking glaze over the edges and crush some salt over the top of the tart (including the outer crust),

7   Slide a large baking sheet under the galette, still on the parchment paper, and bake it in the oven for 25–30 minutes until the courgette has taken on some colour and the edges are golden.

8   Remove from the oven and sprinkle over some lemon zest, then squeeze the lemon juice over the courgette and finish with a drizzle of oil. Sprinkle with thyme leaves and edible flowers (if using). Leave to cool for at least 30 minutes. This can be served warm or at room temperature.

CREAMY LEEK AND TOFU PIE

Makes 1 × 23 cm (9 in) pie or 6 × 10 cm (4 in) individual pies

This pie has the comfort and familiarity of a classic chicken and leek, with tender celery and a creamy mustard-spiked sauce. Puff and flaky pastry give it a light, crisp finish, but you can use the same flaky pastry for both base and lid, or opt for a good shop-bought version to make things even simpler. It's a satisfying, all-in-one pie that comes together quickly and bakes up beautifully.

LEEK AND TOFU FILLING

1. Slice the leeks and celery and finely chop the garlic.
2. Heat the oil in a wide saucepan over a medium heat. Add the leeks, celery and garlic and cook for 5–7 minutes, or until softened and translucent but not coloured.
3. In a bowl or jug (pitcher), whisk together the milk, stock, cornflour, mustard, thyme, salt and pepper until smooth and fully dissolved.
4. Pour the mixture into the pan with the softened vegetables. Stir constantly over a medium heat for 5–7 minutes, or until thickened and creamy.
5. Stir in the tofu pieces and cook for a further 2 minutes to warm through. Remove from the heat and leave to cool completely.

leeks (about 2 trimmed)	250 g	8.8 oz
celery stalks	100 g	3.5 oz
garlic (2½ cloves)	10 g	0.4 oz
olive oil	20 g	0.7 oz
soya milk	200 g	7.1 oz
vegetable stock	250 g	8.8 oz
cornflour (cornstarch)	30 g	1 oz
Dijon mustard	10 g	0.4 oz
chopped thyme leaves	3 g	1 tsp
flaky sea salt	3 g	¾ tsp
ground black pepper	2 g	½ tsp
extra firm tofu, pressed	320 g	11.3 oz

TO ASSEMBLE AND BAKE

6. Preheat the oven to 190°C fan (400°F).
7. Roll out the flaky pastry dough on a lightly floured surface. Cut out a circle or circles large enough to line your chosen pie dish or dishes, with some overhang.
8. Line the pie dishes with the circles, pressing them into the sides and base. Fill each pie with the cooled leek and tofu filling, spreading it out evenly.
9. Roll out the puff pastry dough on a lightly floured surface. Cut out a circle or circles large enough to top the pie or pies. Cover the filling with the pastry, press the edges together to seal and trim any excess pastry.
10. Use a fork to crimp the edges, then cut a small slit in the top of each pie to allow steam to escape.
11. Brush the tops of the pies with baking glaze.
12. Bake in the oven for 22–25 minutes for individual pies or 30–35 minutes for one large pie, or until the pastry is golden brown and crisp. Remove the pies from the oven and leave to cool slightly before serving.
13. Store cooked pies in the refrigerator for up to 3 days. Reheat in the oven at 180°C fan (400°F) for 10–12 minutes for individual pies or 15–20 minutes for large pies or slices, or until heated through. Pies can also be frozen raw or baked – reheat from frozen at 180°C fan (400°F) for 20–25 minutes.

FOR 6 × 10 CM (4 IN) PIES

Flaky Pastry (page 146)	600 g	1 lb 5 oz
plain (all-purpose) flour	for dusting	
Puff Pastry (page 195)	300 g	10.6 oz

FOR 1 × 23 CM (9 IN) PIE

Flaky Pastry (page 146)	300–350 g	10.6–12.4 oz
plain (all-purpose) flour	for dusting	
Puff Pastry (page 195)	200–250 g	7–8.8 oz
Baking Glaze (page 242)	for brushing	

TIP

In place of tofu, you can add pieces of your favourite seitan recipe, or 150 g (5.3 oz) of large chunks of textured vegetable protein – which you will need to rehydrate with 150 g (5.3 oz) hot vegetable stock.

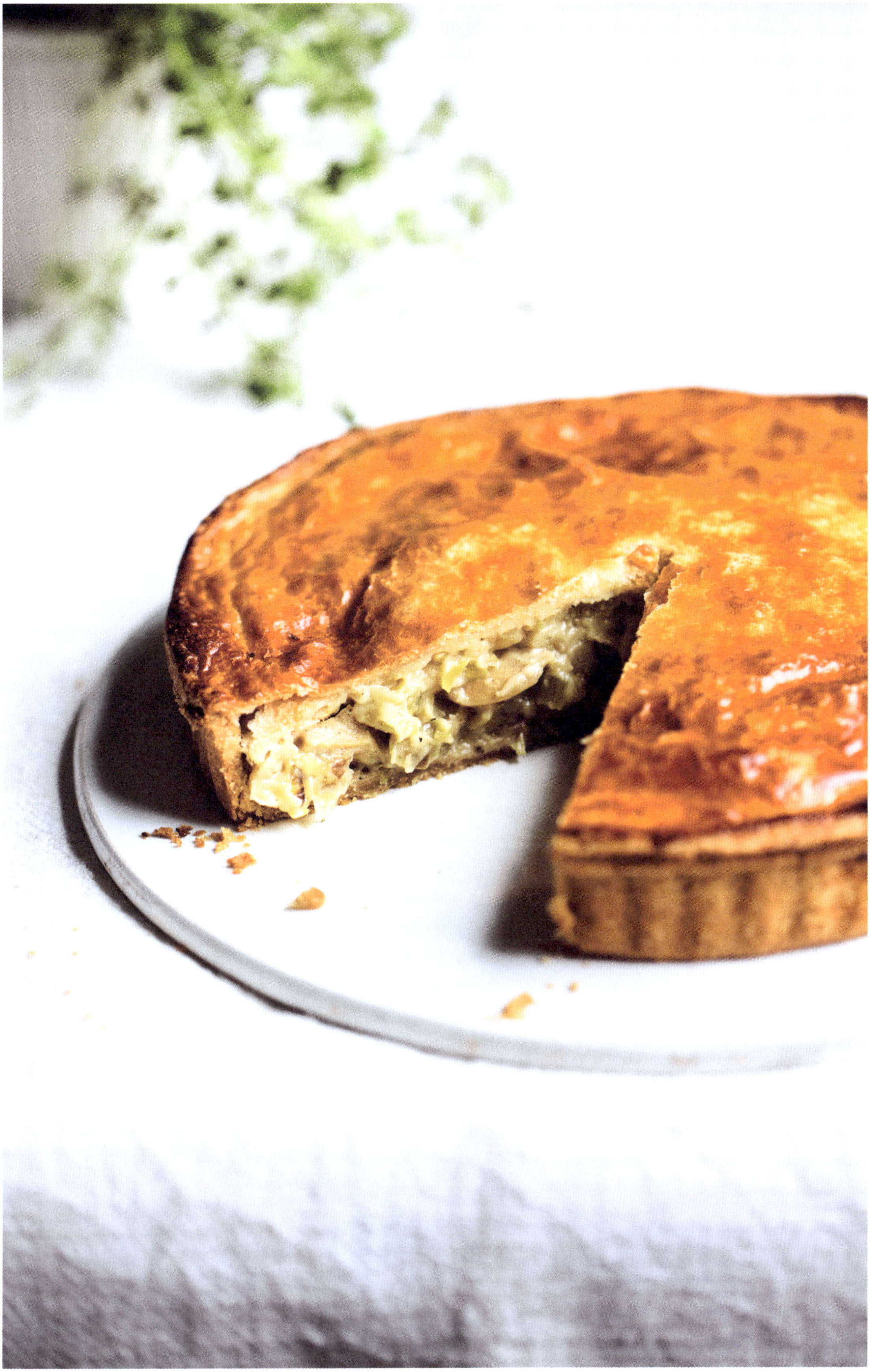

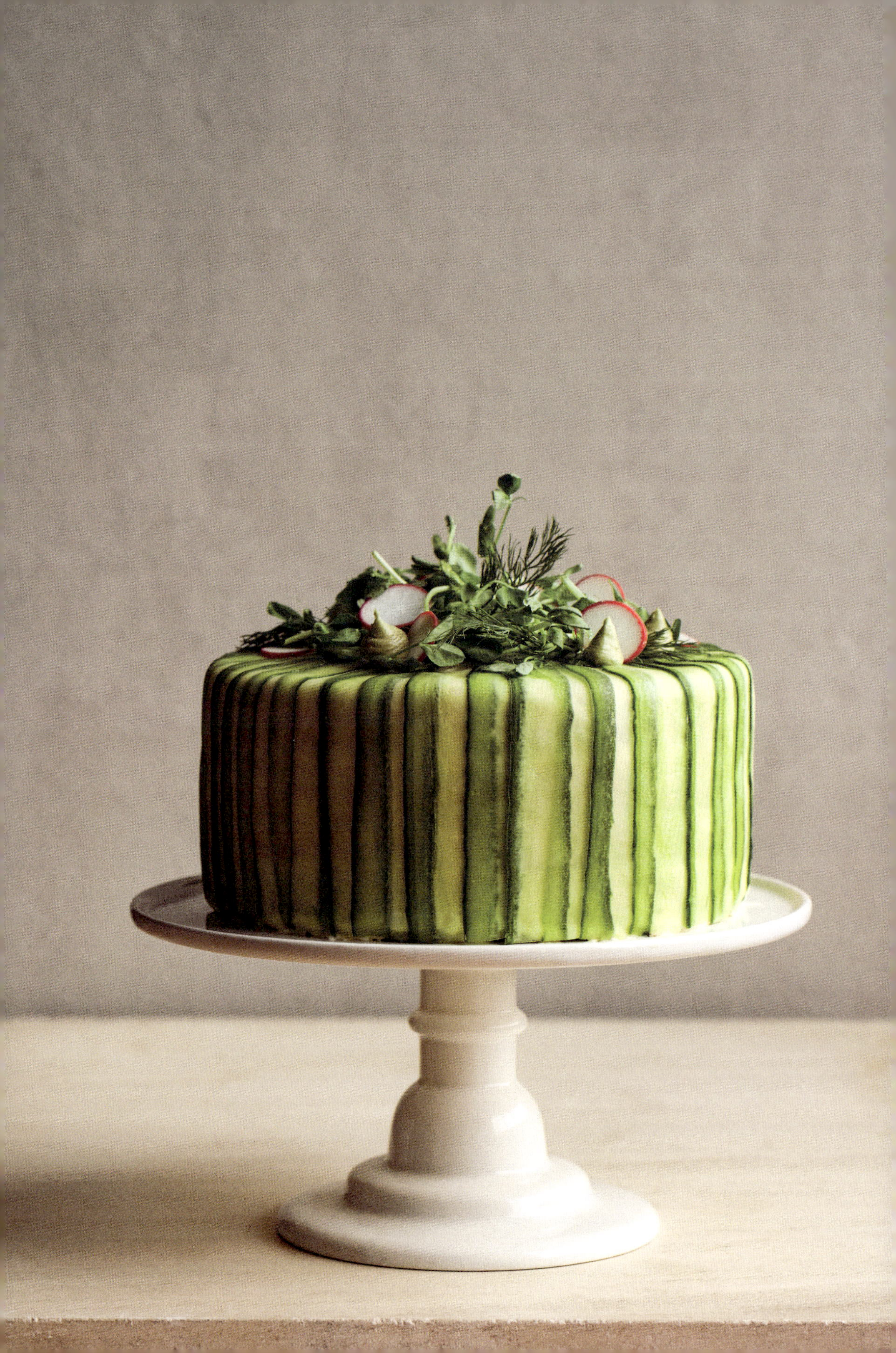

SAVOURY SUMMER GATEAU

Makes 1 × 18–20 cm (7–8 in) four-layer cake

This layered savoury 'cake' is built from rounds of soft, enriched Vrioche (page 56), filled with two contrasting vegetable mousses and finished with a smooth, whipped béchamel 'icing' (frosting). It makes an impressive centrepiece for gatherings and can be assembled ahead of time.

1. Divide the dough in half and shape into two rounds, then place in two greased 18–20 cm (7–8 in) springform cake tins (pans). Press the tops down, then cover with cling film (plastic wrap) or a damp cloth and leave to rise in a warm place for 1½–2 hours, or until the dough has risen to just above the rim of the tins.
2. Preheat the oven to 180°C fan (400°F).
3. Once risen, bake the vrioche in the oven for 20–25 minutes, or until deep golden and hollow-sounding when tapped underneath.
4. Remove from the oven and leave to cool completely.
5. Once cool, trim the domed tops to make them flat, then cut each round in half through the middle to create four even layers. To do this, hold a bread knife steady at the halfway point and rotate the loaf against the blade on your work surface, scoring a guideline. Continue rotating, cutting gradually deeper until the knife cuts all the way through.

Vrioche dough (page 56)	600 g	1.3 lb
olive oil		for greasing

AVOCADO AND PEA MOUSSE

6. Bring a saucepan of water to the boil and blanch the peas for 1 minute, then drain.
7. In an upright blender or in a jug (pitcher) with a hand-held blender, blend the avocado, dill, beans and salt until smooth. Fold in the peas. Chill until ready to use.
8. Thinly slice the tomatoes and set aside to layer with the mousse.

frozen peas	150 g	5.3 oz
ripe avocado (about 1½–2)	200 g	7 oz
dill		6 stems
½ drained 400 g (14 oz) tin of cannellini beans	135 g	3.8 oz
flaky sea salt	5 g	1 tsp
firm tomatoes (2 medium)	250 g	8.8 oz

BEETROOT AND HORSERADISH MOUSSE

9. In an upright blender or in a jug with a hand-held blender, blend the beetroot (1), beans, horseradish, salt and cornflour until smooth.
10. Pour into a small saucepan and cook over medium heat, stirring continuously with a silicone spatula until thickened. Pour into a shallow dish and press cling film onto the surface. Chill until ready to use.
11. Slice the beetroot (2) and set aside to layer with the mousse.

cooked beetroot (1)	90 g	3.2 oz
½ drained 400 g (14 oz) tin of cannellini beans	135 g	3.8 oz
horseradish sauce, or to taste	25 g	0.9 oz
flaky sea salt	3 g	¾ tsp
cornflour (cornstarch)	12 g	1 tbsp
cooked beetroot (2)	200 g	7 oz

BÉCHAMEL ICING

12. Melt the butter (1) in a saucepan over a medium heat. Stir in the flour and cook for 1–2 minutes, stirring constantly, to form a roux.

13. Slowly whisk in the milk, a little at a time, until smooth. Add the bay leaf and bring to a gentle simmer. Cook for 5–7 minutes, whisking often, until thickened to a spoon-coating consistency.

14. Remove the bay leaf and add the salt and pepper. Pour into a shallow dish and place a layer of cling film (plastic wrap) on the surface to prevent a skin forming. Chill in the refrigerator to 5°C (41°F).

15. Once chilled, place the béchamel in a stand mixer fitted with the whisk attachment. Melt the butter (2) in a small saucepan or in the microwave in short bursts until it reaches 50°C (122°F) on a thermometer. Pour it into the béchamel and whisk well – it will start to thicken and take on a thick, icing-like appearance.

Olive Oil Butter (page 55) or shop-bought block butter (1)	30 g	1 oz
plain (all-purpose) flour	30 g	1 oz
soya milk	250 g	8.8 oz
bay leaf	1	
flaky sea salt	2 g	½ tsp
freshly ground black pepper	1 g	¼ tsp
Olive Oil Butter (page 55) or shop-bought block butter (2)	70 g	2.5 oz

TO ASSEMBLE

16. Place the bottom vrioche round on a serving plate. Spread with half the avocado mousse, then layer with half the sliced tomato.

17. Add the second round. Spread with the beetroot mousse and layer with the cooked beetroot slices.

18. Add the third round and top with the remaining avocado mousse (reserving a little for garnishing) and tomato slices.

19. Finish with the fourth round. Press down lightly to settle the layers.

20. Use an offset spatula to apply the whipped béchamel around the sides and over the top as you would an icing. Smooth evenly.

21. Using a vegetable peeler, shave long, thin strips from the cucumbers. Gently press these vertically around the cake, overlapping slightly to fully cover.

22. Garnish the top with pea shoots, radishes and piped dots of leftover avocado mousse.

23. Keep the assembled cake refrigerated. It is best served within 24 hours, although leftovers will keep for up to 2 days. Allow to come to room temperature for 15–20 minutes before serving for the best texture.

cucumbers	2 large
pea shoots	to garnish
sliced radishes	to garnish

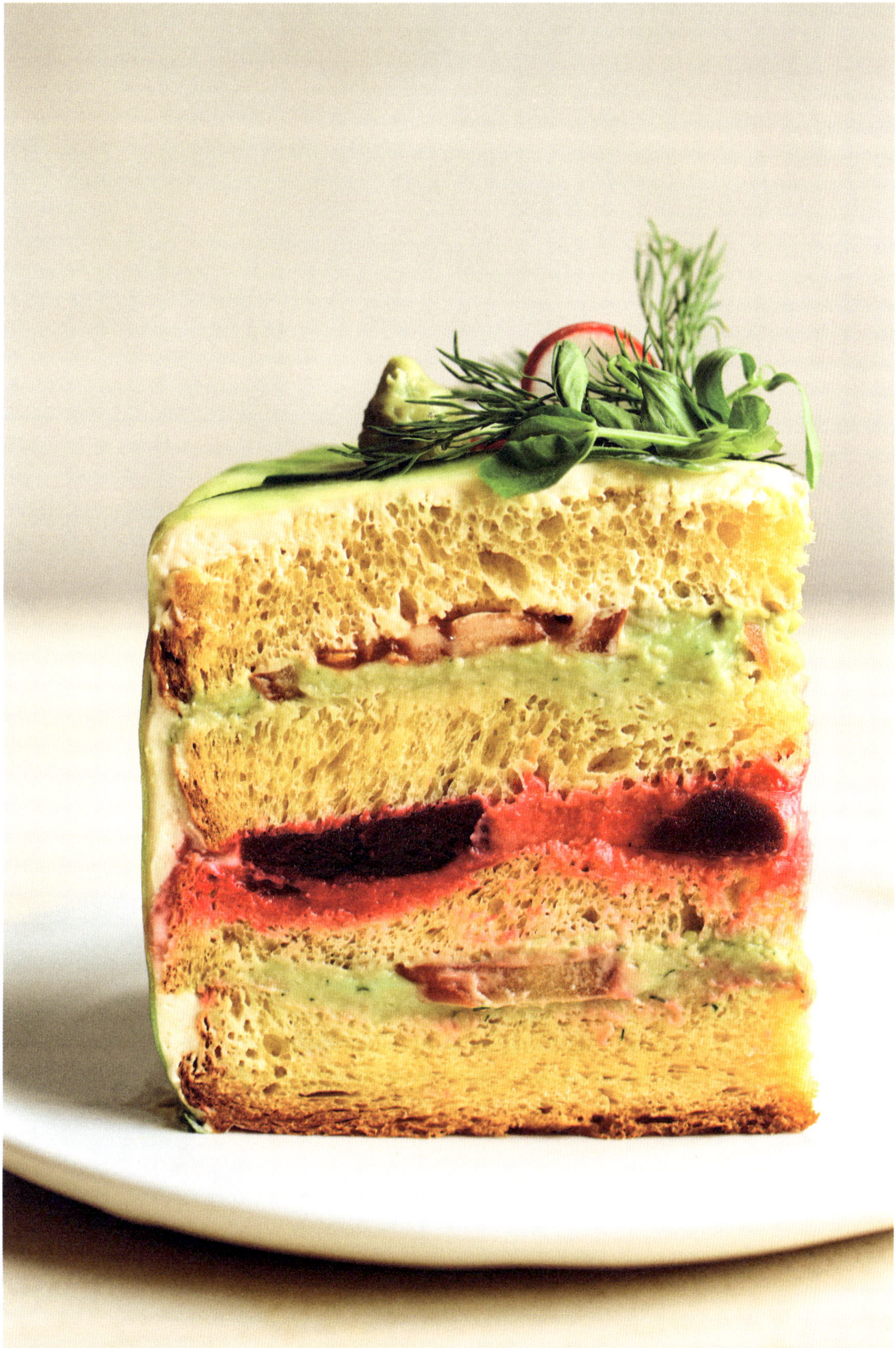

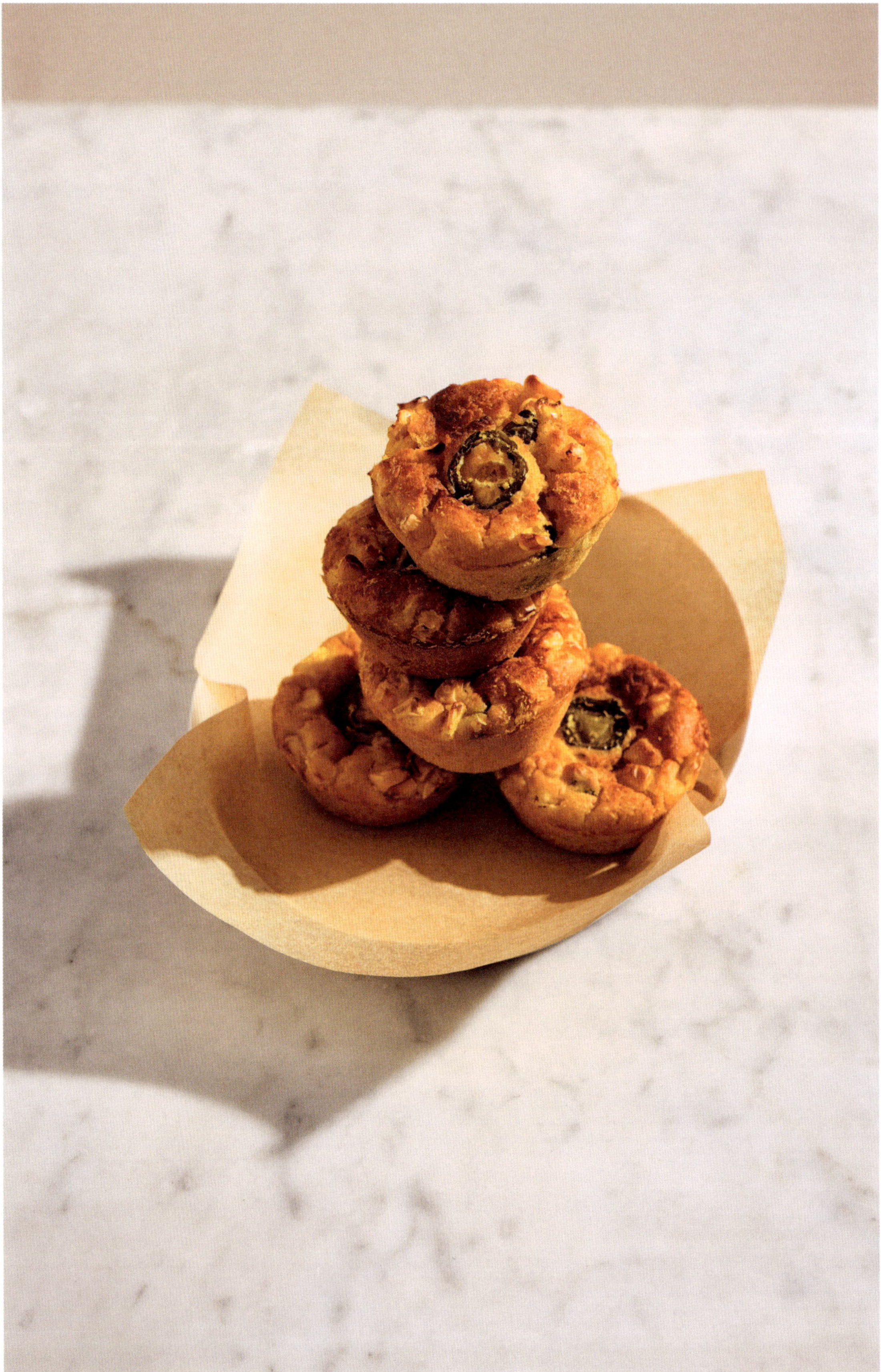

CORN AND JALAPEÑO MUFFINS

Makes 12 muffins

This is pure comfort – warm, golden and full of flavour. This version brings a little extra excitement, with bursts of sweetcorn and the gentle heat of jalapeño, creating the perfect balance of savoury, sweet and spicy.

1. Preheat the oven to 180°C (350°F) conventional (not fan). Line a 12-hole muffin tin (pan) with paper cases.

2. Place the sweetcorn kernels (1) in a food processor or high-powered blender. Add the oil, milk, salt and sugar. Blend for 30–45 seconds, or until smooth and creamy. It should resemble a thick, pourable batter.

3. Whisk together the polenta, flour and baking powder in a large bowl until fully combined.

4. Pour the blended corn mixture into the dry ingredients and use a silicone spatula or large spoon to gently mix until no dry patches remain.

5. Fold in the sweetcorn kernels (2), chopped jalapeños and nutritional yeast. The batter will be thick but scoopable.

6. Spoon approximately 60 g (2 oz) of batter into each muffin case – a standard ice-cream scoop works well here. Top each with a few extra corn kernels and a pinch of chopped jalapeño.

7. Sprinkle each muffin with a little nutritional yeast for a golden, savoury crust.

8. Bake in the oven for 22–25 minutes, or until risen, golden and a skewer inserted into the centre comes out clean. The tops should feel lightly firm and spring back when touched.

9. Remove from the oven and leave to cool in the tin for 5 minutes before transferring to a wire rack to cool completely. Serve warm or at room temperature. These keep for up to 3 days in an airtight container at room temperature.

frozen sweetcorn kernels, defrosted (1)	275 g	9.7 oz
olive oil	80 g	2.8 oz
soya milk	250 g	8.8 oz
fine sea salt	8 g	1½ tsp
caster (superfine) sugar	20 g	0.7 oz
fine or coarse polenta (cornmeal)	50 g	1.8 oz
plain (all-purpose) flour	200 g	7 oz
baking powder	5 g	1 tsp
frozen sweetcorn kernels, defrosted (2), plus extra for sprinkling	100 g	3.5 oz
finely chopped jalapeños, plus extra for sprinkling	70 g	2.7 oz
nutritional yeast plus extra or sprinkling	1 tbsp	

CHEESY SUN BUNS

Makes 8 buns

These sun buns are pure comfort – soft, golden brioche with a molten, cheesy, herb-laced centre that oozes as you tear it apart. The magic happens just before baking, when a frozen puck of savoury, umami-packed goodness is pressed into the fully proved dough, ready to melt into a rich, gooey filling as the bun bakes. The result? A beautifully puffy, golden-topped brioche with a centre that stays irresistibly warm and melty, perfect for pulling apart and devouring while still hot from the oven.

warm water	315 g	11.1 oz
cashews	65 g	2.3 oz
nutritional yeast	5 g	1 tbsp
apple cider vinegar	30 g	1 oz
tapioca starch	35 g	1.2 oz
garlic (1 small clove)	4 g	0.1 oz
dried mixed herbs	1 g	1 tsp
fine sea salt	3 g	¾ tsp
olive oil	10 g	0.4 oz
Vrioche dough (page 56)	400 g	14.1 oz
Baking Glaze (page 242)	for brushing	
maple syup	for brushing	
chives, finely chopped	1 tbsp	

1. Combine all the ingredients except the dough and glaze in a high-powdered blender and leave to sit for 30 minutes to soften the cashews.

2. Blend the mixture on high for 1–2 minutes until completely smooth. The mixture should be creamy with no visible bits of cashew or starch.

3. Transfer the mixture to a small saucepan over a medium heat. Stir continuously with a silicone spatula or whisk. After 3–5 minutes, the mixture will begin to thicken and stretch slightly due to the tapioca.

4. Once thickened and glossy, remove from the heat and cool for 5 minutes. Transfer to a piping (pastry) bag and pipe into 3 cm (1¼ in) silicone dome moulds. Tap the moulds gently on the work surface to settle the mixture and smooth the tops. Freeze the domes until solid – at least 3–4 hours, or overnight.

5. Divide the dough into eight equal portions (50 g/1.8 oz each) and shape into smooth, round buns.

6. Place the buns on a baking tray (pan) lined with baking parchment, spaced at least 4 cm (1½ in) apart. Cover and leave to prove at room temperature for 1–1½ hours until doubled in size and puffy.

7. Preheat oven to 180°C fan (400°F).

8. Once fully proved, brush the tops gently with baking glaze. Unmould the frozen cheese domes and press them firmly into the tops of each bun, until it feels like it has reached the bottom.

9. Bake in the oven for 16–18 minutes, or until a deep golden brown. The cheese centres will begin to soften and sink slightly into the buns.

10. Remove from the oven and very lightly brush with a tiny bit of maple syrup and sprinkly on the chives. Allow to cool for 20 minutes before serving. Best eaten warm when the centre is gooey, but also delicious at room temperature.

11. Store in an airtight container for up to 2 days. Reheat at 160°C fan (350°F) for 5–8 minutes to re-melt the centre. Buns can also be frozen after baking and reheated from frozen.

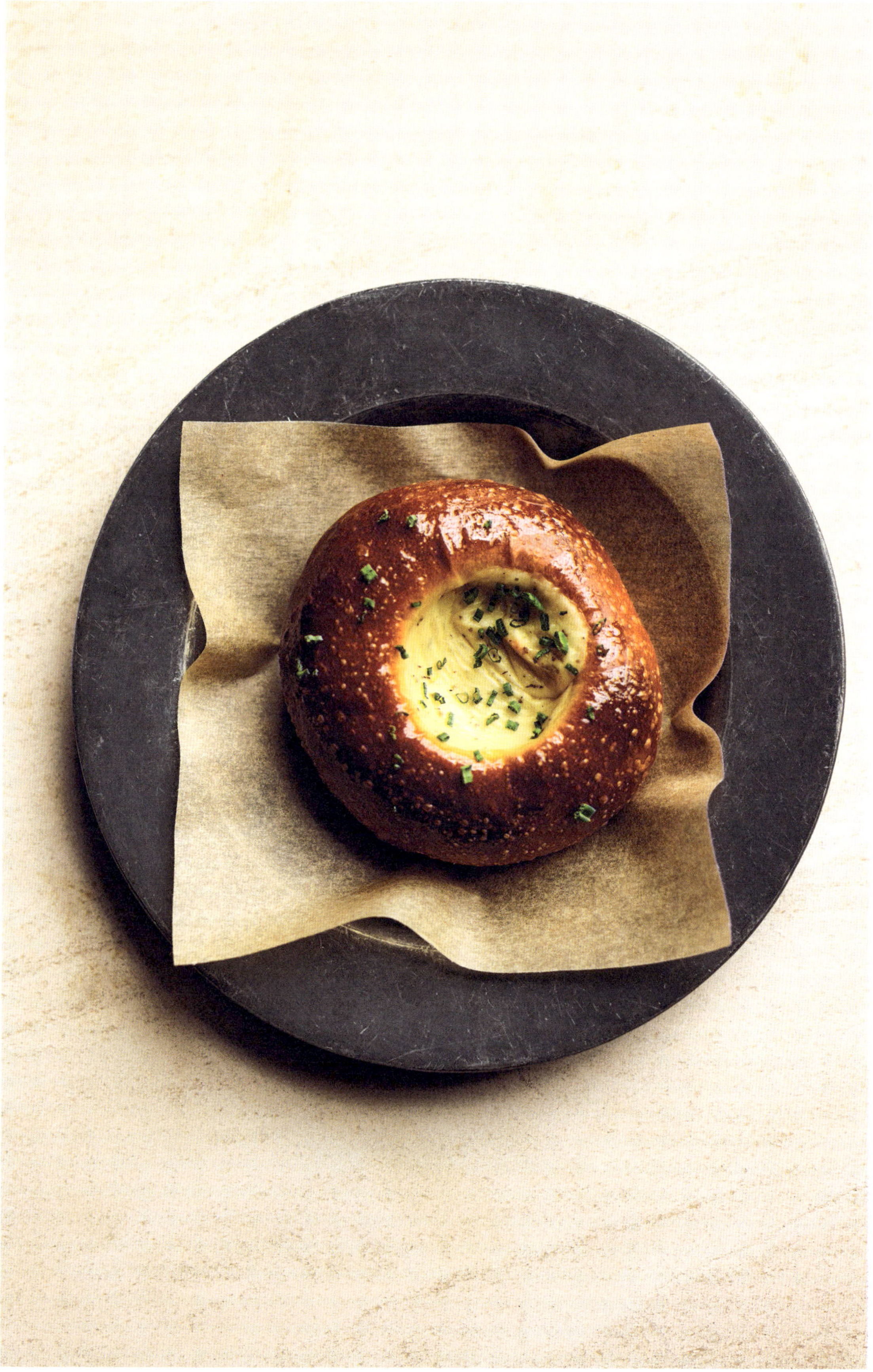

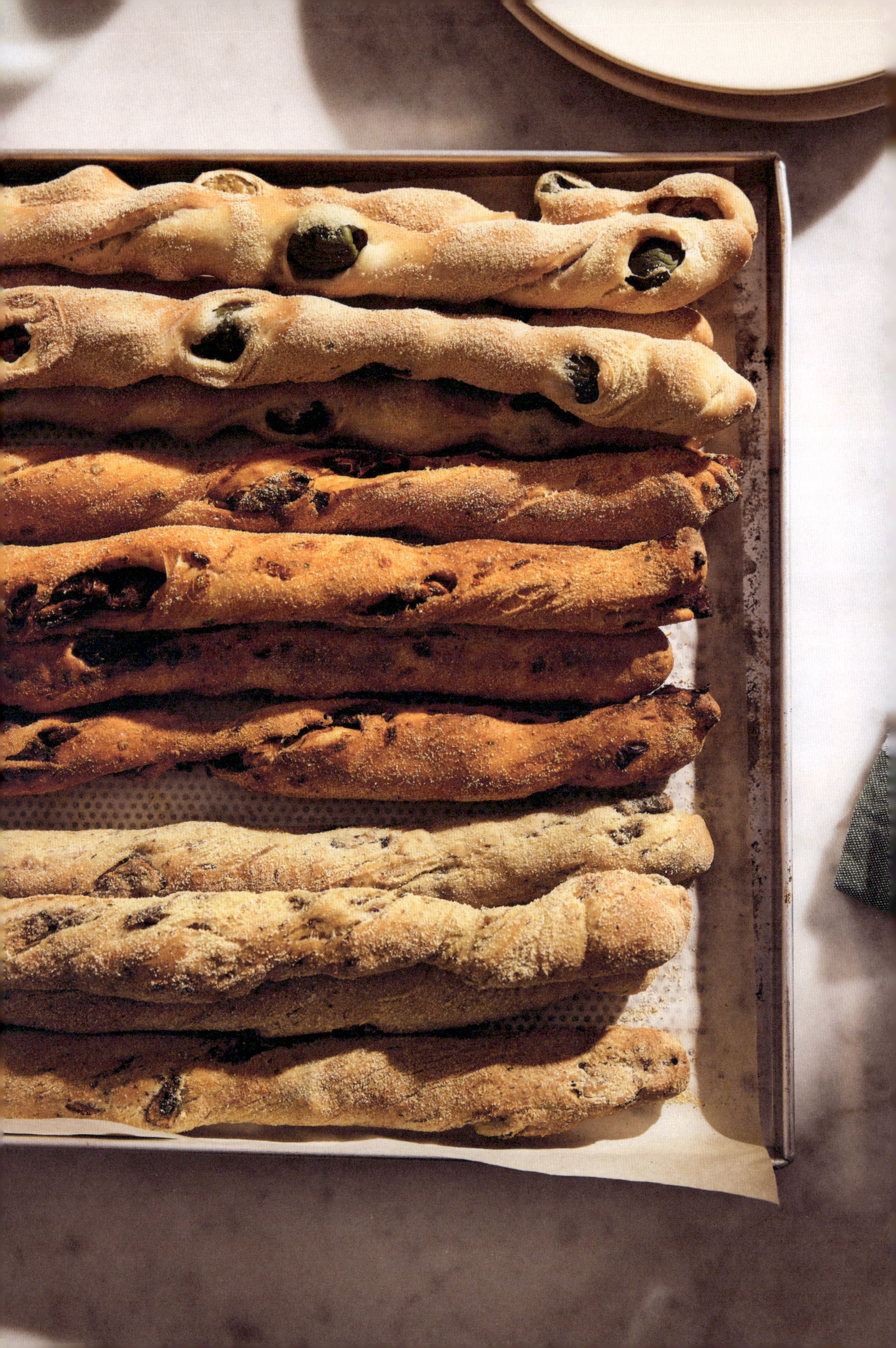

BREAD STICKS

Makes 12 sticks

I've long said that my favourite thing in the Harrods Food Halls is the olive stick – a long, slender bread stick that has become a favourite snack of shoppers. The secret to the perfect olive stick is all in the quality and quantity of olives – about six per 30 cm (12 in), 80 g (2.8 oz) stick is the sweet spot. Harrods uses Sicilian Nocellara olives, prized for their mild, buttery flavour and firm texture, but if they're hard to find, any good, firm olive will work. Too salty? A simple overnight soak in fresh water will mellow them out.

The base dough is beautifully adaptable, lending itself just as well to other bold flavours. Sundried tomatoes bring a deep, concentrated sweetness, while a mushroom and truffle version leans into rich, earthy indulgence. Whether you go classic or experiment, these bread sticks are crisp on the outside, slightly chewy within, and utterly moreish – just try not to eat the whole batch.

OLIVE STICKS

1. Combine the flour, salt, yeast, water and oil in a large bowl. Chop the olives and add to the bowl. Mix with a spoon or your hand until a shaggy dough forms. Cover and leave to rest for 30 minutes at room temperature.

2. After 30 minutes, perform a fold by lifting up one side of the dough and folding it over itself. Rotate the bowl and repeat with each side. This helps gluten development.

3. Rest the dough for another 30 minutes.

4. Repeat the folding process two more times. The dough should become smooth and elastic. Rest again for 30–40 minutes.

5. Press the air from the dough and turn it out onto a lightly floured surface. Divide the dough into 80 g (2.8 oz) portions. Roll each portion into a ball and roll in semolina to reduce stickiness. Rest on the work surface for 10 minutes. Line two baking trays (pans) with baking parchment.

6. Using both hands, roll each dough ball into a long breadstick, about 30 cm (12 in) long, using outward pressure. The olives should be distributed evenly through each stick. The semolina will help create a crisp outer texture.

7. Arrange the sticks on the prepared trays, spaced 2–3 cm (¾–1¼ in) apart. Leave to rest for 30 minutes at room temperature to rise slightly.

8. Preheat the oven to 180°C (400°F).

9. Bake the sticks in the oven for 12–15 minutes, or until evenly golden.

10. Remove the bread sticks from the oven and, if you like, drizzle them lightly with olive oil. Cool before serving.

strong white bread flour, plus extra for dusting	320 g	11.3 oz
fine sea salt	6 g	1¼ tsp
instant yeast	3 g	1 tsp
water	200 g	7 oz
olive oil, plus extra for drizzling	20 g	0.7 oz
Nocellara olives, pitted	330 g	11.6 oz
semolina	for rolling	

MUSHROOM AND TRUFFLE STICKS

1. Finely chop the mushrooms, then sauté them in a dry frying pan over a medium-high heat for 8–10 minutes until they have released their moisture and reduced significantly. Remove from the heat and leave to cool slightly.

2. Combine the flour, salt, yeast, water, oil, cooked mushrooms and truffle paste in a large bowl. Mix with a spoon or your hand until a shaggy dough forms. Cover and leave to rest for 30–45 minutes at room temperature.

3. After 30 minutes, perform a fold by lifting up one side of the dough and folding it over itself. Rotate the bowl and repeat with each side. This helps gluten development. Rest the dough for another 30 minutes.

4. Repeat the folding process two more times. The dough should become smooth and elastic. Rest again for 30–40 minutes.

5. Press the air from the dough and turn it out onto a lightly floured surface. Divide the dough into 80 g (2.8 oz) portions. Roll each portion into a ball and roll in semolina to reduce stickiness. Rest on the work surface for 10 minutes. Line two baking trays (pans) with baking parchment.

6. Using both hands, roll each dough ball into a long breadstick, about 30 cm (12 in) long, using outward pressure. The mushrooms should be distributed evenly through each stick. The semolina will help create a crisp outer texture.

7. Arrange the sticks on the prepared trays, spaced 2–3 cm (¾–1¼ in) apart. Leave to rest for 30 minutes at room temperature to rise slightly.

8. Preheat the oven to 180°C (400°F).

9. Bake the sticks in the oven for 12–15 minutes, or until evenly golden.

10. Remove the bread sticks from the oven and, if you like, drizzle them lightly with olive oil. Cool before serving.

chestnut (cremini) mushrooms	320 g	11.3 oz
strong white bread flour, plus extra for dusting	320 g	11.3 oz
fine sea salt	6 g	1¼ tsp
instant yeast	3 g	1 tsp
water	200 g	7 oz
olive oil, plus extra for drizzling	20 g	0.7 oz
truffle paste	15 g	0.5 oz
semolina	for rolling	

SUN-DRIED TOMATO STICKS

1. Drain and pat dry the sun-dried tomatoes, then finely chop.

2. Combine the flour, salt, yeast, water, oil, tomato purée, dried herbs and chopped tomatoes in a large bowl. Mix with a spoon or your hand until a shaggy dough forms. Cover and leave to rest for 30 minutes at room temperature.

3. After 30 minutes, perform a fold by lifting up one side of the dough and folding it over itself. Rotate the bowl and repeat with each side. This helps gluten development. Rest the dough for another 30 minutes.

4. Repeat the folding process two more times. The dough should become smooth and elastic. Rest again for 30–40 minutes.

5. Press the air from the dough and turn it out onto a lightly floured surface. Divide the dough into 80 g (2.8 oz) portions. Roll each portion into a ball and roll in semolina to reduce stickiness. Rest on the work surface for 10 minutes. Line two baking trays (pans) with baking parchment.

6. Using both hands, roll each dough ball into a long breadstick, about 30 cm (12 in) long, using outward pressure. The sun-dried tomatoes should be distributed evenly through each stick. The semolina will help create a crisp outer texture.

7. Arrange the sticks on the prepared trays, spaced 2–3 cm (¾–1¼ in) apart. Leave to rest for 30 minutes at room temperature to rise slightly.

8. Preheat the oven to 180°C (400°F).

9. Bake the sticks in the oven for 12–15 minutes, or until evenly golden.

10. Remove the bread sticks from the oven and, if you like, drizzle them lightly with olive oil. Cool before serving.

sun-dried tomatoes	165 g	5.8 oz
strong white bread flour, plus extra for dusting	320 g	11.3 oz
fine sea salt	6 g	1¼ tsp
instant yeast	3 g	1 tsp
water	200 g	7 oz
olive oil, plus extra for drizzling	20 g	0.7 oz
tomato purée (paste)	30 g	1 oz
dried basil or mixed herbs	2 g	2 tsp
semolina	for rolling	

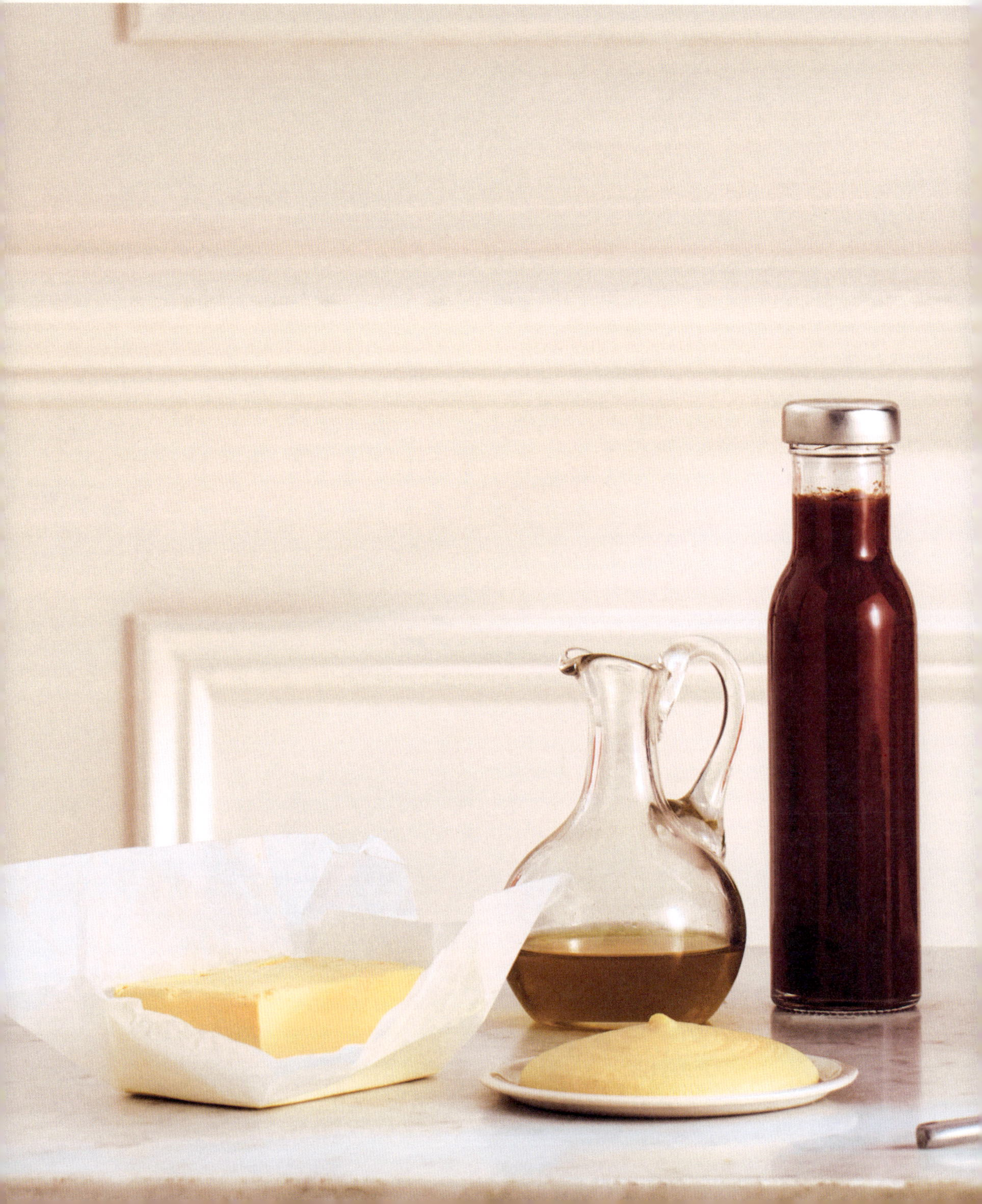

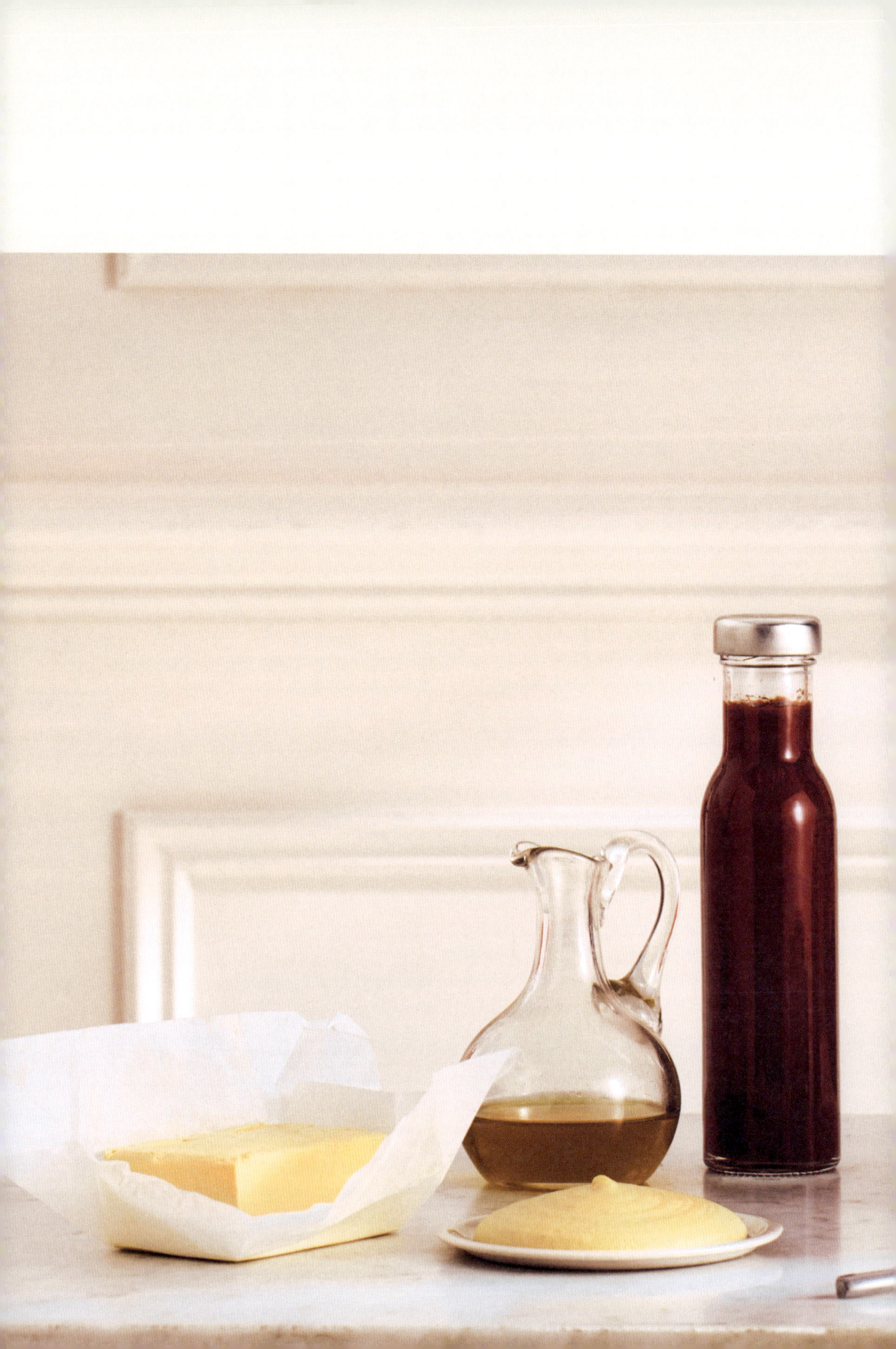

8 A SELECTION OF STAPLES

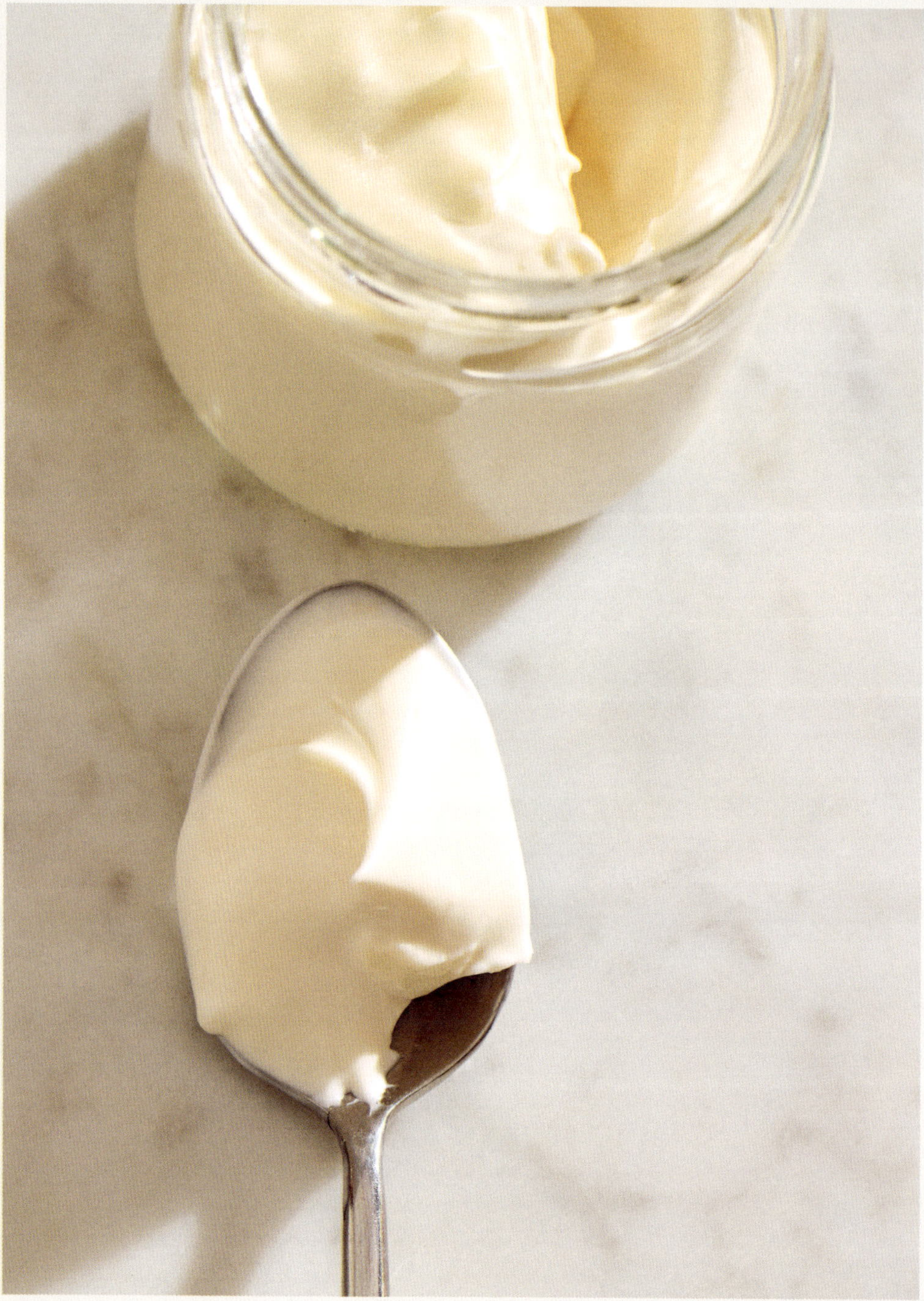

BUILDING BLOCKS
AND SUPPORTS

The following pages contain recipes that provide both support structures and finishing touches: a fail-safe whipping cream that you will find used in myriad recipes across the book; a silky crème pat perfect for filling and topping everything from a sweet yeasted bun to a classic fruit tart; glazes to give a pâtissier-level finish, and of course, sauces such as ketchup and mayo to add sweetness and acidity to classic savouries.

Each batch will be more than enough for one recipe, so I've given instructions on how to store them.

FRESH WHIPPING CREAM

Fresh whipping cream or Chantilly is a versatile staple in the vegan repertoire. This recipe is simple but with a tiny trick. It is best made as a base, stored in the refrigerator and whipped whenever required. It is used to lighten mousses and other creams and can be used in any recipe that calls for a double (heavy) or whipping cream of 35 per cent fat. I have sucessfully used oat milk to make whipping cream, but I much prefer soya milk. Please use deodorised coconut oil and the resulting cream will have a beautiful neutral flavour. Using virgin coconut oil will leave a strong taste and make it prone to spoiling and having an off taste.

Makes 500 g (1 lb 2 oz)

coconut oil (deodorised)	200 g	7 oz
caster (superfine) sugar	40 g	1.4 oz
soya milk	275 g	9.7 oz

TIP

If the cream is not whipping, place the mixture in the freezer for 15 minutes before whipping again. Make sure to chill the mixing bowl before whipping.

1. Add the coconut oil to a microwave-safe bowl and microwave for 30–60 seconds until melted. Alternatively, melt in a medium saucepan over a low heat. Set aside.

2. Add the sugar mixture to the soya milk in a large bowl and use an immersion stick blender or high-powered blender to blend them together.

3. Add the melted coconut oil to the mixture, then, using a thermometer, test the temperature. It should be 35°C (95°F), so warm or cool the mixture as required. Use the immersion stick blender for 30–60 seconds until the mixture has emulsified.

4. Pour the mixture into a shallow dish and press cling film (plastic wrap) onto the surface. Leave in the refrigerator for at least 4 hours to chill and 'crystallise' fully – this is where the solid fat particles cool to the temperature they turn solid and completely solidify. The fat particles should be dispersed throughout the cream in a homogenous, creamy mixture that won't go grainy.

5. Pour the mixture into the chilled bowl of a stand mixer fitted with a whisk attachment, or whisk by hand or with electric beaters making sure to chill your bowl first, until soft peaks are formed that hold their shape. Use immediately or reserve the whipped cream in the refrigerator until needed.

6. To store, transfer to a container, cover with cling film (plastic wrap) on the surface of the cream and use the same day. The unwhipped cream can be stored in the refrigerator in a sealed container or jar for up to 4 days.

CRÈME PÂTISSIÈRE

Crème pât for short! This thick and rich custardy cream is super versatile. It can be folded with fresh Whipping Cream (opposite) to make a luxurious crème diplomat, as in the Tarte Tropézienne recipe (page 126).

Makes 500 g (1 lb 2 oz)

plant-based milk (1)	290 g	10.2 oz
caster (superfine) sugar	90 g	3.2 oz
custard powder	15 g	0.5 oz
vanilla paste (or seeds from 1 vanilla pod/bean)	5 g	1 tsp
cornflour (cornstarch)	28 g	1 oz
plant-based milk (2)	40 g	1.4 oz
coconut oil (deodorised)	30 g	1 oz

1. Combine the milk (1), sugar, custard powder and vanilla paste (or vanilla seeds) in a high-sided saucepan and stir with a whisk to combine. Bring the mixture to a simmer over a medium heat.

2. In a small bowl, combine the cornflour with the milk (2). Mix until the cornflour has completely dissolved and no lumps remain.

3. When the milk mixture in the saucepan comes to a simmer, reduce the heat to low. Pour in the cornflour mixture, stirring continuously. The mixture will thicken immediately. Continue stirring until the mixture comes to the boil and starts to bubble, then remove from the heat.

4. Add the coconut oil to the hot mixture. Whisk gently to melt the coconut oil and incorporate it. The mixture may appear slightly separated at first, but continue whisking until it is fully incorporated, glossy, smooth and clings to the sides of the saucepan.

5. Pour it into a shallow dish and place a layer of cling film (plastic wrap) on the surface to prevent a skin forming. Refrigerate until firm and set. The crème pâtissière can be stored in the refrigerator for up to 4 days.

6. Before using, put the desired amount into a small bowl and whisk until smooth and free of lumps.

CHOCOLATE CRÈME PÂTISSIÈRE

A rich chocolate crème pât, perfect for tarts, layer cakes and other desserts.

Makes 500 g (1 lb 2 oz)

plant-based milk (1)	230 g	8.1 oz
caster (superfine) sugar	90 g	3.2 oz
cocoa (unsweetened) powder	13 g	0.5 oz
cornflour (cornstarch)	13 g	0.5 oz
plant-based milk (2)	30 g	1 oz
dark chocolate min. 65% cocoa solids	130 g	4.6 oz

1. Combine the milk (1), sugar and cocoa powder in a high-sided saucepan and stir with a whisk to combine. Bring to a simmer over a medium heat.

2. In a small bowl, combine the cornflour and milk (2). Mix until the cornflour has completely dissolved and no lumps remain.

3. When the milk in the saucepan comes to a simmer, reduce the heat to low. Pour in the cornflour mixture, stirring continuously. The mixture will thicken immediately. Continue stirring until the mixture comes to the boil and starts to bubble, then remove from the heat.

4. Chop the chocolate and add to the saucepan, stirring until it has fully melted and the mixture is glossy.

5. Pour it into a shallow dish and place a layer of cling film (plastic wrap) on the surface to prevent a skin forming. Refrigerate until firm and set. The crème pâtissière can be stored in the refrigerator for up to 4 days.

6. Before using, put the desired amount into a small bowl and whisk until smooth and free of lumps.

OAT CRUMBLE

A moreish muscovado oat crumble – perfect for topping roasted fruit or cakes.

Makes 400 g (14.1 oz)

extra virgin olive oil	80 g	2.8 oz
plant-based milk	60 g	2 oz
muscovado sugar	50 g	1.8 oz
plain (all-purpose) flour	230 g	8.1 oz
baking powder	4 g	1 tsp
fine sea salt	1 g	¼ tsp
rolled oats	60 g	2 oz

1. Combine the oil, milk and sugar in a jug (pitcher). Blend with a hand-held blender or whisk until smooth and emulsified. This forms your syrup.
2. In a large bowl, whisk together the flour, baking powder, salt and oats.
3. Pour the syrup into the dry ingredients and mix gently with a silicone spatula. The mixture should stay crumbly and not form a dough.
4. Spread the crumble mixture onto a baking sheet lined with baking parchment. Bake according to your recipe or in an oven preheated to 160°C fan (350°F) for around 15 minutes, or until rich golden brown and crisp.
5. Store in an airtight container for upto 1 month.

CANDIED PEEL

A simple recipe for superior pieces of delicious and juicy candied peel, perfect for using in any fruit-based enriched dough or cake, like the Light Fruit Cake on page 102. You won't use shop-bought candied peel again.

Makes 200 g (7 oz)

oranges (organic)		3 large
caster (superfine) sugar	200 g	7 oz
water	500 g	1 lb 2 oz

1. Wash the oranges thoroughly to remove any wax or residue. Using a sharp knife, slice off the tops and bottoms of each orange.
2. Score the orange peel into quarters, making sure not to cut into the fruit. Carefully peel off each quarter, leaving the white pith attached.
3. Slice the orange peel into thin strips, about 1 cm (½ in) wide.
4. Bring a large saucepan of water to the boil. Add the sliced orange peel and boil for 10 minutes. This helps to remove the bitterness from the peel. Drain the peel and rinse under cold water.
5. Refill the saucepan with fresh water, bring to the boil again, and repeat the boiling process for a further 10 minutes. Drain and rinse the peel once more.
6. In the same saucepan, combine the sugar with the measured water. Bring the mixture to a simmer over a medium heat, stirring occasionally.
7. Add the drained orange peel to the syrup. Simmer very gently for 45–60 minutes, or until the peel becomes translucent and the syrup thickens. Stir occasionally to ensure even coating.
8. Remove the saucepan from the heat and let the peel cool in the syrup for 15–20 minutes.
9. Using a slotted spoon, transfer the candied orange peel to a wire rack set over a baking sheet to catch any drips. Leave the peel to dry for several hours, or overnight, until it is no longer sticky.
10. Store in an airtight container at room temperature for up to 4 weeks.

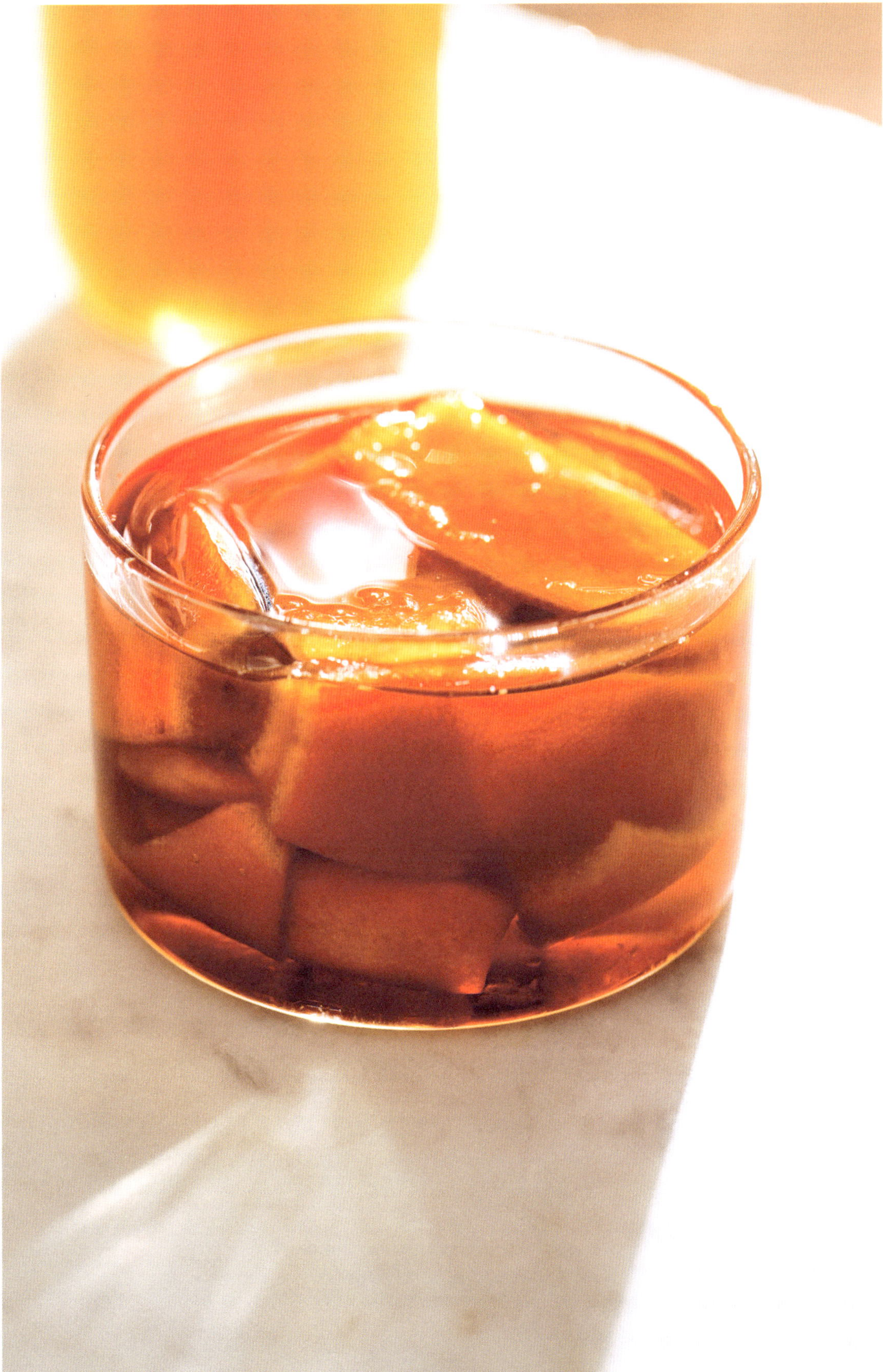

BAKING GLAZE

This is my updated and improved version of a plant-based glaze – it creates an even, golden shine on pastries and enriched breads without darkening too quickly in the oven. The addition of sweet potato gives body and colour without overpowering the flavour.

Makes about 340 g (12 oz)

soya milk	200 g	7 oz
olive oil	70 g	2.5 oz
agave syrup or golden syrup (light corn syrup)	50 g	1.8 oz
cooked sweet potato (page 44)	25 g	0.9 oz

1. Combine all the ingredients in a small upright blender or a deep mixing jug (pitcher) suitable for a hand-held blender.
2. Blend until smooth and fully emulsified – the mixture should be thick but pourable, with a consistent sheen. Try to blend without incorporating too many bubbles, but this can be unavoidable. To remove bubbles, store the glaze in the refrigerator overnight, then skim the foam layer on top.
3. Brush directly onto unbaked pastry or enriched dough just before placing in the oven. For best results, use a natural bristled pastry brush rather than a silicone one, which tends to leave streaks and doesn't give even coverage.
4. The glaze can be stored in the refrigerator for up to 4 days.

TIP

Pour the glaze into an ice cube tray and freeze. Once solid, transfer to a container or bag and store in the freezer for up to 3 months. Defrost cubes as needed.

EXOTIC CLEAR GLAZE

This is a brilliant glaze to help protect cut fruits from the elements and give a tasty and attractive shine to finished bakes. Inspired by the glaze that Pierre Hermé makes with citrus peels and vanilla, which I used to jokingly refer to, along with my colleague who introduced me to it, as the 'eau de pâtissière', this glaze can be melted in the microwave, as its high water content will heat up quickly. If it needs to be reheated on the hob, you will need to break it with a whisk and add a splash of water before reboiling it.

Makes 450 g (15.9 oz)

water	350 g	12.4 oz
agar-agar powder	4 g	1⅛ tsp
caster (superfine) sugar	100 g	3.5 oz
lemon peel		1 strip
orange peel		1 strip
vanilla pod (bean) (upcycle a scraped-out pod)		½ pod
mint		1 sprig

1. Pour the water into a large saucepan. Weigh the agar-agar accurately in a small bowl, add the sugar and mix to combine, then add to the saucepan of water.
2. Peel a couple of strips of lemon and orange and add them to the water along with the vanilla and mint.
3. Bring the mixture to a simmer for 2 minutes, then remove from the heat and leave to infuse for 30 minutes.
4. Strain the mixture through a sieve (fine-mesh strainer).
5. The mixture should be used as it cools – you will notice it starting to thicken. If it cools or clumps, reheat it in the microwave in short bursts or in a saucepan over a low heat. The glaze sets firmly.
6. Set the glaze aside in the refrigerator for up to 2 weeks. When needed, cut a small piece off and heat it in the microwave in short bursts to melt it, or in a saucepan, as noted above.

AQUAFABA AND HUMMUS: TWO WAYS TO USE A CHICKPEA

Chickpeas (garbanzos) – *hummus* in Arabic – are at the heart of this two-in-one recipe. Hummus, the creamy dip now found on tables around the world, has roots in the Levant, with the earliest recorded recipes traced to Syria. For those of us from the region, it's more than a dip: it's a staple. Made well, with soft, cooked chickpeas, good tahini and freshly squeezed lemon juice (sometimes a clove of garlic too, depending on the household), hummus becomes a soft and tangy whip, with depth and subtle bitterness from the sesame, crucial acidity from the lemon juice and added depth and creaminess from extra virgin olive oil.

And then there's aquafaba – the water chickpeas are cooked in. Since its rise to internet fame, aquafaba has been championed for its egg-like properties, particularly for making meringues, foams, mayonnaise and plant-based batters. But while aquafaba can aerate, it does not coagulate like an egg white, so I don't consider it a straight egg replacement, nor do I use it for things like cakes or batters that rely on structural protein.

That said, I do find aquafaba genuinely useful in a handful of preparations – for lightening a dense or whipped mixture, as the base of a mayonnaise or whipped into meringue kisses for an Eton Mess or piped garnish over a pavlova-style meringue.

In this recipe, you'll learn how to make aquafaba from scratch. It is very mild in flavour and is ready to be used, unlike the liquid from tinned chickpeas, which needs to be reduced.

AQUAFABA FROM DRIED CHICKPEAS

Makes about 350 g (12.4 oz)

dried chickpeas (garbanzos)	250 g	8.8 oz
bicarbonate of soda (baking soda)	6 g	1 tsp
water	1.2 kg	2 lb 11 oz

1. Place the chickpeas in a large bowl and cover them with 2–3 cm (about 1 inch) cold water. Stir in the bicarbonate of soda. Leave to soak for at least 4 hours, or overnight in a cool place, so they soften and swell.

2. The next day, drain and rinse the chickpeas. Place them in a saucepan with the measured water and bring to a very gentle simmer over a low heat. Cook for 1–1½ hours, skimming off any foam as necessary. The chickpeas should be very soft and the water should reduce to just cover them. If the water starts to dry out before softening, add a splash more water to cover the chickpeas

3. Once tender, set a strainer over a large bowl and drain the chickpeas. The golden liquid collected is your aquafaba, ready to use with no reduction required. Cool before storing.

AQUAFABA FROM TINNED CHICKPEAS

Makes about 100–130 g (3.5–4.6 oz)

| liquid from 1 × 400 g (14 oz) tin of chickpeas (garbanzos) | about 200 g | about 7 oz |

1. Pour the liquid into a saucepan. Bring to a simmer over a low heat and reduce by about a third. (I check this by pouring the initial liquid into a bowl set on scales to note the starting weight, then check it while reducing by pouring it into the bowl again – 200 g/7 oz should reduce to 100–130 g/3.5–4.6 oz.)

2. Remove from the heat and leave to cool fully before using. Store in a sealed container in the refrigerator for up to 5 days, or in a ziploc bag in the freezer, and use as needed.

CLASSIC HUMMUS

Makes about 300–350 g (10.6–12.4 oz)

cooked chickpeas, plus extra to serve	250 g	8.8 oz
tahini	60 g	2 oz
extra virgin olive oil, plus extra to serve	50 g	1.8 oz
lemon juice	50 g	1.8 oz
fine sea salt	4 g	¾ tsp
ground cumin or paprika		to serve

1. Rinse the cooked chickpeas thoroughly under cold water and drain using a sieve (fine-mesh strainer).

2. Transfer to a food processor or high-powered blender. Add the tahini, olive oil, lemon juice and salt.

3. Blend on high speed for 30–60 seconds, or until smooth and creamy. If the mixture becomes too thick or difficult to blend, add a little extra lemon juice (1 tablespoon at a time) and blend again. The goal is a velvety, spoonable consistency.

4. Spoon into a dish and finish with a few reserved chickpeas, a sprinkle of ground cumin or paprika, and a generous glug of olive oil.

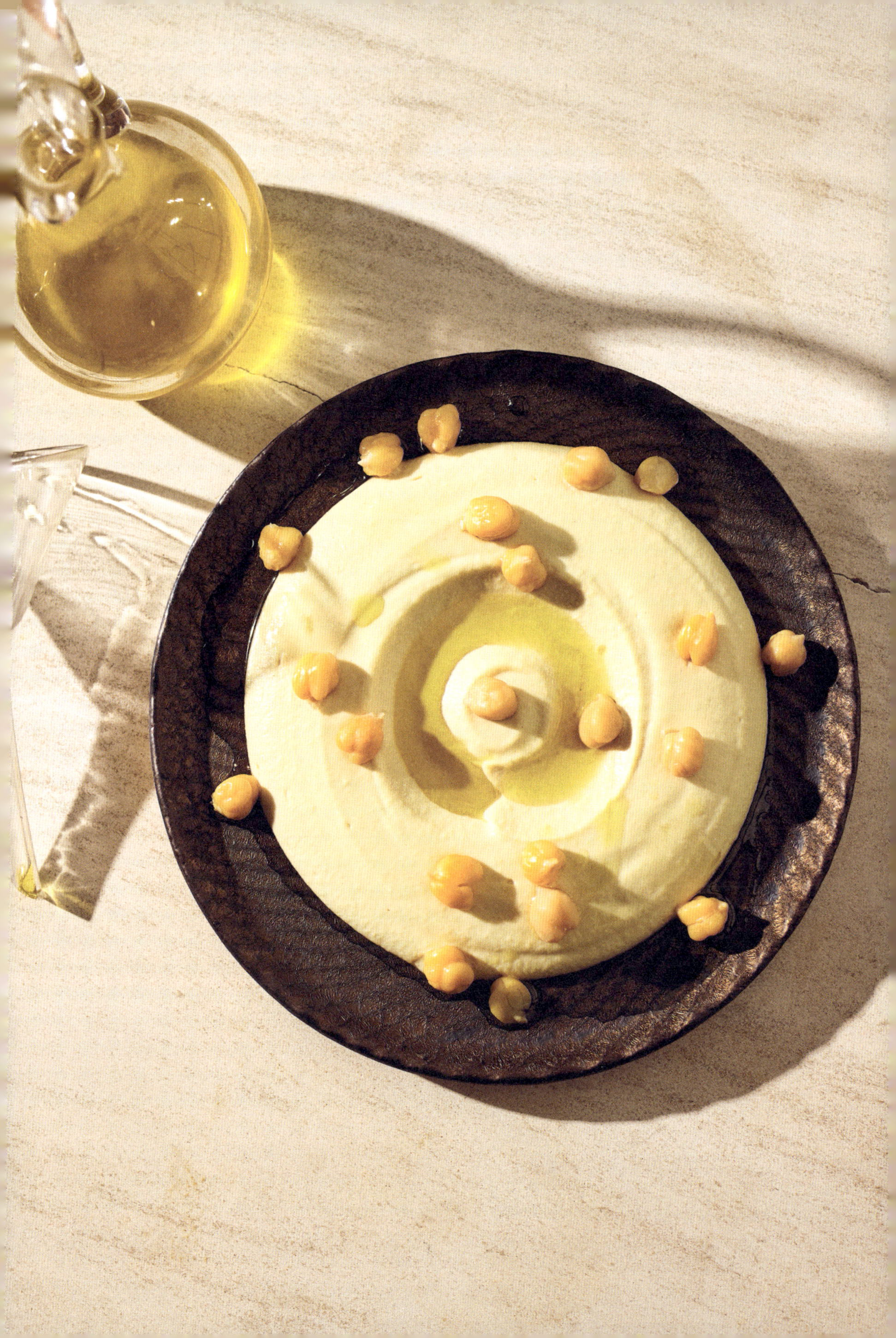

TOMATO KETCHUP

Tomato sauce or ketchup is a favourite condiment for good reason – a sausage roll, hot chips (fries) or a pie can feel incomplete without it. Yet many commercial varieties rely on additives and flavourings, even when labelled as 'natural'. This version returns to basics: ripe tomatoes, vinegar, sugar and spices, gently simmered into something far more honest and flavourful.

Makes 500 g (1 lb 2 oz)

tinned plum tomatoes	400 g	14.1 oz
white or apple cider vinegar	120 g	4.2 oz
water, plus extra as needed	70 g	2.5 oz
muscovado sugar	50 g	1.8 oz
fine sea salt	7 g	1½ tsp
garlic powder	5 g	1 tsp
paprika	2 g	½ tsp
tapioca starch (optional)	3 g	1 tsp

1. Put the tomatoes, vinegar and measured water into a food processor and blend until smooth, then strain through a sieve (fine-mesh strainer) into a saucepan.

2. Add the sugar, salt, garlic powder and paprika, then place over a medium heat, stirring regularly to prevent sticking.

3. Once the mixture begins to bubble, reduce the heat to low and simmer for 20–30 minutes, stirring occasionally, until the ketchup has reduced and thickened to your desired consistency.

4. For a smoother and more stable consistency, mix the tapioca starch with 15 g (1 tablespoon) cold water in a small cup until no lumps remain. Stir this into the ketchup in the final 5 minutes of cooking.

5. Remove from the heat and let the ketchup cool to room temperature. Transfer to a clean glass jar or bottle.

6. Store in the refrigerator for up to 1 month. The flavour will deepen after the first day. This recipe is also suitable for canning.

MAYONNAISE

This simple vegan mayonnaise recipe is a healthier, plant-based alternative to traditional mayo, made with accessible, high-quality ingredients. It's rich, creamy and perfect for sandwiches, salads and for dipping vegetables and crisps (chips).

Makes 240 g (8.5 oz)

aquafaba (page 244)	60 g	2 oz
Dijon mustard	10 g	0.4 oz
apple cider vinegar	15 g	0.5 oz
flaky sea salt	3 g	¾ tsp
garlic (optional, to make aioli)	1 clove	
olive oil	150 g	5.3 oz

1. In a tall jug (pitcher) suitable for a hand-held blender, combine the aquafaba, Dijon mustard, apple cider vinegar and salt.

2. If you'd like to make aioli, very finely chop the garlic and add it to the jug, too.

3. Use a hand-held blender to blend the mixture. As it blends, slowly start pouring in the olive oil in a thin, steady stream until full incorporated and thickened. This slow addition is crucial to forming a thick, creamy emulsion.

4. Taste the mixture and adjust the seasoning as needed.

5. Transfer the mayonnaise to a clean jar or container. Refrigerate for at least 30 minutes before serving to allow the flavours to meld and the mixture to firm up slightly.

6. Store in the refrigerator for up to 1 week.

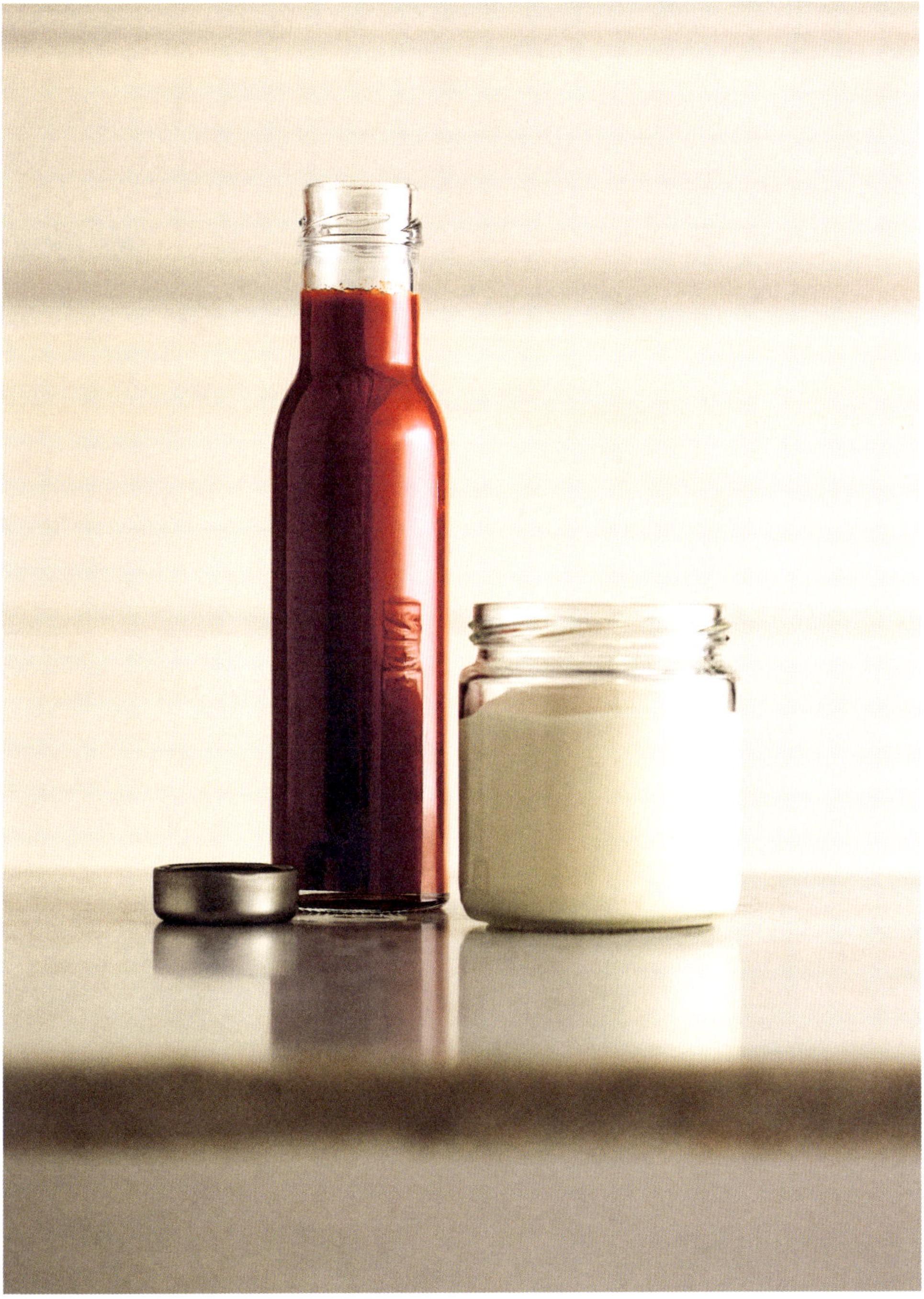

ABOUT THE AUTHOR

Philip Khoury is a globally recognised pastry chef, known for pioneering a new era of plant-based baking from simple ingredients. Born in Australia to Lebanese parents, he trained at Sydney's finest kitchens – including Quay and with Adriano Zumbo – before rising to prominence as Head Pastry Chef at Harrods in London. There, he helped lead one of the UK's largest pastry teams, driving innovation in luxury desserts with a strong focus on sustainability and technique. His debut cookbook, *A New Way to Bake*, won the Fortnum & Mason Award for Best Debut Cookery Book and earned international acclaim for its refined, entirely plant-based approach.

Khoury's work has been featured across global media – from BBC to *The Guardian* – and his creations, such as the 'Beirut Chocolate' bar, have gone viral for their originality and cultural resonance. He has appeared on *MasterChef Australia*, BBC's *Saturday Kitchen* and *Bake Off: The Professionals*. He was awarded the Pastry Innovation Prize by La Liste, and was named an Honorary Fellow of Western Sydney University.

ACKNOWLEDGEMENTS

To my parents – who shaped the way I see the world. My mum taught me to lead with heart and openness, and my dad encouraged me to question what I know and reimagine it. With them, nothing ever felt too big to tackle – just one slice at a time. To my big, brilliant family across Australia, Lebanon and beyond – thank you for grounding me in culture, warmth and flavour. Especially to my nephews and nieces, in whom I see all the world's children.

To Mike – thank you for your steady patience, your quiet wisdom and the calm you bring to every storm. You ground me, lift me and remind me of what truly matters.

Emily Sweet – thank you for betting on me and this vision before it was fashionable. Eve Marleau and Eila Purvis – your trust, support and grace under pressure made all the difference, especially as my delusions had me leave my job and chase a number of dreams halfway through this book. Eila, I will never forget you staying back until 10pm before this book went to print to finalise pages with me. Matt Russell – thank you for capturing my bakes with absolute class. Alexander Breeze – for injecting beauty, precision and energy. And to Evi O – thank you for making the design feel as clear and intentional as the recipes, and for this beautiful evolution of a cover! Thanks to everyone at Quadrille for taking this journey with me again, including Sarah, Joel, Kajal, Diana, Ruth, Becca and Paul.

Adriano Zumbo remains the biggest force in shaping my pastry career – thank you for seeing my potential and letting me run with it. To Kirsten Tibballs – thank you for the skills, belief and generosity. To Peter Gilmore and the team at Quay, Alec Lowe, Jessica Timpano, Anna Polyviou, Giovana Falanga, Alejandro Luna and all the wonderful chefs I've worked with – thank you for the lessons and the inspiration.

Huge thanks to Alexandre, a Frenchman in Perth who takes home-baking of croissants to a level I haven't seen before! Your knowledge of the hand-lamination process and conditions at home helped me craft a method and techniques that result in excellent pastries. Thanks to a little army of recipes testers – Julie, Petrenella, Dreya and Nikunja – who provided much insight to help validate and fine tune the recipes in this book.

To Alistair Birt – mentor, mate, manager – and to the entire pastry team at Harrods: your talent and hard work brought it all to life every day, two floors below the most iconic food halls in the world. Harrods nurtured this slightly rebellious chef and made space for a new kind of creativity. Always grateful.

To all the chefs who led a quiet revolution – who carved a path towards more ethical and expressive pastry when no one was asking for it – thank you Toni Rodriguez.

Pierre Hermé, my great idol and inspiration – from the early days and beyond. Your encouragement means more than you'll know! Thanks also to Dorie Greenspan for your kind words and thanks for your wonderful baking authorship and for being the English translating companion to Mr Hermé. Thanks also to bread whisperer Richard Hart!

And to Ben Liebmann – my strategic compass – who helps me zoom out and see where I can truly add value: you've helped me see myself more clearly.

To the food community in London and beyond – chefs, writers, suppliers, makers (Gurd, Rav, Helen, Lily, Jemma, Terri, Anna and so many more) – thank you for your generosity, talent and humour. You make this work feel like a shared language.

And to every pastry chef out there – thank you for carrying this beautiful, fleeting craft forwards. It's in moments like this, when I'm writing something like this hours before the book goes to print, I realise how much I love my job – something that can, at times, feel so superfluous to the world's needs, yet so crucial… in the end, it's more than cake.

INDEX

A

agar agar 28
    exotic clear glaze 242
almond milk 43
almonds
    almond croissants 66
    grape tart 166–7
    mango lemongrass tart 162–3
    pure pistachio tart 155–6
    roasted almond, pear and saffron trifle 184–6
    strawberry and cream basket cake 118
    stuffed almond croissant cookies 95
Anzac muscovado custard pie 168
apricot tarte tatin 161
aquafaba 44, 243, 244
    aquafaba meringue base [chocolate mousse] 175–6
    mango and vanilla bombe Alaska 180–1
    mayonnaise 246
    pistachio Yule log 139–41
    yuzu meringue pie 152
arrowroot 22
aubergines: nightshade quiche 202
avocados: savoury summer gateau 223–4

B

baking glaze 242
baking powder 29
baklava parfait roll 179
beetroot: savoury summer gateau 223–4
berries, mixed: mixed berry custard Danishes 70
bicarbonate of soda 29
biscuits. *see* cookies & biscuits
Black Forest cake 136–7
bread sticks 231–3
buns
    cheesy sun buns 228
    chocolate-glazed cream bun 79
    vrioche 56–8
butter
    coconut millefeuille 132–3
    laminated pastry 51–2
    olive oil butter 55
    puff pastry 195

C

cacao 41
cakes
    Black Forest cake 136–7
    coconut millefeuille 132–3
    light fruit cake 102
    peach and hazelnut crumble cake 112
    peanut butter and jelly sandwich cake 110–11
    pecan and muscovado Medovik cake 120–1
    pineapple, coconut and lime drizzle cake 107
    pistachio and matcha loaf cake 104
    pistachio and raspberry cream dream 129–30
    pistachio Yule log 139–41
    pure chocolate delice 124–5
    strawberry and cream basket cake 118
    tarte tropézienne 126–7
candied peel 240
cannellini beans
    sausy roll 213
    savoury summer gateau 223–4
cashews
    cheesy sun buns 228
    courgette galette 218–19
    a perfect summer dessert 187–8
cherries
    Black Forest cake 136–7
    pistachio Yule log 139–41
chickpeas 243
    aquafaba 44, 243, 244
    classic hummus 244
chocolate 41
    Black Forest cake 136–7
    chocolate crème pâtissière 239
    chocolate-glazed cream bun 79
    hazelnut and toasted vanilla cookies 88
    mousse: aquafaba meringue base 175–6
    mousse: custard base with whipped cream 176
    mousse: whipped ganache base 175
    pains au chocolat 69
    peanut butter choc chip cookies 86
    pistachio Yule log 139–41
    pure chocolate delice 124–5
cinnamon
    glazed doughnuts 76–7
    macadamia shortbread 91
    orange and maple spiced biscuits 92
cloves: orange and maple spiced biscuits 92

cocoa butter 41
    olive oil butter 55
    pecan and muscovado Medovik cake 120–1
    pistachio and matcha loaf cake 104
    pistachio and raspberry cream dream 129–30
    roasted almond, pear and saffron trifle 184–6

cocoa powder 41
    Black Forest cake 136–7
    pure chocolate delice 124–5

coconut cream: pineapple, coconut and lime drizzle cake 107

coconut, dessicated
    mango and vanilla bombe Alaska 180–1
    pineapple, coconut and lime drizzle cake 107
    coconut millefeuille 132–3

coconut oil 34
    Anzac muscovado custard pie 168
    apricot tarte tatin 161
    baklava parfait roll 179
    crème pâtissière 239
    croissant dough 60–2
    figwell tart 157–8
    fresh whipping cream 238
    grape tart 166–7
    mango lemongrass tart 162–3
    pistachio babka 80
    pure chocolate delice 124–5
    yuzu meringue pie 152

cold-pressed oil 31
    flaky pastry 146

cookies & biscuits
    fig newtons 96
    hazelnut and toasted vanilla cookies 88
    macadamia shortbread 91
    orange and maple spiced biscuits 92
    peanut butter choc chip cookies 86
    stuffed almond croissant cookies 95
    sugar syrup method 85

corn and jalapeño muffins 227
Corn-ish pasty 199–200
cornflour 21
courgette galette 218–19
cranberries, dried: light fruit cake 102

cream
    Anzac muscovado custard pie 168
    apricot tarte tatin 161
    custard base with whipped cream [chocolate mousse] 176
    fresh whipping cream 238
    pure pistachio tart 155–6
    tarte tropézienne 126–7

crème diplomat
    chocolate-glazed cream bun 79
    tarte tropézienne 126–7

crème pâtissière 239
    chocolate crème pâtissière 239
    coconut millefeuille 132–3
    mixed berry custard Danishes 70
    pains aux raisins 72–3
    strawberry and cream basket cake 118
    tarte tropézienne 126–7

croissant dough 60–2
    mixed berry custard Danishes 70
    pains au chocolat 69
    pains aux raisins 72–3

croissants 65
    almond croissants 66
    croissant dough 60–2

cucumber: savoury summer gateau 223–4
custard: savoury royale custard 197

D

doughnuts: glazed doughnuts 76–7

E

equipment 13–14
exotic clear glaze 242

F

figs
    fig newtons 96
    figwell tart 157–8
    a perfect summer dessert 187–8

filo pastry: baklava parfait roll 179

flaky pastry 146
    blind-baked flaky pastry 196
    caramelised onion, pepper and za'atar quiche 209
    courgette galette 218–19
    mushroom and truffle quiche 206
    nightshade quiche 202
    perfect peach pie 148–9
    squash, hazelnut and sage quiche 204
    tempeh and mushroom pie 214–15

flour 18–19

frangipane
    almond croissants 66
    figwell tart 157–8
    pure pistachio tart 155–6
fruit, dried
    light fruit cake 102
    pains aux raisins 72–3

G

glazes
    baking glaze 242
    chocolate-glazed cream bun 79
    exotic clear glaze 242
    glazed doughnuts 76–7
glucose (corn syrup) 39
gluten 45
gluten-free flour 19
golden syrup 39
    baking glaze 242
grape tart 166–7
groundnut (peanut) oil 33
    hazelnut and toasted vanilla cookies 88
    light fruit cake 102
    mango and vanilla bombe Alaska 180–1
    peanut butter and jelly sandwich cake 110–11
    peanut butter choc chip cookies 86
    pineapple, coconut and lime drizzle cake 107
    roasted almond, pear and saffron trifle 184–6

H

hazelnuts
    hazelnut and toasted vanilla cookies 88
    peach and hazelnut crumble cake 112
    squash, hazelnut and sage quiche 204
Hermé, Pierre 117
history of cake 11, 101
hummus, classic 244

I

ice cream
    mango and vanilla bombe Alaska 180–1
    a perfect summer dessert 187–8
icing sugar 39
    glazed doughnuts 76–7
    pineapple, coconut and lime drizzle cake 107
    pistachio and matcha loaf cake 104

J

jalapeños: corn and jalapeño muffins 227

L

laminated pastry 51–2
lecithin 45
    olive oil butter 55
leeks: creamy leek and tofu pie 220
lemongrass: mango lemongrass tart 162–3
lemons
    exotic clear glaze 242
    perfect peach pie 148–9
    yuzu meringue pie 152
limes: pineapple, coconut and lime drizzle cake 107

M

macadamia nuts
    macadamia shortbread 91
    mango and vanilla bombe Alaska 180–1
mangos
    mango and vanilla bombe Alaska 180–1
    mango lemongrass tart 162–3
maple syrup: orange and maple spiced biscuits 92
marzipan: stuffed almond croissant cookies 95
matcha powder
    pistachio and matcha loaf cake 104
    pure pistachio tart 155–6
mayonnaise 246
meringue
    mango and vanilla bombe Alaska 180–1
    yuzu meringue pie 152
milk. *see* plant milk
miso 26
mixed berry custard Danishes 70
muscovado sugar 38, 39
    Anzac muscovado custard pie 168
    pecan and muscovado Medovik cake 120–1
mushrooms
    mushroom and truffle quiche 206
    mushroom and truffle sticks 232
    tempeh and mushroom pie 214–15

N

nightshade quiche 202
nut butter 42
nutritional yeast 46
    cheesy sun buns 228
    olive oil butter 55
nuts 42

O

oat crumble 240
oat milk 43
oils 31–4
olive oil 33
    baking glaze 242
    Black Forest cake 136–7
    blind-baked flaky pastry 196
    Corn-ish pasty 199–200
    fig newtons 96
    figwell tart 157–8
    grape tart 166–7
    mango lemongrass tart 162–3
    mayonnaise 246
    oat crumble 240
    olive oil butter 55
    orange and maple spiced biscuits 92
    peach and hazelnut crumble cake 112
    pecan and muscovado Medovik cake 120–1
    pistachio and matcha loaf cake 104
    pistachio and raspberry cream dream 129–30
    puff pastry 194
    pure chocolate delice 124–5
    pure pistachio tart 155–6
    short sweet pastry 147
    strawberry and cream basket cake 118
    stuffed almond croissant cookies 95
    vrioche 56–8
olive sticks 231
onions: caramelised onion, pepper and za'atar quiche 209
orange blossom water
    baklava parfait roll 179
    figwell tart 157–8
    tarte tropézienne 126–7
oranges
    candied peel 240
    exotic clear glaze 242
    orange and maple spiced biscuits 92

P

pains au chocolat 69
pains aux raisins 72–3
pastries
    almond croissants 66
    baklava parfait roll 179
    coconut millefeuille 132–3
    Corn-ish pasty 199–200
    croissant dough 60–2
    croissants 65
    mixed berry custard Danishes 70
    pains au chocolat 69
    pains aux raisins 72–3
    sausy roll 213
    spinach roll 210
    tarte tropézienne 126–7
    vrioche 56–8
pastry 145
    blind-baked flaky pastry 196
    flaky pastry 146
    laminated pastry 51–2
    puff pastry 194, 195
    short sweet pastry 147
peaches
    peach and hazelnut crumble cake 112
    perfect peach pie 148–9
peanut butter
    peanut butter and jelly sandwich cake 110–11
    peanut butter choc chip cookies 86
peanuts
    peanut butter and jelly sandwich cake 110–11
    peanut butter choc chip cookies 86
pears: roasted almond, pear and saffron trifle 184–6
pecans
    grape tart 166–7
    pecan and muscovado Medovik cake 120–1
pectins 28
peppers: caramelised onion, pepper and za'atar quiche 209
pies & tarts
    Anzac muscovado custard pie 168
    apricot tarte tatin 161
    caramelised onion, pepper and za'atar quiche 209
    courgette galette 218–19
    creamy leek and tofu pie 220
    figwell tart 157–8
    grape tart 166–7
    mango lemongrass tart 162–3
    mushroom and truffle quiche 206
    nightshade quiche 202
    perfect peach pie 148–9

pure pistachio tart 155–6
squash, hazelnut and sage quiche 204
tempeh and mushroom pie 214–15
yuzu meringue pie 152
pineapple, coconut and lime drizzle cake 107
pistachios
pistachio and matcha loaf cake 104
pistachio and raspberry cream dream 129–30
pistachio babka 80
pistachio Yule log 139–41
pure pistachio tart 155–6
plant milk 43. *see also* **individual types**
Anzac muscovado custard pie 168
Black Forest cake 136–7
chocolate crème pâtissière 239
chocolate-glazed cream bun 79
crème pâtissière 239
figwell tart 157–8
grape tart 166–7
light fruit cake 102
mango lemongrass tart 162–3
oat crumble 240
pistachio and matcha loaf cake 104
pistachio babka 80
pistachio Yule log 139–41
pure chocolate delice 124–5
strawberry and cream basket cake 118
yuzu meringue pie 152
polenta: corn and jalapeño muffins 227
potato starch 23
potatoes: nightshade quiche 202
puff pastry 194, 195
apricot tarte tatin 161
coconut millefeuille 132–3
sausy roll 213
spinach roll 210

R

raisins
light fruit cake 102
pains aux raisins 72–3
raspberries
peanut butter and jelly sandwich cake 110–11
pistachio and raspberry cream dream 129–30
rum: light fruit cake 102

S

saffron: roasted almond, pear and saffron trifle 184–6
savoury royale custard 197
caramelised onion, pepper and za'atar quiche 209
mushroom and truffle quiche 206
nightshade quiche 202
squash, hazelnut and sage quiche 204
semolina: orange and maple spiced biscuits 92
short sweet pastry 147
grape tart 166–7
mango lemongrass tart 162–3
yuzu meringue pie 152
shortbread: macadamia shortbread 91
soy sauce 26–7
soya bean products 25–7
soya milk 27, 43
apricot tarte tatin 161
aquafaba meringue base [chocolate mousse] 175–6
baking glaze 242
baklava parfait roll 179
creamy leek and tofu pie 220
croissant dough 60–2
custard base with whipped cream [chocolate mousse] 176
figwell tart 157–8
fresh whipping cream 238
glazed doughnuts 76–7
mango and vanilla bombe Alaska 180–1
olive oil butter 55
peanut butter and jelly sandwich cake 110–11
pecan and muscovado Medovik cake 120–1
a perfect summer dessert 187–8
pistachio and raspberry cream dream 129–30
pure pistachio tart 155–6
roasted almond, pear and saffron trifle 184–6
savoury royale custard 197
short sweet pastry 147
vrioche 56–8
whipped ganache base [chocolate mousse] 175
soya mince 27
sausy roll 213
tempeh and mushroom pie 214–15
spinach roll 210
squash, hazelnut and sage quiche 204
starches 21–3
strawberry and cream basket cake 118
sugar 37–9
sultanas: pains aux raisins 72–3
sun-dried tomato sticks 233
sunflower oil 34
sweet potatoes 44

baking glaze 242
blind-baked flaky pastry 196
flaky pastry 146
stuffed almond croissant cookies 95
vrioche 56–8
sweet shortcrust pastry: figwell tart 157–8

T

tahini: classic hummus 244
tangzhong 56–8
tapioca starch 22
tarte tropézienne 126–7
tarts. *see* pies & tarts
tempeh 26
    tempeh and mushroom pie 214–15
textured vegetable protein (TVP). *see* soya mince
tofu 26
    caramelised onion, pepper and za'atar quiche 209
    courgette galette 218–19
    creamy leek and tofu pie 220
    savoury royale custard 197
    spinach roll 210
tomatoes
    nightshade quiche 202
    sun-dried tomato sticks 233
    tomato ketchup 246
trifle: roasted almond, pear and saffron trifle 184–6
truffle paste
    mushroom and truffle quiche 206
    mushroom and truffle sticks 232

V

vanilla 35
    almond croissants 66
    Anzac muscovado custard pie 168
    baklava parfait roll 179
    crème pâtissière 239
    fig newtons 96
    figwell tart 157–8
    grape tart 166–7
    hazelnut and toasted vanilla cookies 88
    light fruit cake 102
    mango and vanilla bombe Alaska 180–1
    mango lemongrass tart 162–3
    peanut butter and jelly sandwich cake 110–11
    pecan and muscovado Medovik cake 120–1
    perfect peach pie 148–9
    a perfect summer dessert 187–8

pineapple, coconut and lime drizzle cake 107
pistachio and raspberry cream dream 129–30
pure pistachio tart 155–6
roasted almond, pear and saffron trifle 184–6
short sweet pastry 147
vegetables
    Corn-ish pasty 199–200
    nightshade quiche 202
vrioche dough 56–8
    cheesy sun buns 228
    chocolate-glazed cream bun 79
    pistachio babka 80
    savoury summer gateau 223–4
    tarte tropézienne 126–7

W

walnuts
    figwell tart 157–8
    orange and maple spiced biscuits 92
wine: grape tart 166–7

Y

yeast 29–30
    bread sticks 231–3
    croissant dough 60–2
    glazed doughnuts 76–7
    vrioche dough 56–8
yuzu meringue pie 152

Quadrille, Penguin Random House UK, One Embassy Gardens, 8 Viaduct Gardens, London SW11 7BW

Quadrille Publishing Limited is part of the Penguin Random House group of companies whose addresses can be found at global.penguinrandomhouse.com

Penguin Random House UK

Text © Philip Khoury 2025
Images © Matt Russell 2025

Philip Khoury has asserted his right to be identified as the author of this Work in accordance with the Copyright, Designs and Patents Act 1988

Penguin Random House values and supports copyright. Copyright fuels creativity, encourages diverse voices, promotes freedom of expression and supports a vibrant culture. Thank you for purchasing an authorised edition of this book and for respecting intellectual property laws by not reproducing, scanning or distributing any part of it by any means without permission. You are supporting authors and enabling Penguin Random House to continue to publish books for everyone. No part of this book may be used or reproduced in any manner for the purpose of training artificial intelligence technologies or systems. In accordance with Article 4(3) of the DSM Directive 2019/790, Penguin Random House expressly reserves this work from the text and data mining exception.

Published by Quadrille in 2025

www.penguin.co.uk

A CIP catalogue record for this book is available from the British Library

ISBN 978-1-83783-359-7

10 9 8 7 6 5 4 3 2 1

Managing Director, Publishing: Sarah Lavelle
Publishing Director: Kajal Mistry
Senior Commissioning Editor: Eve Marleau
Senior Editor: Eila Purvis
Designer: Evi O Studio
Photographer: Matt Russell
Props Stylist: Alexander Breeze
Food Stylist: Philip Khoury
Copy-editor: Lucy Kingett
Proofreader: Emily Preece-Morrison
Indexer: Cathy Heath
Production Manager: Sabeena Atchia

Colour reproduction by p2d

Printed in China by C&C Offset Printing Co., Ltd.

The authorised representative in the EEA is Penguin Random House Ireland, Morrison Chambers, 32 Nassau Street, Dublin D02 YH68.

MIX
Paper | Supporting responsible forestry
FSC® C018179

Penguin Random House is committed to a sustainable future for our business, our readers and our planet. This book is made from Forest Stewardship Council® certified paper.